ENCOUNTERS WITH INDIGENEITY

Writing About Aboriginal and Torres Strait Islander Peoples

JEREMY BECKETT

ABORIGINAL
STUDIES
PRESS

First published in 2014
by Aboriginal Studies Press
Reprinted in 2026

Aboriginal Studies Press
is the publishing arm of the
Australian Institute of Aboriginal
and Torres Strait Islander Studies.
GPO Box 553, Canberra, ACT 2601
Phone: (61 2) 6246 1183
Fax: (61 2) 6261 4288
Email: asp@aiatsis.gov.au
Web: www.aiatsis.gov.au/asp/about.html

National Library of Australia Cataloguing-In-Publication data:

Author: Beckett, Jeremy, author.

Title: Encounters with indigeneities: writing about Aboriginal and Torres Strait Islander peoples / Jeremy Beckett.

ISBN: 9781922059772 (paperback)

ISBN: 9781922059789 (ebook: pdf)

ISBN: 9781922059796 (ebook: epub)

ISBN: 9781922059802 (ebook: kindle)

Notes: Includes bibliographical references and index.

Subjects: Aboriginal Australians — History. Aboriginal Australians — Social conditions.Aboriginal Australians — Legal status, laws, etc. Aboriginal Australians — Social life and customs. Torres Strait Islanders — History. Torres Strait Islanders — Social conditions. Torres Strait Islanders — Legal status, laws, etc. Torres Strait Islanders — Social life and customs. Indigenous peoples — Legal status, laws, etc — Australia. Indigenous peoples — Australia — Land tenure.

Dewey Number: 305.89915

Foreword

Some contexts of Jeremy Beckett

Because of Jeremy Beckett's former membership of a British Communist youth organisation, the Australian government refused him permission to do fieldwork in Highland New Guinea in 1956. In turning to western New South Wales, in 1956–57, Jeremy could enjoy the counsel of others — mainly students of AP Elkin at the University of Sydney — who were then breaking from 'salvage' anthropology's preoccupation with the least colonised and most 'classical' non-Western societies to write an applied sociology of race relations. However, what eventually set Jeremy apart from such students of the Australian temperate zone as Diane Barwick, James Bell, Malcolm Calley, Ruth Fink, Fay Gale, Judy Inglis and Marie Reay is that after observing colonial relationships in the landlocked, arid, interior of New South Wales he then turned to the Torres Strait (where the music, the dancing and the canoe trips 'met my hunger for the exotic.') (Beckett 2005, p. 85).[1] Both far western New South Wales and the Torres Strait came under effective colonial authorities in the second half of the nineteenth century, but the physical environments and cultural traditions that were thus brought into contact with the British–Australian economy and polity were as different as any that we know of among the colonised peoples of Australia. Few anthropologists working in Australia have cast their net so wide (though the diverse field sites of Ronald and Catherine Berndt — Wiradjuri, Ngarrindjeri, Western Desert, Arnhem Land — come to mind).

Jeremy's interest in two very different parts of Australia is well represented in this collection of essays. However, it is a curious feature of his work that Jeremy has rarely made explicit what he sees as the differences and similarities between his two field sites. In a 1994 reflection on the Murray Island land case (that had culminated in the High Court of Australia's Mabo judgment in June 1992), Jeremy cautioned that the differences between the precolonial social organisation of Aborigines and Torres Strait Islanders are 'not all that striking'. 'Both societies were organised in terms of kinship relations, and were further differentiated in terms of age and gender'; both lacked hereditary chiefs, and the power of senior men was acquired and expressed in their 'leadership in certain religious cults, membership of which was hereditary' (see Chapter 6, p. 129).

What did differentiate the Aborigines of far western New South Wales from the islanders of the Torres Strait was colonial authority's political legacy. Jeremy is recorded as saying in 1964 (shortly after he had been awarded a PhD for his Torres Strait thesis) that, in contrast with Maori, American Indians and Torres Strait Islanders, the Aborigines he had met were remarkably lacking in political organisation.

> Where most people, for example the Torres Strait Islanders, had succeeded in organising themselves so as to provide some sort of counter-pressure to government influence and government policy, some kind of feedback so that the government is forced to find out exactly what the reactions to its policies are, the Aborigines, for most of the history of this country, have been a silent and apparently un-reacting mass of passive objects of various sorts of government policies.[2] (in Sharp and Tatz 1966, p. 360)

In 1965, when reporting how one of his friends ('the Chief') at Murrin Bridge had fared since 1957, he ventured another comparison. Surprised that the unusually entrepreneurial Chief had not, evidently, prospered in material terms, he remarked:

> Re-entering the Chief's home, I was forcibly reminded just how roughly most Aborigines live. In the interim I had lived with Torres Strait Islanders who were better provided with material things on smaller incomes. They had adopted the European virtues of cleanliness and the 'decent home'. Few Torres Straits homes lack a kerosene pressure lamp; here were Aborigines earning three and four times the money with no more than a hurricane lamp, and that often out of service. (Beckett 2005 [1965], p. 102)

Jeremy had needed the permission of the New South Wales Aborigines' Welfare Board to work at Murrin Bridge in 1956. The sympathetic interest of AP Elkin — whose research students were answering questions about 'assimilation' in which the New South Wales authorities had a practical concern — got him through the settlement gate. When he sought the permission of Queensland's Director of Native Affairs to work in the Torres Strait, he found the Queensland government 'proud of Torres Strait'. As Jeremy's subsequent research shows, the practices of the London Missionary Society (LMS), continued by the Queensland government, constituted forms of local native authority — civic and ecclesiastical — that resembled the 'indirect rule' of Britain's African colonies and Fiji.[3] Councils advised the State government, settled internal disputes, and acted as channels of communication between Islanders and government and as 'agents for containing discontent' (see Chapter 8, p. 169). As Jeremy described the result in 1965, while 'things were carefully controlled from above', the Islanders enjoyed 'a substantial degree of local autonomy'. When Jeremy sought permission to work among them, the Queensland officials consulted the Islander local government heads; they 'agreed to my coming' (Beckett 2005, pp. 94–5).

Paralleling these civic structures in the Strait was an ecclesiastical apparatus. In studies included in this book, Jeremy shows how seriously (and competitively) the Islanders, converted by the LMS in the 1870s and 1880s, were taking parish affairs and the offices of the Anglican Church in the 1960s. By the time of the Islanders' victory in the High Court in 1992, Torres Strait Islanders had for more than a century been schooled — by delegated authority in specially designed state and church fora — in 'how to talk to white people'. Notwithstanding that Eddie Mabo was at odds with the Straits' more Christian and suborned Islanders, his High Court litigation evinced faith in the British common law. Such confidence bespeaks the background political culture described by Jeremy.

In contrast, in the pastoral society of western New South Wales in the 1950s, 'bridges' (Jeremy's term in his 1958 thesis) between black and white society had been few. Aborigines were 'vitally involved in' that social order as labourers, 'while yet having few encounters with the white population'. Jeremy summed up the racial stand-off: 'Given the low regard in which the aborigine is held, it is a rare white who will go out of his way to make contact. The Aborigines, for their part, whether out of shyness or lack of inclination, are scarcely more energetic in seeking out white society' (Beckett 2005 [1958], p. 143). Jeremy saw this social distance as the outcome of two phases in the adaptation of the region's Aborigines. In the first phase, they had camped on pastoral properties, as employees, and 'they took as their model the nineteenth century pastoral workers, whose way of life presented many parallels to their own' (Beckett 1988, p. 117). This adaptation had afforded much autonomy, albeit in material poverty. In the second phase, with the division of large pastoral holdings into smaller units, the Aborigines of the region came under the management of government. Rationing by police or by government 'mission' managers characterised a more supervised life, a transition accelerated by the depressed labour market of the Great Depression (Beckett 2005 [1958], p. 46). When Jeremy gives us George Dutton's life story, both adaptive phases are brought into view: the difference between the self-managed working life that had formed drover George and the more supervised life of his descendants had become a gulf of incomprehension and little respect between generations. Dutton was glad to find Jeremy curious about his Law-filled drover's life. However, we should be clear about what made his friendship such a gift to Jeremy's field work. Although anthropology had been developing the 'life-cycle' of a typical individual as a frame for the study of a culture, Jeremy has since made clear that his choice of the individual life as an analytical frame was a move away from anthropology and into history. 'It made no sense to interpret my research in the framework of a life cycle; people's lives, far from being a repetition of previous generations, were marked by radical changes' (Beckett 2005, p. 95). Jeremy's gracefully written biographical essay helped to define 'Aboriginal History' when a journal of that name became possible in 1977.

It has been Jeremy's fate and fortune to be compelled to consider the relative significance of 'culture' and 'history' in explaining the Indigenous diversity — within Australia – that is evident in this book. It is this pressure and opportunity to compare colonial theatres, within the one nation-state, that has made him a singularly historical anthropologist. Each in their own way, the cultural formations of western New South Wales and the Torres Strait illustrate Anthony Hopkins' advice that students of colonial relations should attend to the shared values that settler societies and some indigenous elites held in common. 'These values can be considered, in the language of today, as marking the emergence of a "global civil society", albeit one that was largely a projection of Britain overseas' (Hopkins 1999, p. 235). Let me build on Hopkins by saying: that, in Australia, more than one 'Britain' has been projected; that those so affected are not necessarily or obviously 'elites'; and that the forms of their 'civility' included (in the western New South Wales case) insisting on their civil right to consume alcohol to excess (Beckett 1964).[4] To risk caricature: Jeremy's field work had shown by the late 1960s how British-Australian cultures formed a tropical Barchester in the Torres Strait and Aboriginal larrikinism in western New South Wales.

Anthropology has always been a comparative discipline and therefore has an active sense of the commonalities and differences of the global human. Jeremy came to anthropology in London, a capital of empire where a practitioner of that discipline, under the stimulus of forced and voluntary imperial disintegration in the 1950s, could find that the study of the non-West was becoming a concern for the global dynamics of decolonisation. Thus we see Jeremy, in 1958, citing a study of 'town-natives' in French Equatorial Africa by Georges Balandier to suggest that the drinking he observed in western New South Wales was a means to demonstrate evolué status (Beckett, p. 130). His work has come out of an international literature — sometimes reaching for sociological models of the micro-political (Simmel, Goffman), other times comparing Australia, as a settler colony, with other colonies from which the colonists will never withdraw. He is one of the few to have applied 'mode of production' theory in Australian studies, describing the incorporation and the autonomy of Torres Strait Island peoples in terms that (here, within this book) complement his congregation-centred account.

By the late 1960s, however, Jeremy was wondering whether anthropological research could continue by way of 'community studies, until we had worked out how to conceptualise the system that encapsulated them' (Beckett 2005 [1958]). The work of Eric Wolf showed one way that could be done, and since the 1980s, Jeremy has found Latin American studies fruitful, particularly on the topic of the personal and collective memories of colonised people.

The more one considers Jeremy as an anthropologist, the clearer it becomes that he is a global historian. Like Charles Rowley (who studied Papua New Guinea before turning to Australia in the 1960s) and William Stanner (who wrote on decolonising east Africa and the South West Pacific before returning to Northern Territory studies in the 1950s), Jeremy has written about Australia within an increasing awareness of global colonial situations. Fifteen years ago, Anthony Hopkins challenged writers on Australian history to give up 'the tradition of arranging history so that it fits within national borders' (1999, p. 243). While congratulating British Dominion historiography for overcoming imperial blindness and recognising the place of Indigenous people in each Dominion's history, Hopkins complained in 1999 that:

> even the best of recent studies deal with these events entirely within a national framework, thereby conveying the impression that they are unique. Consequently, Maoris, Aborigines, Indians and others remain subordinated to a historical tradition that purports to emancipate them. An understanding of the imperial context would remove this false sense of isolation, open new possibilities for comparative studies of both settler communities and indigenous peoples, and underline the widespread and growing significance of non-national affiliations in a world divided formally into nation-states. (1999, p. 217)

Jeremy's attention to the diverse historical formation of Indigenous peoples within Australia and his search for a global context in which to make sense of the trajectories of pastoral New South Wales and the Torres Strait have long propelled him in the direction that Hopkins was advocating, as very few historians of Australia have been so propelled. It is not just that these two regions are in Australia, their similarities and differences enriching a story of Australian colonial authority; it is also that they are instances of a global dynamic of colonisation and settler-colonial reckoning with the colonial past. Through what Jeremy has called 'welfare colonialism', the Indigenous people of Australia have acquired dual status: socio-economically deprived citizens of a nation AND honoured bearers of an Indigeneity that is both globally defined and locally instantiated.

Indigenous movements now appeal not only to nation-states but, 'over their heads', to institutions and discourses that formulate Indigenous entitlement and judge nations' responses to its assertion. As the category 'indigenous' has become a more prominent term of political art (in global human rights discourse) it has also emerged as a problematic category of comparative social science and humanities scholarship. Jeremy has found in this climate new ways to historicise his Australian materials. He has been particularly interested in the ways that liberal-democratic political culture — 'welfare colonialism' — affords a certain 'Fourth World' self-representation. The rhetoric in which welfare is claimed and granted in societies such as Australia is 'moralistic', he suggests. To be Indigenous is to present oneself as distinctly deserving.

> This kind of political culture offers indigenous minorities the possibility of transcending their small numbers and powerlessness, while giving governments the opportunity of demonstrating their humanity at what may be relatively small cost. Thus in Australia, Aborigines as well as various immigrant groups have judged it more advantageous to follow this strategy rather than play class or party politics. (Chapter 8, p. 171)

Anthropology is an important participant in a global constituency that is 'grounded in the belief that Indigenous Peoples not only have the right to be different from the rest of the world, but should be assisted to do so', as Jeremy wrote in his introduction to a special issue of Identities: Global Studies in Culture and Power in 1996 (Chapter 11, p. 231). As both propagator and disinterested analyst of the discourse of 'Indigeneity', anthropology is attached ambivalently to global Indigenism. Jeremy has recently reflected on this relationship in an essay that uses the writing of Claudio Lomnitz about Mexico, the nation where 'Indigenism' originated. When colonists and colonised are co-nationals (as they are in Mexico and Australia), he points out, the idea 'Indigenous' performs more than one political service. As Aborigines have been drawn into a revised 'national narrative', they have been invited to be both 'traditional' and 'developing'. They are the settlers' co-nationals as both bearers of an ancient, newly respected culture but also as disadvantaged citizens who must be assisted to modernise. Anthropology — like the colonised, very much shaped by the nation-state, as Jeremy points out — has been of renewed relevance in Australia because it can substantiate Indigenous tradition where public policy has made tradition the basis of entitlements. Anthropology has also been more puzzled (or threatened) about what it can and should say about Indigenous Australians' socio-economic improvement (Beckett 2010). In Australian anthropology, there is (sometimes bitter) debate about the terms in which to represent their suffering.

In using the Mexican case to cast new light on Australian anthropology's political role since the inception of land rights in the 1970s, Jeremy might also have gone back a little further in time to Charles Rowley's leadership of the Social Science Research Council project on 'Aboriginal Policy and Practice' in the 1960s. Before there was a land rights policy or global Indigenism, anthropology seemed to Rowley to offer little to a reformist social science of Aborigines because it failed to account for (indeed, posed few questions about) Aborigines' contemporary behaviour. The standpoint from which Rowley found anthropology so wanting can be conveyed in two quotations.

> Things common to all humanity are more fruitful for the study of government policies than the differences: and most of the attitudes of the Aboriginal minority can be adequately accounted for as likely to have been developed by any minority in similar circumstances. (Rowley 1970, p. 15)
>
> The reactions of these people are those of groups under stress anywhere. If from their many origins there are indeed some cultural predispositions, as well there may be, it is not necessary to postulate these as the cause of Aboriginal actions and attitudes; these may be adequately accounted for by historical and economic factors and by social factors arising from the relationship of the group with government and with non-Aboriginal society. (1970, p. 173)

These words were an intellectual screen against the extant Australian anthropological literature. One of the few anthropologists to get through that screen was Jeremy. Indeed he was Rowley's most cited anthropologist; Rowley was impressed by his descriptions of the mores of the Aboriginal workers of New South Wales and of the Christianity of Torres Strait Islanders, and his chapters on the New South Wales government station Murrin Bridge and on the town of Wilcannia were based largely on Jeremy's Masters thesis (Rowley 1970, pp. 267–86). What Rowley liked was that Jeremy had not asked: what was Aboriginal culture before colonial contact and how much of it is left? Rather, Jeremy saw Aborigines of New South Wales as 'formed to some extent in the frontier experiences', and this perspective obviated reference to 'Aboriginality' in its classic form (1970, p. 317). For Rowley, these Aborigines' suffering was not in their loss of culture, but in their structural exclusion from the benefits of Australian society, including their habits of withdrawal and self-exclusion.

Writing western New South Wales and the Torres Strait into global history, Jeremy has understood 'culture' as the embedded reflexes of people who have been marginalised, but not necessarily disabled, by colonial structures. The people of whom he writes have retained certain resources to live their marginality on terms that are not only sustainable but also — as his convivial descriptions show — share-able with an interested and non-judgmental newcomer.

Tim Rowse, University of Western Sydney

NOTES

1. The work of the cohort who studied Aboriginal conditions in southern Australia in the period of assimilation policy was well represented in Reay (1964).
2. The phrase 'passive objects' would not endear this comparison to 2014 opinion, but Beckett's longevity as an observer/writer has earned him the privilege of apology and self-correction. See Beckett (2005, p. 11), his 1958 MA thesis with new introduction and preface.
3. It is widely agreed that British authority over Aborigines was not 'indirect rule'. Ben Silverstein (2012) has recently challenged that view in a provocative re-interpretation of the Northern Territory's history.
4. The seeds of this ethnography of the civil right to consume alcohol can be found in Beckett 2005 [1958], pp. 125–32.

REFERENCES

Beckett, J 1964, 'Aborigines, alcohol and assimilation', in M Reay (ed.) *Aborigines Now*, Angus & Robertson, Sydney, pp. 32–47.

—— 1988, 'Kinship, mobility and community in rural New South Wales', in I Keen (ed.) *Being Black: Aboriginal Cultures in Settled Australia*, Aboriginal Studies Press, Canberra, pp. 117–36.

—— 2005 [1958], *A Study of Aborigines in the Pastoral West of New South Wales*, Oceania Monograph 55, University of Sydney, Sydney.

—— 2005 [1965], 'The land where the crow flies backwards', in G Gray (ed.) *Before It's Too Late: Anthropological Reflections, 1950–1970*, Oceania Monograph 51, University of Sydney, pp. 38–43.

—— 2005, 'Against the grain: Fragmentary memories of anthropology in Australia, 1956–1970', in G Gray (ed.) *Before It's Too Late: Anthropological Reflections, 1950–1970*, Oceania Monograph 51, University of Sydney, pp. 83–98.

—— 2010, 'National anthropologies and their problem', in J Altman and M Hinkson (eds), *Culture Crisis: Anthropology and Politics in Aboriginal Australia*, UNSW Press, Kensington, pp. 32–44.

Hopkins, AG 1999, 'Back to the future: From national history to imperial history', *Past and Present*, no. 164, August 1999, pp. 198–243.

Reay, M (ed.) 1964, *Aborigines Now*, Angus & Robertson, Sydney.

Rowley, CD 1970, *Outcasts in White Australia*, Australian National University Press, Canberra.

Sharp, IG and Tatz, CM (eds) 1966, *Aborigines in the Economy*, Jacaranda, Brisbane.

Silverstein, B 2012, 'Indirect rule in a settler colony: Race, indigeneity, government,' PhD thesis, La Trobe University.

Contents

Acknowledgments

Aboriginal Studies Press and the author acknowledge the kind permission of the relevant publishers to reproduce the following previously published material in this collection. If anyone believes they have a claim to copyright in this material the publisher would be pleased to hear from them.

'George Dutton's country', in *Aboriginal history*, 1978, 2:1; 'Walter Newton's history of the world — and Australia' in *American Ethnologist*, Volume 20, Issue 4, pages 675–695, November 1993 (Wiley online library); 'Aboriginal Histories, Aboriginal Myths' in *Oceania*, December 1994; v. 65 no. 2, pp. 97-115; 'Autobiography and testimonial discourse in Myles Lalor's "oral history"' in *Telling stories: Indigenous history and memory in Australia and New Zealand*, B Attwood & F Magowan (eds), Allen & Unwin, Crows Nest, 2001; 'Torres Strait Islanders and the pearling industry' in *Aboriginal history*, 1(1), pp. 77-104, 1977; '"Knowing How to Talk to White People": Torres Strait Islanders and the politics of representation' in *Indigenous peoples and the nation-state*, Noel Dyck (ed.), Institute of social and economic research, Memorial University of Newfoundland, St Johns Nfld, pp. 95-112, 1985; 'Rivalry, competition and conflict' in *Anthropology in Oceania*, LR Hiatt and C Jayawardena, 1971; pp 27-46; 'Mission church and sect' in *Mission, Church and Sect in Oceania*, Boutilier (ed.), Michigan UP, Ann Arbor, 1978, pp. 209-29; 'The Murray Island Land Case' in *Australian Journal of Anthropology* 6: 1-2, 1995; 'Aboriginality, citizenship and nation state' in 'Introduction to Aboriginality and the State', *Social Analysis* special issue, no. 24, J Beckett (ed.), 1988; 'Contested images: Perspectives on the Indigenous Terrain in the late 20th century' (Intro) in *Identities: Global studies in culture and power*, vol 3, issue 1-2, Routledge, 1996.

Note about language

Where possible the author has avoided editing the original publications, allowing readers to appreciate for themselves the issues and way of speaking from earlier times. Naturally, as these chapters span a period of several decades, inevitably, there is language used in them which would not be considered acceptable nowadays.

Introduction

The main elements of my career as an anthropologist are quickly told. Graduating in anthropology at University College, London, I came to the Australian National University in 1957, hoping to work in the New Guinea Highlands. For various reasons I found myself instead working for a Master's degree among Aboriginal people in Western New South Wales, and then in 1958 working for a doctorate among Torres Strait Islanders. These have been the places to which I have returned many times.

Neither the Aboriginal people I met, nor the Islanders, could be regarded as 'untouched' by the outside world; rather — like it or not — they had been engaged with it for three generations and more. My task was to identify the forces bearing on them and the social and cultural resources they brought to this engagement: their sense of who they were in the broader scheme of things, as this changed over the years. This necessarily evoked people's memories and rediscoveries of what had happened before, giving rise to histories —albeit conceived amid the confusion of other histories coming from elsewhere — as well as their expectations of what would and should happen in the future.

Coming, like many, accidentally into undergraduate anthropology, I was captivated by the prospect of 'field work'. On the slim basis of tourist trips to Crete and Turkey, only just becoming accessible after the War, I flattered myself that I was good at engaging with people who were not so much other, as different. Anthropology seemed to offer the possibility of 'real field work', in the sense of living at close quarters with people for months, if not years. I have chosen the word encounters for this collection, because this is what I aimed to achieve in my field work. And while no doubt I disappointed some I met, and annoyed others, I have returned many times, renewing old friendships and making new ones.

Writing about these encounters has been another matter, not always attempted soon after the event, but sometimes years later, perhaps with the benefit of hindsight, or in a different frame. Over this period of almost sixty years, much has changed for both Aboriginal and Islander people, as indeed in the world at large. James Clifford has nicely summarised these changes in terms of 'a double history of two unfinished post-war forces working in tensions and synergy: decolonization and globalization' (Clifford 2013, p. 3).

I would add, however, that 'decolonisation' remains unfinished business, often little more than a gesture, in the world's settler colonies, especially when the Indigenous populations are small minorities, as in the case of Australia.

As these changes overtook the lives of Australia's Indigenous peoples, as well as many others in the world, anthropologists had to make what they could of them, in terms of a discipline that was itself changing, partly in response to the forces Clifford mentions, but also to critiques of the old paradigms and diversity of the new proposed in their place.

Already by the time I began, the old definitions of one's field in terms of 'tribe' or 'community' had become increasingly problematic as one's 'people' proved to be externally engaged in wider systems, economic, political, ideological and aesthetic. For my part, I found it difficult to write about Torres Strait, where people lived on physically separated islands, locked in face-to-face relations, and yet their life could not be understood without taking into account the mediated effects of external forces. Today, while each island is still occupied by people, tracing descent from the original inhabitants, 85 per cent of people identifying as Torres Strait Islanders now live scattered among towns and cities on the mainland of Australia. The Aboriginal people I first met in the Far West are also scattered, though not so far afield. With modern communications, scattering does not necessarily mean disconnectedness for either Aboriginal or Islander people, but it does mean that Indigenous connections are now but one among many.

Such changes have not lessened the significance of Indigenous identity for either people, rather the contrary although its significance has become more complex and more reflexive. While families and communities may continue to 'produce' Aborigines or Islanders', it is not as they please. This now occurs in a context of proliferating entanglement with government, and civil bodies, with whom they are engaged or want to engage. Whereas once these bodies attempted to eliminate or at least marginalise Indigeneity, they now seek to incorporate it in some national, lately global framework. Indeed, the formation of Indigeneity is no longer just national. It has become global.

Recognising these developments poses a challenge for an anthropology grounded as mine has been, on the encounter. In several of the chapters included here, I draw extensively on archival sources, to situate my informants' accounts, as well as their recollections of what earlier generations told them, in a political economy frame. Venturing into the fields of cultural and postcolonial studies seems to have taken me even further away from the simple encounter. My inclination has been to situate people in the world without losing them there, but somehow this is getting harder to achieve.

First Western NSW and then Torres Strait

I shall begin with brief sketches of, first Far West New South Wales, and then Torres Strait as I first encountered them; times I scarcely need to add, very different from today.

I found myself with little preparation going off to the Aboriginal Welfare Board's Station at Murrin Bridge in Western NSW, and later, when I discovered there were historical and kinship connections, further west to the township of Wilcannia. The Aboriginal inhabitants of these two centres were a mix of peoples originating from different quarters of the region, whose movements had at various times been affected by the Aborigines Protection — now called Welfare — Board, which had set up and several times relocated managed settlements, and by the changing needs of the pastoral industry which employed most of the men.

White townsfolk seemed to keep Aboriginal people at arm's length, limiting relations to work and commercial transactions. The men were mainly employed doing rough work such as fencing and clearing on stations round about. The law also prohibited the supply of alcohol to Aborigines, except for the few who had exemption certificates and old age pensioners. Others could buy alcohol around the back of the hotel, but while the publican was never charged for the offence, Aboriginal people were often imprisoned.

Against this was a community of familiarity, but there was no one in particular I could go to explain my project, so that in the first instance I must have been taken as connected with the Welfare Board. Collecting the memories of the old people seemed to make sense to the people, and eventually Lance Johnson started to drop by my house, and eventually took me out for a week with his clearing gang. It also seemed to make sense to people that I should collect genealogies. It revealed where they came from, and the overlapping networks of kinship and affinity, which extended throughout the region, though rarely into the non-Aboriginal sector.

Among themselves they maintained an ethos of generosity and egalitarianism, but were divided into those who drank alcohol, and those — mainly women — who did not. Dougie Young's songs, the first of which I recorded at this time, celebrated the escapades of Dougie and his mates, in defiance of the police, 'the people in town', but also the women.

There was another division between anyone under sixty and the 'old people' who lamented the passing of 'the lingo', 'straight' marriages, and putting the young boys, and also girls, 'through the rules'. On Murrin Bridge there was Fred Biggs, who came almost daily to my house, and in Wilcannia there was George Dutton, who I was to know for another ten years. If I had to choose I would regard my encounter with George as the most memorable of my career. But, during my time in the West, I found myself on the one hand trying to understand the Aboriginal life about me, which I began to enjoy, particularly its ribald humour, and on the other hand, listening to the old people's stories, not only for what it told me about their past, but for how they had come to terms with the changes that overtook them.

I had to write my MA in short order, but I was to return to 'the West' many times, and continue to write about it. Meanwhile I had to start a doctoral project, which — through another odd mix of circumstances — sent me to the Torres Strait Islands.

During my first round of field work — between 1958 and 1961 — Torres Strait was quite simply colonial. I had first to get permission from the Queensland Director of Native Affairs in Brisbane, and then from the Deputy Director on Thursday Island, who oversaw movement in and out of the islands, which were classified as reserves. Thursday Island was the headquarters of the pearling industry, although the Department oversaw the employment of its Islander work force. Finally 'TI', as it was always called, was the seat of the Anglican Diocese of Carpentaria, which had most of the Islanders in its spiritual care. 'TI' had once been the domain of whites and a few Asian or part-Asian traders, while Islanders lived on the outer islands. Since the Second World War, Islanders working for the Department were also permitted to live there.

Other Islanders could come into town for medical treatment or to unload pearl shell, but their domain was the 'outer islands'; some thirteen communities, more or less remote from 'TI'. The Department and the Diocese, for the most part, mediated between the Islanders and the outside world but, as I was soon told, elected Islander councillors were in charge of local government and local courts. In earlier times, a resident white school teacher had served as a magistrate, but following a strike in 1936, the Department of Native Affairs had passed this role on to Islanders. As for the church, while the bishops were white, all the priests were Islanders. Councillors, along with police, and priests, received a small wage. It was to the Council Chairman that I had to introduce myself. When I presented myself to the chairman of Mer, Sam Passi, asking how I should conduct myself in the community, his response was 'no colour bar'. I was to find that this was what other islands preferred for white people living among them.

Free to choose which island communities I visited, I went first to Mer, then to Badu, and almost as an afterthought to Saibai; each different from the others, while situated in the same administrative, economic, and ecclesiastical systems.

Torres Strait had been the site of one of the early anthropological projects, the Cambridge University anthropological expedition of 1898, led by AC Haddon. But while its aim was to record memories of a 'savage' culture, the

Islanders had already been involved with missionaries, the marine industry, and the Queensland government for thirty years, and scores of Pacific Islanders, Malays, even Jamaicans, had married into the local population. Haddon in his final volume (1935) had reviewed the documentary history of the Strait, and provided some sense of Islander life as it was around the turn of the century.

Arriving sixty years later, I could kind of pick up from where Haddon left off; there were the same island communities, mostly inhabited by the descendants of Haddon's informants. But much had happened to the people over the ensuing years, particularly service in a home defence force during the Pacific War. The official status of the Torres Strait Light Infantry was in fact ambiguous, but it gave rise to a sense of entitlement in the Australian nation, which in the years that followed seemed not to have been met. These and other events were commemorated in locally composed songs and dances, the particular styles — traditional, Pacific Island, and American popular music — in themselves indicative of an awareness of time and place. And yet the desire to be free to move into the mainstream and the clinging to the certainties of island life were not entirely reconciled. All through the Strait, Islanders celebrated 'The Coming of the Light', when in 1871, the London Missionary Society arrived. But their dances often celebrated warriors in the distinctive feather headdress of 'Darkness Time'. In just about any community one visited, there was some old man or woman who could retail ancestral myths, and one presently learned there was a lively fear of sorcery.

The communities I visited seemed on the one hand taken up with their daily face-to-face relations with one another, while on the other preoccupied with their present and future place in the outside world. As they came to know me, people were for the most part ready to talk. There were also frequent gatherings for community and family celebrations where, as I got to know more of what was going on, I could get some sense of what wasn't being said, as well as what was. On all the islands, great value was given to creativity, with new songs and dances competing with old favourites. As my enjoyment in this developed I found yet another interest in common with Islanders.

The Meriam had virtually given up on the marine industry, getting small amounts of cash from age pensions and child endowment, while putting their energies into their fertile gardens, as well as harvesting fish and turtle. Gardening required both hard work and traditional knowledge, but also awareness of the location of boundaries, which were often hotly contested. There were court books recording disputes going back to the 1890s.

An early administrator had instituted the system of elected local councils, allowing communities to take care of local and customary matters. Mer took advantage of this to achieve a turbulent democracy, with council elections bitterly contested. Most of the Meriam I talked to, particularly the old people, had a sense of a destiny, whether couched in religious or political terms: they would be able to run their own affairs, and be granted 'citizen rights'

Badu was a different story. It had become the main centre for pearling activities, and community life revolved around the coming and going of the luggers which, as well as earning money, also brought back turtle and dugong meat for households and for feasts. All the skippers belonged to one family, who also controlled the council to the extent that, unlike Mer, elections were a foregone conclusion. The Queensland Department, which managed many of the luggers, looked kindly on the situation.

Saibai, while previously committed to the pearling industry, had lately lost their luggers to Badu. With just a monthly cargo boat connecting them with Australia, people expressed concern about the future. In the meantime they used their trading connections with neighbouring Papuan villages to build double outrigger canoes. These they could use for both hunting and trading, though not for pearling. The community was periodically taken up with one occasion or another for feasting and the most extravagant kind of dancing, made even more exotic by bird-of-paradise plumes traded in from Papua.

'Writing Up'

My MA dissertation was hastily written, and in late years I wanted to re-think some of the issues I had written about, as in 'Kinship, Mobility and Community' (1988b). 'Aborigines, Alcohol and Assimilation' (1964), raised a topic I would return to again, reviewing the 'Songs of Dougie Young' in a somewhat different frame (1993). Before going to Torres Strait I had managed to publish a piece about George Dutton and Walter Newton under the title 'Marginal Men: A Study of Two Half Caste Aborigines' (1958). 'Half caste' belonged to an Australia in which notions of race and culture were virtually synonymous. People had assured me that 'full bloods' always refused to initiate boys with white fathers, so that if they claimed secret knowledge they were not to be believed. George Dutton, initiated and with a wealth of knowledge, gave the lie to this.

Having known George Dutton for another ten years after our first meeting, I wrote a fuller account of his life, 'George Dutton's Country'. The first piece in this collection, it explores the same theme of marginality, but is informed now with archival material, documenting the political economy of the region, as he grew from boyhood to manhood, as both a 'flash' stockman and initiated Aboriginal man. Nowadays we might talk in terms of cultural hybridity. Certainly, there must have been compromises that he had to make in negotiating this path. In one such, omitted from this paper, he described how a dying uncle, who was 'clever', wanted him to take over his powers. Later when he was driving home he was pursued by a kangaroo that carried his uncle's spiritual powers. It pursued him for a while, but since as he said, he 'didn't like the idea', it eventually bounded away into the trees.

As he grew older, the 'Aboriginal option' grew beyond his reach, although he treasured the memory of it, welcoming the arrival of researchers who would write it down and take care of it.

I have selected two other papers, discussing the situation of George Dutton's generation, poised between old and new ways of thinking about their world. Many years after my first attempt, I returned to Walter Newton's 'History of the World — or Australia', but viewing it now in terms of what not only anthropologists but also historians and writers in the emerging field of cultural studies were writing about the cultures of the colonisers and the colonised. I was by now deriving much inspiration from recent writings about Latin America's Indigenous peoples. 'Aboriginal History, Aboriginal Myth', written about the same time, takes up much the same problem, but looks comparatively at what Australianists had been writing on this topic.

What I had written about George Dutton gave rise many years later to another kind of assignment. Myles Lalor came from the north coast of NSW, but he had somehow found his way to Wilcannia, marrying a Wilcannia woman. Being a traveller like George, the two of them would compete with their stories of faraway places they had visited. Myles had read my article about George, and on a visit to my house in Sydney late one night, he proposed that I should do his 'oral history'. *Wherever I Go: Myles Lalor's 'oral history'* (Beckett 2000) was largely made up of transcriptions of the tape recordings I made at that time. But in 'Autobiography and testimonial discourse in Myles Lalor's oral history' (Chapter 4) I comment on, and attempt to place, this mode of literary production in the emerging genre of Indigenous writing in Australia, comparing it with what was coming out of North and Central America. One of the matters discussed in this paper is whether the speaker speaks for 'his people'. What Myles shares with George Dutton, whose name comes often into our conversations, is that they both speak for and about themselves.

I have been running ahead of myself, however, and must now turn back to what I was writing about the Islanders during the same period. I did not complete my book, *Torres Strait Islanders: Custom and Colonialism* until 1987, but published a number of articles, both before and after, several of which are included here.

Reading back, I am struck by the seeming absence of individual voices like those of George Dutton or Myles Lalor. Let me hasten to add that this was not because there were no people I got to know well; rather the reverse, so that the papers try to encompass many voices, talking sometimes to, sometimes over one another, as well as to me.

Life in the Strait for me and for the Islanders, was a matter of coming to terms with these overarching institutional structures of government, church, and economy, as well as the still scarcely known mainland Australia. The Queensland Department of Native Affairs (DNA), as it called itself when I was first in the Strait, had been a formidable presence in Islander lives since the late nineteenth century. The marine industry had played a dominant role in the regional economy for even longer. Mission Christianity had had a foothold in islands since 1871, though the London Missionary Society had handed its flocks over to the Church of England, which still enjoyed a monopoly in most communities at the time, though it was soon to encounter competition from Pentecostalism.

What was remarkable about the Strait was that, while white people occupied the dominant positions in all three institutions, Islanders, in the form of community councillors, boat skippers, and priests, mediated between the people and the authorities. The three papers here are attempts to understand how Torres Strait people engaged with this triple order from the vantage point of their various communities. Behind the generalisations are countless conversations, which have been worked into the narrative.

The first offering takes a political economy approach to the pearling industry, characterising the use of cheap non-European labour as internal colonialism. Torres Strait Islanders eventually became the main source of this labour. The DNA oversaw their employment but also managed community-based luggers on their behalf. The later part of the paper looks at the case of Badu, where, at the time of my field work, a family of boat skippers extended their influence into other community institutions.

'Rivalry, Competition and Conflict' is concerned with a community I call Kawa (the word simply means island). Describing the doings of individuals in a small, rather introverted community, I have decided to preserve the anonymity of the island and the actors, although none of them is now alive. Striving to maintain equality, the Kawans seem forever to be squabbling, but it must be noted that this is done largely through community institutions which, when all is said and done, everyone supports in principle.

'Mission, Church and Sect' was written for a combined meeting of historians and anthropologists with an interest in Oceania, a frame certainly appropriate to the nineteenth century history of Torres Strait, and it draws on the archival sources for that period. However, by the mid-twentieth century, Islanders looked to Australia, rather than the Pacific, and from this standpoint, their standing as Christians seemed somewhat ambiguous. Were the Anglicans, who had taken over from the London Missionary Society in 1914, a proper church or just another mission? Was the Pentecostalism which some had joined while working on the mainland, as they claimed more civilized than the established church? But was Pentecostalism a real church or just a sect which most Christians disregarded? Back on Mer, people wondered whether an island community could really accommodate more than one religious congregation?

In the new millennium, community and church are no longer synonymous. Islanders not only on the mainland but in the Strait, while overwhelmingly Christian, belong to a great variety of denominations. Buried for the moment in all this was the question of where to situate the beliefs that had pre-existed Christianity, but still retained some kind of validity in the present. This was to come into play with the Mabo cases, discussed later.

Something of the Kawans' contentiousness can also be found in a piece I wrote about Mer's 'robust' electoral politics, 'Elections in a Small Melanesian Community' (Beckett 1967). 'Knowing How to Talk to White People' (Beckett 1985) (presented to a conference of scholars working with indigenous people in North America and Norway') takes up Islander politics at a later period, in the 1980s. By this time the federal government had decided to intervene in the Indigenous field, giving local politicians the opportunity to play federal off against state (but also of course giving the space for the two governments to score off one another through their Islander clients).

By this time the Torres Strait marine industry was virtually defunct, and a majority of Islanders had gone to the mainland in search of work. Those remaining in the Island communities were now increasingly dependent on funding from one or other government. Representing one's community now required much more economic and political experience than previously.

Negotiations with government officials were conducted behind closed doors, excluding other Islanders, as well as the anthropological observer. Fortunately, on Mer, back in the 1950s, I had become friendly with the late George Mye, who was starting out on a political career which — with occasional interruptions — lasted through to the 1990s, by which time he was described as an 'Elder Statesman'. (One of his last acts, before his death in 2013, was to speak before the United Nations.) Over many years he would give me his take on the way things were in regional politics — though, ever the politician, it was always his side of the story. He had, for example, long found it difficult to work with the director of the state department, but he found he could work with Bob Katter, who became the state minister in the 1980s.

The majority of Torres Strait Islanders live on the mainland, mainly in North Queensland, though there are sizeable numbers in the Northern Territory and Western Australia. However, given that the mainland is defined as Aboriginal country, Islanders living there find it difficult to get a hearing. I have attended a number of conferences of mainland Islanders, where discussion has focused almost entirely on affairs in the Strait. The resolutions were usually ignored by the official representatives based in the Strait. The famous Mabo case, initiated by a long time absentee from Mer, caused consternation, not least among Meriam.

There is now a considerable literature on this case, including barrister Brian Keon-Cohen's insider account (2011), and Paul Burke's book on the changing role of the anthropologist, subtitled 'From Analysis to Expert Testimony' (2011). I was one of the expert witnesses in question, but my involvement was not as someone engaged to research a claim, as is often the case now, but as someone with long-standing acquaintance with the Meriam going back to the days before the idea of native title seemed a possibility. 'The Murray Island land case' (Beckett 1995) offered here, attempts a different perspective on what happened.

Many Meriam had viewed Koiki Mabo and his case with suspicion, but eventually came to terms with it, once the High Court had handed down its decision. Koiki Mabo, who died before this, was buried with due ceremony on his ancestral land. However, while the Meriam are assured of native title, Queensland has reasserted its presence with a version of the Deed of Grant in Trust legislation of the 1980s: those who want the state to build them houses have to give the state a forty-year lease on their land. The community is divided on the question, but Badu has lately signed on to the arrangement.

The issue that I raised in a latter part of this chapter is still with us: in what terms can anthropologists press the argument for cultural continuity? And as I ask late in the chapter, 'at what point does traditional become traditionalism?'. In this connection, it is worth looking at the latter day status of the Meriam Malu–Bomai cult for a people who were practicing Christians, since it seemed for not only them, but also non-Islanders to clinch the 'Mabo' case.

Although the London Missionary Society had attempted to suppress anything to do with the old cult, it was evident that many Meriam retained a certain regard for the chants and dances over the years, performing them from time to time. Moreover non-Islanders had not only been eager to see these performances, but also filmed them in 1967 by the Commonwealth Film Unit. So much outside attention must have confirmed the Meriam sense that they had something special. People may have somehow believed in both Christianity and Malu-Bomai, without ever having explicitly to choose between them, as the London Missionary Society pastors had once demanded. It seems to have taken an ordained priest of the Church of England, who was also a descendant of one of the officials of the cult, Father David Passi, to come up with a resolution (Sharp 1996).

Whatever the thoughts of the early Europeans on the significance of the cult, those of recent writers, as well as the High Court's decision, seemed to indicate that in the post-colonial world other people's beliefs were to be respected, in a new cultural, particularly religious pluralism.

While few Australians knew anything about Islanders, often confusing them with Aborigines, there were widespread ideas about what Aborigines were like, even though few had ever met one. For most of colonial history, Aboriginal people had had to live with settler notions of who and what they were, while their voices went unheard. The realisation of this led me to shift my gaze from the Indigenous minority to the settler majority, or least those among the latter — including anthropologists — who had articulated a view that was intended to be authoritative. In 1988 I edited a collection, under the title *Past and Present* (Beckett 1988a; 1994) in which I and others explored 'The construction of Aboriginality', mainly as it had been done by scientists, anthropologists and policy makers as well as by the first generation of Indigenous writers.

I was also becoming aware that while Aborigines and Islanders were increasingly liberated from the old colonial restrains, they were becoming increasingly dependent on other forms of government, particularly the welfare system. The old 1970s model of 'internal colonialism' that I had used to characterise the old pastoral and pearling industries no longer applied. Moreover, jobs like fencing that had employed men around western New South Wales had become mechanised, as had the work of railway fettling which had provided work for the Islanders who came down onto the mainland. These trends turned my attention from the mainstream capitalist economy to that section of it that provided welfare for such categories as the old, the incapacitated, and the unemployed. In 'Knowing How to Talk to White People' (Beckett 1985), I had referred to 'welfare capitalism'; I now adopted the term Robert Paine coined for the situation of Saami in Norway to apply his 'welfare colonialism' to the situation of Aboriginal people and to Islander people living in the Strait.

Trying to make sense of this took me outside the areas that anthropologists usually frequented to consider what economists and political scientists had written about welfare systems in the developed capitalist countries of the twentieth century. Australia's welfare system was less generous and less comprehensive than Britain's at that time, but by the 1980s it had something of the same features. Its attempts to bring Indigenous people into the nation came up against the fact that, having been so long 'colonised', Aboriginal people (and also Islanders) could not be simply transformed into citizens by legislative act, even had they wanted to do so. Moreover, in a post-colonial era Indigeneity had to be respected, if not compensated for past oppression.

Writing now some twenty-five years later, with the continuing disappearance of the jobs that Indigenous people used to do, it seems that welfare dependency has become one of the features that defines them. With welfare budgets now coming under review, there is some risk that this becomes a primary feature while the nation celebrates the emergence of a small Indigenous middle class by way of saving the nation's face from its post-colonial critics.

Thinking about Aboriginality in the 1980s eventually led me to the realisation that Indigeneity was becoming a global phenomenon in the 'late twentieth century'. Indeed the word was only then coming into the lexicon. I had long been interested in what anthropologists had been writing about Latin America, and taking advantage of a sabbatical leave spent some months at the Colégio de México reading the Spanish language literature, before moving on to New York, where I knew colleagues working in Latin America. My visit coincided with the establishment of a new journal, *Identities: Global Studies in Culture and Power*, and I was asked to write a short piece for a special issue that was concerned with indigeneity in various parts of the world. I took as my point of departure the Zapatista uprising in Mexico, an event that had just lately taken the world by surprise. My main point was that, while the Indigenous has in one sense always been with us, it had taken on a discursive salience in the late twentieth century. I was later to write an entry for the *International Encyclopedia of the Social and Behavioural Sciences* under the heading 'The fourth world' (Beckett 2001). (The forthcoming edition will have a new entry under 'Indigeneity'). Remarkably, the second piece takes me back to the Zapatistas, who are still with us. James Clifford's book, *Returns*, cited in my opening, also gives it particular attention, suggesting that it resonated with global developments, while following its own path.

In terms of the particulars, the situation of Indigenous people in Mexico or Ecuador, or even in parts of the United States, might seem too different from that of Aboriginal or Islander people in contemporary Australia, to make comparison useful. For my part, I look for how the conjunctions between the two worlds work out. Sider and Dombrowski have usefully coined the term indigenism: referring to the political middle ground arising out of the engagement of Indigenous and non-Indigenous meanings, in which understandings are sometimes reached, but sometimes left contested or simply unresolved (Dombrowski 2010). Spirituality — a familiar trope of indigenism — is a case in point, when old Indigenous beliefs are subjected to some kind of rehabilitation in the wider world. Thus, the meaning of Mer's Malu-Bomai cult, which I discussed earlier, might have been contested even among the Meriam themselves, while allowed to remain unresolved by the outside world.

This takes me back to the idea I began with, the encounter with people who as I put it are 'not so much other as different'. An anthropologist is expected to be a sympathetic listener. But when I eagerly wrote down George Dutton's stories about 'the country', I could scarcely share the meanings they had for him, although I enjoyed the excitement of being taught. Did he expect me to believe in the *muras*, or was he simply content to have someone to record the knowledge of which he was so proud? I did not ask him such questions, nor he me. The Kawans wanted to tell me their side of the story in their squabbles, but they did not ask me to take sides.

Perhaps there is something of this in all field work encounters; we hope to learn something of one another, but not too much. But then isn't life like that?

REFERENCES

Beckett, J 1958, 'Marginal Men: A Study of Two Half Caste Aborigines', *Oceania*, vol. 29, no. 2, pp. 91–108.

—— 1964, 'Aborigines, Alcohol and Assimilation', in M Reay (ed.) *Aborigines Now*, Angus & Robertson, Sydney, pp. 32–47.

—— 1967, 'Elections in a Small Melanesian Community', *Ethnology*, vol. 6, no. 3, pp. 332–44.

—— 1985, 'Knowing How to Talk to White People: Torres Strait Islanders and the Politics of Representation' in N Dyck (ed.), *Indigenous Peoples and the Nation-State,* Institute of Social and Economic Research, Memorial University of Newfoundland, pp. 95–102.

—— 1987, Torres Strait Islanders: *Custom and Colonialism*, Cambridge University Press, Cambridge.

—— 1988a, *The Past and Present: The Construction of Aboriginality*, Aboriginal Studies Press, Canberra.

—— 1988b, 'Kinship, Mobility and Community in Rural New South Wales', in I Keen (ed.) *Being Black: Aboriginal Cultures in Settled Australia*, Aboriginal Studies Press, Canberra, pp. 117–36.

—— 1993, 'I Don't Care Who Knows: The Songs of Dougie Young', *Australian Aboriginal Studies*, no. 2, pp. 34–38.

—— 1995, 'The Murray Island Land case', *The Australian Journal of Anthropology*, vol. 6, no. 122, pp. 15–31.

—— 2000, *Wherever I Go: Myles Lalor's 'Oral History'*, Melbourne University Press, Me.bourne.

Burke, A 2011, *Law's Anthropology: From Ethnography to Expert Testimony in Native Title*, ANU E-Press, Canberra.

Clifford, J 2013, *Returns: Becoming Indigenous in the Twenty First Century*, Harvard University Press, USA

Dombrowski, K 2010, 'The White Hand of Capitalism and the End of Indigenism As We Know It', *The Australian Journal of Anthropology*, vol. 21, no. 1, pp. 129–140.

Haddon, A C 1935, *Reports of the Cambridge Anthropological Expedition to Torres Straits, vol. 1: General Ethnography*, Cambridge, The University Press.

Keon-Cohen, B 2013, *A Mabo Memoir: Islan Custom to Native Title*, second edition, Zemvic Press, Malvern, Victoria.

Lalor, M 2000, *Wherever I Go: Myles Lalor's 'Oral History'*, Melbourne University Press, Melbourne.

Sharp, N 1996, *No Ordinary Judgment*, Canberra, Aboriginal Studies Press.

Smelser N J, J Wright and P B Baltes, 2001, *International Encyclopaedia of the Social and Behavioural Sciences*, Pergamon, Elsevier.

Chapter 1

George Dutton's Country:
Portrait of an Aboriginal Drover

I first met George Dutton in the winter of 1957. I had come to the little town of Wilcannia, on the Darling River, in the course of a study of part-Aborigines in the far west of New South Wales. My assignment was to investigate their place in 'outback' Australian society. I had not intended to search for remnants of the Indigenous culture — indeed, my advisers had led me to believe that there would be none. But I found a dozen old men and a few women who had been initiated, and I was soon devoting a part of my time to working with those who were ready and articulate enough to tell me something about the 'dark people's rules'. It was frustrating, time-consuming work, and I might not have attempted it had it not given me an occasion for being among Aborigines who were suspicious about, and more or less uncomprehending of, my interest in their present-day affairs. I found, moreover, that it provided the basis for a closer relationship than I could achieve with any of the younger generation.

I had already heard of George Dutton while working on the Lachlan. When I came to Wilcannia, everyone agreed that he was the man to see: 'He knew forty lingos!' They directed me to the outskirts of town, where a score or so of scrap iron humpies stood scattered in the saltbush and mallee scrub. Some youths in cowboy hats and high-heeled boots led me past the wrecked cars, over the broken glass and rusty tins, to a rough single-room shanty, just big enough for the two beds in which he, his small son and two daughters slept. Dutton was sitting outside playing cards, a tall, emaciated half-caste of about seventy, his long, sallow face sunken with the loss of his teeth, under his broad brimmed stockman's hat. I stated my business but he was unresponsive, saying he might come and see me tomorrow.

I felt I had been fobbed off, but he came. He explained that he wasn't going to talk in front of the young people because they only made fun of the old ways. He dictated a few myths and then drifted away to a poker school. Rather to my surprise, he didn't ask me for any money or even seem to expect payment. But I had to pursue him to get more. It took some time to convince him that I wanted more than the few folk tales that had proved enough to satisfy the tourists he had met before. Perhaps also it took time for him to marshal the knowledge that had lain so long untapped. I kept off ritual, having found other old men very reticent on the subject. At last one day, when we were drinking in the hotel, I asked him whether he had been 'through the rules', which was the way Aborigines in these parts described initiation. He answered noncommittally, as I feared he would. But when we stopped by the lavatory on the way out, he showed me that he had been circumcised. He then gave me a detailed account of the young men's initiation, though it was some time before he would discuss the higher rites.

As time went on, the character of our work changed. I was still eager to learn what I could about tribes that had gone undescribed, but I was becoming interested in the man himself and ready to let him take his own course. The culture was dead, but its exponent was alive and accessible. Much of his talk was about the country, which he knew both in its mythological associations and as a drover. I had to send for large-scale maps to follow the tracks that the Dreamtime heroes — the *muras* — and he had followed. In the arid back-country, both Aboriginal and stockman must be able to recognise landmarks that seem nondescript to others, and they travel slowly enough for each feature to make its impression on them. I have heard drovers in bars rehearsing each step of a route, remembering what had happened here and there along the way, as though they were Aborigines 'singing the country'. The country provided the link between George Dutton's life as a stockman in white society and his life as an initiated man in black society. For him at least, it seems to have mediated the conflict between the two worlds.

George's country was not Wilcannia, but the 'Corner', the arid country to the north-west where the three states meet. He had not been there for some years, and we were soon seized with the idea that he should 'show me the country'. He also had the notion that we should find opals at the end of some *mura* track, since the old people used to say that opal was *mura*'s blood. Unfortunately, however, I had no car. We managed to get a lift as far as Tibooburra the following January, but that was as far as we could go. Even so, the trip was worthwhile. We saw a few of the places that had been no more than names until then. And though many old timers were dead, while others had left in the general drift from the region, there were still a few of George's generation with whom I could hear him reminisce and talk myself. It was not until several years later that the Australian Institute of Aboriginal Studies (now AIATSIS) provided me with a Land Rover to go up to Cooper's Creek. George was in his eighties by then and frail. I was half-joking when I asked him whether he was coming. 'By Jesus Christ, I'm coming!' he said. And he persuaded his youngest son to join us. Despite his enthusiasm, he found the heat and the journey gruelling. With his failing sight, he could barely recognise the drought-ravaged country he had not seen for forty years. At Innamincka Station, there was not one Aboriginal person where once there had been hundreds.

After 1958, I was caught up in other work and able to make only brief and infrequent visits to the far west — in 1961, 1964, 1965 and, finally, 1967. One by one, the old people died, and each time I left George wondering whether I would see him again, but each time I came back he was there, thinner, coughing more and seeing less, but mentally as alert as ever. His friend Myles Lalor, who had droved through the same country and who took down many of his letters, predicted in 1964 that we wouldn't have the old man with us much longer; later he said, 'He's nearly died a dozen times but he won't give up.' George never lost his zest for the old stories, especially when he was recording them on tape. He was by now a seasoned informant, working with NWG Macintosh, Stephen Wurm and Luise Hercus (McCarthy and Macintosh 1962; Hercus 1970). In 1968, I sent Harry Allen, a prehistorian, to see him, but this time it was too late. He was too ill, though he dictated a short letter: 'Me and Harry can't do much here now. I can't get around to help him along, but I'll send him a word when I get strong ...' He died in November of the same year, the last initiated man in the far west.

I found the same restlessness and love of travel among other Aborigines of George's generation, though none had travelled so widely as he. This does not, of course, support the notorious 'walkabout' myth. They had not grown up as hunter-gatherers, and I doubt whether they were much more peripatetic than white pastoral workers, whom Anthony Trollope had earlier called the 'nomad tribe' (Ward 1962, p. 9). Though the white settlers exploited the country in ways different from their Aboriginal predecessors, they nevertheless reproduced the conditions for nomadism, at least among the proletariat. The prevalence of seasonal and contract work, the need to drive stock across vast distances, the monotony of life on remote stations and the shortage of women were all conducive to moving on. And, for some at least, the way of life acquired a certain glamour. There are Australian folk songs that are little more than lists of places where shearers have shorn or drovers have travelled (Ward 1962, pp. 177–9). These conditions survive today only in the most remote areas, but they were still active when Dutton was a young man. Aborigines, in addition, had to cope with periodic official harassment, forcing them to move on or take flight.

More than others, Dutton responded to the combined pressures of white and Aboriginal society in his zest for travel. And in his old age it mattered more to him than it did to others. Once, when he was arguing with another man who had misremembered my name, he clinched the matter by saying, 'Dammit, I've *travelled* with the bloke!'

When George Dutton was born, the traditional order still held, but it was breaking up by the time he reached maturity and the memory of it died with him. Yet he was not a tribal Aboriginal. His parents' generation had already made the adaptation to pastoral settlement, grafting the institutions that they valued onto station life. They had, in Elkin's (1954, p. 324) words, 'woven station activity and certain European goods into their social and economic organization and into their psychology without upsetting the fundamentals of their social behaviour or belief'.

This adaptation appears differently according to whether it is viewed from the settlers' perspective or that of the Aborigines. Elkin (1951) sees the Aborigines as pursuing a strategy of 'Intelligent parasitism'. The term has unfortunate overtones — doubtless unintended — and the notion credits them with more freedom of choice than they necessarily had. They were indeed able to use European resources to underwrite Aboriginal activities, but only because the arrangement suited the settlers.

In terms of the wider system, we have what may be called internal colonialism, a regime that preserves traditional institutions in order to maintain a supply of cheap labour (Protector of the Aborigines 1883).[1] In New South Wales as elsewhere, the pastoral industry could not have survived recurrent droughts, recessions and labour shortages without Aboriginal help. Many stations supported permanent communities in order to be assured of a supply of cheap but skilled labour that could be taken on and laid off at will. Aboriginal women, for their part, provided domestic labour and sexual release for the solitary males who made up the white workforce. Thus the pastoralists had nothing to gain and something to lose by disrupting their peons' ties to community and country, or teaching them the virtues of monogamy and thrift. Cultural difference obscured and legitimised exploitation, but at the same time it assured Aborigines of an area of autonomy.

When the *modus vivendi* broke down, Dutton's people moved into the phase that Elkin (1951) has called 'Pauperism'. This refers to an indigence that is as much cultural as economic, a net loss of material and mental things, and a life that is wholly mundane. Also lost are the occasions for self-determination. Until they can reconstruct their identity, Aborigines are distinguished from other Australians by external factors: the colour bar and the uninvited attentions of welfare and protection agencies.

The transition is poorly documented and little understood. Ultimately the determining factors are to be found in the white sector, and there are many instances of direct suppression of custom — even of language. But sometimes the agents of destruction have been the Aborigines themselves, responding to diffuse and indirect pressures from within the community, as well as from without (e.g. see Berndt 1962; Stanner 1960). Often, as in the far west, the decimation and dispersal of Aboriginal populations have been crucial (Elkin 1951, p. 170). But the dispersal must be understood in terms of changes in the rural economy of the far west, which were themselves reproduced in other parts of Australia. I refer to the subdivision of the large pastoral properties and the decline in the proportion of wage labourers to self-employed smallholders. In those parts of northern Australia where the population has been neither decimated nor dispersed, and Indigenous institutions have not been suppressed, the transition may not take place.

Although many anthropologists have worked among Aborigines at the first stage of integration, few have described them in these terms. Ronald and Catherine Berndt (1951) have given some impression of it in the early pages of their South Australian study and Mervyn Meggitt (1962) has stressed the settlement environment of his *Desert People*. However, WEH Stanner (1960) has given it the most direct and vivid treatment in his biography of a Port Keats Aboriginal, Durmugam. In the far west of New South Wales, the phase had ended by or before 1920 and there was no question of my observing it, but it was the setting for the early years of Dutton and his generation. By the time they were born, Europeans had already settled the land, which may explain why none of them could give me a coherent account of local organisation. Theirs was a world of sheep stations, wayside hotels and rare, dusty townships, but also of regulated marriage, bush camps and secret rituals.

During these times, Aborigines had the freedom and occasion to travel further afield than their forebears did. This increased mobility brought into contact tribes that had hitherto been separate. There were more cups from which to drink, even if the contents were somewhat adulterated. The white sector likewise offered new experiences and opportunities, as well as restrictions. Some Aborigines made more of their opportunities than others. The half-caste was perhaps better able to penetrate the white sector and, in this part of Australia at least, suffered no disabilities in the Aboriginal community.

The names and location of the tribes of the far west are a matter of some confusion. Dutton's own account (Map 1.1) does not coincide exactly with that obtained by Tindale from field and documentary sources, and there seems to be no way of resolving the differences at this date. However, the general picture is clear enough. The tribes to the east of the Darling were linguistically and culturally homogeneous and may be classified together under the heading of Wiradjeri (Capell 1956, p. 42). They do not concern us here, except to note that they differed from the people of the Darling and the country to the north and west, who may be classified as Bagundju. According to Dutton,

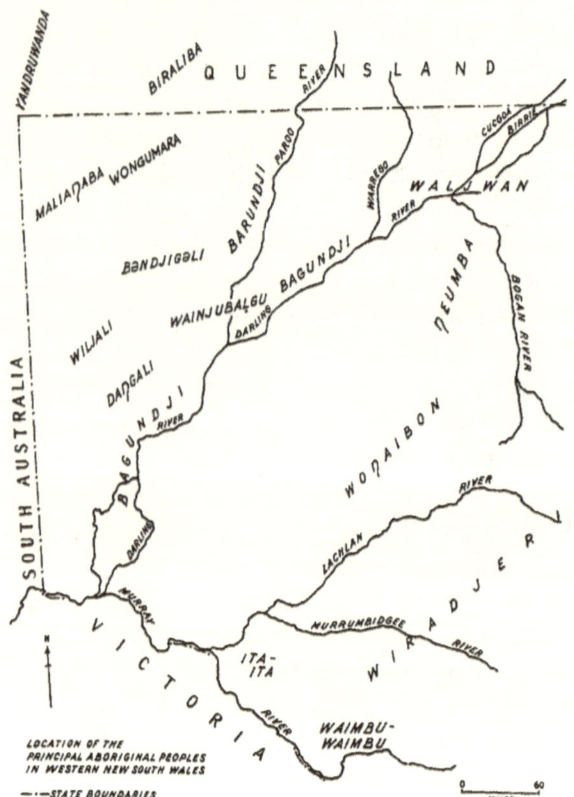

Map 1.1. Distribution of language groups, western New South Wales.

Bandjigali, Danggali, Bulali, Wiljali, Wiljagali, Wainyubalku, Barundji and Bagundji people all spoke variants of the one language. They also employed the same kinship terminology, which Elkin (1939, p. 43) recorded under the name Wijakali.

The people of the 'Corner' — Maliangaba, Wadigali, Gungadidji and Wonggumara — differed again. They are mentioned only in passing by earlier writers, and Maliangaba is the only group about which I could obtain much information (Beckett 1968). Though their languages were not like Bagundji, their kinship terminology and social organisation were similar. But, like the peoples of south-western Queensland and north-eastern South Australia, they practised circumcision and a form of the *wiljaru* rite. Elkin (1931, p. 53) has classified them with these northern and western neighbours as part of the Lakes Group, but since some of the northern members of the Bagundji group also practised a variant of the *wiljaru* without cicatrisations *(jama — i.e. 'clean' — wiljaru)*, one should be wary of setting up boundaries. Mythical *mura* tracks run from the Paroo to Lake Frome in South Australia, and from White Cliffs to Bulloo Downs in Queensland. Aborigines around Tibooburra travelled over into South Australia as far as Parachilna for red ochre and exchanged grinding stones with people on the Cooper. Dutton and other informants made little mention of contacts with the Darling River people, but this may have been due to the disrupting and decimating effects of white contact upon the latter, already advanced by the time they were born.

Hardy (1969) has documented the settlement of the far west in detail. Europeans began to establish pastoral runs along the Darling early in the 1860s. By the end of the decade, the banks of the river had been taken up and newcomers were pressing into the arid areas to the north and west. By 1880, almost all the country to the state borders had been carved up into vast pastoral properties. Wilcannia was a flourishing town of substantial stone buildings, its prosperity based on its situation as a port for the river traffic which linked the region with the coastal cities. But the back-country stations were so far from such centres that they were obliged to be self-supporting for long periods. Stations that had become established and prosperous employed scores of workers, maintaining their own workshops, smithies and stores. CEW Bean, who explored the region before the First World War, described such stations as being more like villages (see Bean 1945, pp. 73–6).

During the 1880s, discoveries of gold in the Tibooburra area and of opals at White Cliffs created a brief mining boom bringing hundreds of prospectors — Chinese as well as European — into the area. The boom was short-lived, however, and towns such as Tibooburra, Milparinka and White Cliffs soon dwindled into tiny centres, serving the vast pastoral hinterland. Only Broken Hill proved to have the deposits to support a large-scale permanent mining industry. With its more or less static population of around 30,000, it has been the region's only city — though one that has offered few openings to Aborigines.

Here, as elsewhere, settlement resulted in some violent clashes between white and black. Dutton had heard of several (see below), and Hardy (1976, pp. 117–22) has found documentation for many more. The settlers did not go out of their way to publicise such things, but Bean's account of events along the Darling is indicative:

> It did not matter who was shot. Every blackfellow that was killed was considered a pest. He would get you as soon as he possibly could ... The law at this time could hang a man for killing a blackfellow. But there was nobody to enforce the law if the squatters did not take it into their own hands. (Bean 1911, pp. 259–61)

In the long run, white settlement was incompatible with the Aborigines' hunting and gathering economy. Intensive grazing, interference with water supplies and the shooting of game undermined the old mode of existence. But the Aborigines had become dependent upon European goods before they lost their access to wild foods. Their eagerness for such things as flour, tea, tobacco and sugar was as intense here as elsewhere, and as potent a source of friction as the conflict over land. In other parts of Australia, the economy had no place for Aborigines, but the pastoral industry of the far west could make use of them. By December 1882, the newly appointed Protector of the Aborigines could report that, 'The males are employed by the squatters in the district, bringing in the horses and general knockabout work for which they receive food, clothes and tobacco.' (Protector of the Aborigines 1883) Aborigines camped near the homesteads, providing a pool of cheap labour which could be tapped as the need arose, as well as expert knowledge of the country. Aboriginal women worked in the homestead kitchens and became the concubines and casual sexual partners of white men. An old white stockman told me that, 'All the jackaroos had two or three gins in those days, and if you looked cross-eyed at them you were sacked on the spot.' One can scarcely assess the extent of miscegenation at this date. Half-castes were a sizeable minority in the Aboriginal population by 1915 (see Table 1.1). Persons with some European ancestry outnumber 'full-bloods' by approximately ten to one in the present population, but often both parents are of mixed descent, and miscegenation seems to have occurred less frequently over the last twenty-five years.

It seems unlikely that the 'station blacks' would have commanded much status or respect in the eyes of white people (see Ward 1962, p. 186; Hardy 1976, p. 183), but from their ranks there emerged a new generation — mainly half caste — who were not tied to the one station, but rather formed part of the region's itinerant proletariat (Hardy 1976, pp. 199–200). They had been reared by their black mothers and ignored by their white fathers; in most case, they had been initiated, but they had also acquired the manners and style of the white stockman. This is not to suggest that they became indistinguishable from their white workmates or that they were accepted on terms of equality. It seems unlikely that they could escape the pervasive Australian prejudice against 'mongrelisation', but it may be that with enough 'cheek' they could achieve acceptance in the egalitarian setting of the roadside hotel and the stockman's camp. In Tom Collins' *Such is Life*, a novel set in the western New South Wales of the 1880s, the half-caste is a sturdy fellow, as capable as any of treating his employer with cool insolence (Collins 1944, p. 10). Neither employers nor workers confined Aborigines to any particular class of occupation. In 1911, Bean wrote:

> [T]he Australian worker of his own accord regularly recognizes his obligation to the blacks, drawing a firm distinction between him and

other dark-skinned people. Shearers who will not work beside a Hindoo or American negro, will work readily with an Australian black or a New Zealand Maori. (Bean 1911, p. 26; see also Ward 1962, p. 122)

Section 16(I)(g) of the New South Wales *Rural Workers Accommodation Act 1926* required separate accommodation for Asiatics and Pacific Islanders, but not for Aborigines. The old practice of serving Aborigines their meals 'on the woodheap' instead of in the men's huts had gone by the time Dutton began working, though it persisted in Queensland.[2]

By the 1880s, the white population had increased and the black population had declined to the point where Aborigines were no longer a numerical threat. There is no way of estimating the Aboriginal population before contact, but the first police enumeration for the Protector in 1882 reported a mere 561, including twenty-eight half castes, from the Darling to the Queensland and South Australian borders (see Table 1.1). Even allowing for some omissions, notably in the Paroo area, the figure could scarcely have exceeded seven hundred, which was less than the population of Wilcannia alone. It seems safe to conclude that bullets and disease had already accounted for many, and the decline continued, as Table 1.1 shows. But for the moment the survivors were still able to hold ceremonies and marry according to the old rules. It was into this world that George Dutton was born.

Table 1.1: Location of Aboriginal population in far western New South Wales, 1882 and 1915 (number of half-castes shown in brackets)

Location	1882	1915
Milparinka	152 (2)	33 (7)
Mt Gipps Station (near Broken Hill)	61 (3)	–
Tibooburra	187 (21)	17 (10)
Pooncaira	52 (2)	26 (4)
Menindie	–	21 (7)
Wilcannia	109	5
Torrowangie Station	–	16 (8)
Cal Lal	–	11 (11)
Broken Hill	–	5 (3)
Wanaaring	–	32 (9)
White Cliffs	–	13

Sources: Police enumeration, by police sub-districts and stations, in the second report of the Protector of the Aborigines, to 31 December 1882, and in the Aborigines' Protection Board's Annual Report for 1915. No enumeration was reported for the Paroo region in 1882, although it seems likely that there were Aborigines living there. If this assumption is correct, the population decline is greater than the totals indicate.

Dutton was born on Yancannia Station some time during the 1880s. Yancannia, situated about 50 miles [80 kilometres] north of White Cliffs, was one of the first stations to be established in this part of the country. Aborigines had attacked it a number of times in earlier years (Hardy 1969, p. 141), but now all was quiet. His father, after whom he was named, was a white stockman; his mother was Aboriginal.

> I don't know much about my father. I just seen him. They reckoned he was a good feller. He left me money, but I never got it. People wanted me to fight for it, but I never bothered. He was run over by a dray up in Queensland. My step-father was living with my mother all the time. He reared me. Him and my father used to work together, they were great mates. Of course, a lot used to sell their women. My mother died when I was about seven. My old step-father and I, we travelled up into Queensland, two or three times to Cobham Lake, down this way [Wilcannia], through Wonominta. We travelled for the pleasure of it. The Gaiters [a white family] wanted me to go to school in Tibooburra. I was about ten then. My old father would have left me behind, but I didn't like it and cleared off after a week.

That was all the education Dutton ever had. Looking back, he considered this action decisive: 'I might have been doing all right for myself now, but I'd never have known about the dark people's stories.'

This was his education during the next few years as he travelled about the country with his step-father, who taught him all he knew. The old man was a Maliangaba. George's mother had been a Wonggumara, but he himself was Bandjigali, because he was born in Bandjigali country. Tribal boundaries did not restrict their travels 'for pleasure', but Tibooburra, Milparinka and Yancannia were the main centres. The station was his father's place of work and the two townships were in his father's tribal country. It was here, when he was about sixteen, that he went through the *milia* circumcision ceremony.

> They were chasing me for a year before they got me. I was keeping away from them, working down at Connulpie. Someone came and said: 'Your father wants to see you. He's in Milparinka.' When I came there they were holding a big meeting in a barn. I ran outside. 'Don't try those bloody capers on me,' I said. They told me not to worry. My father said, 'Let's go down to Mt Brown.' We set off, but there was a big mob following behind us. 'What's happening?' I said. 'They're going to put me through.' 'No,' he said, 'Don't worry, it isn't for you. You'll be *dahra,* you'll have to go back to Yancannia for that.' (Beckett 1968)[3] We camped and the other mob came up and joined us. The next morning they started a game of *gudjara* [played with throwing sticks] and every now and then someone would make a grab at me, but I was too bloody quick. 'Don't try these capers on me,' I said. There was another young feller, about sixteen, they were going to put through with me. I said to him, 'Let's get away.' We sneaked off early the next morning, but they followed us. 'Where are you going?' they said. 'Rabbiting,' we said — of course we weren't. 'You better come back, your father's sick,' they said. We came back. My father was lying down and the doctor, the old clever man, was sucking things out of him. It was only a

trick: he wasn't sick really. 'I'd like you to go through while I'm alive,' he said. Then my *malandji* [a male cross-cousin who serves as the guardian during the ceremony] said, 'You ought to go through the rules. I've been through.' So I agreed. But they kept us there two months till a mob came down from Queensland.

I have published Dutton's account of the *milia* elsewhere (Beckett 1969), so I shall not repeat it here. As he described it, it was a solemn affair but revealed no mysteries. There was no attempt to terrorise the neophytes and the operation was painless.

When the two boys were released from their seclusion and had gone through the final rites, they set off for Queensland with some Wonggumara and Gungadidji friends. Years later, the old man showed me the spot where they had been surprised by a station owner, eating one of his sheep:

> I travelled from Cobham Lake right up through Milparinka, Tibooburra, Nerialco. We stopped off at the stations on the way. We were going up to Conbar where they were going to put a Bundamara boy through. It was like showing you how to circumcise so you can get your own back. They compel you to go. When we got up there they had him caught and everything. That night they had the singsong. They speeded things up. We sang the *milia* all night and put the feller through. We came home then, stopping round Nockatunga for a few weeks.[4] They had a big corroboree there. Then my mate got a job there. They asked me to take two hundred head of goats from Noccundra to Windorah …

In these last few sentences, we have foreshadowed the pattern of George Dutton's career for the next twenty-five years. He went through the *milia* around the turn of the century, and from then until the 1920s he roamed far and wide, droving and participating in the ceremonies of the various tribes he encountered. Early in our acquaintance, he insisted on my taking down a list of the places where he had gone, the names of his employers and the work he had done. He dictated without a pause and had evidently worked it all out at some time. His account is interesting to follow with the assistance of Map 1.2.

> I was working on Cobham Lake one time. I started from Cobham Lake in 1902 and went right off to Windorah. I got a job off Mr Hackett to go to Balkarara Station. We picked up a thousand head of bullock there and took 'em off to the Bluff [near Birdsville]. Then I left Mr Hackett. I took a job at Haddon with Mr Frew but he sold the place so I had to shift over to Arrabury Station and worked there with Mr Lindsay for twelve months, breaking in horses. I went to Farina with a mob of horses, with McLean the drover. I left him and went with Jim Sidi the Afghan, carting copper from Nunamudner[5] mine with twenty-five head of camels. After I was finished there I came back to Nockadoo Station. I worked there twelve months. Then I left there and went over to Durham Downs Station, to put the horse

paddock up. After I'd finished there I went to Orient Station to work for Mr Eastern. I left there and I came back to a place they call Nerialco Station to work with Mr AC McDonald as a stockman. After I was finished there I took a team of bullock on, working for the same station. Then I went down with fifty head of horses to Meningie in South Australia, other side of Adelaide. I left AC McDonald down there. I worked for the council there for about three months. Then Mr McDonald wanted me to come back to Grasmere Station [NSW]. I caught the boat at Meningie and came across to Adelaide. I caught the train there to go up to Broken Hill and took the mail to Carungoo Tank where the boss met me. I handled fifty head of horses for the sale and twenty head of riding hacks. I went to Nerialco Station and took five hundred head of cattle from there to Maree with a feller called Billy Hillston. I stayed at Finniss Springs for about eleven months. Then I got a job with eight hundred bullocks from Crown Point [NT]. We brought them to Yandama Station [NSW]. Then we picked up a mob there to take to Cockburn and we came back to Yandama Station. I done 5 mile [8 kilometres] of fencing with another dark chap. I went from there to Mount Pool Station. I done 6 mile [9.7 kilometres] of fencing there with another dark bloke, friend of mine. Then I went to Eurithinna scrub-cutting. Then I went up to Bransbury Station. I got a job off the owner, Mr Charlie Austin. We had two bullock teams, me and a feller named Ted Baldwin, and we came across to Yandama Station. We picked up 11 ton [tonnes] of wool there and took it to Broken Hill. When we were finished we went across to Langawira Station in New South Wales and picked up 11 ton of wool there and took it to Broken Hill. Mr Austin sold the teams in Broken Hill and took me across to Olary Down in South Australia, to pick up sixty head of poor cattle. I took them out for Mr Austin to Mootwingie Station — Mr McFadden owned it. From there I went to Polamacca Station. I stopped there two days, then carried my swag up to Tibooburra. I got a job on Yancannia Station. Then I went from there with a fellow named Tom Larkin to Lake Elder [SA] with two thousand sheep. I left there and I went back to Tibooburra and stayed there prospecting for gold. It was 1914 and I enlisted there to go to the war — me and a dark fellow named Albert Hebsworth. We couldn't pass (see Idriess 1936; Hardy 1976, p. 195),[6] so we went back to Nerialco and got a job there again with Mr McDonald. We both stopped there for twelve months. Then we parted and I went down to Finniss Springs. I did some dogging down there for about twelve months ...

For some reason — perhaps related to his marriage — Dutton did not leave New South Wales after 1925; he still worked as a drover, but mostly within a 150 mile [240 kilometre] radius of Wilcannia, which became his home. Apart from his one visit to the coast at Adelaide, George Dutton's country could be roughly bounded by the Flinders Range in the west, the Channel Country in the north and the Paroo in the east, with the southern boundary running through Wilcannia and Broken Hill. This is all more or less desert country, in which the oases are rare stations and even rarer townships, like Birdsville,

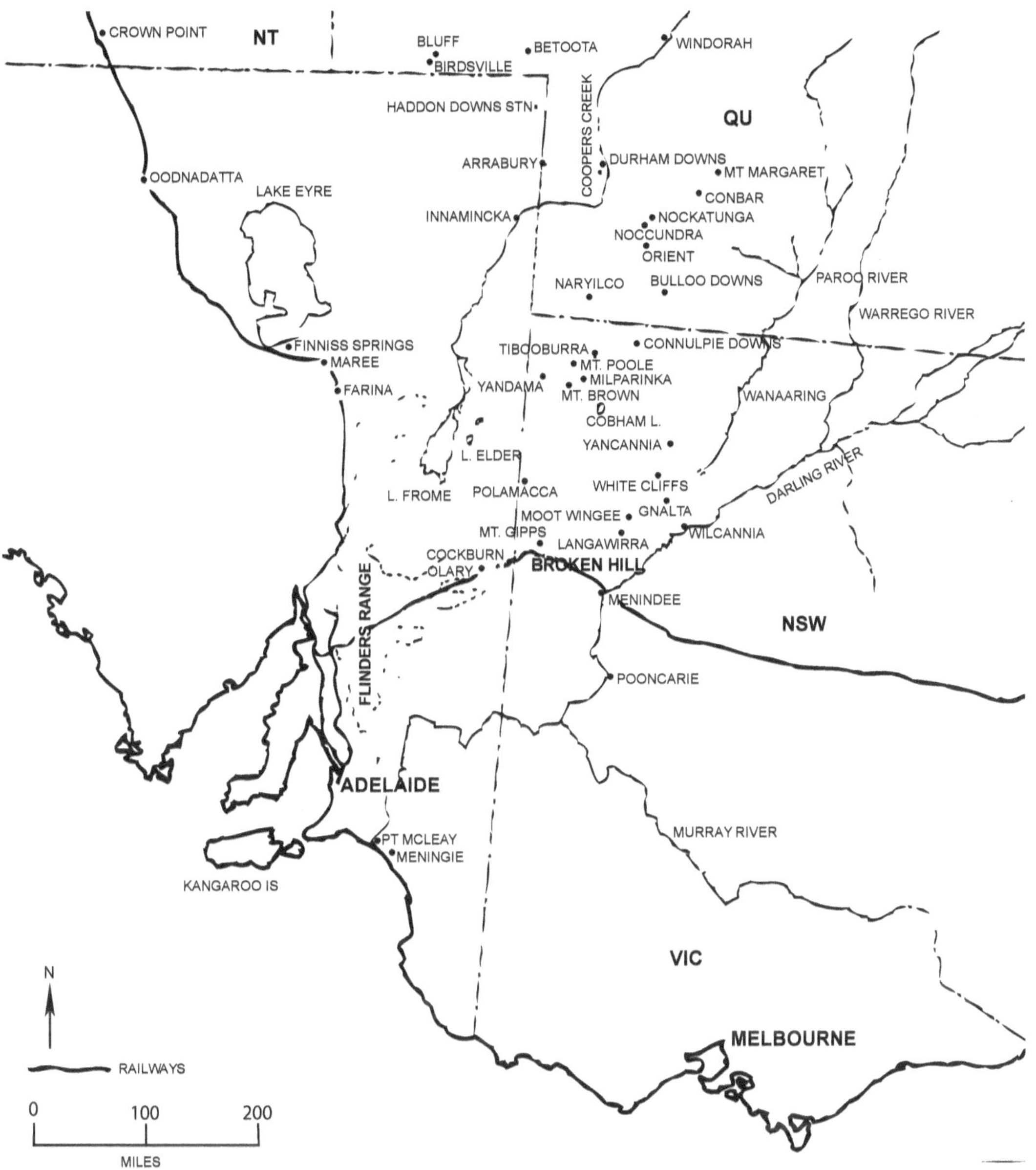

Map 1.2. George Dutton's country.

Farina, Maree and Windorah. Broken Hill is the metropolis, but for stockmen it is a place of transit. Many of the stations named were Kidman property at some time, though Dutton never encountered the man himself.[7] For much of the time, he was working the droving routes — sometimes called the 'Y' — that linked the relatively lush but isolated Channel Country with the rail-heads at Maree and Broken Hill.

It would seem that Dutton had no lack of employers, and his white contemporaries remembered him as a 'smart man' — which is to say skilled in his handling of horses and stock. He was 'flash' too, with his clothes made to measure for him in Broken Hill and long-necked spurs. He worked with Aborigines, Afghans and whites. AC McDonald gave him a state schoolboy to 'train up' for a while. He claimed to have had a short spell as a head stockman somewhere, and when a white worker refused to take orders from him the boss backed him up. He addressed the station owners as 'Mister', but this seems to have been the general practice at that time (Berndt and Berndt 1964, p. 203) and it didn't stop him from answering them back:

> AC McDonald was a good old fellow, but I had a barney with him once. I'd just unyoked the bullocks for the night when he came and asked me why I was camping there. 'I'm the bullock driver,' I said. 'Don't give me any of that talk,' he said. I told him to go and get fucked and left him the next day, but we made it up later. He left Albert Hebsworth and me two blood horses, but we missed out — someone burned the letter.

Dutton does not seem to have made any lasting friendships among his white workmates. But during the years that I knew him, I never saw him more at ease than when he was among his old droving associates. Late in the evening, when he had become a little drunk, he prefaced a contradictory remark with, 'Well, I'm only a poor old blackfeller, but …', only to be reassured with, 'You're white enough for us, George.' But there were whites who would 'call your colour' in the hope of starting a fight. George recalled several such incidents, although he said he had never been directly involved. He said that on some Queensland stations they tried to give him his meals 'on the woodheap' with the local blacks: 'I told them if I wasn't good enough to eat inside I wasn't good enough to work on the place.' Initially he told me that he had gained his point, but years later implied that he had walked out.

Dutton's travels, though usually prompted and directed by his participation in the pastoral industry, had a dual character. The routes he followed as a drover were often those travelled by the *muras*, who had created the waterholes at which he watered his stock. The stations where he worked often had Aboriginal camps, where he heard new languages and saw new ceremonies: 'I saw corroborees at Innamincka, Durham Downs, Cobham Lake. I started learning then. Only after I came back I started to learn our own stories'. In 1965, Luise Hercus met a Point McLeay man who remembered George Dutton, and said that he was a 'special mate' of Albert Karloan. Ronald and Catherine Berndt later used Albert Karloan as their principal informant, writing down the same myth that Dutton had heard years before and always remembered (Hercus 1970). But it was his time in the northern Flinders Ranges that seems to have been the high point of his career:

> When I went down to New Well [on Stuart's Creek Station, near Finniss
> Springs] among the Arabanna mob, they asked me if I was a *wiljaru*. 'No,'
> I said. 'Have you been through the first rule?' 'Yes.' I told them my father
> and all my people were *wiljarus* and I had to go through then. They offered
> me a wife, wanted me to marry bad, but I didn't want to. I didn't want to
> marry from a strange country. Too far away. Too far for me to take her
> back to her own country to see her relations.

Although he used to say, 'Where I put my hat down, that's home,' Dutton —
like most of the Aborigines I know — could not consider living away from his
own people permanently. Perhaps he also felt uneasy among strange tribes.
He told me grim tales of *kadaitcha* men in these parts and claimed to have seen
a man killed for revealing *wiljaru* secrets. He was amazed and disgusted to see
Arabanna eating fat cut from the chest of a corpse as part of a funerary rite.
And when I asked him about subincision he just laughed and said, 'Bugger that
game!' But he stayed long enough to master the language and learn several of
the song cycles, which he could remember more than half a century later.

When he was back among his own people, he found he was a senior man.
'Two or three of my mob saw me lying down with the marks on my back.
"He's a *wiljaru*!" They were pleased then and asked me to come out with
them. Then they started singing the song in our way and I started singing
the way I was taught.' This was about 1905, when ceremonial activity was
drawing to an end in New South Wales due to the decline in and dispersal of
the Aboriginal population. The survivors, whether they had been through the
milia or *dalara,* whether they were *wiljarus* or *jama wiljarus*, joined together.
Which form they followed depended on who was running it. Whether as an
innovation or by tradition, if a boy from one tribe was put through the rule of
another tribe, the latter must reciprocate at a later date. Dutton thought that
the last *dalara* ceremony had occurred about 1902 and the last *milia* in New
South Wales around 1914. But there were still new ceremonies to see up in
Queensland and over in South Australia, and he pursued them long after his
other countrymen had given up. Speaking of one, he remarked:

> Yes, well, poor old bugger, he didn't know anything. He was my country-
> man too, you know, but he knew bloody nothing, though he was a *jama*.
> Now look, I'm the only man in New South Wales — and old Hebsworth
> that died up there in Bourke — we're two bloody half-castes, but we been
> through more bloody *muras* than any other man. We went through the
> *milia,* through the *waradjeri* with the Jandruwanda mob; then he went
> through the *maragandi* — that was up on Bulloo Downs — and I went
> through the *wiljaru*. He beat me by one, and I beat him by one. It's like that
> song, 'I've been everywhere ...'

Dutton saw his last ceremony, the *dulbiri mura* (Beckett 1967, p. 458) at Yandama Station in 1925. By 1930, he was the only surviving ritual leader in New South Wales. About this time, the Queensland government removed the Nockatunga Aborigines to a settlement further east, thus depriving the region of one of its main centres. Everywhere the numbers were declining. Dutton knew that somewhere to the west the life was still going, but too far from home where he now had a wife and children. He was married twice:

> The first one I was just living with her. I met her at Nerialco. She was a full-blood, had three kids. I went with her about ten years. Reared the three boys — there's one living now up in Queensland. I came down to Gnalta to see my auntie [his mother's sister]: I always had to look after her and give her money. When I got back she had a kid. I said, 'Fuck it, the father can have her.' The grandmother was mad after me so I said all right. The man came back, but he said it was all right, he'd had enough. I went up to Nockatunga with this woman. Then I started taking cattle down to Maree. When I came back me and her had an argument — she was a terrible jealous woman, didn't even want me to talk to other men. So I left her and went off to Maree. She took another bloke then. My second wife was a half-caste girl, born on Yandama Station. I'd just come back from South Australia in 1925 to see her father — I knew him, he'd come from Yancannia. Her father and uncle wanted me to marry her. She was booked up for me. I didn't want to, but the old feller said, 'You better stop with us and help us out.'

He stayed with this wife, having three sons and three daughters.

When George Dutton married for the second time, the country was different from what it had been in his youth. Both the Aboriginal life and the pastoral economy had changed. The most dramatic change was the disappearance of the Aboriginal population. The decline between the first New South Wales police enumeration of 1882 and the last of 1915 (see Table 1.1 above) is dramatic and, if anything, understates its extent. Dutton knew it well enough: 'At Polamacca in 1901 there was a big mob of blackfellers, two hundred men without the women and kids. When I went back in 1910 there were only two boys left and graves all round.' The Spanish Flu epidemic of 1919 accounted for more lives. When we looked about the old Tibooburra camping ground, now occupied by one old couple, he recalled the two hundred who had lived there in his youth. When old Frank Miller, a Wonggumara, sang a *mura*, George wept to hear the names of so many who were dead.[8] But the final dispersal was effected not by natural causes, but rather by white people.

The subdivision of pastoral properties, already begun before the First World War, intensified after it in the soldier settlement program. The small, family-sized blocks needed few if any permanent workers, and with the hazards of drought and fluctuating prices had neither the need nor the means to support an Aboriginal camp. Yandama Station supported a small community into the 1930s, but in the west, as elsewhere (Hausfeld 1963), the 'station blacks' were becoming fringe dwellers or clients of the Aborigines Protection Board (Hardy 1976, pp. 176, 186, 194–5). Hitherto the board had left the Aborigines of the far west to the care of the station owners and the police, but it now began to extend the policy of bringing them onto settlements. As the Great Depression set in, Aborigines who had supported themselves all their lives had to go onto the settlements because the agencies distributing unemployment relief considered them the Board's responsibility.

Economic hardships also brought about a deterioration in relations between white and black. In Tibooburra, where the two were about equal in number, tensions became apparent in late 1934. A Mr Allan Angell wrote to the local member of parliament asking whether it was compulsory to admit Aborigines to a registered hall, and to admit Aboriginal children to public school where they would be 'intermixed in classes of white children'.[9] The inquiry was referred to the Department of Education and the Aborigines Protection Board. The department replied that Aboriginal children were required to attend school, but added that 'Their attendance at public school with white children is allowed by the department unless objection to their presence is lodged by the parents of the white children.'[10]

Early in 1935, Mrs J Angell submitted a petition, with seventeen other signatures, requesting the removal of Aboriginal children on the ground that they were physically unfit to sit with white children in a small classroom, being subject to many diseases that whites did not have.[11] In May, the minister approved the removal of all children of Aboriginal descent.[12] But evidently Mr Angell had not intended that Aboriginal children of white appearance, from decent and respectable homes, should be excluded.[13] Several part-Aborigines who had been among the signatories were dismayed to find their children shut out along with the rest. A meeting of parents then requested the minister to readmit all children until the Protection Board could provide alternative facilities.[14]

The Protection Board took no action until 1937, when Mrs Angell submitted a second petition, with nine other signatories, requesting either separate facilities for Aborigines or their removal to the Menindie settlement.[15] In April 1938, the board responded to this clamour by sending a truck and forcibly removing the Tibooburra Aborigines 300 miles [482 kilometres] east to the Brewarrina government settlement.[16] Dutton and his family were among those deported. His account of the place tallies closely with that of its long-term resident, Jimmy Barker (Matthews 1976, pp. 154–60, 212–16). The labour market was already saturated and employers preferred the workers they knew to strangers, who consequently had to live on the meagre board rations. To a man like Dutton, the situation was intolerable: 'I told the manager, "This is no good to me." "You can't go," he said. "I'm going to," I said, and we loaded up the turn-out straight away.' When he saw Tibooburra again, George sought out the man who had led the agitation to have the Aborigines removed. 'I called him out of the pub. "You're the bloody bastard that had all the people turned out of their homes," I said. But he said he didn't have nothing to do with it.'

The Duttons were not the only ones to leave the settlement. Once economic conditions improved, many of those who had earlier lived independently moved off, if only because so great a concentration of Aborigines in one place ensured a high level of unemployment. However, Wilcannia now became the focus, both for the Darling River people who had been on the Menindie settlement, and for the people from the Paroo and the 'Corner' who had been on the Brewarrina settlement. Few returned to Tibooburra or the other townships of the 'Corner', which were all sadly reduced in population.

Wilcannia itself had fallen below one-third of its three thousand peak. With the laying of the Sydney–Broken Hill rail line through Menindie and the termination of the river traffic, it dwindled into a small service centre for the surrounding stations. Its own Aborigines had vanished long before, but within a few years it found itself with an immigrant population of some two hundred, no longer on the decline but increasing rapidly. The government, having failed to draw the Aborigines to its new model settlement near Lake Cargelligo, built a number of cottages, but sited them across the river at the insistence of the white population. The Aborigines soon tired of the black soil that turned to mud as soon as it rained and the periodic floods that cut them off from supplies. Many preferred to squat on the drier ground of the town's outskirts, even if it meant living in scrap iron humpies and doing without a water supply or sanitary service. It was here that I found Dutton in 1957.

Wilcannia at that time still depended on the pastoral industry, and most of the inhabitants were directly engaged in it. No one was obviously wealthy; the majority were working class. The main division in town followed racial lines. The Aborigines were pastoral workers too, mostly unskilled and in such casual contract work as fencing and mustering. A few were drovers, but motor transportation had deprived the drovers of much of their work in this part of the country. Although young Aborigines affected the dress of the mounted stockman, few had much to do with horses. The Land Rover had replaced the horse, and there was no scope for 'smart' horsemen. I found it hard to assess work opportunities. What was clear was that many Aborigines — particularly adolescents — were not working for a considerable amount of the time. During the late 1960s, when the far west was gripped by drought and the adolescent population had increased, there was no doubt about the lack of work. Subsequently, unemployment has exceeded 70 per cent.

Black and white bought their food at the same stores. Their children attended the same schools. The Greek cafe was open to everyone. But Aborigines always sat down the front in the cinema. There was a separate lavatory for Aboriginal children in the state school and there was segregation in the hospital. A few young Aborigines played in the football team, but they could not join the team for a beer after the match because the law then forbade the supply of liquor to Aborigines. It was effective to the extent that it kept them out of the bars, but it did not prevent the back-door supply of cheap wine in large quantities. The police were never able to catch the suppliers, but they kept busy rounding up Aborigines for being drunk or in possession of liquor. I have described elsewhere the endless running battle between Aborigines who were determined to drink and the law whose reprisals set off renewed defiance (Beckett 1964). It was a part of a general pattern of police harassment. In addition to their normal duties, the police had to act on behalf of the Aborigines Welfare Board, issuing rations to the indigent, reporting on cases of child neglect, enforcing school attendance, dunning defaulting husbands and fathers for maintenance, pursuing vagrants and so on. I could not see the police records, but there was no question that the Aborigines were their most regular customers. As often happens, constant interaction had produced a sardonic familiarity between the two, but it was the kind of familiarity that allowed the police to enter Aboriginal homes unceremoniously or sit with their truck headlights shining on a group talking, for as long as they cared.

From 1943, it was possible for Aborigines to obtain a Certificate of Exemption from the disabilities normally imposed on them by the New South Wales *Aborigines Protection Act*.[17] The certificate was commonly known as a 'dog licence', but a number of men and women had obtained one. Most of them, like Dutton, were old people who could not otherwise become eligible for a Commonwealth age pension. Since it was winter, we spent quite a lot of our time yarning round the fire in the hotel bar. The townspeople were not particularly friendly, but there was a motley collection of transients who would sometimes join the circle.

Later the government repealed the liquor prohibition in the Act, but the situation did not change much. As George said in one of his letters, 'It's open slather in the bar for the dark people and they are no better off as there seems to be more in gaol now than before.' After several riotous months, the hotels established their own colour bar and George wrote, 'The pubs are closed on us again but we can buy as much wine and beer by the gallon and dozen at the store. It makes one think, doesn't it.' In the end, only one hotel served Aborigines and the publican issued and revoked his own exemption certificates. For the few who had once been assured of their rights, the situation had deteriorated. George, thinner, bearded and ragged, may have seemed less presentable than in earlier years. He told me with bitterness how the owner of one of the other hotels had refused even to allow him to warm himself at the fire.

Had life continued as it was when he was young, Dutton would have been a man of some standing. Among his own people, he would have been a senior man and a ritual leader. Among whites, he would have been an 'old timer', or what is known in Australian country towns as 'an old identity'. In the event, he was neither. He had tried to set himself up as 'King of the Darling', but such honorifics — hollow at the best of times — meant nothing to the younger generation, white or black. The Aborigines knew he could speak a lot of languages, but even if they could understand some of the languages themselves they were more embarrassed than pleased to hear them spoken in public. His stories of strange tribes and customs had no appeal. He tried to teach his sons, and one young man he had taken droving complained that George had kept him awake all night with his stories, but he could make no impression on them. Children fell into uncontrollable giggles when he sang the old songs. I would have expected him to take consolation among the few survivors of his own generation, but he did not. He dismissed them, sometimes unjustly, as know-nothings. He resented any time I spent with them and would ask, sardonically, whether I had picked up anything good. Often, too, he would dismiss them as *myalls* — timorous, unsophisticated blackfellers, unable to stand up to white people. Possibly, having at last found white people who would actively seek him out and provide an appreciative audience, he feared rivals. He relished the status of expert, frequently rounding off a recording with a remark like, 'Now if there's anyone who knows more stories than me, he's a good man.'

Many Aborigines have the notion that anthropologists exploit their old people, extracting their lore for a few packets of tobacco and selling it to the newspapers for large sums. The notion is exaggerated, if not quite false. I gave George something when I could, more by way of a gift than as payment. He never asked for money except once when he was in trouble, and somehow a gift seemed a more appropriate expression of appreciation for his 'helping' me. Yet there were times when I wondered whether I was exploiting our friendship. I was reassured when, fairly late in our acquaintance, he told me how a white man, seeing us in the bar together, had suggested he was taking me for a few quid by spinning tall stories. 'You know,' he said, 'they don't understand what we're doing.' He was on a mission to get his knowledge recorded. When he was dictating something he considered important, the sense of urgency and authority was unmistakable.

What Dutton considered important were certain rituals and myths. They were always connected in some way with the country. He had no interest in the yarns about rainbow serpents and hairy men that the other old people told. There was no strain of speculation or mysticism. His delivery was matter of fact and his approach dogmatic. (An example of Dutton's narrative style appears in the Appendix to this chapter). At the same, he did not lack feeling for sacred places. He adamantly refused to camp overnight at Mootwingie and prevented his son and me from finding the rock engravings there. Discussing his nominal conversion to Catholicism, Dutton said he 'squared it' with certain myths, but he attempted no syncretism. He was unimpressed by the attempts of his cousin, Walter Newton, to integrate the whole corpus of myths and restate them in terms of a battle between good and evil (see Beckett 1958).[18] Of Catholic beliefs he remarked, 'Of course, a man can't be sure; it's only what you hear.' In one letter, he wrote to tell me of the rumour that the people of another settlement had 'turned Christians':

> There is one bloke got bit by a snake down there. Well the first thing he done was pull out his Bible and started to read. At that the snake started to cough and the bite did not affect the man. Then there was an old lady look-ing after a child and didn't have any milk to give the child so she looked around and there upon the table stood a tin of milk ... Well old pal, if they don't hit the lunatic asylum shortly I don't know nothing. I don't think the God done anything for me.

He seemed to have no such scepticism about 'the dark people's stories'.

Whatever the old ways meant to him, Dutton clearly had an acute sense of cultural deprivation in the modern setting. Around 1927, when the old order was dying, he had been baptised into the Roman Catholic Church, perhaps as a substitute. 'I like their way. Hymns were like the *mura* and the *guluwiru* was like God. I squared it up with the story of Crow and Eaglehawk.' (Hercus 1970) Despite his scepticism, he liked attending mass. But he never went near the church in Wilcannia. He objected to the way the priest 'wanted to boss the dark people around'. Referring to the priest's attempt to check drunkenness, he tartly remarked that the man drank himself. In search of cultural variety, he turned to the 'Ghans' and Chinese and, as they disappeared, the Greeks. He had found his way to the Greek Club in Broken Hill and loved to hear strange languages and customs discussed. But in Wilcannia he found life empty and featureless. His own people lived without order or meaning. Discussing the old ways, one night, he said:

> The dark people take no interest in it, don't want to learn. And a lot of the dark people round this part of the country, Jerry, between you and I, they don't know what they are. They don't know whether they're *gilbara* or *magwara* [the moieties], you understand what I mean? That's how they come to marry into one another, but they don't know. All they know is how to read a comic. [At this point his son interjected, 'Can you read a comic?',

but the old man brushed aside this jibe.] And furthermore, they don't know anything about it, they can't tell you. They go down to the picture show and have a look at the picture. Tomorrow you ask them what did they see? They couldn't tell you the story, what it was or anything, nothing.

One of his contemporaries had put it even more succinctly: 'They know nothing and they don't talk about anything.'

The reader may find a certain irony in an Aboriginal turning to white people to preserve the culture that his own people were rejecting. He knew well enough what the early settlers had done and the effects of white contact. Discussing a massacre near Wilcannia, he said: 'Those poor fellers didn't know anything. They fired into 'em. They tried to get away but they couldn't. Just for nothing. Raped the bloody women, one thing and another, rode 'em and shot 'em as well. All for nothing.' He had heard of similar shootings around Tibooburra and Cobham Lake. I asked him if the settlers had used poisoned flour:

> Oh yes, round Coongee Lake, there's bloody thousands died there. Paddy-paddy water hole ... There might have been a bit of bloody spearing, and they had to defend their bloody selves, but no need for 'em to go on that far. They only had to shoot one or two and scare 'em. But they shot the whole bloody camp.'

In these last few sentences there is evidence of the accommodation that had already set in when Dutton was born — not a sullen accommodation to superior force, but a recognition that the settlers 'had to defend themselves'. At another time, he remarked:

> It's not so bad that the whitefeller came, but it spoiled the people. It made 'em ashamed to talk their own lingo, and marry wrong. They don't learn from the old people, can't talk their own lingo. Some of them can't even ask for a bit of bread or meat. They were better off in the old days, camped on their own, working on stations. They always had a bit of money. They knew who their aunties and cousins were. Now they got educated they think they're better than other people. They're always telling lies.

Even in this, he laid part of the blame on his own people: 'There was too much boning and poisoning.' And explaining the disappearance of *clever men*, he said, 'The grog settled it.' Dutton was not harking back to some golden age of tribalism, which he had never experienced, but to the time of the big pastoral holdings, a period of accommodation to white settlement in which his people still retained their own social order and cultural resources. Now the Aborigines had abandoned their identity only to find themselves in the position of delinquents and outcasts in Australian society. In 1914, when he volunteered for the army, there seemed to be a place for men like himself. In

1957 he said, 'These darkies have got no right to go fighting for the whites that stole their country. Now they won't let 'em into the hotel. They've got to gulp down plonk in the piss house.'

His view of life may have been soured by the sickness and family troubles that increasingly beset him. His wife had gone insane and his eldest son died suddenly, following an encounter with the police; the old man spent all his savings bringing the body back to Wilcannia — it was the only time he asked me for money. Cataracts were destroying his sight and he suffered from chronic bronchitis that several times turned to pneumonia. In his last years, infirmity confirmed him to the settlement, where the only visitors were the police — no friends of the Dutton family.

Strangely, in the last year of his life he was able to re-establish contact with some of his old friends in South Australia. Luise Hercus, while working in Marree and Port Augusta, recorded a number of messages for him, including his reply when she visited Wilcannia. She played him a Southern Aranda man singing the Urumbula (native cat) cycle, which George had learned at New Well. Between verses, the singer said, 'Tom Bagot singing now. The Urumbula. You remember, George?' George replied, 'Well Tom, it's a long time since I left New Well, and the time we had the Wandji-wandji corroboree, you remember that? You was a smart man and I was a smart man ... I hear a lot of them went out to it, a lot of the people. That's one of my songs now, Tom, but I am getting very short-winded now.'

He also heard the voice of Andrew Davis, the Banggala-Gugada man who had been his sponsor in the *wiljaru*. Davis, with Tom Bagot, sang part of the Wandji-wandji cycle. 'That's the Wandji-wandji. George Dutton knows it. I put him through it. He knows. You get a big hiding in that corroboree, you have a rough time in that corroboree ...' George replied: 'Well Tom, I'm really glad you and Andrew Davis singing that Wandji-wandji corroboree and I am very glad to hear you. I can't sing a song for you just now, but I'm very sorry to hear that Tom Marsh [a southern Aranda] went off. Well, some day we might meet again — course I'm crippled now, old fellows. Well, I'll say goodbye to you once more, Tom, Andrew.'

The European settlement of the far west brought about the cultural as well as material dispossession of the Aborigines. Dutton, however, grew up in a period of temporary respite, with his people continuing to regulate marriage, initiate young men and perform rituals under conditions of cultural dualism. The settlers were now secure in their possession of the land, but still dependent on a reserve of cheap black labour. The stations of the 'Corner' region were big enough to support small Aboriginal communities, which sewed the knots of the social and ceremonial network. The missionaries and schoolteachers who were suppressing traditional activities elsewhere had not yet reached the far west, and the pastoralists did not care. If anything, they stood to gain, for the cultural difference facilitated the economic exploitation of black men and the sexual exploitation of black women. However, cultural difference did not mean an insurmountable social barrier. Some Aborigines — particularly half-castes — were able to enter the ranks of the drovers and shearers and become 'smart men'. Nor did this require a drastic change in their identity, for in the fluid conditions of the frontier, work was the primary mode of identification, and society made few other demands.

Dutton travelled both as a drover and as an Aboriginal. The country provided the unifying ground for this dual life, but the two perceptions of it were distinct and unassimilable. For the Aboriginal, the land was an artefact that had taken final form through the deeds of mythical heroes: songs and ceremonies celebrated their deeds and gave renewed particularity to places. The European's purpose was to change the country, which he saw as virgin: it was an economic resource, to be measured and bounded, but as yet outside the sphere of human action and meaning. His equipment for giving particularity to place was of the most rudimentary kind; often he took a native name that meant little or nothing to him. This dissociation[19] of the two worlds gave Aborigines a defence in their accommodation to conquest. While accepting (as they must) the white man's law, they could also plead their continuing need for blackfellow law. Maddock (1977, p. 27) has explained such two-law thinking among Northern Territory Aborigines as assertion of 'human equality and cultural value and of the need to remain in touch with one's past if one is to remain truly human'.

By the time Dutton reached maturity, the dual order was disintegrating. As Aboriginal life failed, he tried to extend his foothold in the European sector, only to find that this too was changing. The depressed townships of the 'Corner' that had now become the centres of Aboriginal life brought demands that many — the Duttons among them — could not meet. Officialdom moved in, and they began their descent into economic and social marginality, their only defence a self-destructive defiance.

Under these conditions, cultural dualism meant nothing. But with the arrival of anthropologists Dutton once again could proclaim its validity. He was not primarily interested in serving as an informant: strings of seemingly unconnected questions exasperated him. He had his own message and his own way of communicating it. In showing us the country, he was telling us who he was, and what his rightful place was in it.

APPENDIX: THE BRONZE-WING PIGEON, TOLD BY GEORGE DUTTON

One time when the old pigeon came down — the *madi* they call him, but he was a man then — he came down all the way from the Bulloo right away down

to Mt Brown. He camped there and he come over to Mt Pool. There was a big
mob of people camped there, all mixed. Then a kid said, 'Who is that skinny
looking man?' (He was talking Wonggumara.) He turned round and he said:
'I'm only just travelling.' An old feller said to him, 'Come closer, make your
camp.' Anyway, he had a feed — they give him the tucker. 'Good!' he said.
(He was talking Gungadidji now.) He turned in that night. He took the water
bag down. Then he said to the water, 'Come this way, water.' So all the water
came in from three water holes into the bag and the bunyip too. He started off
that night. When he got to Good Friday: 'I think I will camp here.' Then he
went on to Tibooburra: 'I think I'll camp here.' Then he went on from there
to Ngurnu. When the Mt Pool fellers got up next morning — no water. 'Hey,
get up! No water here. Come on, well follow that bloke.' So they set to work
and followed him. 'Oh, bugger him!' Anyway, away he went. He went from
Ngurnu to Jalbangu. He went from Jalbangu to Woodburn. Then he went
from there to Tickalara. Then he went from there to Little Dingara. Then he
went from there to Draja [Bransbury Station]. Then he went from there to
Warali. Then he went from there to Graham's Creek. Then to Paddy-paddy,
then just this side of the *Wipa* hole. He camped in the creek and made his camp
there. He hung his water bag up. The snake started to move: he bust the bag.
Then the old Bronze Wing away he goes and banks the water up so the water
won't get away. Then the water washed the bank away. He tried to bank it up
with a boom. 'Ah, bugger it, let it go.' It all ran into Paddy-paddy. He called
it the *gugu* then. Then he went on to Madawara (*gidgee*) Creek. He went on
from there to what they call *Wipa* hole. He left all his feathers at Widhu [Hook
Creek]. Then he went up from Hook Creek to Walbinja and this is where he
died. He's standing up as a stone, but the gold is away to one side.

Acknowledgments

This chapter was first published in 1978 in *Aboriginal History,* vol. 2, no. 1.
The photograph of George Dutton published in the original paper has been
omitted from this chapter.

NOTES

1. I have applied Wolpe's model of internal colonialism to the northern Australian pearling
   industry and suggested its applicability to the cattle industry (Beckett 1977). In work as
   yet unpublished at the time of writing, Heather Goodall, a graduate student in history
   at Sydney University, has shown its value in explaining the situation of New South
   Wales Aborigines into the 1930s.
2. Myles Lalor tells me that at least one station persisted with the 'woodheap' practice into
   the 1950s.
3. Dutton's stepfather meant that he would be put through the Bandjigali initiation which,
   like that of the Darling River Aborigines, involved tooth avulsion and hair depilation,

Dutton subsequently participated in these rites as an initiated man and recorded the songs for me.

4. Nockatunga Station seems to have had the largest concentration of Aborigines in south-western Queensland at that time.

5. I have been unable to locate these places on the map, and it is possible that my spelling is incorrect.

6. It seems that the Australian Army rejected Aboriginal volunteers during the early years of the First World War, though they accepted at least a few part-Aborigines later on. There is a story among older Aborigines that the army adopted this policy after the Kaiser had sneered at them for using black troops.

7. Several of my own informants encountered Kidman and spoke well of his treatment of Aboriginal workers. According to one, he believed that Aborigines brought good luck.

8. Personal names were taken from those of sites along a *mura* track. A name thus brought to mind a place, a mythical event and a human being — living or remembered.

9. The correspondence is to be found in the Tibooburra Public School file in the archives of the NSW Department of Education. I am indebted to Mr Jim Fletcher for bringing these to my attention. Mr Angell's letter was dated 19 December 1934. For a less informed account of the affair, see Hardy (1976, pp. 219–21).

10. Tibooburra file, dated 6 February 1935.

11. Tibooburra file, dated 16 March 1935.

12. Tibooburra file, dated 3 May 1935.

13. Tibooburra file, dated 28 May 1935.

14. Tibooburra file, dated 31 May 1935.

15. Tibooburra file, item undated.

16. Tibooburra file, dated 29 April 1938. The Tibooburra deportation was not an isolated case. The Pooncaira Aborigines were deported to the Menindie settlement about the same time and under similar circumstances (Pooncaira Public School File, Department of Education).

17. At that time, Aborigines (as defined by the *Aborigines Protection Act 1909–1943*) could not legally purchase or possess alcohol, and under a 1936 amendment the board had acquired power to remove campers to a reserve or managed station. The Aborigines Welfare Board's 1952 Annual Report noted that Aborigines living off reserves were now eligible for Commonwealth unemployment and sickness benefits and age, invalid and widow's pensions, but these rights were not extended to reserve and station residents for some years. Exemption from the provisions of the Act, a policy change stemming from the adoption of an assimilation goal in 1940, was granted on an individual basis, ostensibly as a recognition of attainment of a suitable manner of life, but certificates could be withdrawn by the board. In the far west, exemptions were often granted to avoid the inconvenience of supplying board rations to individuals dispersed in towns.

18. Newton's was one of the few attempts I have seen at syncretism. However, it does not get very far before encountering the problem of the geographical particularism of Aboriginal myth, and its absence in Christian myth.

19. Stanner (1960, p. 96) noted the same dissociation in Durmugam.

REFERENCES

Aborigines Protection Board (NSW) 1904–59, *Annual Reports*, Votes and Proceedings of the Legislative Assembly, 1884–1903; Joint Volumes of Papers Presented to the Legislative Council and Legislative Assembly.

Aborigines Welfare Board (NSW) 1940–56, *Annual Reports*, Joint Volumes of Papers Presented to the Legislative Council and Legislative Assembly, 1940–1966.

Bean, CEW 1911, *Dreadnought of the Darling*, Alston Rivers Ltd, Sydney.

—— 1945, *On the Wool Track*, Alston Rivers Ltd, Sydney.

Beckett, J 1958, 'Marginal men: A study of two half caste Aborigines', *Oceania*, vol. 29, no. 2, pp. 91–108.

—— 1964, 'Aborigines, alcohol and assimilation', in M Reay (ed.), *Aborigines Now: New Perspectives in the Study of Aboriginal Communities*, Angus & Robertson, Sydney, pp. 32–47.

—— 1967, 'Marriage, circumcision and avoidance among the Maljangaba of western New South Wales', *Mankind*, vol. 6, no. 10, pp. 456–64.

—— 1977, 'The Torres Strait Islanders and the pearling industry: A case of internal colonialism', *Aboriginal History*, vol. 1, no. 1, pp. 77–104.

Berndt, RM 1962, *An Adjustment Movement in Arnhem Land*, Mouton, Paris.

Berndt, RM and Berndt, CH 1951, *From Black to White in South Australia*, Cheshire, Melbourne.

—— 1964, *The World of the First Australians*, Ure Smith, Sydney.

Capell, A. 1956, 'A new approach to Australian linguistics', *Oceania Linguistics Monographs* 1.

Collins, T 1944, *Such is Life*, Furphy Foundry, Sydney.

Elkin, AP 1931, 'The social organization of South Australian tribes', *Oceania*, vol. 2, no. 1, pp. 44–73.

—— 1939, 'Kinship in South Australia', *Oceania*, vol. 9, no. 1, pp. 41–78.

—— 1951, 'Reaction and interaction: A food gathering people and European settlement in Australia', *American Anthropologist*, vol. 53, no. 2, pp. 164–86.

—— 1954, *The Australian Aborigines: How to Understand Them*, Angus & Robertson, Sydney.

Hardy, B 1969, *West of the Darling*, Jacaranda, Brisbane.

—— 1976, *Lament for the Barkindji: The Vanished Tribes of the Darling River Region*, Rigby, Adelaide.

Hausfeld, RG 1963, 'Dissembled culture: An essay on method', *Mankind*, vol. 6, no. 2, pp. 47–51.

Hercus, L 1970, 'George Dutton in South Australia', unpublished manuscript.

Idriess, I 1936, *The Cattle King: The Story of Sir Sidney Kidman*, Angus & Robertson, Sydney.

Maddock, K 1977, 'Two laws in one community', in RM Berndt (ed.), *Aborigines and Change: Australia in the '70s*, AIAS, Canberra, pp. 13–32.

McCarthy, FD and Macintosh, NWG 1962, 'The archaeology of Mootwingee, western New South Wales', *Records of the Australian Museum*, vol. 25, no. 13, pp. 249–98.

Meggitt, MJ 1962, *Desert People: A Study of the Walbiri Aborigines of Central Australia*, Angus & Robertson, Sydney.

Protector of the Aborigines 1883, *Report of the Protector, to 31 December 1882*, Votes and Proceedings of the Legislative Assembly, New South Wales.

Rowley, CD 1971, *The Remote Aborigines*, AIAS, Canberra.

Stanner, WEH 1960, 'Durmugam: A Nangiomeri', in JB Casagrande (ed.), *In the Company of Man*, Harper & Row, New York.

Ward, R 1962, *The Australian Legend*, Oxford University Press, Melbourne.

Chapter 2

Walter Newton's History of the World — or Australia

Colonised people have not only to endure their situation but to make sense of it. The task is not an easy one, because colonialism is built upon a cultural contradiction. The colonisers, in Gerald Sider's (1987, p. 7) words, are caught between 'the impossibility and the necessity of creating the other as the other — the different, the alien — and incorporating the other within a single social and cultural system of domination'.[1] The colonised, correspondingly, are caught between 'distancing [themselves] from domination and engaging with domination to struggle against it' (1987, p. 7). I would also see them alternately contesting the attributed otherness that structures domination and embracing it as a basis for resistance; again, they may contest incorporation as a threat to their autonomy or embrace it as a basis for making claims on the new order.

This contradiction underlies not only what the colonised say about themselves but how they go about saying it. Their otherness is a matter not just of their internal constitution but of whom they are 'other' to. What, then, is the appropriate way to speak about the difference, and whose way is it? Is the colonisers' knowledge the only way of understanding the colonisers and perhaps the colonised as well? Is local knowledge still valid for local things? Can it even — by renegotiating meanings — be made commensurate with the colonisers' knowledge to form a unitary understanding?

Until recently, anthropologists took only a passing interest in what Indigenous people said about colonisation. However, over the last decade or so, they — along with historians and students of comparative literature — have brought the culture of colonialism into focus (Seed 1991). The literature on Latin America is particularly rich (e.g. see Hill 1988; Nash 1979; Taussig 1980, 1987), as is that on the island Pacific (especially Kaplan 1990; Sahlins 1985). Some Australianists have also turned their attention to such matters (e.g. Koepping 1988; Kolig 1989; Rose 1988), but while — contrary to earlier opinion — it is clear that Aborigines have tried to make sense of colonisation, it also seems that they have resisted bringing it into the framework of 'The Dreaming' — the term anthropologists use to gloss the central body of beliefs and practices by means of which Aborigines conceptualise a cosmic and social order. There are, however, a few exceptions.

One such exception has been lying unquietly in my notebooks for many years, ever since an Aborigine called Walter Newton dictated to me what he called a 'history', though he was uncertain whether it was a history of the world or just of Australia.[2] He had lived most of his life apart from Aboriginal people, but he made the history out of the Aboriginal stories he had heard as a child. These he reworked into a long narrative that set up a dialogue with the Bible and concluded with the heralding of European colonisation. In this article, I want to show how Newton made his 'history', and in particular how he used myths formed in a traditional Aboriginal society to make sense of colonial Australia — if not 'the world'.

Culture and colonisation

The contradictions of colonisation evoke a push toward dialectical resolution, which Roger Rasnake has characterised in the following terms:

> The subjects' model addresses the present situation with a consciousness of transformation [as] well as an awareness of the past. Symbolic forms, and especially myths, thus picture the past as an arena in which the present situation of paradox was created. Myth becomes history — the mythic vision becomes imbued with a consciousness of time and transformation — and, at the same time, history becomes myth — 'real' events in the past … are modified and shaped not only to conform to principles of order in a particular cultural tradition but also to express the contemporary perception of the meaning of past events; and this is done in such a way that the remembered transformation creates a contradiction, or a paradox, that is yet to be resolved. (Rasnake 1988, pp. 139–40)

Where are these symbolic forms to come from? What is the cultural material with which the colonised have to work? Whose past is to be invoked? The possibility that Indigenous knowledge could be brought to the task was obscured for some time by a tendency to regard the savage mind as not merely without history, but inimical to it. Claude Levi-Strauss (1966), in his well-known distinction between the 'hot' societies of Europe and Asia and the 'cold' societies of the primitive world, describes the latter as seeking 'by the institutions they give themselves' to annul 'the possible effects of historical factors on their equilibrium and continuity in a quasi-automatic fashion' (1966, pp. 233–4). If this were the case, the culture of the 'primitive' would indeed have nothing to say about colonisation, and the colonised could make sense of their situation only by adopting the culture of the colonisers. However, recent work — notably in South America (Rasnake 1988, p. 138; Turner 1988, p. 235) — makes it clear that the 'savage mind' is capable of historical consciousness and can even bring mythical consciousness to bear on the historical fact of colonisation.

Marshall Sahlins (1985), while accepting Levi-Strauss's characterisation of the savage mind, has sought to bring the ancient Hawaiians in from 'the cold'. He describes them as encompassing 'existentially unique events' — notably the arrival of Captain Cook — in the conceptually familiar (1985, p. 146), but he argues that 'in action or in the world … the cultural categories acquire new functional values. Burdened with the world, the cultural meanings are thus altered. It follows that the relationships between the categories change: the structure is transformed' (1985, p. 138).

Sahlins is dealing with a protocolonial situation: the Hawaiians were still in control of their lives and had time to collect their thoughts between encounters with Europeans. As long as the unique event came 'raw', in the sense of being unencumbered by intrusive meanings, they could 'cook' it according to their own recipes. The model ceases to be adequate once the stranger becomes a permanent presence, establishing external linkages, introducing new social and cultural forms, and imposing cultural hegemony as well as political domination (cf. Thomas 1989, p. 64). It is now a matter of encompassing not single, meaning-free happenings, but a plethora that — so to speak — bring their own meanings with them. At some point, Hawaiian culture ceases to be coextensive with the culture of Hawaiians — or whoever the group happens to be. It organises only a part of their lives — perhaps just their memories — and exists for them relative to other ways of knowing, against which it is self-consciously compared and reified under such rubrics as 'custom' and 'tradition'. Discussing one such situation in Fiji, Martha Kaplan writes that:

> Between models of enduring indigenous encompassment of the novel, and of the encompassment of the 'other' by a powerful colonial hegemony, there is a space. In this space are the histories of people making new articulations between systems of meaning. (Kaplan 1990, p. 14)

At this point it seems better to break the mould of the totally integrated, endlessly encompassing, indestructible culture and begin thinking in terms of a field in which various cultural formation sometimes compete, and sometimes coexist, articulated perhaps in a makeshift fashion but also separated by disjunctions. One's view depends on where one stands in this field.

Articulations are negotiated through a combination of trope and political manoeuvre, and they may come unstuck if one or the other is ineffective. Those articulations that get into the ethnographies are but the residues of a cacophony of improvisations, most of which — for whatever reason — have failed to catch on. The improvisers — the *bricoleurs* — are unusual individuals, often loners and eccentrics, whose personalities, positions in the world and experiences of it give them an idiosyncratic perspective. Carlo Ginzburg (1982) writes of the sixteenth-century miller who is the subject of his *The Cheese and the Worms*:

> In the eyes of his fellows, Menocchio was a man somewhat different from others. But this distinctiveness had very definite limits. As with language, culture offers to the individual a horizon of latent possibilities — a flexible and invisible cage in which he can exercise his own conditional liberty. With rare clarity and understanding, Menocchio articulated the language that history put at his disposal. (1982, pp. xx–xxi)

The significance of most such individuals is not so much that they change anything, as that they explore the possibilities — the margins — of their cultural environment.

Walter Newton was such an individual. Not only did his life straddle a radical discontinuity in the history of his people, but shifts in the structures of incorporation and exclusion first singled him out and then left him stranded in the space created by the disengagement of black and white. Unlike most of his contemporaries, he was not initiated; also unlike them, he served in the Australian army during the First World War. His experiences imbued his Aboriginal knowledge with new meanings and new incomprehensions. And when he heard stories from the Bible, his Aboriginal knowledge came to exist relative to it, enabling him to set up a dialogue and make his history.

His history can be read in a number of ways: first, it can be examined as a text, in terms of its internal relations; second, it can be read against a knowledge (mainly anthropological) of Aborigines in general and those of Newton's own country in particular; third, it can be read against a knowledge of Australian colonialism, particularly as manifested in one region; and finally, it can be read in the light of Newton's life, which gave him his idiosyncratic perspective on the two worlds. I understand his history as an attempt to negotiate the contradiction between otherness and incorporation; my reading will end up reproducing this contradiction (cf. Young 1990, p. 146), albeit self-consciously and in a critical mode.

History in a cold climate

It is scarcely surprising that Levi-Strauss should take the Australian Aborigines as his prototypic cold society. Nineteenth-century writers who worked from an evolutionary perspective regarded the Aborigines as 'a Stone Age people' whose culture was an anachronism that must crumble at the touch of civilisation. The classic ethnographies likewise reported a society that was rigidly conservative. TG Strehlow, Levi-Strauss's main source, wrote of the Aranda: 'Tradition and the tyranny of the old men in the religious cultural sphere have effectually stifled all creative impulse,' leaving them 'not so much a primitive as a decadent race' (1947, p. 6). AP Elkin, another of Levi-Strauss's sources, stated that, in Aboriginal society, 'the individual is trained not to show curiosity, indeed, not to be curious' (1951, p. 164). Again, Lauriston Sharp (1951) not only predicted the demise of the Yir Yiront social organisation as a result of the introduction of steel axes, but argued that the people had 'no recollection' of the battle of Mitchell River although it had caused the death of 30 people only 70 years earlier (1952, p. 70).

Colonisation does seem to have left some Aborigines in a state of helpless immobility, but this can be explained in terms of physical and social devastation rather than cultural rigidity. Others, more favourably situated, adapted their strategies to the new circumstances with remarkable flexibility. The silence of the Yir Yiront may have been elective rather than amnesiac; in any case, there are Aborigines who do recall massacres (e.g. see Morphy & Morphy 1984). More generally, it is clear from recent work that Aborigines produce — and probably always have produced — historical and quasi-historical accounts of events that occurred beyond living memory (Rose 1984).

Assessing the earlier statements would require more space than can be spared here, but we should consider that their authors mistook the highly structured areas of Aboriginal life — kinship, totemism and cosmology — for the whole. As Sahlins (1985, p. xiii) has remarked, a society may include 'evenementially hot areas, and other areas relatively cold'. Terence Turner (1988, p. 235) has similarly argued that mythical and historical modes of consciousness often coexist, even among the supposedly cold societies of South America.

Modern ethnographies nevertheless suggest that while Aborigines receive welfare payments, drive trucks, visit cities and participate in complex negotiations with government, their 'high culture' remains discrete and historically impervious; it evidently has no place for Europeans, and its only response to colonisation is a peremptory 'No comment!' Thus Kenneth Maddock's northern Australian informants told him they wanted to live under both blackfeller and whitefeller 'laws' (that is, cultural orders), but kept the two 'apart in thought and action' (1977, p. 22).

'Blackfeller law' is virtually synonymous with the Dreaming, a term of Aranda (Arrernte) origin under which Australianists subsume the fundamental features that Aboriginal religions seem to share. The Dreaming is articulated in stories that recount the deeds of beings often glossed as 'ancestors', but having features and powers that mark them off from ordinary mortals. They travel the country, forming and naming it, ending perhaps by 'turning into' topographical features. The landscape thus affirms the 'truth' of the stories, which may also record the 'origin' of some feature of human existence —

perhaps death or the initiation of boys. Aborigines ritually commemorate incidents in the story, whether by miming or by reproducing designs that derive their meaning from the story, or by singing the names of the places along which the 'ancestor' travelled.

The protagonists of the stories may remain immanent in particular places on the earth or in the firmament, and become accessible through ritual — for example, for the purpose of healing the effects of sorcery (Munn 1969, p. 90). They may also manifest themselves destructively if their places are disturbed without the mediation of ritual. Yet they are not normally accessible. The Pintupi oppose the Dreaming to what is 'visible' and 'true' in the everyday sense of these words, situating it 'parallel to everyday life' yet transcendent to the immediate and the present (Myers 1986, pp. 49, 51). In an important sense, however, it also exists in a 'past' — a 'creative epoch' (1986, p. 48), when 'the structure of the world and life was fixed once-and-for-all' (Stanner 1966, p. 151). Consequently, there is what Maddock (1982, p. 105) calls a 'metaphysical discontinuity between men and powers'. Fred Myers writes:

> The Dreaming denies creative significance to history and human action, just as it denies the erosions of time. It represents all that exists as deriving from a single, unchanging, timeless source. All things have always been the same, forever deriving from the same basic pattern. The Dreaming, which cannot be altered by human action, is the very image of self-direction and the source of a given autonomy in human life. (1986, p. 52)

This does not mean that, as some earlier writers supposed, nothing could be changed. Thus, in north-west Australia, Aborigines moving into country whose owners had abandoned their ritual custodianship assumed responsibility for it and extended the ancestral tracks (Kolig, 1981). Western Desert Aborigines could join a new ritual community, based on a commonality 'discovered' in the various local stories (Myers 1982). But, to quote Myers again, 'the concept of The Dreaming organizes experience so that it *appears* to be continuous and permanent' (1986, p. 53). Innovation consists of 'finding' what was always there. In Stanner's (1979, p. 64) words, the Dreaming is 'part of a moving system, accompanying it like a shadow, in continuous correspondence with it, being modified as life modifies'.

But if novelty in itself is not an impediment, there are limits to what can be 'found'. Tracks can be extended, and new rituals and kinship systems adopted; it is even possible to incorporate bottles and Macassar boats into Arnhem Land iconography. Yet horses and bullocks have not joined the ranks of totemic animals, and the automobile has no place in the Dreaming. The 'Captain Cook' and the 'Ned Kelly' of the Aboriginal stories from the Victoria River Downs bring the things of the colonial world, as the ancestors brought the things of Aboriginal world, but unlike the latter they are not inscribed on the landscape (cf. Rose 1984).[3] Stanner's informant, Muta, seems to be suggesting a fundamental incommensurability when he says that, 'White man got no dreaming, him go 'nother way' (Stanner 1979, p. iv).

This issue is posed with particular sharpness in the case of Christianity. Some movements in Western Australia, for example, seem to have incorporated biblical elements such as Noah's Ark and Jesus (Kolig 1988, p. 377). Kolig characterises the usual Aboriginal response to mission Christianity as lukewarm, concluding that such incorporations are random and without philosophical commitment (1988, p. 376). Nevertheless, Aborigines are sometimes ready to recognise a likeness between their religion and that of the missionaries. Usually they do not go further, but they occasionally make attempts at articulating the two, even at situating them within a single field.

To date, the best-documented case is to be found in Ronald Berndt's *An Adjustment Movement in Arnhem Land* (1962). This 'attempt to integrate the traditional world with the outside world' (1962, p. 24) occurred on an isolated Methodist mission in 1957. Some senior initiated men proposed that the showing of certain hitherto hidden ritual objects, called *rangga*, obligated white people to reciprocate with books and education, because these were 'valuable and precious' to Aborigines (1962, p. 40). Although the *rangga* had been shown, they were to remain important: 'We have two minds to think: we worship two Gods. The European Bible is one way: but these *rangga* here on the Memorial are our Bible, and this is not far from the European Bible' (1962, p. 77). Despite the equation of the two 'Bibles' in this sermon, Berndt reports that the leaders no longer regarded the Dreamtime beings as creative or supremely important: echoing mission teaching, it was said that they had come after the Christian creation and were 'not gods, but prophets' (1962, p. 72). He states, however, the Aborigines had not 'adopted Christianity in a wholehearted or exclusive fashion' but were 'endeavouring to blend it with their own religion' (1962, p. 82).[4] Remarkably, the only Christian motif they had drawn into their iconography was the cross, which already had a place in the Indigenous repertoire (1962, p. 63).

Berndt considered the movement untypical of Aboriginal Australia, pointing to the intense missionary indoctrination under conditions of isolation from other European contacts and to the inclusion of Aborigines at the lower levels of the church hierarchy. He also remarked that, unlike most Aborigines, those of coastal Arnhem Land had long been in contact with Macassar trepangers, and had inscribed their presence in the iconography (1962, pp. 13, 28). In other words, this Aboriginal culture was not as 'cold' as, say, that of Strehlow's Northern Aranda (Berndt 1962, pp. 13, 28).

In view of what is to follow in this article, one can doubt whether the movement was as unusual as Berndt suggests, or whether it can be explained satisfactorily in terms of contingent circumstances. The conditions under which such innovations become possible are probably complex, including not just the intellectual constraint that the Dreaming may impose but the nature of the Aborigines' exposure to other ideas and the situation of the innovators in Aboriginal and colonial society, particularly — recalling Strehlow and Elkin — the power of the elders to stop something being said or done.

Walter Newton's history comes out of a different milieu. Colonisation had wrought devastation, to the point where rituals had ceased and the tradition was faltering. Yet he attempted to articulate the Dreaming with the Bible not only by situating them in a single field but also by proposing correspondences between the two in what amounts to a dialogue. Unusually, as least so far as the Australianist literature is concerned, he went on to situate conquest within the Dreaming.

Walter Newton's people

I met Walter Newton about the same time that Berndt discovered his movement in Arnhem Land, during the course of a study of Aborigines[5] in interior south-eastern Australia.[6] The region had been subject to pastoral and mining settlement for almost a century (Hardy 1969, 1976), and the Aboriginal population, reduced in numbers and increasingly cut off from traditional sources of food, now supported itself through casual and seasonal wage labour. Their location in government-administered settlements or squatter camps on the fringes of tiny towns gave spatial expression to a lopsided dialectic between white exclusion and Aboriginal separatism (Beckett 1964, 1978). A few nuclear families and individuals (of whom Newton was one) lived in the white section, but at the cost of distancing themselves from other Aborigines.

Most of them were of mixed descent, and they manifested few of the characteristics that one might expect from a reading of the classic ethnographies. They had a robust sense of Aboriginality, but in the sense of maintaining a distinctive lifestyle rather than a cultural tradition (Beckett 1964). Under official and unofficial pressure to adopt the norms of Anglo-Australian culture, members of the younger generation tried to distance themselves from the 'wild Jacky-Jacky' image that constituted the touchstone of Aboriginality for white Australians. A slightly old-fashioned, idiomatic English was the usual — and, indeed, for the rising generation, the only — means of communication. Young people said they were 'ashamed' to hear 'the old lingo'. Denying or not knowing their totemic clans and moieties, they used British names, including patronymics usually taken from some white genitor (who had rarely also been a pater) or patron back in the early years of settlement. They might remember a few myths, but as curiosities, not as ways of understanding the world in which they lived.

The sense of discontinuity was confirmed by the presence of men and women who had been through initiation rites 50 or 60 years before. They were ready — even eager — to, as they put it, 'teach' me about their language, the old marriage rules and the less secret places and rites (Beckett 1958, 1968, 1978). They also dictated a score or so of myths in English, interspersed with passages in the vernacular. Their insistence that these stories were 'true', as evidenced by the presence of this or that feature of the landscape or heavens, and the peremptory 'That's the story' with which they greeted my requests for explanation, gave me the impression of a culture that was valid for them, requiring neither apology nor explanation. It was otherwise with Newton's stories, which I initially considered less authentic.

Newton was the only Aborigine in Broken Hill, a mining town some hundred miles [160 kilometres] from the place where I was working. Although I had heard of him, I did not meet him until I went travelling with the most highly initiated man in the region, who did not get on with Newton and warned me I would hear nothing worthwhile. He grudgingly agreed to introduce us, but left soon after.

Using the terms I had learned from earlier interviews, I explained that I was interested in 'the dark people's stories' and had heard that he knew some. Almost immediately, he launched into his 'History of Australia', dictating for several hours while I wrote and pausing only while I caught up or queried a vernacular word. The next day, he added a few points, answered some questions I had thought up overnight and gave me some details about his life. I never saw him again.

He told me he had been born on a remote pastoral station, around 1890, the only child of a local Aboriginal woman.[7] He said that his father, whose name he bore but whom he had never seen, was an Englishman, a former lawyer and convict.[8] When Walter was about ten, his mother married an Aboriginal man and moved away, leaving him with the white manager of the station. Presumably because of these events, he was not initiated. His first job was to ride on the manager's buggy, opening and closing the gates as it went from paddock to paddock. Later, he became a skilled horsebreaker. He was also one of the few Aborigines to be admitted into the Australian army during the First World War, serving in the Light Horse Regiment in Palestine (Huggonson 1990).[9] Although he was mainly occupied in looking after the horses, he said he had seen plenty of fighting, with 'bullets coming thick all round'. It was presumably his army service that enabled him to get a job in the Broken Hill mines,[10] but he returned to bush work after a couple of years. In middle age, he had returned to a menial job on the Broken Hill municipal council, and was now drawing an old-age pension.

He recognised as kin several of the families with which I had been working, but he never visited them, complaining that their camps were too dirty and full of drunks. He had a few contacts with white neighbours and said he visited the war veterans' club on Anzac Day to meet old comrades. But the only close attachment he admitted to was 'Mr Tapp', the station manager and later owner who, as he told me, had taken him as a boy and employed him intermittently in later years. Edward Tapp had also taken Newton to the war with him,[11] later getting the younger man a job with the council and finally an old-age pension, both hurdles for Aboriginal people at that time.[12]

Newton had no warning of my visit, yet he dictated his history almost without a pause, as if he had rehearsed it. He said that with time on his hands he had been thinking over the stories he had heard as a child. He said he would like his history to 'favour' several families to whom he was related, and it seems he had tried to tell his story to a kinsman who came to the house but who proved unresponsive. However, he had no hesitation about telling it to a white stranger who claimed to be studying Aboriginal lore. Nor did he seem to anticipate scepticism, for at one point he remarked that, 'If the astronomers and geologists [he needed help with these words but had evidently heard them before, perhaps on the radio] follow what I'm saying, they'll find it true.'

I reproduce Walter Newton's history below in his own words.[13]

The History of Australia – or the World

When the history of the world — or Australia — began, the people all represented an animal. That's where they got their marriage from.

The first people were burned. There was a big flame. They were drawn into it. Some were saved, the best-behaved, I suppose. They came out as animals — ducks and goannas, emus, kangaroos. The people what was saved — may have been a thousand, I don't know — they spread out. Every couple claimed themselves as an animal of some kind. Men and women had to be relations: *makwara* [one matrimoiety] — duck, kangaroo, bandicoot, goanna, mulga snake, native companion, eaglehawk [that is, totemic matriclans]; *kilpara* [the other matrimoiety] — emu, carpet snake, fish, lizard, black snake.

All *kilpara* had to be related, had to be uncles [a cross-generational classificatory term meaning mother's brothers and sisters' sons], sister or brother. *Makwara* were related just the same. That's where they got their marriage from. *Makwara* could marry an emu. All their children would fall on the mother's side. Your aunties' [that is, father's sisters'] kids were cousins, but you could marry them, not the kids on your mother's side.

The second time the people were drowned, and this is where they were saved. The Holy Eaglehawk came and he punished the people. First of all the people in Broken Hill — all where the mine is now — the people were punished and buried here. Their veins turned into silver. That was the Wilyali [a tribe]: the boulders on one side of the hill, that's their flesh. There came an explosion, earth flew up and covered the bodies. Wilya-wilyaru means trillions of people.

The Guluwiru Udarpa [presumably another name for the Guluwiru; see below], his guards built a home for him. All the rest were living around — the Wainyubalku, Barundji, Bakundji, and the Malyangapa, Gungadidji and the rest, further out.

Dinya — that's the fog — was the master of the sections of these people. He was in charge of them; in fact, he was an overseer. But he misled the people instead of teaching them right. So God had to punish the people. First of all he had a word with Dinya and took his power away from him, had a bit of a scrap with him, and in the excitement and the scramble a big fog came along and he [Dinya] sneaked away so the people couldn't see him. He threw a boomerang which came back and showed him how to get away. He wandered up to Queensland. The Guluwiru made him lose his memory so every time he went away he came back to where he started.

God certainly picked out a number to go on in the world again. He stood them apart, and he punished the people all round him. There were convulsions, the ground blew up. They were standing up and he said, 'You can stay as you are.' He threw dust over them and they're now formed into rocks. That's Ganduwandi. They rose up a thousand feet high. He made a flat top. Just a little bit — 300 yards away from his temple at Noontherungie — that's the Holy Jerusalem of Australia. At one end it's rough and cliffs. That's where the people were saved. They had to live there.

The Holy Dirda — he's a great black hawk, 15 feet [4.5 metres] across his wings — he was the head. Next to him was the Holy Bilyara — that's the eaglehawk. The next lord [that] was under him was the Holy Waku [the crow]. It was him that caused the destroyment of the people before they were burned. He came to the two young women's home, and they had two babies, just toddling about. The two young women were going down to get *nardoo*, and they asked the Holy Waku if he'd mind the kids while they were away. He thought he might get one of the women to come back [he had sexual designs on her]. He pinched the kids to make them cry. Both of the women came running back. That was no good. There was a tree in front of the camp. He bored a little hole in the trunk. He kneeled down and he blew in it and said, 'Now grow!' The tree shot up. 'Now lower,' he said. It came down. Then he planed it to make it smooth. Then he blew it up again. Then he said, 'You'll do,' and lowered it. He built a big nest in the fork of the tree and he put the children on it. He blew on it and up [it] went with the two kids on. It went up—oh—a hundred feet, and they [the mothers] had no hope of climbing up it. The mothers stood below, and they ran to the head camp and told them, and messages were sent around, and they [the people] came in like water. The people tried all sorts of ways to cut the children down, but they couldn't. So they had a talk and they thought of the Virgin Lady, and she had a grown-up son. The two women told her. She says, 'Yes, I was expecting that. It's got to happen.' She already knew about it. He [the son] explained to the two mothers, 'You can all lie away from where the children are, to give me space to get there.' (This was ahead of Christ; this came before.) He hypnotised the people and put them all to sleep so they could not see him there. He came while they were sound asleep and got them [the children] down — him being a virgin's son. He told the kids to keep quiet till he got away. He pointed to the women: 'This is your mother! This is your mother! When I give you the signal you can call out "Mamma".' He got away and gave the signal. They woke up and yelled and hopped about with gladness. Then a great big fire bursted out.

The Holy Dirda and Bilyara and Waku drifted away from the people. The Waku started death. He met a woman one day. She was wearing the widow's *copai* [baked white clay] cap. 'Where's your husband?' 'He's dead,' she said, 'but he's going to rise again in three days.' 'He can't do that,' said the Waku. 'When he dies he must die altogether.' He went along to the grave. The husband was just crawling out. 'Go back!' he said. 'Die altogether!' He was after widows. That's why we die. If he hadn't done that we might live forever.

[Newton then told me the story of Crow and Eaglehawk, which I foolishly failed to record since I already had a version from another informant. The main events are as follows: Crow is camping with Eaglehawk and the latter's son. He stays back, feigning illness, while the others go hunting. The boy returns with a possum, which he refuses to share with Crow. Crow kills him by a trick. Eaglehawk, returning, guesses what has happened but beguiles Crow into digging a grave. He then buries Crow. Crow emerges and pursues Eaglehawk, killing him by another trick. Eaglehawk is brought to life again and overtakes Crow, who has retired for the night inside a *maimai* or leaf hut. He sets fire to the shelter, and Crow emerges black. These events all occurred on a hill near Mundimundi station.]

The people grew in numbers and came back. The Holy Guluwiru came and punished the people. He crucified the people. He done that at Mayala Lake: took all their water and they all perished, Wainyubalku and Bakundji. He went from here [Broken Hill] to Mootawingie and made ranges and waterholes. He went a few miles from there, and his bodyguard caught a kangaroo, and that kangaroo — one kangaroo — fed thousands of people, like in the Bible. But he said to the bodyguard, 'Don't interfere with the stomach. Take it over there, about 300 yards [275 metres]. I'm going to do something you can remember me by.' They were laughing and talking with happiness. They looked over to the stomach. It had grown enormous. He said, 'There's something you can remember me for.' By an hour's time it was 50 feet [15 metres] high and 100 yards [90 metres] across. About two hours later, it was 100 feet [30 metres] high and about 200 yards [180 metres] across. Later it was 150 yards [140 metres] high. He waved his hands and formed it into a solid rock, and it's as smooth as this bucket, and all the shapes of the stomach are there. He named it Yunda-ano. It's the other side of Mootawingie, standing out from the other hills, not a tree or a weed grows on it.

Then he went from there and he came to Goondiwindi. Then he called his daughters to him. They were the seven virgin sisters who are now stars in the sky, called *wirduwirdulanya*. He also had seven sons, called *barlugu malimali* or *gagugagulanya*. They had been camping around among the tribes, but the people wouldn't interfere with them. They were going around teaching the people to come right, but the Dinya misled them, like I told you. When the people were gathered together, they said good bye to the people: 'But we'll always be looking down on you. There'll always be seven worlds and another seven worlds.' We call them stars.

Then God made a great rain and a thunderstorm. There was a tribe living at Tibooburra and another at Mt Brown, and God destroyed them with lightning. Then he caused a convulsion which threw them all in a heap and all their eyes blew out of their heads and flew about 30 miles [48 kilometres] from there to a place out from Mt Arrowsmith. You can pick up natural eyes there. White people call them cat's eyes.

Then he brought a great rain and the whole of the land was under water. Those he couldn't kill or get near were drowned. But the good people were able to stop on Noontherungie and Koonenbury Hill, and God made sure there was enough food for them.

While all the land was under water, God got the Holy Devil and his wife. The land was just flat with no drainage in it, no creeks or rise and fall in the ground to make the creeks run either way. There were no rivers, no lakes. God gave the Holy Ngatji [the Rainbow Serpent] instructions to bore out lakes and make a river. That's why the River Darling is like a snake's track. They bored out lakes. They coiled around and scooped out land to make sand hills. And they made channels to drain into the lakes, such as creeks. To make the water run this way and that they rose the ground up. Now this was done right through Australian land. They lived at Peak Tank for a week and that formed Peak Hill. And they said, 'We'll go back to our children.' They went from there, past Yancannia Station to a place called Birndiwalpi. When they came there they said, 'Oh, we can hear our children playing.' When they [the children] saw their parents they were excited and ran down into the burrow. And there was an ordinary big snake, a poisonous snake, *murna* they call him, just beside the burrow. The two Holy Ngatji said, 'We'll sneak up on this *murna* and kill him.' But something woke him up just as they were on him, and he made off down his hole. They just grabbed a couple of feet of his tail. That's how they got the *mura* [a sacred song], and they dance a corroboree to that. They sharpen emu leg bones, and anyone who'd done wrong had to push the bone through their cock and balls.[14] This was because they'd eaten carpet snake before it was given them to eat. The hole at Birndiwalpi was only the outdoor of the real house. They went right down through like a big rabbit burrow or tunnel, and followed their children back to the Paroo [River]. Everywhere was smaller then. God made the ground and creeks bigger after.

The Guluwiru then just flew into a big cloud and went to heaven. And he told them before he left, 'I won't be down among you people anymore. You old folks may live to see what'll happen. There'll be a new race of people coming in years to come, and they're going to control Australia. They're going to own it. They're called *miri batjubatju* — that means white face. And the dark people, the *winbuwimbaku*, will be under them.' He wouldn't call them white, the colour of their skin, because he reckoned that was impertinent — and the old folks when they were alive didn't like you calling them black.

[We broke at this point and resumed the next day, beginning with some biographical details, given above.]

We'll start off from where God left the people. I told you how he said the whites would come and the dark people would be under them, as it is now. Now he said, 'There's a place not far from here that's going to be called — I'm going to name it — Corona, that is at the Queen of England, owned by the Crown. There's a clump of trees that God put, called *gardi* trees. They're the only trees round there — same as those that grow around Tibooburra area. Just by that clump of trees they had their cookhouse; you can see them now, the different rocky stones, the nardoo colour, the red ochre, and you can see them there.

Tales retold

Although Newton had something new to say, he said it in an old way. His history was made of 'the old people's stories', and he was at pains to establish his authority as a bearer of this authentic Aboriginal tradition. He recalled: 'I used to go and hear the old people's stories. I loved listening to them. I was always asking for stories. I'd run errands for them so they'd tell me my favourites.' But unlike his contemporaries, he was not content simply to tell the stories. He approached them self-consciously as needing interpretation, and he saw himself as the one who could lay bare meanings that had gone unrecognised: 'Other people don't give you the right meaning of it.'

Apart from the final episode, announcing the coming of white people, I believe that Newton did make his history out of the mythology of the region. Some of the stories I had heard from other Aborigines, and a variant of one was recorded by an anthropologist who worked around the Darling River in the 1930s (Tindale 1939). Overall, they retain a family likeness to much other Aboriginal mythology in that they describe how 'Dreamtime heroes' (called *muras* in this part of the country, like the songs and stories associated with them) brought form to the landscape and to human affairs by performing deeds that linked the concerns of latter-day humanity (food, sex, children and so on) with world-shattering and world-forming events. The stories give meaning to features of the landscape and the sky, which in turn give substance to the stories. The two snakes, or *ngatji*, are AR Radcliffe-Brown's 'Rainbow Serpents' (1930), known throughout Aboriginal Australia and associated with springs, bores, floods and thunder.

In the course of interpreting the stories, however, Newton changed them — sometimes unconsciously, sometimes perhaps consciously. There are some differences between his rendering of certain episodes and those of his contemporaries. He omitted an episode about a 'talking turd' and one in which Crow sends his penis underground to copulate with the two unsuspecting women — stories that his contemporaries found comical. Perhaps he was prudish or shy, or he may have thought that such ribaldry was out of keeping with the solemnity of his undertaking.

A more important innovation was his attempt to arrange the myths in sequence and as a single narrative. The other storytellers did not make this attempt, and they resisted my promptings to do so. Newton announces the beginning and explains the origins of totemism. Thereafter, he has difficulty in maintaining a sense of sequence, often achieving no more than a simple chronicle. For example, the sequence of fire, flood and eruption seems arbitrary. Perhaps he is trying to create narrative momentum so that the history can encompass the fact of colonisation in its final instalment. However, the episode in which the Guluwiru foretells the coming of Europeans is clearly a conclusion — and not merely because it appears at the end. Guluwiru's departure from the scene of mythological action is a closure for all that has gone before. Nothing is done thereafter; the rest is fulfilment.

Cataclysms punctuate the narrative. Their inclusion is scarcely surprising in a region that is liable to bushfires, droughts and floods, and that experienced volcanic eruptions and earthquakes a long time ago but within the period of human occupation.[15] Fire, water and sky often feature in Aboriginal mythology and ritual, but in this context they function much as they do in the mythology of aboriginal South America, destroying undifferentiated primordium so as to give way to a socially and symbolically differentiated world (cf. Sullivan 1988,

p. 80). Out of the fire emerge the 'best behaved', organised according to social totemism so that they can 'marry straight'. (Fire later fixes the libidinous Crow in his bird form and marks him with its consuming power.) After rainstorm and flood, the landscape is formed.

There are some differences in the use of place names. Like his contemporaries, Newton has 'spatially anchored' (Harry Hoijer, cited in Basso 1984, p. 32) the main events of his history by naming the places where they happened. Some of the names are English, but familiar to the Aborigines; others are Aboriginal, but had been adopted by the settlers; others are used only by Aborigines.

Discussing narratives they recorded in Western Australia, Stephen Muecke and colleagues (1985, p. 98) conclude that 'when historical accounts are collectively constructed by Aborigines, a (perhaps the) major task is to establish the names of places and the right sequence of moves among them', with this representing 'the work of authority in the text and the codification of appropriate knowledges'. The same can be said of the stories told by both Newton and his contemporaries, including accounts of droving trips as well as of the travels of the *muras* (Beckett 1978, pp. 14–15, 29–30).

But there is more to naming than this. Some of the narratives I heard — called *muras*, like the protagonists — were little more than listings of the names of the country the *muras* had travelled. I heard place names chanted and also recited as what the performer called 'dark people's poetry'. These narratives were a matter not so much of naming the country as of telling how the *muras* had named it. Other renderings of the two snakes story included scores of names; Newton included only a few, and mentioned the act of naming only as an afterthought at the end of the second interview (in a passage not included above): 'the Ngatji named the places ... That's how they got the names.' However, he did not forget to mention the Guluwiru's naming of the kangaroo's stomach after it had been turned to stone. And he made a particular point of the Guluwiru's naming of the place associated with the Queen of England: 'that's going to be called — I'm going to name it — Corona.' This, of course, is not an Aboriginal name.

Writing about the Murngin, Nancy Munn has suggested that the 'naming power' of two heroines is indicative of their autonomy: 'With naming power they can "create" the world through imposing upon it a social identity, by socially objectifying it and giving it a power of its own. Thus they can change the merely "lived in world" into the "thought about" world' (1969, p. 180). The same can be said of the Aborigines in Newton's country, the more so in that individuals derive their personal names from the places in the stories. Newton's history seems to surrender naming power in the country at large, but to retain it at the two strategic points. I shall return to this matter later.

Newton has in any case to go beyond what can be authorised through names, for he purports to tell the history not just of the region but of Australia as a whole. It would obviously be impossible to connect the tracks and stories of the region to those of the rest of the continent, even if he knew them. Instead he transcends particularity when, having told how the two snakes formed his part of the country, he adds, 'Now this was done right through Australian land.'

He is also telling the 'history of the world', which cannot be encompassed in this way because the world already has its own stories. His strategy is to bring 'the old people's stories' into dialogue with what he takes to be the master discourses of the dominant culture. When he calls his narrative 'a history', he proposes, at the very outset, a commensurability of white with black knowledge, and he suggests that scientists and clergy will confirm what he says. Geology and astronomy, like the mythology, are concerned with the formation of landscape and firmament by non-human forces in 'another time'. They conceive these forces quite differently, of course; in any case, Newton knew too little about them to do more than propose a dialogue. The Bible he knew better, and the task of bringing it into articulation with the Dreaming was that much easier, because the Bible consisted of stories and its forces were personified. By rendering the old people's stories as a continuous narrative, he made the dialogue that much easier.

The central figure in this history is the Guluwiru, who is also called God. He stands at the apex of a hierarchy of command and now looks down on us from above. According to Newton's contemporaries, the Guluwiru was certainly an important figure, and some equated him with God. He had created all the waterholes, placing a rainbow serpent in each, and when he opened his water bag the rain fell. He had also placed his voice in the bullroarer used in the region's highest initiation rite.[16] He was not, however, a ruler or a punisher, nor did he dwell in the sky. It would seem that Newton elevated him, either by identifying him with the biblical God or by equating the two.[17]

Dreaming Time and Bible Time

The conjunction of elements from the Dreaming and the Bible cannot be adequately understood as syncretism, if by that term is meant only a mechanical, arbitrary melding (cf. Rasnake 1988, p. 156). The conjunction must be understood as an attempt to negotiate the contradiction that colonisation sets up between otherness and incorporation, by initiating what I have called a dialogue. It is metaphorical in the sense of asserting 'a similarity in a difference and, at least implicitly, a difference in a similarity ... the provision of meaning in terms of equivalence or identity' (White 1978, p. 72). Thus Noontherungie is the 'Holy Jerusalem of Australia' and all the *muras* are entitled 'Holy', although some are 'good' and others 'bad'. The rainbow serpent, identified with the serpent in the Garden of Eden, becomes the 'Holy Devil', although he does nothing bad. ('Holy' is almost certainly a calque for *mura*, which is prefixed to the names of heroes in some vernacular texts of the region.)[18]

Several times, Newton asserts that an event in his history is like one recorded in the Bible — for example, Christ's and the Guluwiru's feeding of the multitudes. At other times, the way of telling seems to suggest a correspondence of his stories with biblical ones — for example, of the flood episode with the Noah story and of the other cataclysms with God's destruction of Sodom and Gomorrah. The ascension of the Guluwiru and the seven brothers and sisters resonates with the Ascension of Christ; the Virgin's son's words to the children, 'This is your mother', resonate with Christ's words to Saint John at the crucifixion. Crow's libidinousness (his desire for widows) brings about death (the Fall). In this way, the Dreaming and the Bible become reflections of one another. Sin and punishment appear in the Dreaming, while the Bible becomes a record of miracles and cataclysms.

Difference is defined in terms of spatial separation. Noontherungie is in Australia; Jerusalem is in Palestine: to each his Holy Land. But the people of the Bible are now in Australia, occupying the land formed by the *muras* and ruling over the people for whom the Aboriginal law was made. Here is the concrete problem at the heart of Newton's history. Note how, at the outset, he states his theme as the history of the world and then changes it to 'the history of Australia'. How can he tell the history of Australia without telling the history of the world? But how can he tell the history of the world using stories that refer only to Australia?

He establishes another difference in terms of time, however. In metaphor, while one thing is expressed in terms of another, it remains the primary referent. Newton asserts the priority of the Dreaming in temporal terms: 'This was ahead of Christ; this came before.'[19] In other words, the events of Aboriginal mythology do not simply replicate, still less mimic, those of the Bible, but are *sui generis*. The Aborigines' prior occupation of Australia provides a basis for asserting the priority of Dreaming events. This projection of the sequence of occupation of Australia back into mythological time is made possible through the mediation of the land that Europeans own but Dreaming heroes created. The Dreaming and the Bible are domains of the same kind and of the same value, but when Europeans come onto Aboriginal land, the events of the Dreaming are 'senior' to those of the Bible — perhaps as in Aboriginal society one sibling is senior to another.

The relationship between them approximates that described by Erich Auerbach (1957, p. 64), in which events are linked — not temporally or causally, but vertically to a divine providence. In Newton's history, this role of providence is filled by a person who is sometimes called the Guluwiru and sometimes called God. Whether this person is also the God of the Bible, rather than 'like' him, remains unclear — understandably, perhaps, because the possibility of mediating the contradiction between otherness and incorporation turns on the question. The use of the two names — indifferently it would seem — suggests that they refer to one person; if there are two persons, then they reflect one another. Both are rulers and both dwell in the sky, from whence they can look down on the world; both can transform the face of the earth, punish the people and reward them. Perhaps what we have is an ambiguous, Janus-faced personage, like the Andean 'gringo-gods' (Silverblatt 1988, p. 189), who contains rather than mediates the contradictions of colonialism.

The final episode of the history physically situates this contradiction, for the person who announces the coming of the whites is identified as the Guluwiru, and it is the Guluwiru who exercises 'naming power' over the place. Yet the name that he gives invokes the imperial British Crown (and, by association, the Church of England). It seems as though the Guluwiru is revitalised through access to this symbol of colonial power, and by his participation in the act of colonisation. The Dreaming is enabled to survive the colonial rupture into the new epoch. The Dreaming encompasses colonisation, but only through itself being encompassed.

Myths of conquest

If Guluwiru-God told Aborigines about colonisation before it happened, the event was grounded in the Dreaming. Such claims to foreknowledge occur in the history of colonisation from the time of Cortes and Moctezuma (Todorov 1984, p. 74) and may be understood as, among other things, assertions of the validity of Indigenous knowledge. However, they entail a kind of responsibility for conquest, which in some traditions is elaborated into a story of a primordial blunder.[20] This admission enables a people to retain a sense of control over their destiny, but at the cost of admitting that their ancestors were foolish, unless they are prepared to declare colonisation a benefit.

Given the repeated reference to wrongdoing and punishment in Newton's history, it might be possible to read the coming of the whites as the latest in a series. There is an Old Testament resonance to the telling of these events, but when I asked Newton what the people had done to deserve punishment, he replied, 'Doing the wrong thing, marrying anyway, doing rude things. They didn't take any notice of what the old people told them.' Note also that after a preliminary statement of the punishment theme, the text begins with an account of the marriage system. For all those in his generation, this — rather than ritual — had become synonymous with the Aboriginal order, which had disintegrated during their lifetime.[21]

The disasters that overtook the people were punishment not simply for sexual impropriety but for disobedience. Indeed, the idea of authority comes out much more strongly in Newton's history than in the stories of his contemporaries. They did not associate the Guluwiru with punishment, although they recognised this idea in the person of a kind of tribal vigilante.[22] Newton represents him as a ruler, at the apex of a political hierarchy, described in the idiom of the sheep station and the authorised version of the Bible. Fog (Dinya) becomes 'master of the sections of [the] people'; the Holy Dirda is 'the head' or 'overseer', and under him are the Holy Bilyara and then the Holy Waku. The white boss, whose coming the Guluwiru-God foretells, is thus prefigured in the history; inasmuch as 'the people' are represented as wayward and disobedient, he fills the vacuum left by the Guluwiru-God's 'Ascension'. Authority, then, becomes the vehicle for continuity.

Throughout Newton's history, the Guluwiru-God is represented as punishing the people. They 'married anyway' and did 'rude things'. It thus becomes possible for Newton to say that the imposition of white people's law was a judgment upon Aborigines for breaking their own law, but he does not say this and the prophecy is not made in the form of a threat. Colonisation is nevertheless a fulfilment, and so legitimate. To echo the Virgin Mother in one of the earlier stories, 'Yes … It's got to happen.'

This line of interpretation has a further implication. The breakdown of the marriage system and of the old people's authority that occurred during Newton's earlier years as a result of colonisation is resituated in the Dreaming. Similarly, the violent retribution that these transgressions call down stands in place of the violence of the colonists. By incorporating history into myth, Newton denies the colonists' agency and so absolves them of responsibility.

From the vantage point of the 1990s, I think Aboriginal readers and their friends would expect Walter Newton's history to contain a hidden polemic. They would look particularly for intimations of the Aboriginal land rights movement that was to emerge in western New South Wales twenty-five years after he told it. Certainly, in his description of the silver lode in the Broken Hill mines as people's veins and the hills around it as their flesh, we have a chilling metaphor for the violence of white Australia against land and people.

If this is what Newton intended, the message was indeed concealed. But well it might be, because at that time Aboriginal people were politically prostrate: they had no voice and few advocates. Although Newton was born after the shooting had stopped, the old people from whom he heard the stories were a terrorised generation and (unlike Sharp's Yir Yiront) they did keep the memory, though they were slow to talk about it (Beckett 1978). They also knew at first hand the power of officialdom to break up families and disperse communities, and of the police to imprison and abuse Aboriginal people

It is scarcely surprising, then, that they did not articulate the possibility of recuperation in my hearing, or even perhaps among themselves.

Nevertheless, when my other informants recited the names that the Dreaming heroes had bestowed, they were not only 'spatially anchoring' their stories but also asserting a continuing relationship with the land, contesting the right of the settlers to bestow their own names or to appropriate Aboriginal names without the meanings that accompanied them. Newton's history can be read in the same way, but his argument seems to follow a different and in some ways a bolder direction. His bringing the Dreaming stories into conjunction with the Bible can be seen as what Homi Bhabha (1985) calls 'hybridity' because it reverses 'the effects of colonialist disavowal so that other "denied" knowledges enter upon the dominant discourse and estrange the basis of its authority' (1985, p. 156); specifically, it challenges Christianity's claim to be the one true religion and the claim of white Australians to a monopoly of knowledge. Further, by what Silverblatt (1988, p. 173) might call a 'colonial irony', it draws upon the authority of the scriptures to restore the failing authority of the Dreaming to a position of parity.

The conjunction may also permit the formulation of a social alternative. When Newton brings native and settler together under the Guluwiru-God, he situates them not only in the same place — the land that the Dreamtime heroes formed — but in the same moral space, achieved by the overlapping of Dreaming and Bible time. Both have a right to be there.[23] Perhaps this is what is meant when the Guluwiru-Gods says it is 'impertinent' to refer to the colour of people's skin, whether black or white.

There is a further possibility. The Guluwiru-God makes sure there is enough food for the 'good' people during the inundation, and after taking away the water he makes waterholes and feeds the multitudes. Thus it becomes possible to say — though it is not said explicitly — that this obligation has passed to the new owners of the land. The kangaroo meat, autochthonous food of the country, satisfied the people's hunger; the kangaroo's stomach, turned to rock, satisfies the land hunger of the colonists, but the Guluwiru-God transforms it to commemorate his bounty to the people.[24]

It is remarkable in this connection that the Guluwiru-God (and presumably Newton) reserves his 'naming power' for the two moments at which the moral relations between Aboriginal people, himself and, by implication, settlers are defined: the feeding of the multitudes and the heralding of colonisation. In the first instance, the name is Aboriginal; in the second it is not merely English but invokes the imperial Crown, an Aboriginal exercise of naming power over a symbol of colonial power, but in the cause of colonisation.

Reading the history 25 years later, when Aborigines were engaged in political struggle, a young relative of Newton concluded that the man had been 'a bit of an Uncle Tom'. Its polemic, if it can be called that, asserts the value of Aboriginal knowledge and cultural ties to the land, but within the colonial order it claims only respect and perhaps sustenance for the Aborigines. This, I think, was why Newton thought that scientists and the heads of the churches would confirm his history, and why he was ready to tell it to me.

A history of Walter Newton

The sad truth was that white people would have dismissed the myths as fairy stories and the equations with the Bible as mimicry (Bhabha 1984). Even my declared interest was not what Newton supposed: I was looking for anthropological data, not truth. The Aboriginal families he also thought to benefit with it — whether his contemporaries or their children or grandchildren — would have scarcely been more responsive. The intermediate generation seemed to have rejected the past in the course of wresting control over marriage from their seniors. For those over 70, by contrast, the stories recalled a way of life, a 'two laws' situation in which, as one put it, 'the people knew who they were'. They had no expectations of a revival, but they guarded its memory jealously and spoke disparagingly about one another's expertise. Newton, not having been initiated, lacked the authority to tell the stories, and the changes to which he subjected them transgressed the norms regulating their use. In the words of an initiated contemporary, he knew 'bloody nothing'.

Those who did 'know' were not unwilling to consider equivalences between the Dreaming and the Bible. One old woman had astonished some nuns with her assertion that the Christian God was the same as the Guluwiru, and a highly initiated man had allowed himself to be baptised into the Roman Catholic Church after 'squaring up' what he had heard of the Bible with Crow and Eaglehawk. The same man showed me a stone that was the 'Sacred Heart' of a *mura* called Ngaridi. However, these equations were arbitrary in the sense that they had no impact on Dreaming or Bible stories. The fact was that these people knew little about the Bible and had had few opportunities to learn because there had never been a mission in the region and contacts with clergy were brief and infrequent.

Newton's experience, in this as in other respects, was different. The 'old people's stories' had evidently made a deep impression on him, and something of the delight and excitement they had held for him as a child was apparent in his retelling — particularly of the two incidents in which parents and children are reunited. Their truth, moreover, was attested for him by the features of the country where he had lived for all but a few years of his life. Because he had not been initiated, they lacked the dramatic reinforcement of ritual and the deeper meanings revealed to those who had, but if Aboriginal ritual had never brought him into the presence of the Dreaming, Christian ritual had brought him into the presence of God. By the time I knew him, he was no longer attending church but, as he explained, he had 'got interested in religion' in Palestine: 'They taught me a bit about it. It was Church of England mostly. I liked their way. I've got the Bible they gave me. I can't read it, but I keep it.'[25] If he could not read the Bible, the truth of its stories had been attested in the same way as the Aboriginal stories — by the places he had seen in the Holy Land.

The particular circumstances of Newton's career gave him a particular perspective on the Bible, as on the old people's stories. He experienced the pressures of incorporation to a greater degree than his contemporaries, yet his appearance ensured that he remained the Aboriginal 'other' — albeit an exceptional one. His marginal situation corresponds to the popular stereotype of the half-caste, as one caught between the two races, but not to the reality for his half-caste contemporaries who began as, and remained, Aborigines (Beckett 1978). He was a child of conquest, but his marginality derived rather from his lack of an Aboriginal step-father to sponsor his initiation and from his quasi-adoption by the station manager, Tapp, who later sponsored him in white society. This society allowed him only the slenderest of footholds: it allowed him to undergo experiences that he could share with white but not with black, but without allowing him to be white.

Like his white contemporaries, but unlike his fellow Aborigines — who were mostly rejected by the armed forces — Newton 'went away to the war'. In his investigation of trench warfare's impact on the imagery of English pastoral poetry, Paul Fussell (1975, p. 63) observes that 'dawn has never recovered from what the Great War did to it'. Similar transformations are apparent in Newton's history. The cataclysms in the myths, which Aborigines who lived long after the volcanic eruptions could only imagine, became a terrifying, destructive reality in his experience of bombardment in Palestine. Simultaneously discovering the Bible in the Holy Land — the very place where it all happened — he came to understand the cataclysms as expressions of divine wrath. Returning from the war, he worked for a while in the Broken Hill mines. Going underground, as no other Aboriginal did, he witnessed at first hand the assault upon the silver lode, which was the veins of people punished by the Guluwiru-God, and the surrounding hills, which were their flesh. Perhaps this explains why he left after a couple of years, though he said only that he had 'got tired of it'.

After leaving the mines, Newton once again became Tapp's client, and was to remain so for the rest of his life. It is tempting to see this man as a surrogate for the father whose name Newton bore: 'I never ever saw him — Mr Tapp knew him.' The labour market did not foster enduring relations between employer and employee but, in any case, most Aborigines seemed to share the Australian pastoral workers' independent attitude toward bosses. When Newton's cousin wanted to denigrate the history, he tartly suggested that 'Walter should stick to Mr Tapp!'

In the early days, when farms were much bigger, employers found it easier and often advantageous to cultivate Aboriginal clients. It also seems likely that some Aborigines welcomed the security such dependence brought. According to Myers (1986, particularly pp. 220–2), Pintupi men readily entered into such relations with whites, modelling them on the 'looking after' relations obtaining between older and younger men, particularly in ritual matters. In the case of Newton, it was the other way around. He had never been 'looked after' by an older Aboriginal man. It was Tapp who had 'looked after' him. Tapp, however, was not only patron but, for much of the time, also employer. In this central relationship, as in the army, Newton experienced hierarchy with greater intensity than most of his contemporaries. He himself had been a station overseer in the early years of the war. In the absence of Aboriginal authority, these experiences enabled him to hierarchise the Dreaming and to equate the Guluwiru with God on the one hand, and with the white boss on the other.

Tapp's patronage won Newton the rank of private in the Australian Light Horse, though his acceptance could scarcely have been secure: several Aborigines were decorated, but a man from the same region as Newton had been released, reportedly because he was 'too dark' (Huggonson 1990). The same uncertainty attended the privileges and comradeship supposedly due an Aboriginal veteran after the war, and some who had been decorated found it difficult to adapt to civilian life. Newton took up his entitlement to a position in the mine but quit after a few months. Otherwise the economic prospects were meagre. After being in demand during the war, Aboriginal workers again took second place to returning soldiers; in any case, the subdivision of the big pastoral properties reduced the demand for workers and eliminated the overseer's position that Newton had occupied earlier. He spent some years on his own, looking after a tank on a remote sheep property, until the renewed labour shortage created by the Second World War enabled him to get back into Broken Hill.

He never returned to the Aboriginal community, however. A relationship with an Aboriginal woman broke up after a few months. A niece remembers him visiting his mother, but says, 'He didn't mix up much with the coloured.' When I met him, he admitted kinship with several families but described himself as his mother's only son, although the children of a half-sister lived not far away.

In psychological terms, one might attribute this alienation to his early separation from his mother. But structural factors worked towards the same end. His lack of an Aboriginal father (or step-father) resulted in his not being initiated; his association with a white patron resulted in his being initiated by war — which, according to the nationalist ideology of the time (Kapferer 1988), 'made men' of young Australians. Newton could sustain this form of manhood, however, only by dissociating himself from his Aboriginal kin. No Aboriginal people were present when he died in 1962; the funeral was paid for by the Returned Soldiers League (RSL).

For all this, he remained an Aboriginal, identified with an outcast people and forever at risk of having — as Aboriginal people put it — 'his colour called'. Indicative of his contradictory situation was his refusal to drink alcohol, to indulge in a practice by which whites displayed their manhood but Aborigines their inferiority. However, it was not only this negative aspect of his Aboriginality that had to be denied, but everything that required the company of Aboriginal people in order to be expressed. The only part of his Aboriginality accessible to him was the old people's stories. With these, towards the end of his life, he set about trying to mend the self that life on the margins had fractured.

Newton's involuntary isolation from the white community and his elected isolation from black society left Newton not only the solitude but the intellectual space in which to construct his history. The outcome was not a private fantasy: he worked with and through what he had heard from the old people and from the army padre. But his isolation freed him from the constraints that they would have applied under other circumstances. He kept the Bible the padre had given him, but he could not read it and so did not come under the constraints that it would have imposed. At the same time, he was able to give rein to his immature understanding of the Dreamtime. Situated in the space between ignorance and authorised knowledge, the two traditions took the form of stories. They were commensurable: first because, as Roland Barthes (1977, p. 79) has written, narrative 'is simply there like life itself ... international, transhistorical, transcultural' and second because they were grounded in Holy Lands, both of which Newton had seen. Yet for us, as for his Aboriginal contemporaries, the joins in the history — and in his mended self — show through.

Conclusion

I began with the contradiction at the heart of colonialism, which constructs the colonised as the other while incorporating them into a single social and cultural system of domination. It is something that the colonised must experience, albeit in varying ways and with varying intensities, and make sense of with whatever cultural material is at hand. The initial response to contact may be, as Sahlins has suggested, some kind of cultural encompassment. As 'contact' becomes colonisation, however, the production of culture becomes pluralistic. Encompassment may continue, but the culture of the colonised comes to exist relative to the culture of the colonisers. Indigenous knowledge is no longer self-evident; it must be assessed relative to the knowledge of the colonisers, and if it is not to be abandoned as worthless, it must either be consigned to a separate domain or made commensurate with the knowledge of the other through some kinds of articulation.

The culture of Aborigines, I have suggested, is by no means as 'cold' as some anthropologists — and some Aborigines themselves — have implied. Nevertheless, while traditionally oriented Aborigines may come to pragmatic terms with whitefeller law, they do not — if the ethnographies are right — attempt to encompass it within the transcendent meanings of the Dreaming. Black, like white, regard the two knowledges as discontinuous. If an explanation of colonialism is attempted, it is in terms of human rather than supernatural agency, whether in the form of circumstantial accounts or of schematic stories, such as those about Captain Cook.

Berndt's Arnhem Landers, by contrast, proposed commensurability between 'the two Bibles'. As Morphy (1983, p. 112) glosses Berndt's account, their aim was to 'exchange perceptions of value'. By revealing valued knowledge, they were also giving white people the opportunity to enter into a relationship with the Dreaming. The colonial environment of these Arnhem Landers was relatively benign in that their land had not been expropriated nor their labour exploited. Nor had their culture come under direct assault from the mission. The main instrument of incorporation was the distribution of European goods, on which they were becoming dependent. However, they experienced this relationship as exclusion rather than inclusion, through their apprehension of what white people knew and they did not. The leaders of the movement, who had collaborated most closely with the mission, seem to have felt the sense of exclusion most acutely (Berndt 1962, p. 39).

Newton's situation was similar, but he had no sacred objects to reveal: they were no longer made and he would not have had access to them if they had been. The commensurability he proposed was between the old people's stories and Bible stories, and in this sense he too was inviting me and, notionally, scientists and 'the heads of the churches' — perhaps white people in general — to participate in a unified, if still segmented, relationship with the land. Bridging the discontinuity that he had experienced in his own life required him to take up a self-conscious, reflexive approach to Aboriginal culture. It was no longer enough to tell the stories as his contemporaries did; he had to discover 'the right meaning'. He did this by 'finding' parallels with the Bible and by elevating the Guluwiru until he could reflect the qualities of, if not become one with, the biblical God. The result is unique in the literature, if not in the Aboriginal reality.

Up to a point, Newton's history can be read as Aboriginal tradition encompassing both the fact of colonisation and the meanings it brought with it, undergoing transformation in the process. But this gesture came not from some tribal elder, steeped in the lore of his ancestors, but rather from a fatherless son who was never initiated and who spent the later part of his life in isolation from Aborigines. And it was not a whole culture that encompassed these things, but rather the memory of it and a tradition that had retained some vitality because it consisted of stories. Even for the teller, however, these stories could no longer stand on their own. If they were to regain the authority and sense-making capacity he believed they should have, they had to be situated in the same ontological domain as the Bible. To tell them, one had to tell the Bible stories as well. In order to sustain the authority of the *muras*, Newton had to let the Guluwiru foresee colonisation and consecrate it with his naming power. Corona, with its trees, coloured rocks and red ochre, is the substantiation of this articulation.

The outcome was a new myth that resituated the significant events of history in 'another time' and represented them in forms that, while they encompassed latter-day experience, were marvellous in the old way. It can scarcely be counted a statement of protest, for it removed the violence of colonisation and the moral responsibility for it from the sphere of human agency. Nevertheless, by situating Aborigines in the same moral space as white people, it enabled them to make claims on the new order. Moreover, it proclaimed the validity of Aboriginal knowledge, and in doing so situated the history of Aboriginal Australia in the history of the world without losing it there.

Postscript

In the 1980s, Aborigines from Walter's country laid claim to Mootawingie, a large rock engraving and painting site, which had been declared a national park. In rebutting the archaeologists' assertion that the site was prehistoric because living Aborigines knew nothing about it, they produced one of Newton's stories, taken from my notebook. By this time, the authorities recognised myth as a basis for such a claim. References to the Bible and the heralding of colonisation were omitted because they might have cast doubt on the authenticity of the source. The claim was successful.

Acknowledgments

Versions of this article have been read at anthropology seminars of the Graduate Center, City University of New York; the universities of Western

Australia and Adelaide; Macquarie University; Rice University; the University of Texas, Austin; and the Australian National University. My thanks to those who commented. My thanks also to those who read earlier drafts, including Mervyn Meggitt, Francesca Merlan, Barry Morris, Tim Rowse, Gerald Sider, Sheila Shaver and two anonymous readers for the *American Ethnologist*, where it was published in 1993, vol. 20, no. 4, pp. 675–95.

NOTES

1. Along somewhat similar lines, Edward Said (1979, p. 58) describes the West's perception of the East in terms of a 'median category' that allows one to see new things as versions of previously known things.
2. I published a note on Newton and his history at the time (Beckett 1958).
3. In Australian popular history, Captain Cook is an eighteenth-century explorer and Ned Kelly a nineteenth-century outlaw. In the Aboriginal stories, they generally remain Europeans and do not become features of the landscape. In one Aboriginal story, however, Captain Cook acts like a Dreamtime hero and ends as a feature of the Sydney landscape. He is followed by other Captain Cooks who act like whites and have no such apotheosis (Mackinolty & Wainburranga 1988).
4. The two statements are not entirely consistent. In a personal communication in 1989, Ronald Berndt told me that it was not the Aborigines but the missionaries who had demoted the heroes of the Dreaming.
5. These Aborigines were affiliated with a number of Aboriginal 'mobs', including the Bakundji; their linguistic relatives the Wainyubalku, Barundji, Bandjigali, and Wilyali; and the neighbouring Malyangapa and Wongkumara.
6. This was the 'far west' of the state of New South Wales, including the region to the north and west of the Darling River, up to the South Australian and Queensland state borders. It was a semi-arid region, given over to sheep raising. Populations were sparse. Except for the mining town of Broken Hill, with a population of about 30,000, settlements were widely dispersed in towns of fewer than 1000 residents.
7. His mother was a Wainyubalku from around the tiny town of White Cliffs.
8. Walter Newton Sr may have been a convict, but it is unlikely that he had been transported from Britain, because the practice ceased in 1854.
9. The Australian armed forces were prevented by law from recruiting men 'not substantially of European origin or descent', but as manpower became scarce, they accepted Aborigines who had 'one European parent'. Some 400 served in the First World War (Hall 1989, p. 2).
10. Employment in the Broken Hill mines was closely controlled by the union, and was normally reserved for the sons of miners; however, exception was made in the case of returned soldiers.
11. The embarkation roll of the Australian Imperial Force places the two names side by side, recording that they joined up on 2 February 1917.
12. In the 1950s, Aborigines were only entitled to old-age pensions if they lived apart from other Aborigines and could find Europeans to vouch for their good character.
13. I wrote the history down at his dictation. The punctuation is mine, suggested by pauses in the delivery or by what seemed to be the ends of episodes or stories.
14. Other informants described this as the *Dulbiri Mura*, a ceremony they said was performed to stop married couples from quarrelling.
15. Jeannette Hope, an archaeologist who has worked in the region, informs me that Tower Hill, near Warrnambool in Victoria, erupted about 6,000–7,000 years ago. She also mentions eruptions near Mt Gambier in South Australia about 4,000 years ago (personal communication 1989).

16. I refer to the *wilyaru*, which in variant form linked the north-west corner of New South Wales with north-eastern South Australia (see Beckett 1978).
17. The case invites comparison with the case of Baiami, the 'sky god' of Aborigines to the east of Newton's country. Around the turn of the century, anthropologists debated whether he was an artefact of primitive monotheism or of Christian acculturation.
18. Luise Hercus tells me that some of the texts she collected in the region entitle mythological protagonists *mura* (personal communication 1990). Others use 'old man', a form that an informant of mine translated simply as 'the old Crow, Eaglehawk, etc.'.
19. Wainburranga's Captain Cook is similarly likened to Adam and Eve, but he is said to have been 'there first' (Mackinolty & Wainburranga 1988, p. 356).
20. The motif is widely distributed but is particularly associated with the Melanesian Cargo Cult (for example, Lawrence 1964). There is one report of it from northern Queensland, though the region's history of contact with Melanesians might suggest diffusion (Seligman 1916).
21. Marie Reay was told by older Aborigines in northern New South Wales that 'wrong marriages' were the 'ruination of the Aboriginal race' (1949, pp. 107–8).
22. I refer to the *dinawala*, persons similar to the *kadaitcha* man of Central Australia.
23. My interpretation parallels Adorno's (1988, p. 30) reading of Guaman Poma's description of colonial Peru.
24. I am indebted to Gerald Sider for this reading.
25. The nominal roll of the Australian Imperial Force lists Newton's religion as 'Church of England'. Those without a previous affiliation were often assigned to this category, but if this was the case with him, it nevertheless resulted in his attending that church while in the army.

REFERENCES

Adorno, R 1988, *Guaman Poma: Writing and Resistance in Colonial Peru*, University of Texas Press, Austin, TX.

Auerbach, E 1957, *Mimesis: The Representation of Reality in Western Literature*, Doubleday Anchor, New York.

Barthes, R 1977, *Image, Music, Text*, S. Heath, trans, Noonday Press, New York.

Basso, K 1984, '"Stalking with stories": Names, places, and moral narratives among the Western Apache', in E Bruner (ed.), *Text, and Story: The Construction and Reconstruction of Self and Society*, Washington, DC: American Ethnological Society, pp. 19–55.

Beckett, J 1958, 'Marginal men: A study of two half caste Aborigines', *Oceania*, vol. 29, no. 2, pp. 91–108.

—— 1964, 'Aborigines, alcohol and assimilation', in M Reay (ed.), *Aborigines Now*, Angus & Robertson, Sydney, pp. 32–47.

—— 1968, 'Marriage, circumcision and avoidance among the Maljangaba of north-west New South Wales', *Mankind*, vol. 6, pp. 456–64.

—— 1978, 'George Dutton's Country', *Aboriginal History*, vol. 2, pp. 2–31.

Berndt, R 1962, *An Adjustment Movement in Arnhem Land, Northern Territory of Australia*, Mouton, Paris.

Bhabha, H 1984, 'Of mimicry and man: The ambivalence of colonial discourse', *October*, vol. 28, pp. 125–33.

—— 1985, 'Signs taken for wonders: Questions of ambivalence and authority under a tree outside Delhi', in F Barker (ed.), *Europe and Its Others*, University of Essex Press, Colchester, pp. 89–106.

Elkin, AP 1951, 'Reaction and interaction: A food gathering people and European settlement in Australia', *American Anthropologist*, vol. 53, pp. 164–86.

Fussell, P 1975, *The Great War and Modern Memory*, Oxford University Press, Oxford.

Ginzburg, C 1982, *The Cheese and the Worms: The Cosmos of a Sixteenth-Century Miller*, Penguin, New York.

Hall, R 1989, *The Black Diggers: Aborigines and Torres Strait Islanders in the Second World War*, Allen & Unwin, Sydney.

Hardy, B 1969, *West of the Darling*, Jacaranda, Brisbane.

—— 1976, *Lament for the Barkindji: The Vanished Tribes of the Darling River Region*, Rigby, Adelaide.

Hill, J (ed.) 1988, *Rethinking History and Myth: Indigenous South American Perspectives on the Past*, University of Illinois Press, Urbana, IL.

Huggonson, D 1990, 'Too dark for the Light Horse', *Education*, 13 April, n.p.

Kapferer, B 1988, *Legends of People, Myths of State*, Smithsonian Institution Press, Washington, DC.

Kaplan, M 1990, Meaning, agency and colonial history: Navosavakadua and the Tuka movement in Fiji', *American Ethnologist*, vol. 17, pp. 3–22.

Koepping, K-P 1988, 'Nativistic movements in Aboriginal Australia: Creative adjustment, protest or regeneration of tradition', in T Swain and D Rose (eds), *Aboriginal Australians and Christian Missions*, The Australian Association for the Study of Religions, Adelaide, pp. 397–411.

Kolig, E 1981, *The Silent Revolution*, Institute for the Study of Human Issues, Philadelphia, PA.

—— 1988, 'Mission Not Accomplished: Christianity in the Kimberleys', in T Swain and DB Rose (eds), *Aboriginal Australians and Christian Missions*, Australian Association for the Study of Religions, Adelaide, pp. 376–90.

—— 1989, *Dreamtime Politics: Religion, World View and Utopian Thought in Australian Aboriginal Society*. DM Verlag, Berlin.

Lawrence, P 1964, *Road Bilong Cargo*, Manchester University Press, Manchester.

Levi-Strauss, C 1966, *The Savage Mind*, University of Chicago Press, Chicago.

Mackinolty, C and Wainburranga, P 1988, 'Too many Captain Cooks', in T Swain and DB Rose (eds), *Aboriginal Australians and Christian Missions*, Australian Association for the Study of Religions, Adelaide, pp. 355–60.

Maddock, K 1977, 'Two laws in one community', in RM Berndt (ed.), *Aborigines and Change: Australia in the '70s*, AIAS, Canberra, pp. 13–32.

—— 1982, *The Australian Aborigines* (2nd ed.), Penguin, Ringwood.

Morphy, H 1983, 'Now you understand', in N Peterson and M Langton (eds), *Aborigines, Land and Land Rights*, AIAS, Canberra, pp. 110–33.

Morphy, H and Morphy, F 1984 'The "myths" of Ngalakan history: Ideology and images of the past in northern Australia', *Man*, vol. 19, pp. 459–78.

Muecke, S, Rumsey, A and Wirrunmarra, B 1985, 'Pigeon the Outlaw: History as texts', *Aboriginal History*, vol. 9, pp. 81–100.

Munn, N 1969, 'The effectiveness of symbols in Murngin rite and myth', in RF Spencer (ed.), *Forms of Symbolic Action*, American Ethnological Society, Seattle, WA, pp. 178–207.

Myers, F 1982, 'What is the business of the "Balgo Business"? A contemporary Aboriginal religious movement', MS, files with the author.

—— 1986, *Pintupi Country, Pintupi Self: Sentiment, Place, and Politics among Western Desert Aborigines*, AIAS, Canberra and Smithsonian Institute Press, Washington, DC.

Nash, J 1979, *We Eat the Mines and the Mines Eat Us: Dependency and Exploitation in the Bolivian Tin Mines*, Columbia University Press, New York.

Radcliffe-Brown, AR 1930, 'The Rainbow Serpent in south-east Australia', *Oceania*, vol. 1, pp. 342–7.

Rasnake, R 1988, 'Images of resistance to colonial domination', in J Hill (ed.), *Rethinking History and Myth*, University of Illinois Press, Urbana, IL, pp. 136–56.

Reay, M 1949, 'Native thought in rural New South Wales', *Oceania*, vol. 20, pp. 89–118.

Rose, DB 1984, 'The Saga of Captain Cook: Morality in Aboriginal and European law', *Australian Aboriginal Studies*, vol. 2, pp. 23–39.

—— 1988, 'Jesus and the dingo', in T Swain and D Rose (eds), *Aboriginal Australians and Christian Missions*, Australian Association for the Study of Religions, Adelaide, pp. 361–75.

Sahlins, M 1985, *Islands of History*, University of Chicago Press, Chicago.

Said, E 1979, *Orientalism*, Random House, New York.

Seed, P 1991, 'Colonial and postcolonial discourse', *Latin American Research Review*, vol. 26, pp. 181–201.

Seligman, CG 1916, 'An Australian Bible story', *Man*, vol. 29, pp. 43–4.

Sharp, L 1951, 'Steel axes for Stone Age Australians', in E Spicer (ed.), *Human Problems in Technological Change: A Casebook*, Russell Sage Foundation, New York, pp. 69–90.

Sider, G 1987, 'When parrots learn to talk, and why they can't: Domination, deception, and self-deception in Indian-white relations', *Comparative Studies in Society and History*, vol. 29, pp. 3–23.

Silverblatt, I 1988, 'Political memories and colonising symbols', in J Hill (ed.), *Rethinking History and Myth*, University of Illinois Press, Urbana, IL, pp. 174–94.

Stanner, WEH 1966, *On Aboriginal Religion*, Oceania Monographs 11, University of Sydney, Sydney.

—— 1979, *White Man Got No Dreaming: Essays, 1938–1973*, ANU Press, Canberra.

Strehlow, TG 1947, *Aranda Traditions*, Melbourne University Press, Melbourne.

Sullivan, L 1988, *Icanchu's Drum: An Orientation to Meaning in South American Religions*, Macmillan, New York.

Taussig, M 1980, *The Devil and Commodity Fetishism in South America*, University of North Carolina Press, Chapel Hill, NC.

—— 1987, *Shamanism, Colonialism, and the Wild Man: A Study in Terror and Healing*, University of Chicago Press, Chicago.

Thomas, N 1989, 'Taking people seriously: Cultural autonomy and the global system', *Critique of Anthropology*, vol. 9, no. 3, pp. 59–69.

Tindale, N 1939, 'Eagle and Crow Myths of the Maraura Tribe, Lower Darling River, NSW', *Records of the South Australian Museum*, vol. 6, pp. 243–60.

Todorov, T 1984, *The Conquest of America: The Question of the Other*, Harper & Row, New York.

Turner, T 1988, 'Ethno-ethnohistory: Myth and history in native South American representations of contact with Western society', in J Hill (ed.), *Rethinking History and Myth: Indigenous South American Perspectives on the Past*, University of Illinois Press, Urbana, IL, pp. 235–81.

White, H 1978, *Tropics of Discourse: Essays in Cultural Criticism*, Johns Hopkins University Press, Baltimore, MD.

Young, R 1990, *White Mythologies: Writing History and the West*, Routledge, London.

Chapter 3

Aboriginal Histories, Aboriginal Myths:
An Introduction

Until the 1970s, Aboriginal people in Australia were virtually without a voice. Administrators, missionaries, scientists and novelists spoke of them, and occasionally for them, with such authority as to make a native voice seem unnecessary — even impossible. It was as though Aborigines were incapable of articulating their hopes and their history. The last twenty-five or so years, whatever their disappointments, have seen the creation of a public space within which Aboriginal people can speak to other Australians and to one another. The faces of several Aboriginal spokespersons have become familiar to television viewers, and Aboriginal writers, painters and playwrights have found a sizeable audience, Aboriginal and non-Aboriginal. But an older and less educated generation has also been able, through the use of a tape recorder and an editor, to collect their memories and tell their stories to the world at large. Sally Morgan's *My Place* (1987) tells how a young Aboriginal graduate of the 1970s enabled her mother and grandmother to confront their lives and articulate their Aboriginality.

This was a painful and difficult process because the bureaucratic terror and daily oppression that the two older women had experienced had forced them not merely to conceal but to repress their Aboriginality. The authorities weighed particularly heavily on them because their European ancestry and appearance rendered them candidates for assimilation; but not every Aborigine suffered to this extent. People who 'looked Aboriginal' were less pressured and so better able to talk about their Aboriginality, at least within the confines of home and bush camp, if not yet in public.

The experts who wrote about Aborigines up to the 1970s largely ignored such talk, due to the intellectual priorities of the time — particularly the reconstructionist emphasis in anthropology — but also to the belief that a people who situated all the formative events of their world in a mythological

'Dreamtime' must be without history. Thus, according to Lauriston Sharp, the Yir Yiront had 'no recollection' of the 'battle of Mitchell River', although it had caused the death of some 30 people only 70 years earlier (1952). WEH Stanner (1966, pp. 139–40) reported a similar forgetting among the Murimbata. The implication was that the Aborigines, existing in a world of endless repetition, lacked the capacity for linear thought, and so could conceive neither of a past or a future that was different from what they knew. Generalising from such reports, James Urry (1980, pp. 2–3) concluded that history was a construction of the past that was alien to Aboriginal thought, a conclusion Tony Swain (1994, p. 3) has lately endorsed.

Howard and Frances Morphy (1983) have questioned this conclusion, retailing Aboriginal accounts of killings from their own fieldwork, yet such notions have not quite disappeared. In 1989, Erich Kolig remarked on the apparent inability of traditionally oriented Aborigines to conceive of political alternatives to colonisation: 'having given up their armed struggle against white intrusion, Aborigines seem to have entered a phase of political inertia, or perhaps better described as catatonia, from which they emerge now by participation in the [Australian] political process'. Kolig attributes this change not (as I am inclined to do) to the changing conditions of colonialism, but to an 'internal revision of the Aboriginal world view' in which 'politics directed at reshaping society as a whole, leaves behind religiously inspired ideas, goals and methods' (1989, pp. 156–7). This change was not easily achieved, because the religion was enormously conservative and did not tolerate rival knowledge. Contradictory knowledge was either incorporated into the dogma or it was suppressed and wiped away (1989, pp. 104–5).

Such thinking has a considerable genealogy, stretching back at least to AP Elkin (1951) and TG Strehlow (1947), who provided much of the material for Claude Levi-Strauss's 'Cold Society' (1966).[1] I have reviewed this debate (in Chapter 2) and will not repeat the argument here, except to note that, at least for Levi-Strauss, the ability of cold societies to encompass change is not at issue; rather, this encompassment is achieved by making change retrospective and, so to speak, 'freezing' it in some mythological 'Dreamtime' (Levi-Strauss 1966: 233–34; cf. Sahlins 1985). Examples of this range from the Arnhem Landers' encompassment of the Macassan traders in ritual and iconography (Berndt 1962) to New South Wales war veteran Walter Newton's retelling of 'the old people's stories' to include European colonisation (Chapter 2). And as Deborah Bird Rose (1994) shows, Aborigines of the Yarralin community found a place for the outlaw Ned Kelly.

This, however, leaves outstanding the question as to whether this is the only way that Aborigines — or at least 'traditionally oriented' Aborigines — can articulate memory: are there no narratives that could be called histories?

Is a rudimentary historical consciousness not a condition of human existence? David Carr (1986, p. 3) has indeed suggested the existence of 'a non-thematic or pre-thematic awareness of the historical past which functions as a background for our present experience, or our experience of the present', and which may (but need not) provide a ground for the historian's history. Confronted with Levi-Strauss's cold society, Carr considers the possibility that 'for such cultures, linear and narrative organization is characteristic of ordinary experience, but that this organization does not get projected onto the larger-scale time of long-term social events'. However, he is dissuaded by the claim of Levi-Strauss and others that 'the conceptual systems they describe cover all aspects of the lives of those who subscribe to them, not merely a part of them' (1966, p. 180).

The Australianist literature, along with much of classical anthropology, has tended to support this view, taking the grand structures of reciprocity, kinship and mythology to apply to the whole of Aboriginal culture. But an alternative understanding is possible if we think of cultures as complex and heterogeneous. Maurice Bloch, criticising Geertz's representation of time in Bali, has argued that two cognitive systems coexist, one organising ritual activity and the other practical activity (1977; for a South American parallel, see Rappaport 1990, p. 14).[2] Although he might not accept quite this formulation, Marshall Sahlins (1985, p. xiii) has observed that a society may have 'evenementially hot areas, and other areas relatively cold'. With this in mind, it becomes possible to suppose that so-called cold societies always had their warm patches, if only to provide people with the discursive means of coming to terms with contingencies, rather as — as the ethnographies of the 1960s demonstrated — Aborigines needed to do more than invoke the rules to accomplish a marriage (Meggitt 1962; Hiatt 1965).

The question is not just whether Aborigines remembered things from day to day or year to year: the ethnographies are full of ritual and marital transactions that dragged on over decades, and Lloyd Warner's Mahkarolla seems to have no difficulty in putting together a life story that extended back to his years in the bush (Warner 1958, pp. 467–90). Nor does memory necessarily die with those who experienced it. In Merlan (1994), an Aboriginal informant retails accounts of the early days of settlement, heard from those who had experienced them. Even in the traditional domain, Stanner (1966, p. 140) obtained accounts — albeit hazy — of rites abandoned before his informants were born. This, however, leaves outstanding the question of how such memories are articulated and framed.

Compared with Sahlins' (1985, p. 35) Polynesians, Aborigines do not seem inclined to 'heroic history', though the term 'epic' is not altogether inappropriate for the oral accounts of Pigeon the Outlaw (Muecke et al. 1985) — not to mention Colin Johnson's (1979) ironic literary reworking of the story. However, without pre-judging the issue, we should not scorn to look at humbler, less structured forms such as jokes, songs, genealogies and stories as possible means by which Aboriginal people have stored and organised their pasts and their futures. Rose (1989, p. 147) has reported of the Victoria River Downs Aborigines:

> There is no Yarralin history as such, there are stories. There are stories that belong to people because they were witnesses to the events recounted, because their parents or other forebears were witnesses and passed the knowledge on to them. Stories are true because the ways in which they account for the particular are proved through experience.

We need to think of people drawing on a diversity of forms in the process of making sense of their lives and, once colonisation intrudes, these forms need not be only traditional. The colonial encounter brings with it its own cultural forms which in due course become available to the colonised. These include the missionaries' Bible — or perhaps one should say Bible stories. They also include the kind of knowledge about the Australian past that features in primary school syllabuses, illustrated magazines, civic ceremonies and television, which falls short of academic linear history, but includes exemplary stories and fetishised 'historic' (rather than historical) events such as Captain Cook's 'discovery' of Australia or the outlaw Ned Kelly's defiance of authority.

If there seem to be a number of ways of framing the past, how and why do those doing the speaking adopt one form rather than another? Terence Turner and Jonathan Hill have confronted similar problems in the analysis of South American narratives by rethinking the categories of history and myth (Turner 1988; Hill 1988). They dispense with the old criterion of what is true (or credible) set against what is untrue (or incredible). Instead, they posit a single domain of social consciousness. For Hill, this is differentiated in terms of structure and agency, with myth having a preponderance of structure and history a preponderance of agency (Hill 1988, p. 6). According to Turner (1988, pp. 243–4):

> The characteristic move of mythic thought is the projection of the existing order of experience as its own formative principle, but in a fantastic, asocial form inaccessible to the world of ordinary social life. This means in practice its projection as a peculiar form of time: a dual time, in which the original coming-to-be of the existing sociocosmic order, or some aspect of it, is represented as a qualitatively distinct mode of time, which not only precedes but continues on another level, to frame the complementary mode of time, that of everyday social activity, in which the social world is directly lived, known and recreated.[3]

By contrast, 'The operative principle in "historical" modes of consciousness ... is an openness to contingency, an awareness that the existing social order emerges as the effect of particular actions and events even as it constrains them'. History, then, is 'rooted in a consciousness of creative social agency as a property of contemporary social actors (or at least *potentially* contemporary actors in the sense of persons belonging to a social world and time continuous with those of the historians and their audiences)' (Turner 1988, p. 244). Following Rina Lederman, Turner sees history as keeping alive the possibility of alternatives (1988, p. 245). These are alternatives that are within the reach of human agency — a sense that presumably changes with historical conditions. One might suggest that myths posit ideal alternatives, and so provide standards against which the morality of latter-day conduct can be measured, even if it is not changed.

Turner argues that, in the supposedly cold societies of South America, myth and history often coexist, rather than the latter succeeding the former, because they answer different levels of questions:

> Myth is an attempt to mutate the *essential* properties of social experience in terms of a series of 'generic events', at a level transcending any particular context of historical relations or events; history, by contrast, is concerned precisely with the level of particular relations among particular events. (1988, p. 252; cf. Austin-Broos 1994)[4]

These are types, so that many stories may be said to fall somewhere in between the two, rather than being classified as either myth or history. Indeed, any story worth telling — and certainly any story worth repeating — must have some measure of meaning beyond its particularity, even if that meaning falls short of the 'generic'. Almost any story has a plot, in Hayden White's sense of 'a structure of relations by which events are endowed with meaning by being identified with parts of an integral whole' (1987, p. 9). We also need to take seriously White's assertion that historical narrative — indeed, perhaps all narrative — consists of the moralising of events (1987, p. 24; cf. Rose 1984), Despite these qualifications, I shall argue later that Turner's and Hill's distinctions help us to perceive the discriminations some Aborigines have made in talking about their powerlessness, and formulating a response to the fact of colonisation.

The collection in which this paper was originally published examines what Norman Whitten (1988), in a South American connection, has called 'the intersections of indigenous creativity and the mythic-historical framing mechanisms for such creativity' (1988, p. 284). The occasion of these intersections is the attempt on the part of Aboriginal people to negotiate a position in a creole nation-state. A full exploration of this theme would include appropriations of Anglo forms, such as the novel and the linear history (e.g. see Johnson 1979, 1983; Miller 1985). Here, however, we shall confine ourselves to stories told by Aboriginal people who have not undergone Australian schooling or become familiar with the discourse of Australian indigenist politics, but who are or were direct heirs to the discourses of the 'Dreaming'.

The 'Dreaming', despite its objectionable genealogy and its narrow ethnographic grounding (Wolfe 1991), has become so firmly established in the literature and in Aboriginal indigenist discourse that it can scarcely be displaced, and is best treated as a gloss. It is perhaps time to look again at the differences among Aboriginal mythologies and cosmologies, but meanwhile it seems possible to recognise general uniformities around the idea of a 'metaphysical discontinuity between men and powers' (Maddock 1982, p. 105), whereby beings gave form to the earth and the heavens, and order to human existence. This 'creative epoch' (Myers 1986, p. 48) occurred in 'another time' which was 'long ago' but is somehow still existing, if normally unseen.[5]

By way of an initial exploration, I shall discuss some stories I heard from Aborigines in New South Wales in 1957, and then re-analyse some of the so-called Captain Cook stories, which have been reported and discussed by several writers, but about which there may be more to say. The first set of stories comes from a time when Aborigines had no legitimate presence in Australian society, and the concept of land rights was almost inconceivable. By contrast, most of the Captain Cook stories seem to have emerged in the more liberal climate of the 1970s and 1980s.

Before doing so, however, something should be said about the general conditions under which these stories were made and told. Turner (1988) suggests that narratives of the kind I have been discussing 'typically order the events they recount according to schemata representing the processes that constitute the structure of the ongoing situation of contact', and they must be 'understood as programs for the orientation of action within the situation of contact and as keys for the interpretation of interaction within that context' (1988, pp. 240, 241). I shall then outline the milieu within which Aborigines interacted with other Australians and told their stories.

Over the last century, all but a handful of Aborigines — none of them considered here — have been dependent on the settler economy for the basic necessities of life. This has been in part due to the seduction of the commodity, but primarily due to the destruction of the Indigenous foraging economy as a result of settlement. At the same time, Aborigines have been subject to a regime of domination, instituted at times through terror and sustained through official and unofficial surveillance and control. Whether or not Kolig's (1981) Aborigines were in 'a state of catatonia' until the recent period, it is certain that the regime denied them political expression when it assumed responsibility for their welfare. Since the 1970s, both the rhetoric and the practice of governments have changed. At the national level, Aborigines have been enfranchised and empowered — albeit within structures that the state itself has established. Locally, the picture is variable, ranging from communities owning their traditional land under land rights laws to squatters living under conditions of insecurity. Notwithstanding land rights and outstations, Aboriginal people are, if anything, more dependent on the settler economy than they were thirty years ago, with the difference that this dependence is now mediated through the structures of self-determination, which the state has established to solve 'the Aboriginal problem'.

There are two ways of conceptualising the Aboriginal presence in Australian society. According to the one just outlined, they occupy a position that is defined primarily in terms of subordination and dependence. Within this frame, the Aboriginal voice is counter-hegemonic, in the sense of contesting and resisting, but within the terms set by Australian cultural hegemony. There is an alternative view, which argues that essential Aboriginal qualities, such as spirituality and an affinity with the land, are the wellsprings of Aboriginal survival and resistance. Accepted uncritically, this amounts to a romantic essentialism, yet it is important to grasp that Aboriginality arises not simply in reaction to colonial domination, but out of a space in which Aboriginal people are able to produce and reproduce a culture that is theirs. Whether that culture is 'traditional' in the fetishised sense of the old anthropology is beside the point; it is no less Aboriginal if it concerns the lives and adventures of local identities, or the wanderings of particular families. What is critical in the present discussion is that it provides them with the means to reinterpret meanings emanating from the dominant society, and to redistribute the effects of external forces. A society that can redistribute the wages paid to particular employees can also reinterpret the message of consumerism.

Each Aboriginal space has its own history, but perhaps one can say in general terms that each is the product of a dialectic — albeit unequal — of engagement and disengagement between coloniser and colonised. Gerald Sider (1987, p. 11) has written of the 'fundamental *cultural* contradiction of the process as a form of incorporation, of bonding together, and simultaneously domination as a form of creating distance, difference and otherness'. Ironically, the Aboriginal strategy has been the same, if differently driven, and although the two strategies have not always been in synchrony, there have been moments of mutual disengagement that have left Aborigines a little space to 'be themselves'.

The distance most whites have maintained in dealing with their Aboriginal workers and wards, and the tendency for many to be transient, has ensured that longstanding, multistranded relations have been concentrated mainly among Aboriginal people. At the same time, there have been individuals who have lived intimately with Aborigines over a long period. Such persons — who might be partners, station owners, missionaries or anthropologists — have found themselves impinging on Aboriginal space. Whether their intrusion has been for good or ill, they have sometimes found themselves hearing the kinds of stories that concern us here. Some of the stories were told to them, perhaps in answer to a request or a question; others may have come up in general conversation, perhaps just to pass the time.

I shall discuss seven stories, four of them coming from the period before Aboriginal enfranchisement and three recorded in recent years.

Alf Barlow

My first stories come from Alf Barlow, a Wainyubalku man from the Paroo River, a sparsely populated area of sheep country in north-west New South Wales, which had been settled before he was born, some time in the 1880s. Barlow dictated a number of myths to me, mainly consisting of Dreaming tracks. He also told me two stories, which I reproduce here.

> 1. A whitefeller and a blackfeller were looking for cattle one time, near Tea Creek — that about 50 miles [80 kilometres] from Bedourie [in south-western Queensland]. The blackfeller was looking around the bush. He saw a *makudja* [a black, hairy goblin] in a tree and rode on. The whitefeller [coming behind] sang out, 'Hey wait on, there's a man here!' 'Alright, you can catch me up,' that's the blackfeller talking. 'By gee you've got big whiskers!' He [the white feller] tried to pull his beard to pull him out of the tree. While he was doing this, the *makudja* was fixing his liver [i.e. by magic]. The black feller sang out, 'Come on, leave him.' He got on his horse, then the whitefeller came after. 'By gee, he's pretty tough, that little fellow.' 'Oh you don't want to touch him.'
>
> They rode on for a couple of miles and he [the white feller] started to feel crook. When he got home, he tied his horse up and went to bed. Tea came and they were asking where he was. They sang out for him. 'I'm very crook in the guts.' That night he died.
>
> The blackfeller never told them what happened.
>
> 2. Some whitefellers were trying to raise a bore at Mumbiowey, that's near Innamincka. There was an old white *ngadji* [a rainbow serpent] there — down here they're black. At last he made a big disturbance like a big wind — threw down the scaffolding, blew away their tent. They saw his mouth all red. They thought it was lightning.

The rainbow serpent appears in the literature for most parts of Australia (Radcliffe-Brown 1930), as well as southern Papua. Springs, bores and lightning are evidence of its presence; the winding course of rivers is evidence of its movement. As in the famous Arnhem Land story of the Wawilak sisters (Warner 1958, pp. 242–8), it can rear up and swallow humans. Although mythology often associates rainbow serpents with particular places, they can also be regarded as an active and unpredictable element in the cosmology, inasmuch as rivers change their course and springs appear and disappear. The goblin-like creature seems also to be widely known in Aboriginal Australia, but is little described in the literature. It is associated with rocky hills, and is not normally dangerous, but better kept at a distance — as in the story. Rather like the serpent, it is somewhat unpredictable.

Barlow's two stories make a pair, having the same triadic structure: the whitefeller is the protagonist, through ignorance disturbing an autochthonous superhuman being; the superhuman beings of the country are the antagonists, responding violently when disturbed. The blackfeller is a presence, in that he knows about these things, but he has no influence over events. In Story 1, he tries but is ignored, and the next time keeps the truth to himself. In Story 2, there is no mention of a blackfeller in the party, but only blackfellers know what really happened, and evidently they allow the whitefellers to go on thinking it was all a matter of natural causes — even though they 'saw' the serpent's red mouth.

The agency of the Aborigine in this story is not absent, but it is frustrated. Its implied intent, however, includes both resistance and collaboration. In the first story, the Aborigine tries to warn the whitefeller, but Aboriginal knowledge is discredited. In the second story, we have to assume that Aborigines tried to explain the sacred character of the spring, or would have done if they thought it would do any good. Whether or not the Aborigines wished to protect the whitefellers from harm is unclear. What is clear is that they wanted to protect the country and its denizens from inappropriate treatment. Barlow told me that as a child the old people had told him to cover his tracks when going to a spring, for fear that white people would find it and sink a bore, driving away the *ngatji*. Since the names of such places were also the names of Aboriginal people, linking them with others along the songlines, we can see them as resisting the erasure of their cultural presence from the landscape. What is also clear, however, is the powerlessness of the Aborigines. They can only intervene if the settlers listen. By refusing to listen, the whites deny Aboriginal people agency. They do not affect the outcome of the story, however; it is left to the superhumans to act.

Barlow's stories are exemplary, in the sense of allowing for other instances of the same kind of thing. I did indeed hear other such stories of whites inappropriately intruding on things that Aborigines only approached after ritual precaution. They are not identified as parts of a larger narrative. Nevertheless, they can be read in terms of an unarticulated narrative of displacement. At one level, the two stories point in different directions: in the first, the *makudja* lives and the white man dies. In the second, the white men survive — albeit somewhat scared — but the spring is desecrated and the *ngadji* is driven off. One might argue that the death of one man doesn't stem the desecration of Aboriginal places — which, as Barlow well knew, had been going on for almost a century. At another level, then, the stories bear witness to the erasure of Aboriginality from the landscape.

Even so, there remains what Aborigines still know, even if they cannot speak. Barlow, however, saw this disappearing with the younger generation, of whom he remarked, 'They know nothing and they don't talk about anything.' Yet a secularised intimation of it remained in the words of a fifteen-year-old who I had asked to define the difference between whitefellers and blackfellers. He replied immediately that whites were smarter when it came to making cars and radios, but blackfellers got on better in the bush.

The stories may be read as leaving open the possibility that the Aborigines' agency would be restored and the country saved if white people started listening. Perhaps that was why he told me the stories. But at that time, there seemed little prospect of such a thing.

Fred Biggs

Fred Biggs was about the same age as Barlow. A Wongaibon or Ngiemba, he had been born on a sheep station in the arid backcountry between the Lachlan and Darling Rivers in western New South Wales.[6] He spent approximately the first half of his life in the backcountry, and the second half living as a recipient of rations on three government settlements, the second and third of which were off his own country.

Biggs had worked with Ronald Berndt some fifteen years before he met me, and he readily assumed the role of anthropologist's informant when I turned up. However, he had not had much occasion to recall what he knew in the intervening years, and it came back to him in bits and pieces, as my notebooks attest. Before we finished, however, he had communicated an unusually tricky kinship system and a dramatic account of his initiation, back in the 1890s.

Wongaibon religion centred on the sky world, inhabited by the creator Baiami, to whom Biggs usually referred as God. The strategy revealed in this statement is complex, for in the face of white Australian assumptions of superior knowledge, it asserts a parity of European, Aboriginal and — notionally — other knowledges. Biggs situates the Aboriginal and European God in a unitary domain, but the domain is segmented in the sense that 'God' can be understood differently. And the nature of the difference is left undefined so that one set of meanings can penetrate, even dominate, the other.[7] A somewhat younger Wongaibon man, Dave Harris, who had not been initiated but had been around the 'old people', said to me, 'There's God alright ain't there. I believe in God meself, although I can't read or write, I'm only going by the old blackfeller. Every nation in the world believes in God, only in a different way ... we all know there's a God. Must've been.'[8] In the case of Biggs, there was no doubt that his God was Baiami, and God's law was the performance of initiations and marrying straight, as in the time of his youth.

Both of these practices had long ceased by the time I met him, and Biggs mourned their passing. At the end of a dramatic account of his own initiation, he concluded, 'I'm very sorry it's all finished'. As for the marriage rules, people now were 'like dogs'. How had this happened? When I asked him why the initiations had ceased, back in the 1920s, he exclaimed sadly, '*goi, goi, goi*' — *goi* meaning white people. But he meant that the example of white people had caused the Wongaibon to go astray; the choice had been theirs.

Biggs had no stories of conquest as such, but reading back through my notebooks, I find a series of statements — virtual one liners — given in answer to my questions or coming up in conversation, which lend themselves to articulation as a narrative. On one occasion I asked whether the settlers had shot Aborigines in the early days. He said there had been no shooting in his part of the country, though he knew it had happened elsewhere. Whites had 'made friends with the people', giving them food and tobacco, but then, 'Of course, they knew they were onto a good thing, getting the land.' What Aborigines got in return was food and tobacco, and small reserves of land which Biggs, like many Aborigines of his generation, believed had been bestowed in perpetuity by Queen Victoria.

A distinctive feature of the Baiami cult was the scope it gave to the 'clever men'. In Aboriginal English, the word 'clever' carries the connotation of wonderful powers, beyond the capacity of ordinary folk, but also attributed to the heroes of mythology. Biggs described to me the wondrous feats they performed during his initiation, and their ability to travel over long distances, and to project long strings from their testicles, from which they projected themselves into the sky world, where they were able to break the celestial waterbag and make rain (see also Berndt 1946–47, 1947–48). They are comparable in some respects to the rainbow serpents and the hairy men, in the sense of being an active and unpredictable force in the world — with the difference that they are human, even though empowered by a personal totem.

Biggs claimed that the clever men were by no means powerless in the face of the settlers. He told me how, when a farmer was shooting Aboriginal dogs for killing sheep, a clever man stopped his revolver from shooting straight and 'sent him mad for good'. In another anecdote, Aborigines had to restrain a clever man before he killed all the whites in the town. Biggs described one — Charlie Martell — as a 'second God' who could escape from the police and other enemies.

Why, then, did they not stop the settlers from coming? Biggs blamed the clever men on the coast: 'They had God's power. They ought to have been able to stop the ships in the middle of sea.' This displacement of blame brings to mind the way in which station Aborigines in Arnhem Land blamed 'wild Aborigines' for provoking the settlers into a massacre (Morphy and Morphy 1983), and perhaps also the way Walter Newton connected colonisation with the misdeeds of the Aborigines (Chapter 2).

But Biggs had his strictures for the local clever men as well, for he claimed that in the end — which is to say the early years of this century — they turned their powers against their own people, and each other: 'They were too clever to live!' Apart from one old woman who lived in another town and was credited with lesser powers, there were no clever people any more.

We might expect a bad ending to a story that had Aborigines succumbing to the settlers' blandishments, aping foreign ways instead of their own and turning 'God's power' against their own people instead of the invaders. Biggs had one. Telling me how God had burned the country with fire 'so nothing lived', he continued, 'Next time it be with water [i.e. a flood]. Punishing wickedness. It's coming — I thought it was coming last winter [when the river had overflowed its banks].'

Aborigines in the Kimberley seem also to have predicted an end of things, a notion that conflicts with the anthropological conceptualisation of Aboriginal cosmology of endless reproduction (Koepping 1988; Kolig 1989). Whether autochthonous belief in fact allowed for an ending is impossible to say; the anthropologists may simply have got it wrong. What concerns me here is that it provides a satisfactory, if depressing, ending to a story of failure and loss. Biggs is not really concerned with the deeds or fate of the settlers; they are apparently friendly, but their gifts of food and tobacco are deprived of moral value because 'they knew they were onto a good thing, getting the land'.

Biggs focuses on Aboriginal rather than settler agency, or its failure at key moments when it might have been exercised. Instead, he inculpates his own people — the clever men on the coast but also those in his part of the country — and the people in general for failing to keep up the old ways. They failed to use the powers that God had given them, and when they did act, chose wrongly. God — or Baiami — was still in his sky world, along with the water bag and the beings who guarded it, but there were no longer any clever men to communicate with him and release his power. God would nevertheless intervene soon. As in Barlow's stories, the closure is effected by superhuman agencies that the Aborigines know about, with the difference that this will happen in the future.

Self-inculpation, which I take to constitute the plot of the narrative I have articulated for Biggs, is a familiar trope in the stories of the colonised. It is, for example, a common element in Melanesian Cargo Cult stories. It consists of a contradictory double movement. On the one hand, it asserts the integrity and value of the colonised, *vis-à-vis* the colonisers. Their subjection is their own fault, rather than being due to the superiority of the invaders; things could have been different. In the same way, the diseases that decimated the Wongaibon at certain periods are not attributed to the whites who introduced them, but to the power of sorcerers working within.

To uphold such a position, one has to have a sense of the power of the society, a sense that — to judge by Biggs' account of his initiation — seems to have been impressed on him by the terrors of the ritual and the wonders that the clever men performed. By blaming the clever men and Aborigines in general for the misuse of this power, Biggs is able to go on believing in it; to do otherwise is to admit that it could not withstand the power of the settlers.

Comparing Biggs' reconstructed narratives with Cargo stories in which the trope of self-inculpation often occurs, one is struck with an important difference. In the Cargo story, not only could things have been different at the beginning; they could be different in the future through the redeeming agency of the ancestors, or some hero of myth. For Biggs, there was no redemption. Perhaps as Diane Austin-Broos has suggested (pers. com.) the character of Aboriginal cosmology is 'intractably non-redemptive'; however, the experience of dependence during his lifetime would have given him little reason to think otherwise.

Too Many Captain Cooks

I now want to turn from my own material to some of what have come to be known as the 'Captain Cook stories'. They have a wide distribution across northern Australia, and appear sporadically elsewhere. Maddock has pointed out that they are factually incorrect: Cook did not land where they say he landed, and never came into the interior; however, as Reynaldo Ileto (1979, p. 183) has remarked in another connection, their 'real concern is not the reconstruction of events but the articulation of meaning'. I would further argue that, with two exceptions I shall reserve to the end, they are expressions of a historical consciousness, in the sense that they are about human agency.

The stories are quite diverse, so let me first turn to the one thing they have in common: the name of Captain Cook. Since it is historically unfounded, we can treat it as a trope, but its rhetorical use cannot simply be understood in terms of the Aboriginal domain. For whatever the academic historians may write for their colleagues, the Australian state has made of him an icon in the course of celebrating its beginnings as a British colony and its destiny as a creole nation. His representation as the one who 'discovered Australia' for generations of school children and the public at large condenses in his person, and in a single act of possession, the whole colonial story. In the early 1900s, the Catholic-Irish element proposed that Australia should celebrate the date of

Cook's landing rather than Empire Day (the precursor to the present Australia Day).

That Captain Cook is primarily celebrated as a traveller may have recommended him to people whose own stories were about travelling. But their appropriation of this historic and historical name can be read as an attempt to authorise what they are saying; it also enables them to turn stories of particular events into a paradigmatic narrative of colonisation, while stopping short of the generic. Whitten (1988), contesting the view that ethnic (specifically Indigenous) minorities tend either towards assimilation or enclave formation, suggests that:

> nationalist (or colonial) culture and ethnic bloc culture should be inter-preted as complementary and mutually reinforcing systems of symbols sustained by dialogic discourse … The dialogic discourse seems to create synthetic symbolic Units … which in their rhetorical conjunction, bring forth a predicative link that carries the double act of assertion and denial. (1988, pp. 303–4)

This perhaps attributes a degree of calculation to the story-maker that is inconsistent with the need to believe the story oneself and make others believe it. We need also to consider the way in which Aborigines use names in other contexts. I referred earlier to the use of 'God' to refer to the Aboriginal sky being, Baiami. Biggs, telling one of the old stories, began: 'Crow was Jesus Christ, onetime' to suggest, I think, that both were supremely and equally 'clever'. (Walter Newton similarly linked Aboriginal and Biblical heroes, see Chapter 2.) It should also be remembered that in Biggs' and Barlow's part of the country, as elsewhere in Aboriginal Australia, the names of places were also the names of people — in other words, the function of personal names was as much associative as individualising.[9]

I shall begin with the two 'first contact' stories which, if they are not consistent with the documentary record, have the same theme of disordered exchange and bafflement that we find in the logbooks of Dampier, Cook and other explorers of the early period.[10] In one, Cook comes ashore, and gives the 'wild Aborigines' clothes and ship's biscuit. As he returns to his ship, they come out and throw them after him. The second, more complex story has him offer them tobacco, tea and a johnnycake, all of which they reject, and boiled salt beef, which they accept. When the party prepares to leave, the Aborigines, who have concluded that the whites are the spirits of the dead returned, are overcome with grief, calling Cook 'Father'.

Although we have no indication of the tone in which the stories were told, it is easy to imagine later generations, who had come to be dependent on the items that the old people rejected, finding it comical that their ancestors should have failed to recognise their value. Such stories are widespread, and are usually an occasion for laughter, even when — as in a recent film about the Pintubi — the storyteller is talking about his own ignorance. What kind of laughter is evoked is another matter, whether it be mockery, embarrassment or irony.

But the stories can also be viewed at another level. As Maddock (1988, pp. 25–6) has suggested, the picture of a people given to exchange among themselves, rejecting gifts from outsiders, suggests something more important is being talked about. Certainly among Melanesians, a gift is not refused lightly (Young 1983). Similarly it is unlikely that the Aborigines would have refused the gifts just because they failed to appreciate the utility or the items offered. If the refusal was not tantamount to a declaration or war, it was certainly a refusal to make friends, and to resist what Bourdieu (1977, pp. 190–4) has called the gift's 'symbolic violence'.

It is not only the whites who are actors in these events, but Aborigines too. And it is possible to see the stories as self-inculpatory, in the sense that Aborigines missed a historic opportunity, and thereafter were destined to live in want of the good things that they could have had for the asking. In the second story, their grief at Cook's departure might be read as a belated recognition of the value of at least one of his gifts.

The belief that the members of the party were the dead returned occurs a lot in the literature, but its implications have not been given much thought. Such an event reversed the normal course of events in which the dead went away for good, and could thus be taken as the beginning of a new epoch. This may have been its significance for the storytellers, although they probably no longer believed that whites were ghosts. This rupture may also have marked an end to reciprocity, which would explain why the Aborigines in the second story took the beef, but gave nothing in return. In other words, they entered into a relationship of dependence with their new 'father' — a one-sided transaction of the kind Stanner (1958) perceived in the Cargo belief. Fred Myers (1986) has argued that the Pintupi maintained a nurturing relationship between the generations, and tried to model their relations with Europeans along the same lines.

For Maddock (1988, p. 27), however, the story implies that there must be some kind of reciprocation, and since the storytellers did, willy-nilly, accept the white man's gifts in the end, this seems a reasonable conclusion to reach. The storytellers, having had a rather different experience of colonisation, would have perceived that the whites got their land and their labour in return for the tea, tobacco and so on. Perhaps, like Fred Biggs, they wanted to suggest that Captain Cook 'knew he was onto a good thing'. If the storytellers saw it in this way, then we may see the Aborigines in the first story not as stupid myalls, but as still-free agents who were smart enough to spot the hook in the bait.

I next look at a recent text published by Deborah Bird Rose of a long monologue by Hobbles Danaiyairi (1984), a man from the Yarralin community on Victoria River Downs. With the publication of her powerful *Hidden Histories* (1991), which draws extensively on his circumstantial accounts of white atrocities and abuse, we can take the first text as an attempt to generalise from the local peculiarities to embrace the whole of Australia.[11] Captain Cook provides the vehicle for this discourse: as a great traveller, he can traverse the length and breadth of the continent. However, he is not so much an explorer or gift-giver as a settler, a 'hard man' who takes the country for his livestock, killing Aborigines indiscriminately and sparing only those who will work for him. As on Victoria River Downs, these get little for their labours and are denied medical attention when they get sick. In this telling, then, the hero of creole Australia is turned into a villain.

The Aborigines attempt to resist the invasion, but they are unable to withstand firearms. Henceforth they are the victims, and Captain Cook the unchallenged protagonist. They retain a sense of the immorality of the colonisation, which Hobbles spells out at some length, but they do not — unlike Barlow and Biggs — look to a superhuman agency for a resolution. The memory of violence and abuse is still fresh for Hobbles, but speaking in an era of land rights, and in the Northern Territory where they have been realised most extensively, he is able to imagine an alternative, and claim back the land. What Rose calls the 'Saga of Captain Cook' is an explicitly political statement — except that the names of particular settlers are replaced by a long-dead, depersonalised and displaced figure from colonial history.

Rose concludes that the Saga has the same structure as the Dreaming myths, with which Hobbles is also familiar, but it is not a myth. Captain Cook, as an immoral being who instituted conditions that must be changed, cannot be incorporated into an account of the Dreaming — of what is, always has been and will be. I will add that, as confirmation of this exclusion, Captain Cook does not undergo an apotheosis; he does not become part of the landscape or the firmament, as the heroes of Aboriginal mythology do. He simply goes away. However, Hobbles speaks of Captain Cook's 'Law', in the form of a book brought from England (Rose 1984, p. 32). Northern Territory Aborigines use 'Law' to refer to the Dreaming, but they also speak of 'whitefeller law' (e.g. Maddock 1977) as regulating the European domain in which they have to live. Unresolved is the question of whether the two are constituted similarly or differently.

It seems to me that the Saga needs to be read with the stories of Ned Kelly, (see Rose 1988, pp. 369–71; 1994):

In the very beginning when the earth is still covered with water, Ned Kelly arrives at the Northern Territory in a boat. Like Noah — though it is not clear whether the storyteller made the parallel explicit — he sees a leaf and realises there is dry land. He and his band of angels go about shooting police. They also teach the Aborigines to make tea and cook damper, and there is feeding of the multitude that reminds us of the New Testament. The police eventually catch and hang him, but on the third day he emerges from the grave and with a great noise and shaking of the earth he flies up into the sky.

Ned Kelly here is, I take it, identified in some way with the celebrated bushranger, who was hanged in 1880. Although Australia has dedicated a day to him, it credits him with a characteristically Australian resistance to injustice, if not all authority. In the Aboriginal version he does not actually confront Captain Cook, but he does shoot the police. One can imagine the Aboriginal story-makers concluding that the enemy of their enemy was their friend. In any case, he does not shoot Aborigines, and brings them good things.

Even though Ned Kelly 'really existed', Rose (1988) calls this story a myth — and indeed it meets Turner's (1988) criteria. Unlike Cook, Kelly leaves his mark on the land, and he undergoes an apotheosis. He does not go away or simply die, but becomes part of the firmament. As Rose concludes, 'While Captain Cook is dead, Ned Kelly lives.' In other words, Kelly is equated with the heroes of the Dreaming; thus, as in Barlow's and Biggs' stories, it is a superhuman being — in this case, a white one — that challenges the colonists, in the person of the police.

The Aboriginal appropriation of Kelly is, of course, achieved at the price of anachronism, if we think of the 'Dreamtime' as situated before the coming of whites. The incorporation of a white man is again an anomaly, if we think of the 'Dreaming' as being an Aboriginal domain. However, if we recall Kolig's (1981, p. 43) and Myers' (1986, p. 268) work, the inappropriateness of this observation becomes evident. Both report how Aborigines 'discover' that the tracks of the ancestors passed through the country where they now happen to be, or where they have found new friends; the new is found to have always been the case. Rather than talking of 'the Dreaming', then, we are better off, as Rose suggests here, with Stanner's felicitous 'everywhen', or the 'onetime' with which Fred Biggs began his stories.[12] Biggs' assertion that 'Crow was Jesus Christ *onetime*' achieves a similar 'anachronism' at a single stroke. (As I shall remark in a moment, however, some Aboriginal narratives are 'diachronised'.)

When Aborigines 'discover' that a previously unknown track has 'always' been there, they recognise something that is cognate with what they already know; by contrast, the Ned Kelly story takes on board things and people of another kind. These are, however, those parts of the European presence that Aborigines want to keep, as distinct from what they would prefer to do without. The desired is fixed in the domain of myth; the undesired is left to history, the domain of human agency, where it is open to change. Recalling the first contact stories, discussed earlier, we might see this as another attempt to solve the problem of how Aborigines can get what they want from white people, without having to pay the high price demanded. Ned Kelly doesn't get anything in return either, although his gifts are accepted.

The final Captain Cook story I want to consider presents a somewhat different configuration of the same moves. For Paddy Wainburranga, also from the Northern Territory, there is not one but many — 'too many' — Captain Cooks. The first, however, is like Ned Kelly in the last story. He was around at the time of Satan, 'a long time ago. Like a million years ago ... He was like ... Adam and Eve. But Adam and Eve were only "half way" — Captain Cook was there first ...' (Mackinolty and Wainburranga 1988, p. 256). It is worth noting that the storyteller is 'diachronising' his actors. Koepping (1988, p. 403) remarked on this tendency in some Kimberley stories. Walter Newton did much the same in his 'history of the world'. The principle of sequence — of who was where first — is, one might say, integral to the experience of colonisation.

The 'first' Captain Cook came from the other side of New Guinea, coming with two wives and a donkey and a goat. He was involved in law and ceremony, belonging to one of the moieties and having his songs, designs and corroborees. But he also had 'white man's power, white man's things. Blackfellas never had any of those things.' (Mackinolty and Wainburranga 1988, p. 357) These included paddles for canoes, clothing, axes and steel knives. He travelled 'all over the world', ending up in Sydney where he made the harbour, but not the bridge. Mortally wounded after a battle with some enemies, he is buried under an island in Sydney Harbour, with quantities of pre-decimal currency. The story then goes on to talk about other Captain Cooks, who were murderous and rapacious, as in Hobbles' Saga. It ends optimistically with, 'But now we've got the culture back.'

Like Ned Kelly and the Captain Cook of the First Contact stories, Paddy Wainburranga's first Captain Cook does not receive anything in return for his bounty. The story even states that he brought his two wives with him when he came. What he appropriates is the pre-decimal currency. Taking a long shot, I would link the withdrawal of the old money in 1966 with the roughly contemporaneous award of equal wages for Aboriginal pastoral workers and the Referendum that, in popular belief if not strictly speaking, gave Aborigines their rights. In other words, he is taking away the money Aborigines never got and ushering in a new, more just era.

Much of what I have said about the Ned Kelly story is also applicable to Wainburranga's 'first' Captain Cook. The latter is a more complex, ambiguous figure: he does not come from Australia, but is integrated into the Aboriginal social order. In due course, he makes Sydney Harbour and is buried there. He thus undergoes an apotheosis — although we are not told whether he is 'alive' like Ned Kelly. This Captain Cook has the same Australia-wide and global associations as his namesake in the school history books, with the difference that he does not take the land, but brings the Aborigines things they did not have before — including some things such as canoe paddles that we think of as being Aboriginal.

I understand these two stories as an attempt to situate in the domain of mythical certitude those things that came with the settlers, and upon which Aborigines have become irretrievably dependent, while at the same time situating in the domain of history — and therefore of mutability — the violence and expropriation that accompanied settlement. But if the land is returned, the flour and tea and steel tools, which were the insufficient repayment for the land — at least according to Fred Biggs — come as gifts without reciprocation. This seems to leave Aborigines in a state of dependence. Where Aborigines are not dependent (and where they have something to give) is what they know.

What Aborigines Know

The 'blackfellers' in Alf Barlow's two stories know things about the country that the 'whitefellers' do not know, and refuse to credit when the blackfellers try to tell them. Here, at least, the blackfellers have the advantage, since at least from their point of view, these things are worth knowing, and — according to the stories — are worth white people knowing. All the storytellers discussed in this chapter are taking a similar stand, and in each instance what they know is not something of interest only to Aborigines, but something of common concern: they are giving the Aboriginal side of the story of the country, God, Captain Cook or Ned Kelly — figures white people think they know all about, but don't.

Recognising the dialogical character of these stories, we can perceive another reason why the maker of the Ned Kelly story, Paddy Wainburranga (and likewise Walter Newton), attempted to diachronise their narratives. They are at pains to situate their stories in relation to the Bible and to colonial history. Paddy Wainburranga sets up coordinates between his story and the Bible, but claims priority for his, much as Walter Newton claimed the Aboriginal 'feeding of the multitudes' happened 'before' Christ's miracle (p. 25). However, Ned Kelly's resurrection seems to have happened after Christ's.

Notwithstanding the dialogic character of the Aboriginal stories, which — as I have suggested, following Whitten (1988) — attempt to create synthetic symbolic units, engaging nation and Indigenous minority, the attempt is one-sided. Black and white may have Captain Cook and Ned Kelly in common, but the black versions transgress white notions of historical propriety. It is only by seeing past the Captain Cooks and Ned Kellys of the history books that the message can come into focus. But one can understand why so many Aborigines gave up trying to communicate their message, even to their own children.

Conclusion

Kolig's (1981) image of the 'catatonic' Aborigine is scarcely confirmed by the stories we have considered here. Apart from the tellers of the first contact stories, who are unknown, all are traditionally oriented to the extent of having been initiated, yet all recognise the possibility of alternatives to the present situation, if only in the apolitical form of 'what if …?' The difference is that Hobbles Danaiyairi and Paddy Wainburranga made their stories in an era of land rights, something Biggs and Barlow could scarcely have imagined.[13]

Only Biggs comes near to establishing a position outside the universe of domination from which to propose alternatives to the colonial order, but it is grounded in the past dereliction of the clever men to stop the invaders and the bleak possibility that the world will soon end. It should be noted also that he situates the white man's gifts in the history of contingency rather than myth. The first contact story might be read the same way. By contrast, the Ned Kelly and 'first' Captain Cook stories have removed commodities from the domain of history; they are fixed in myth and thus non-negotiable. Their stories are thus grounded in the reality of Aboriginal dependence on European commodities.

In these stories, Aboriginal agency is situated in the past: the armed resistance in Hobbles' Saga, the failed clever men in Biggs' tale, the unheard blackfeller in Barlow's and the unwilling recipients in the first contact stories. In the present, it is either God or the whites who will act.[14] But, stepping outside the frame of the story, we can say that the storytellers are agents, even if their agency consists only of telling stories to anthropologists.

The act of telling stories to anthropologists or other sympathetic listeners must not be left out of our analysis (cf. Rose 1989). It is indeed a mode of dialogue distinctive of creole nation-states, where anthropology often occupies a mediating position between the state and the Indigenous minority. As a good listener, the anthropologist promises (though the promise is often broken) a hearing for Aborigines, and the possibility of another kind of relation with whites — whites who are more like Hobbles' Ned Kelly or Wainburranga's first Captain Cook.

The assumption that there are whites who are not simply 'onto a good thing' like Biggs' 'friendly' settlers, or murderous usurpers, like Hobbles' Captain Cook, is of course a bold one. It is, however, a necessary condition of any kind of political action for people who amount to less than 2 per cent of the population, and who have until recently been without political leverage. This does not amount to capitulation, as long as it retains a sense of an Aboriginal interest. The position of Indigenous minorities such as the Aborigines is, however, profoundly contradictory. What Norman Whitten (1988) has perceived for Indigenous South Americans has a wider relevance: they resist and are contained, yet release their own powers 'to reconstitute and reproduce not only themselves but also the system of domination and their dynamic, forceful, resistant place within it' (1988, p. 283).

Acknowledgments

Earlier drafts of this paper were presented to a small seminar on Aboriginal histories at Sydney University in 1990, attended by several of the contributors to the collection in which it originally appeared, and to the anthropology seminars at the Australian National University and the Northern Territory University. I gained considerably from the comments of colleagues on these occasions. Diane Austin-Broos, Francesca Merlan and Alan Rumsey have also helpfully commented on the penultimate version of this paper. It was first published in 1994 in *Oceania*, vol. 65, no. 2.

NOTES

1. For a genealogy of the 'Dreaming' in anthropology, see also Wolfe (1991).
2. Bloch's critique seems to have provided a point of departure for Patrick Wolfe's (1991) critique of the use of the 'Dreaming' in Australian anthropology.
3. It may be necessary to note that this distinction would assign the grand historical narratives of Hegel and Marx to the mythological end of the scale, notwithstanding the absence of gods.
4. Here again, this distinction takes a decidedly Rankean view of history, assigning Marxist or any other search for 'historical laws' to the mythological end of the continuum.
5. Stanner (1962) and Myers (1986) have provided the best ethnographically based accounts of Aboriginal religion. For a comparative reconsideration, see Swain (1994).
6. Biggs, with another man, was the principal source for Ronald Berndt's 'Wuradjeri magic and "Clever Men"' (1946–47; 1947–48) (although to me he identified himself as Ngiemba); he was also the source of my account of Wongaibon kinship (Beckett 1959).
7. For a parallel instance, also from New South Wales, see Walter Newton's *History of the World* (Chapter 2).
8. Harris's monologue, which I recorded in 1964, is held in the Sound Archive of the Australian Institute of Aboriginal and Torres Strait Islander Studies, Tape no. LA 627.
9. In Western society too, naming serves both functions, identifying individuals with family through surnames and sometimes also given names. Among Catholics, individuals are also associated with saints, while the names of national heroes are chosen in some societies.
10. Stone's (1974) documentary source book opens with two such instances.
11. Walter Newton likewise strove to generalise the old stories about his country to construct a history of Australia, if not the world.
12. In her study of Ngiyampaa language, Tamsin Donaldson reports the adverb *maradhal* as situating something 'far back in time', and with the suffix *-bu*, as 'as far back as

possible' or as the 'in the beginning' used to introduce myths (1980, pp. 77–8). These forms would seem to be the Aboriginal forms of Biggs' 'onetime'.

13. Biggs, did, however, imagine the possibility of Ngiyembaa knowledge being taught in schools, perhaps as a result of our collaboration.

14. Francesca Merlan informed me that in language texts she had collected from Victoria River Downs, she was struck by the enormous preponderance of grammatical agentive marking on the noun 'whitefeller'.

REFERENCES

Austin-Broos, D 1994, 'Narratives of the encounter at Ntaria', *Oceania*, vol. 65, no. 2, pp. 131–50.

Beckett, J 1959, 'Further notes on the social organization of the Wongaibon of Western New South Wales', *Oceania*, vol. 19, pp. 200–7.

Berndt, R 1946–47, 'Wuradjeri magic and "clever men"', Pt I, *Oceania*, vol. 17, pp. 327–65.

—— 1947–48, 'Wuradjeri magic and "clever men"', Pt II, *Oceania*, vol. 18, pp. 60–86.

—— 1962, *An Adjustment Movement in Arnhem Land, Northern Territory of Australia*. Paris: Mouton.

Bloch, M 1977, 'The past and the present in the present', *Man*, vol. 12, pp. 278–91.

Bourdieu, P 1977, *Outline of a Theory of Practice*, Cambridge University Press, Cambridge.

Carr, D 1986, *Time, Narrative and History*, Indiana University Press, Bloomington, IN.

Donaldson, T 1980, *Ngiyambaa: The Language of the Wangaaybuwan*, Cambridge University Press, Melbourne.

Elkin, AP 1951, 'Reaction and interaction: A food gathering people and European settlement in Australia', *American Anthropologist*, vol. 53, pp. 164–86.

Hiatt, L 1965, *Kinship and Conflict: A Study of an Aboriginal Community in Northern Arnhem Land*, ANU Press, Canberra.

Hill, J 1988, 'Introduction', in J Hill (ed.), *Rethinking History and Myth: Indigenous South American Perspectives on the Past*, University of Illinois Press, Urbana, IL.

Ileto, R 1979, *Pasyon and Revolution: Popular Movements in the Philippines, 1840–1910*, Ateneo de Manila University Press, Quezon City, Manila.

Johnson, C 1979, *Long Live Sandawara*, Hyland House, Melbourne.

—— 1983, *Doctor Wooreddy's Prescription for Enduring the Ending of the World*, Hyland House, Melbourne.

Koepping, K 1988, 'Nativistic movements in Aboriginal Australia: Creative adjustment, protest or regeneration of tradition?', in T Swain and D Rose (eds), *Aboriginal Australians and Christian Missions*, Australian Association for the Study of Religions, Adelaide.

Kolig, E 1981, *The Silent Revolution*, Institute for the Study of Human Issues, Philadelphia, PA.

—— 1989, *Dreamtime Politics: Religion, World View and Utopian Thought in Australian Aboriginal Society*, DM Verlag, Berlin.

Levi-Strauss, C 1966, *The Savage Mind*, University of Chicago Press, Chicago.

Mackinolty, C and Wainburranga, P 1988, 'Too many Captain Cooks', in T Swain and DB Rose (eds), *Aboriginal Australians and Christian Missions*, Australian Association for the Study of Religions, Adelaide, pp. 355–60.

Maddock, K 1977, 'Two laws in one community', in RM Berndt (ed.), *Aborigines and Change: Australia in the '70s*, Australian Institute of Aboriginal Studies, Canberra, pp. 13–32.

—— 1982, *The Australian Aborigines: A Portrait of Their Society*, Penguin, Ringwood.

—— 1988, 'Myth, history and a sense of oneself', in J Beckett (ed.), *Past and Present: The Construction of Aboriginality*, Aboriginal Studies Press, Canberra.

Meggitt, M 1962, *Desert People: A Study of the Walbiri Aborigines of Central Australia*, Angus & Robertson, Sydney.

Merlan, F 1994, 'Narratives of survival in the post-colonial north', *Oceania*, vol. 65, no. 2, pp. 151–74.

Miller, J 1985, *Koori: A Will to Win: The Heroic Resistance, Survival and Triumph of Black Australia*, Angus & Robertson, Sydney.

Morgan, S 1987, *My Place*, Fremantle Arts Centre Press, Fremantle.

Morphy, H and Morphy, F 1983, The "myths" of Ngalakan history: Ideology and images of the past in northern Australia, *Man*, vol. 19, pp. 459–78.

Muecke, S, Rumsey, A and Wirunmarra, B 1985, 'Pigeon the Outlaw: History as texts', *Aboriginal History*, vol. 9, pp. 81–100.

Myers, F 1986, *Pintupi Country, Pintupi Self: Sentiment, Place, and Politics Among Western Desert Aborigines*, AIAS, Canberra and Smithsonian Institute Press, Washington, DC.

Radcliffe-Brown, AR 1930, 'The Rainbow Serpent in south-east Australia', *Oceania*, vol. 1, pp. 342–7.

Rappaport, J 1990, *The Politics of Memory: Native Historical Interpretation in the Colombian Andes*, Cambridge University Press, Cambridge.

Rose, DB 1984, 'The Saga of Captain Cook: Morality in Aboriginal and European law', *Australian Aboriginal Studies*, vol. 2, pp. 23–39.

—— 1988, 'Jesus and the dingo', in T Swain and D Rose (eds), *Aboriginal Australians and Christian Missions*, Australian Association for the Study of Religions, Adelaide, pp. 361–75.

—— 1989, 'Remembrance', *Aboriginal History*, vol. 13, pp. 135–48.

—— 1991, *Hidden Histories: Black Stories from Victoria River Downs, Humbert River and Wave Hill Stations*, Aboriginal Studies Press, Canberra.

—— 1994, 'Ned Kelly died for our sins', *Oceania*, vol. 65, no. 2, pp. 175–86.

Sahlins, M 1985, *Islands of History*, University of Chicago Press, Chicago.

Sharp, L 1951, 'Steel axes for Stone Age Australians', in E Spicer (ed.), *Human Problems in Technological Change: A Casebook*, Russell Sage Foundation, New York, pp. 69–90.

Sider, G 1987, 'When parrots learn to talk, and why they can't: Domination, deception and self-deception in Indian–white relations', *Comparative Studies in Society and History*, vol. 29, pp. 3–23.

Stanner, WEH 1958, 'On the interpretation of Cargo Cults', *Oceania*, vol. 29, pp. 1–2.

—— 1966, *On Aboriginal Religion*, Oceania Monographs 11, University of Sydney, Sydney.

Stone, S 1974, *Aborigines* in *White Australia: A Documentary History of the Attitudes Affecting Official Policy and the Australian Aborigine 1697–1973*, Heinemann, Melbourne.

Strehlow, TG 1947, *Aranda Traditions*, Melbourne University Press, Melbourne.

Swain, T 1994, *A Place for Strangers: Towards a History of Australian Aboriginal Being*, Cambridge University Press, Melbourne.

Turner, T 1988, 'Ethno-ethnohistory: Myth and history in native South American representations of contact with Western society', in J Hill (ed.) *Rethinking History and Myth: Indigenous South American Perspectives on the Past*, University of Illinois Press, Urbana, IL, pp. 235–81.

Urry, J 1980, 'Aborigines, History and Semantics', *Journal of Australian Studies*, vol. 6, pp. 68–72.

Warner, WL 1958, *A Black Civilization: A Study of an Australian Tribe* (rev ed.), Harper Collins, New York.

White, H 1987, *The Content of the Form: Narrative Discourse and Historical Representation*, Johns Hopkins University Press, Baltimore, MD.

Whitten, N 1988, 'Historical and mythic evocations of chthonian power in South America', in J Hill (ed.), *Rethinking History and Myth: Indigenous South American Perspectives on the Past*, University of Illinois Press, Urbana, IL.
Wolfe, P 1991, 'On being woken up: The Dreamtime in anthropology and in Australian settler culture', *Comparative Studies in Society and History*, vol. 33, pp. 197–224.
Young, M 1983, *Magicians of Manumanua: Living Myth in Kalauna*, University of California Press, Berkeley, CA.

Chapter 4

Autobiography and Testimonial Discourse in Myles Lalor's 'Oral History'

One of the criticisms levelled against anthropology is that Western-trained researchers impose their own reality on their subjects. I would argue, nevertheless, that a challenging — and to me redeeming — feature of anthropological fieldwork is the way it subverts the researcher's preconceptions and, to a greater or lesser degree, remakes the project in its own image. Our subjects are not inert, and have a way of setting their own terms — even making demands that send us off doing thing we never intended to do. Right at the beginning of my career, I found myself being required by one of my best Aboriginal informants, named George Dutton, to take down the details of his career as bush worker and ritual leader. His story formed the basis of the first article I published. Many years later, in 1987, a much younger friend of this man — also Aboriginal — named Myles Lalor proposed that I should do what he called his 'oral history'.

I had a tape recorder to hand and we started straight away. He recorded some four hours of reminiscences the same evening, and another three a week later. He then went back to Broken Hill, the New South Wales town where his family lived, and made further recordings, some with his daughter as audience, some on his own. He died about twelve months later, aged sixty-two, leaving me to edit some seventy thousand words of transcription without the benefit of his advice or wishes. I have just finished this task, for better or worse (see Beckett 2000).

Myles' story might be called an autobiography, but it includes political content of a kind that some critics have called testimonial. In Australia, as in other places, the 'voice' of an Indigenous person is in a sense political, whatever the content. Correspondingly, the kinds of framing and interpretation that I required to make the text accessible outside a specialist audience — which I think Myles would have wanted — are likely to incur the reproach of distorting if not appropriating his voice and, in particular, his Aboriginality. As is the way with identity politics, various critics — Indigenous but also non-Indigenous — have appointed themselves the guardians of what one might call an 'alternative' cultural capital.

In the latter part of the twentieth century, a structural opposition between the settler majority and the Aboriginal minority in Australia became part of a global discourse of indigeneity under the aegis of the United Nations and other international governmental and non-governmental bodies. There are two strands to this discourse, which I might designate as colonial victimisation and cultural authenticity. The former, deriving its legitimacy from the anti-colonial struggle of the post-Second World War period, represents the oppression of, and discrimination against, Indigenous peoples within nation-states as a latter-day colonialism. Although in its earlier phase this discourse was dominated by the non-Indigenous civil rights advocates, it now gives priority to the previously unheard Indigenous voice, 'the voice of the voiceless'. The latter stresses cultural difference not just from some dominant national culture, but from modernity in general. Thus Indigenous peoples claim and are credited with special qualities such as spirituality, care for the environment and non-acquisitiveness, which many in the West think of themselves as having lost. In this global formulation, the various Indigenous groups are interchangeable — yet, paradoxically, it is their particularities that are required for authentication. These particularities are cultural capital, to be deployed by nation-states, international media and the various Indigenous mobilisations. Representations of the Indigenous are, then, critical, and control over it — including the 'native voice' — is contested.

There has been a heightened interest in the writings and transcribed oral depositions of Indigenous people among both scholars and concerned readers in recent years, and I shall look at some of them before coming on to Myles' story. A remarkable feature about these writings is that in a great many, if not most, instances, the editors, interlocutors and facilitators who have been instrumental in the diffusion of the Indigenous voice have been non-Indigenous; for the most part, the readership has not been Indigenous either. At the same time, there has been an increasing awareness of the political position of such cultural mediators; some critics have questioned whether, good intentions notwithstanding, their interventions have compromised the authenticity of the Indigenous voice — even appropriated it.

Some of this anxiety stems from a preoccupation with the difference between Indigenous and non-Indigenous to the point of disregarding the common ground that makes communication possible. There is also some tendency to regard Indigenous subjects as ingenuous, rather than having their own agenda and being capable of effecting their own reverse appropriations when the occasion arises.[1] But, either way, an awareness of the conditions under which an utterance — particularly an extended utterance such as an 'oral history' — is produced is essential to an understanding of what is being said. It is also necessary to have an awareness of how this utterance stands in relation to communication within the Indigenous and non-Indigenous domains and, since extended narratives are unusual in either, how these come to be articulated.

The life-course narratives of Western people who are not writers, or perhaps even literate, have long been the concern of social historians and sociologists. Correspondingly, Indigenous life histories have been the preserve of anthropologists and ethno-historians; recently, however, they have come within the purview of what is called comparative literature. In the United States, Native American work has received its share of attention, particularly from Arnold Krupat and Hertha Dawn Wong (see Krupat 1989, 1992; Swann and Krupat 1987; Wong 1992). For Krupat, Native American autobiographies are:

> interesting both for the model of the self and the model of the text they propose, the first of these more nearly collective, the second more nearly dialogic than what has been typical of Euramerican autobiography ... the self most typically is not constituted by the achievement of a distinctive, special voice that separates it from others but, rather by the achievement of a particular placement in relation to the many voices without which it could not exist. (Krupat 1989, p. 196)

He argues further that, viewed as a 'textual representation of a situated encounter between two persons (or three, if we include the frequent presence of an interpreter or translator) and two cultures, Indian autobiographies are quite literally dialogic' (1989, p. 133). I am left uncertain as to whether the collective nature of the Native American self derives from Krupat's reading of the autobiographies, or his assumptions about Indian society as the milieu in which Native Americans achieve a sense of self; either way, I am left with a sense of prescription: this is how their autobiographies ought to be. However, the suggestion poses some interesting questions that I shall take up again later on.

Latin Americanists have formed some rather similar notions, but in a context of more fundamental, and at times violent, conflicts between Indigenous and non-Indigenous. Some of their thinking has formed around what has come to be called testimonial discourse. These writers, also exponents of comparative literature rather than anthropology, have addressed the kinds of problems I have outlined and have posed some interesting questions — most recently in a collection of essays entitled *The Real Thing* (Gugelberger 1996; see also

Gugelberger and Kearney 1992) — that I shall try to follow up with the Australian case, and Myles' autobiography in particular.

The Latin Americanists have designated testimonial discourse a genre 'marginal to literature'. First coming into currency in Cuba in the 1960s with the publication of the autobiography of the runaway slave Esteban Montejo (Barnet 1973), its most celebrated example is the autobiography of the Guatemalan activist and Nobel Prize winner Rigoberta Menchu, *I, Rigoberta Menchu: An Indian Woman in Guatemala* or, in its more eloquent Spanish title, 'I am called Rigoberta Menchu, and this is how my consciousness was born',[2] produced in collaboration with a Venezuelan anthropologist, Elisabeth Burgos-Debray, and first published in Spanish in 1983 (Burgos-Debray 1984). I should add that there are others, which some consider better, and of late some awkward questions have been raised about this book.

Since a number of scholars are active in the field, there are also many definitions, but let me start with George Yúdice, who was among the first. He begins by asserting that 'testimonio' has contributed to the demise of the intellectual/artist as 'spokesperson for the voiceless'. By contrast, the *testimonialista* speaks, addressing a specific interlocutor in the first instance. But while the story is personal and told in the first person, the story is shared with the community to which the speaker belongs, without the speaker speaking *for* that community, thus performing an act of 'identity formation that is simultaneously personal and collective'. Yúdice continues by stating that 'testimonial writing may be defined as an authentic narrative told by a witness who is moved to narrate by the urgency of a situation'. It is

> first and foremost an act, a tactic by means of which people engage in the process of self-constitution and survival. It is a way of using narrative discourse whose function is not wholly pragmatic ... but just as significantly aesthetic (in so far as the subjects of testimonial discourse rework their identity through the aesthetic), though the aesthetic does not usually correspond to the definitions of the literary as legitimised by dominant professional, educational and publishing institutions.

Testimonio has also to be free of the master discourses, and the testimonialist has to be in dialogue with a politically committed or empathetic transcriber/ editor, who does not unduly control what is said through leading question or doctoring the text (Yúdice 1991).

The term 'authentic', to which several of his colleagues object, alerts us to the dependence of all this on recognition by non-Indigenous, and in many cases non-Latin American, scholars. It seems to me that Yúdice and some of his colleagues are at risk of conjuring up an 'unspoiled Indian' — what Alcida Ramos (1994), in a somewhat different context, has called the hyperreal Indian — who doesn't talk to mining companies or communist ideologues, and doesn't get mixed up with the wrong kind of non-Indigenous interlocutor. Even speaking Spanish (or whichever is the language of the dominant group) is compromising.

Here, of course, is the contradictory element in testimonio, for in most of the instances that have come under scholarly attention, it is delivered not to the testimonialist's own people, but across a cultural — including linguistic — divide, apparently driven by some urgent situation to seek a sympathetic listener who will in turn provide access to a wider audience. Menchu, for example, told her story to a Venezuelan anthropologist in Paris who, according to Kay Warren (1997), did not know Guatemala well and spent only a short time with her.

Oddly, although a good deal is said about the editor/interlocutors and their variable but generally suspect influence on the testimonio that eventually appears in print, almost nothing is said about the readership, which may include Indigenous intellectuals but is mainly non-Indigenous. What should be said is that the readership is of crucial importance, given the political incapacity of most Indigenous peoples to not only raise the consciousness of their own people but also to appeal to non-Indigenous sympathisers. This appeal may be directed to a national or a transnational constituency, such as an Indigenous rights organisation or a church network — whoever is in a position to exert pressure. Over the last thirty years, applied or anticipated outside pressure has been a major factor in the politics of indigeneity, and Indigenous mobilisations have increasingly been directed towards making their grievances news — preferably television news, as in the case of the recent Zapatista uprising in Chiapas Mexico (e.g. see de la Grange and Rico 1997). Up to a point it seems to work; it is hard to say how far in most cases, though the Menchu autobiography won her the Nobel Prize and her cause a lot of international attention, which may have assisted the move from military to civilian government in Guatemala.

The point is, however, that unlike the stereotypical anthropologist's informant who is induced to provide information, the testimonialist wants urgently to get a message across to some audience. (I would add that this situation is not as unusual in ethnography as its critics seem to think.) This brings into focus the question of how the testimonialist stands in relation to some wider collectivity. For Yúdice, as we have seen, the message witnesses an experience that is both personal and collective (Yúdice 1991). And, as I noted earlier, Krupat has more generally argued that Native Americans (along with most of the world's peoples) tend to construct themselves as persons, which is to say as a bounded entity invested with specific patterns of social behaviour, normative powers and restraints, rather than as individuals who have interiorised consciences, feelings, goals, motivations and aspirations

(Krupat 1992). The testimonialist, however, is often displaced, in Paris, Mexico City or, in Myles' case, Sydney. And, as Santiago Colás (1996, p. 166) has remarked, he or she is not identical to other members of the community, at least in the sense of having chosen to speak. How this has come about is one of the questions that need to be asked. Is it simply a question of being in the right place at the right time, or of having a catalytic experience, or of possessing an unusual capacity for telling a story?

It is not altogether surprising that scholars trained in literature should focus upon the testimonial voice, even though they are at pains to distinguish it from the authorial voice of Western literature, since they regard the autobiography as 'the quintessential form in which the so-called centred subject has been constructed in the West' (Jameson 1996, pp. 180–1). Situating the testimonial voice in some kind of *gemeinschaft,* which is opposed to the West's *gesellschaft,* becomes critical if they are not to fall back into conventional literary analysis. Even so, Thomas Luckman's (1991) characterisation of biography, including autobiography, seems applicable to testimonio, at least to the extent that it integrates 'short-term into long-term temporal sequences' which are *'individual* rather than social', and are 'tailored to fit an individual lifetime rather than institutional times' (1991, p. 161, emphasis in original). This then raises the question of how the testimonio came to take this form: either the narrative form was already to hand, or it was articulated in dialogue with an interlocutor, though not necessarily in a form imposed by the latter. What is certain is that such extended narratives do not just come naturally. Raymond Williams (1980, p. 25), discussing nineteenth-century British working-class writing, remarked: 'Very few if any of us could write at all if certain forms were not available. And then we may be lucky, we may find forms which correspond to our experience.' In this case, they wrote autobiographies 'because the form coming down through the religious tradition was of a witness confessing the story of his life, or there was the defence speech at a trial when a man tells the judge who he is and what he had done'.

The testimonialist may not have to make the transition from the oral to the written, but he or she still has to integrate short-term into long-term temporal sequences, a practice that may well be a departure from everyday discourse, or that makes explicit what is normally left implicit. If the form for a long-term sequence is not readily to hand, probably it is the interviewer that provides it, through questions and in editing the text, perhaps obscuring this intervention in the final version, as Miguel Barnet seems to have done with the autobiography of Esteban Montejo (see Sklodowska 1996, p. 88). But it may rather be the unusual situation — a tape recorder rolling, an interested listener and an uninterrupted period of time in which to talk — that induces the speaker to expand an already existing narrative form, or to bring off an impromptu bricolage. However, it has still to make sense, first to the listener and, if the listener is to be the means of access to a wider audience, to others who may not have the local knowledge that the listener — an anthropologist, perhaps — does.

With rather more sensitivity to the hybrid nature of the situation, Colás has suggested that:

> The resistance value of the testimonio as cultural practice and artefact, far from resting on the absolute identity between a people, their representative, the interlocutor, and the foreign sympathiser, seems rather to derive from the tension generated by the disjuncture between these different subjects. (Colás 1996, p. 170)

Colás sees Menchu's self-presentation accordingly:

> both presents the appearance of being a 'genuine' Guatemalan Indian and frustrates our expectation with regard to the proper contents of such an identity. She tricks us by being a Euro-North American Marxist and Feminist in Indian clothing. Not the stability of her identity, nor the fixed truth of her discourse, but the protean character of these ... lend her work such 'dangerous' power. (Colás 1996, p. 170)

For Colás, the testimonialist may or may not intend this effect, although he seems to think that Menchu, moving in ever-widening circles outside her native culture, is aware of her 'protean' and 'hybrid' qualities. John Beverley similarly remarks on the 'performative transvestism' in 'her use of traditional Mayan women's dress as a cultural signifier to define her own identity and her allegiance to the community she is fighting for' (Beverley 1996, p. 278).

It seems to me that Colás is raising some interesting questions when he draws our attention to the tension generated by the disjuncture between 'a people, their representative, the interlocutor, and the foreign sympathiser' (Colás 1996, p. 170). Warren has remarked on the complexity of the Maya experience of the military terror in Guatemala, and the different positions that various individuals found themselves in during this time (Warren 1997, p. 22), and she implies that Menchu is obscuring important differences and diversities when she claims that, 'My story is the story of all poor Guatemalans. My personal experience is the reality of a whole people.' (Burgos-Debray 1984, p. 1) This indeed has been the reproach of anthropologist David Stoll (2007) in a recent book. More generously, Richard Gott (1999, pp. 17–19) has suggested that Menchu was using her own story to provide a generalised account for a fairly ignorant non-Latin American audience.

As I suggested in my introduction, however, the preoccupation with difference and disjunction tends to obscure the conjunctions which enable the testimonialist to work with interlocutor and to reach a non-Indigenous audience, and still sustain some kind of recognition among at least sections of his or her own people. Without these conjunctions the testimonio is impossible, even though the speaker's rhetorical strategy may be to deny them. It seems to me that the tension to which Colás refers is also to be found in the space between conjunction and disjunction.

I have dwelt upon the Latin Americanist writing on testimonio because I have found it helpful to ponder the questions they ask as I try to come to terms with the Australian material, and Myles Lalor's oral history in particular. The last quarter of the twentieth century also saw a proliferation of Indigenous biography and autobiography in Australia and, on a smaller scale, similar kinds of commentaries — particularly on the part of Mudrooroo, who has written poetry and novels under the name Colin Johnson. Mudrooroo comments on the extent to which any kind of non-Indigenous involvement distorts Aboriginal discourse, even if it is only self-censorship. One of the few books produced under an Aboriginal control of discourse is Bob Bropho's *Fringedweller* (1980), which shows a mixture or ignoring of European genres, being both a polemic and an autobiography. Mudrooroo (1990) comments that it 'is not so much the story of Bob Bropho as of the people living on the fringe. Community is foremost, and the cover illustration is not the smiling face of the author, but a family pressed together into a collective whole.'

Sally Morgan's (1987) autobiographical *My Place* has been by far the best-selling Aboriginal work, and perhaps on this account has provoked the only sustained debate. This has centred on Morgan herself, with critical scrutiny focused mainly on the tension occurring between her and her kinfolk, and the Aboriginal community at large (see Attwood 1992; Birch 1993; Huggins 1993; Rowse 1993; Tarrago 1993; Michaels 1994). There is no question of translation or transcription, since Morgan was working in her first — indeed her only — language, and she wrote the book herself. An editor worked on the manuscript but we do not know what changes were made and, in any case, this has not been made an issue. As for the readership, which has numbered in the hundreds of thousands in Australia and also in North America and Europe, it is overwhelmingly non-Indigenous.

Morgan might almost have taken Menchu's subtitle in the sense that her book is about the birth of her Aboriginality. In this case, however, it is not military atrocities that form this consciousness, but a series of small incidents that arouse her curiosity about the Indigenous origins that her family has tried to conceal from her. This need to know builds up to a state of urgency in herself, rather than in a collectivity. The stories that she eventually induces them to tell reveal the oppression that her mother and grandmother's generations suffered, and which, though abating by the time she was born, still cast a shadow over her childhood. 'Coming out' as an Aboriginal person in the 1970s was not the dangerous act that it could have been for her mother 30 years before — and indeed for Morgan, the budding artist, it might be considered a smart career move.

In eliciting the stories of her grand-uncle, mother and grandmother, which mediate the experience of being Aboriginal of earlier generations, Morgan herself is the interlocutor, privileged by being 'family', and thus able to press where outsiders might have felt diffident: the identity which she is discovering is, after all, her birthright. The accounts are in English and, although nearer to Aboriginal English than Morgan's own narrative, they probably needed editing but not translating. However, rather than standing on their own, they are incorporated into Morgan's own autobiographical narrative, which, Bain Attwood suggests, takes the form of 'an inexorable movement towards the discovery of her real self'. He dubs this as a 'romantic view of an individual life', while in somewhat similar vein Eric Michaels refers to Morgan's 'Protestant self' and Mudrooroo claims it is 'an individualised story, and [that] the concerns of the Aboriginal community are of secondary importance' (Attwood 1992, p. 167; Mudrooroo 1990, p. 149). But even if this is so, the life and the self are realised through and in relation to other people.

My Place is accessible to non-Indigenous readers in the form of an autobiography but also a mystery story, though they are reminded that the characters are real people when the dark secret that would have been revealed in a novel is left as a suspicion. What also makes *My Place* so accessible to non-Aboriginal readers is that the young Morgan is very much like themselves. Although we know from the start that she is 'really Aboriginal', her realisation of it is delayed, and she takes us with her through the voyage of discovery, getting to know her mother's and grandmother's past little by little and in due course meeting other members of the family, until eventually we go north to meet the ' real Aborigines'. Meanwhile, the author, who is in so many respects 'like us', mediates these encounters. She is also, through her own story and that of her Aboriginal kinfolk, quietly delegitimising her white antecedents. It comes as a literary surprise when Morgan declares her Aboriginality, leaving the reader as 'other' (Michaels 1994, p. 173). One can read this, and perhaps is intended to read it, as subverting the assimilationist scenario that ruled during her childhood, and is still the expectation of many non-Indigenous Australians: this Aboriginal woman is still 'like us' in all sorts of ways, and yet declares her difference. However, she practises her Aboriginality as a painter, which has proved the most acceptable aspect of indigeneity to the wider community.

What makes Morgan accessible and acceptable to non-Indigenous readers, however, is almost bound to set up a tension between her and other Aboriginal readers. The fact that she and her mother were able to 'pass' as white, so that she had later to discover her Aboriginality, has not pleased those who, whatever their appearance, have always lived as Aboriginal people (see particularly Huggins 1993). This said, Michaels also perceived a tendency in her book to construct a pan-Aboriginality (Michaels 1994, p. 174); certainly, kinship and spirituality are represented as transcending or transecting diversity, as is so often the case in Aboriginal writing.

Myles Lalor's 'oral history' sets up a different set of conjunction and disjunctions among the subjects. There is as yet no readership, so I shall focus on the tension in Myles' story between him and myself as non-Indigenous interlocutor, between him and the Aboriginal people who are, as you might say, his significant others, and between the two of us *vis-à-vis* the readership we anticipate.

Let me begin with the circumstances attending Myles' proposal that I should 'do his oral history'. I had known Myles for almost thirty years when he came to my house that evening. I had met him first in Wilcannia, a small township on the Darling River, where he lived with his wife and children, working as a truck driver, stockman and all-round labourer. From the late 1960s through the 1980s, he spent long periods in Sydney, and from time to time he would drop round to my house. These were convivial occasions, but did not have much to do with my current research interests so I did not write anything down. What, then, was different about this particular occasion, and wherein lay the urgency?

Myles was already suffering from the heart ailment that would kill him within the year, and it may be that he wanted to leave some lasting record of his life, but he never said anything of the kind. What he did mention was that he had just looked up his personal file in the records of the New South Wales Aborigines Protection Board that had control of people like himself during the early part of his life. At one stage he had been taken from his family and placed in the Kinchela Home for Aboriginal Boys. Myles had been in the home only from the age of twelve to fourteen years, and had absconded several times, but he had wanted to see what they said about him. When he arrived at my house, he was still angry about what he had read, and he wondered what they had said about his mother, who had also been institutionalised, along with several of her siblings, years earlier. Since these reports of long-dead officials were in writing, one can imagine that he might want to have his side of the story in equally permanent form. Talking to his daughter, he said: 'I feel like burning the bloody thing but then I think, maybe a hundred years from now, someone will pick it up and wonder.'

But if it was his and his mother's reputation that he was immediately concerned about, he quickly widened the narrative to include the many other Aboriginal people who had similar experiences. The authorities made a practice of 'removing' Aboriginal children in those years; there were various pretexts, but underlying them was the view that Aboriginal children would have a better future if brought up away from the unsuitable environment provided by their families and communities. In recent years, historians have seen this as a strategy to disrupt the reproduction of Aboriginal culture and identity, and some have called it genocide. In his narrative, Myles repeats the move from his own case to that of other Aborigines, with the difference that he represents his own experience as less damaging than theirs; thus he observes that, while he had only been in Kinchela for a short time, many of them had been taken as infants and sent out into the world not knowing where they came from or who their kinfolk were. The opening up of the archives was a response to people such as this, and the demand for restitution by those who have come to be called the Stolen Generations was already building up. Myles also perceived the removal of children as a tactic in a wider strategy of control, explaining how the police and officials could coerce Aboriginal women with the threat of taking away their children; he even claimed that his father, who had been killed in the war, had been recruited under the same duress. In his telling, this state practice becomes the quintessential assault on Aboriginal sociality.

Early on, Myles states, 'I'm classified as Aboriginal wherever I go', but his Aboriginality resides in the first instance in his colour. Morgan tells how she discovers the Aboriginal descent that has been hidden from her; in the process, her white antecedents are by one means or another delegitimised, leaving her finally with an immaculate Aboriginal pedigree. Myles tells a different story, describing how the hatred of colour, which was unconcealed in Australian national ideology in the years when he was growing up, corrupted relations among his Aboriginal kin. There is a paradoxical calculus to his pedigree: he remembers two great-grandfathers, both of whom were alive when he was a child. The one on his mother's side was white, 'an Englishman'; the one on his father's side was black. He mentions no Aboriginal antecedents on his mother's side, and no white antecedents on his father's side: they existed but they do not get mentioned. One can read this as an instance of the way race played out in Australian society in the 1930s: families who identified as white denied their Aboriginality. Thus his father's family kept their Aboriginal grandparents hidden on the edge of town and disowned their son's child by an Aboriginal woman. For Myles, kinship was not the bond that transcended difference among Aboriginal people, but a travesty that he left behind him as soon as he could. His Aboriginality begins with his 'showing too much colour' and continues as he lives on the reserve, sees the police targeting the Aboriginal homes and, in due course, comes under the control of the Aborigines 'Persecution Board' as his mother had before him.

Of his father's mother, Myles recalls: 'You used to see the hurt on her face for me to sit on her verandah ... and call her granny, but I only did it out of devilment.' As this passage reveals, when he talks about victimisation he also talks about the way he fought back. Similarly, his account of the brutality and poor teaching in the boys' home is also a story of the way in which he coped with them; in this way, he distances himself a little from the others:

> I didn't spend a lot of time in Kinchela because I went walkabout from there a couple of times ... I got up one morning just on sunrise, I dressed and I walked through the bloody paddocks of corn so as no bastard would see me, right into the country, 14 mile [22.5 kilometres]. I was off the road, walking rows of corn, and of course it wasn't hard to dodge the bastards from the home because they had a little yellow Bedford truck. You could see the bastard coming miles away. Plenty of time to squat down and let it go past. It took me until dark to get to Kempsey. There was a train standing there, so I jumped in the bloody train. I suppose I was lucky, no ticket or anything. There's an old woman there with a heap of bloody kids, heading to Sydney. The poor old conductor must've thought I was one of hers, because I got right through to bloody Sydney.

Here we have a characteristic feature of autobiography, as set down by Luckman: 'In addition to those elements of an individual life that are predetermined by a social structure and those that are simply contingent, there are those that are the result of his own actions—and *those* are guided by biographical schemes that were internalised by him.' (1991, p. 164, emphasis in original)

Earlier I referred to the critics who characterised Morgan's autobiography as 'romantic' or 'Protestant'. Myles' story has the same quality: his survival depends on his own determination, not some community that stands behind him and helps him out. In much of Myles' recordings with me, travel can be read as a metaphor for self-determination. His absconding from the boys' home is only the beginning. And when, after being brought back for the second time, the authorities go one better and send him 1000 kilometres away, to a place he has never heard of and people he does not know, he manages to get himself sent home, but then some years later makes his way back there of his own accord and eventually marries into the community. He moves beyond the territory normally traversed by Aboriginal men of his natal or adoptive communities, to find work and make friends — almost always Aboriginal, including lovers, whom he will in due course leave but not forget. Travelling is also knowledge in the sense that he can hold forth about the places that he has been, often in fine detail and always named. And with the places go the people, also named.

Once we get started, Myles knows what stories he wants to tell, scarcely stopping for me to change the tape. Now and again I ask a question, maybe just to clear up a confusion, sometimes to show him that I know what he is talking about, occasionally to raise a matter that I think may be interesting. But if I ask questions that he doesn't want to answer, he will say so, and once, when I have sent him off at a tangent, he abruptly stops and gets back onto the course he wants to follow, reminding me that I am the one who is going to have to straighten all this out.

Nevertheless, I am an interlocutor in a sense: as these stories are told to me we have eye contact, and he laughs a lot, though the laughter is often sardonic, and my laughter, also to be heard on the tape, indicates that he has left the space for me to join in. After so many years, we have done a lot of talking; he has also read some of the pieces I have written. So you might say the ground for this dialogue has been laid. In particular he knows about my work with a much older man, long since dead, who brought us together in the first place. 'Old George', as we always called him, had been initiated according to several Aboriginal rites, spoke a dozen languages, and had learned the mythological tracks over a vast area of country, including the Flinders Ranges and the Birdsville Track (see Chapter 1). Myles also knew this country but in a secular way as a truck driver and bush worker, and they spent a lot of time arguing about the various places. Myles has never been initiated, a practice that had ceased in his part of the country long before he was born, and he does not presume to talk about the mythology even if he knows it.

When Myles talks to his daughter some weeks after the sessions with me, he adopts a different, familial tone, referring to a trip they made to Uralla, the town where he was born: to them 'it's pretty little town', he teases, mimicking their voices; to him it's 'a bastard of a place'. Again he is the one who holds the floor, though the daughter gets to ask a question occasionally, and despite the playfulness he intends to instruct — about the way life was for Aboriginal people when he was growing up and when he was a child. Some of the stories about the oppressiveness of the authorities he has already told me, but they loom larger in the recording, whether because he has been brooding about them or because he has been holding back the tide of anger in the presence of someone who, though a friend, is still white. On the tape he recorded on his own, the witticisms, the playfulness and laughter fall away. Some of what he says seems to be intended to gratify workers in the Aboriginal Medical Service, where he had worked some years earlier, but at other times the bitterness and brooding that underlie the earlier stories come to the surface. Although he has attacked the government's record throughout the recordings he did with me and his daughter, he only attacks white people as a group on the tape he recorded alone: 'I still have a lot of things I want to do, but problems are stuck in front of me, not by the blacks but by the whites, who have the black chuck the problem up to me. It's left to the black to put that problem right. I'd notice that all the way through it's the white who's the expert, the black knows bloody nothing.'

How did Myles put together this long, sustained narrative? How, for a start, does it compare with everyday talk among his Aboriginal contemporaries in the town where he lived? What they would have recognised would have been the individual stories, or 'yarns' to use the local term; indeed, I recognised some of them myself, having heard them before. Yarning was a common pastime among Aboriginal people in the far west of New South Wales, a way of passing the time in bush camps in the days before transistor radios, but also in town, before television reached the bush in the 1970s, and in gaol. The stories ranged from ephemeral gossip to crafted anecdotes with a punchline, typically a smart retort to some overbearing individual, that 'rhymed it well' and that might be repeated several times to savour its wit. Such stories might already be known to some of the listeners, but they didn't seem to mind the repetition.

Recalling Yúdice's reference to the aesthetic of testimonio, I should explain that Myles was a stylish raconteur, ornamenting his delivery with the swear words that are standard in rural Aboriginal English, though he never used them to convey their literal meanings.[3] He took his time in the telling, savouring the detail. Reported speech was a regular feature, with the characters rendered in different voices — sly, pompous, dumb, gossiping. There were well-turned phrases such as 'I was an occasional drinker, but I wasn't an occasional gambler'. In this art, he was perhaps better than most, but not quite out of the ordinary.

Our project was nevertheless out of the ordinary, if only for its length. Among Aboriginal people, the competition between the speakers — particularly when there was alcohol flowing — meant that sooner or later someone else would want his turn and butt in. The situation of the recording session and the understanding that he had the floor to do his 'oral history' created the space in which to construct a more ambitious narrative. But this, of course, did not provide him with the framework for it.

When I was interlocutor, Myles strung his yarns together in a sequence that was roughly chronological but also, because he was talking about travelling for much of the time, topographical.[4] Indeed, the itinerary may be said to determine the sequence, inasmuch as many of the incidents he describes could have happened at any time. At one point in his narrative, when he is still a long way off the Birdsville Track, which he had often talked about before, he pauses to promise that later on — that is, when his narrative lands him there — he will take me through all that country where old George travelled, and in due course he does, telling it in a kind of counterpoint, rather as the two of them used to argue about their conflicting memories, 'like he was talking yesterday and I was talking today'.

I don't think his narrative would have taken this form if he had not been telling it to someone who knew George Dutton. With his daughter, who was only a child when the old man died, there is less about country, but the chronology remains: his early childhood, hard times in Uralla during the Depression, the oppressiveness of the authorities. He went over some of the ground he had covered with me, though with further details which had perhaps come to mind after we had talked about them.

It is Myles' past that is being recorded here, whether for me or the family or the world at large, and one can read his 'oral history' as autobiography, in the modern sense. There is a dwelling on childhood — something that Krupat (1992) says is uncharacteristic of Native American autobiography — and some sense of personal development flowing from certain key events. For example, at one point he speculates that he was drawn to old men such as George because he had lost his father early in life. The recurring 'Protestant' theme of self-reliance can also be read as the lesson he learned early in life, through his rejection in his own birthplace and lack of family support. Throughout a lifetime of displacement and disconnection, his own sense of self is the primary source of continuity.

Displacement in one way or another, as I suggested earlier, is the experience of many if not most testimonialists. It is also a common experience for Aboriginal people. Morgan calls her autobiography *My Place* although it is her grandmother, mother and grand-uncle who were physically displaced; Myles was likewise displaced in the first instance by his relatives and the authorities, but later by his own choice. For such people, the stereotypical *gemeinschaft* of Krupat and Yúdice's formulation is not an option. Displacement and a need to constitute the self in a new way, and with conscious deliberation, problematise the relationship with any collectivity, at least to the extent of having to make explicit what might otherwise be left implicit. This may go some way towards explaining why testimonial narratives so often take the autobiographical form.

Myles' narrative consists of a dialectic between himself as subject and the Aboriginal world with which he identifies and is identified with. This is because this world is his own articulation. In identifying as Aboriginal, his credentials are his appearance. This is critical for a travelling man such as himself for, as he tells it, when he goes beyond the places where he and his name are known he can get some kind of recognition from the local Aborigines, though there may be some who do not want to know him. By the same token, he has to expect rejection from many of the whites, though he does not avoid them on this account, developing the front to come to terms with them when the occasion arises. Some figure in his stories: employers, some of whom were 'all right', doctors in the medical service who will talk to you on an equal footing, as well as the police and the welfare board officials. It is Aboriginal sociality he wants to remember, however, naming the individuals whom he has known during his travels and the places where they live. The names of the people, and his rehearsing in fine detail where exactly their houses were situated, and often what they said on a particular occasion, even mimicking their voices, stand for the 'community' that Mudrooroo perceives on the cover of Bropho's book.

Frederic Jameson (1996, pp. 185–6), discussing the Third World testimonial novel, heralds the dispelling of the 'authorship' of the old centred-subject-private-property type, and the instituting of 'some new collective space between named subjects and individual human beings':

> Anonymity here means not the loss of personal identity, of the proper name, but the multiplication of those things; not the faceless sociological average or sample or least common denominator, but the association of one individual with a host of other concrete individuals.

But it is Myles' life course rather than a pre-existing community that articulates this world of names: in this life, he has travelled far and wide so that the people who live in one place may not know those who live in another place he talks about, and with his death this world falls apart, unless it has been recorded in some lasting form, which is what he seemed to want to do in his oral history.

Myles is prepared to generalise, beyond his own experience and that of the people he knows, about the experience of being Aboriginal in settler Australia. But, despite a strong sense of the opposition between black and white, and a sceptical commitment to various Aboriginal causes and organisations, he stops short of political rhetoric. He has a bitter disquisition on 'the white man's morals', but does not articulate the nature of Aboriginal difference. On the contrary, there is a sense of the plurality of the Aboriginal world.

In contrast to most Aboriginal writers, including Morgan, Myles makes little of traditional knowledge. He refers to such matters when he is talking about his times with 'the old people', but it is as an outsider who is puzzled and amused, not as an heir to this knowledge. He mentions them, he says, because he knows I am interested. Even with his great friend George Dutton, he admits there were times when they were just not on the same wavelength. It is not just the difference in age. Myles can imagine some of the stories the old man tells about the past, like his people's forced removal from Tibooburra to the Brewarrina settlement in 1936, and the subsequent flight of him and his family, travelling by night to avoid the authorities. But he says Wilcannia township, where they both lived, 'just didn't exist as far as George was concerned'. 'But if you go the opposite way (back toward Tibooburra) every hill existed. And when you get talking to him you get beat then, because he talking about something that was bloody vital when he was a young fellow, but you can't see it the way he's seeing it.' The nexus of people, place and myth has disintegrated and, separated from one another, they have changed. In his history, Myles rearticulates the nexus in a secular sense but he knows that it won't last out there in the real world. Again, unlike Morgan and many other Aboriginal writers, he does not deploy the trope of spirituality, although at one point he says he could tell such stories (and had in fact done so, the first time I met him).

As for the disjunction between him and me, this is not so much stated as implied in the subject matter. I would gloss it in terms of race, in a relatively unmediated form, but also of class, as implied in the stories he tells of a life as an Aboriginal man who has been a stockman and truck driver and much beside. As a middle-class white academic, I have never experienced such things, but I know something about them if only because he has told me on earlier occasions, and I did once have a hair-raising ride with him in the Ivanhoe to Wilcannia mail car, of which he reminds me. But the conjunction between us resides finally in the fact that I have known some of the people he is talking about. This, of course, is not going to be the case with other readers, for whom as editor I have had to make the history accessible.

Myles Lalor's oral history does not as yet have a readership. It has been my job to find him one, bearing in mind the strictures placed upon non-Indigenous editors and interlocutors, particularly those who may be presumed to have their own academic and ideological agendas. For the most part, his meaning is clear and, as I have suggested, his narrative is sufficiently connected for him to speak for himself. I have had to take the risk of tidying up the false starts, the sentences that go awry, the repetitions; otherwise, reading will become wearisome. I have also provided some factual background for the reader who does not know what kind of a place Uralla is, or how the mallee camp in Wilcannia came about, or what the government policy on Aborigines was during the years when Myles was growing up. But these passages will be marked as mine, and the purist is free to skip them if they seem intrusive. What I cannot eliminate is the part I played in Myles' discourse, through being his audience and interlocutor during the first rounds of recording, and because of the memories we shared. On his visits, Myles often arrived with gifts — Aboriginal gifts such as wild meat or emu eggs — and once he made johnnycakes on the electric stove; in a way his oral history was also an Aboriginal gift.

Acknowledgments

Earlier drafts of this paper were presented to the anthropology seminars at the universities of Lund, Tromsø, Stockholm and Sydney. My thanks to colleagues for their comments and suggestions. It was first published in 2001 in B Attwood and F Magowan (eds), *Telling stories: Indigenous history and memory in Australia and New Zealand,* Allen & Unwin, Sydney.

NOTES

1. John Beverley (1996, pp. 272–3) makes this point in connection with debates over the autobiography of Rigoberta Menchu.
2. The Spanish original is *Me llamo Rigoberta Menchu y asi me nacio la conciencia.*
3. Myles heard the recording of our first session in the presence of my wife, whom he had not previously met; he expressed some embarrassment at the amount of 'swearing', though he did not reduce it once he got into the swing of the next recording.
4. This corresponds to the Bakhtinian concept of 'chronotope', which Pam Morris glosses as 'the spatio-temporal matrix which shapes any narrative text'(1994, p. 246).

REFERENCES

Attwood, V 1992, 'Portrait of an Aboriginal as an artist: Sally Morgan and the construction of Aboriginality', *Australian Historical Studies*, vol. 25, no. 99, pp. 302–18.

Barnet, N (ed.) 1973, *Esteban Montejo: The Autobiography of a Runaway Slave*, Pantheon, New York.

Beckett, J 2000, *Wherever I Go: Myles Lalor's 'Oral History'*, Melbourne University Press, Melbourne.

Beverley, J 1996 'The real thing', in GM Gugelberger (ed.), *The Real Thing: Testimonial Discourse and Latin America*, Duke University Press, Durham, NC.

Birch, T 1993, 'Half-Caste', *Australian Historical Studies*, vol. 25, no. 100, p. 458.

Bropho, B 1980, *Fringedweller*, Alternative Publishing Cooperative, Sydney.

Burgos-Debray, E (ed.) 1984, *I, Rigoberta Menchu: An Indian Woman in Guatemala*, Verso, London.

Colas, S 1996, 'What's wrong with representation?' in GM Gugelberger (ed.), *The Real Thing: Testimonial Discourse and Latin America*, Duke University Press, Durham, NC.

de la Grange, B and Rico, M 1997, *Marcos la Genial Impostura*, Aguilar, Mexico City.

Gott, R 1999, 'Sacred text', *London Review of Books*, vol. 21, no. 11, pp. 17–19.

Gugelberger, GM (ed.) 1996, *The Real Thing: Testimonial Discourse and Latin America*, Duke University Press, Durham, NC.

Gugelberger, GM and Kearney, M 1992, 'Voice of the voiceless: Testimonial literature and Latin America', *Latin American Perspectives*, vol. 19, no. 3, pp. 3–14.

Huggins, J 1993, 'Always was, always will be', *Australian Historical Studies*, vol. 25, no. 100, pp. 459–64.

Jameson, F 1996, 'On literary and cultural Import-Substitution in the Third World: The case of the testimonio', in GM Gugelberger (ed.), *The Real Thing: Testimonial Discourse and Latin America*, Duke University Press, Durham NC, pp. 180–1.

Krupat, A 1989, *The Voice in the Margin: Native American Literature and the Canon*, University of California Press, Berkeley, CA.

—— 1992, *Ethnocriticism: Ethnography, History, Literature*, University of California Press, Berkeley, CA.

Luckman, T 1991, 'The constitution of human life in time', in J Bender and D Welbery (eds), *Chronotypes: The Construction of Time*, Stanford University Press, Stanford, CA.

Michaels, E 1994, 'Para-ethnography', in E Michaels (ed.), *Bad Aboriginal Art*, Allen & Unwin, Sydney, pp. 165–76.

Morgan, S 1987, *My Place*, Fremantle Arts Centre Press, Fremantle.

Morris, P 1994, *The Bakhtin Reader: Selected Writings of Bakhtin, Medvedev, Voloshinov*, Edward Arnold, London.

Mudrooroo 1990, *Writing From the Fringe: A Study of Modern Aboriginal Literature*, Hyland House, Melbourne.

Ramos, A 1994, 'The hyperreal Indian', *Critique of Anthropology*, vol. 14, no. 2, pp. 153–71.

Rowse, T 1993, 'Sally Morgan's caftan', *Australian Historical Studies*, vol. 25, no. 100, pp. 465–8.

Sklodowska, E 1996, 'Spanish American testimonial novel: Some afterthoughts', in GM Gugelberger (ed.), *The Real Thing: Testimonial Discourse and Latin America*, Duke University Press, Durham, NC, pp. 84–101.

Stoll, R 2007, *Rigoberta Menchu and the Story of All Poor Guatemalans*, Westview Press, Boulder, CO.

Swann, B and Krupat, A (eds) 1987, *I Tell You Now: Autobiographical Essays by Native American Writers*, University of Nebraska Press, Lincoln, NE.

Tarrago, I 1993, 'Response to Sally Morgan and the construction of Aboriginality', *Australian Historical Studies*, vol. 25, no. 100, p. 469.

Warren, K 1997, 'Narrating cultural resurgence: Genre and self-representation for pan-Maya writers', in DE Reed-Danahay (ed.), *Auto/ethnography: Rewriting the Self and the Social*, Oxford University Press, Oxford, pp. 21–46.

Williams, R 1980, 'The writer: Commitment and alignment', *Marxism Today*, vol. 24, no. 6, p. 25.

Wong, HD 1992, *Sending My Heart Back Across the Years: Tradition and Innovation in Native American Autobiography*, Oxford University Press, New York.

Yúdice, G 1991, 'Testimonio and postmodernism', *Latin American Perspectives*, vol. 18, no. 3, pp. 15–31.

Chapter 5

The Torres Strait Islanders and the Pearling Industry: A Case of Internal Colonialism

The Torres Strait Islanders are Australia's Melanesian minority. Currently numbering some ten thousand, they are today found throughout the continent, but their homes are a score of islands that lie between Cape York and the southern coast of New Guinea. The Islanders' first known contacts with Europeans occurred early in the seventeenth century, but they did not have to come to terms with a permanent white presence until the middle of the nineteenth century. This was not the catastrophe for them that it was for so many mainland Aborigines. The Europeans came mainly to exploit the region's marine resources, and so had no occasion to displace Indigenous communities or encroach upon traditional means of livelihood. They did, however, need labour, while Islanders wanted the goods that could be obtained by working. This exchange relationship provides the key to an understanding of post-contact Torres Strait society, and of that society's relationship with the rest of Australia.

Although meshed into the mainland economy for more than a century, the Torres Strait has remained an enclave of under-development with its own distinctive structure.[1] This had been due less to geographical isolation or cultural backwardness than to the nature of the marine industry and the place of the Islanders in that industry. The industry — which is to say pearling and trepanging — has always been marginal, able to survive only through access to cheap labour. Lacking any alternative, Islanders have worked for small wages, but this they could only do as long as they could supplement their earnings with seafood and garden produce. They were thus anchored to their communities, which became part of the industry's support structure.

The Torres Strait is part of Queensland, and the state government's 'native affairs' agency has been a powerful political force there.[2] Until recently, however, its activities consisted largely of maintaining and regulating the arrangement just described, and the Indigenous communities that lay at the back of it. In relation to the rest of Australia, the policy did perpetuate the Islanders' status as a distinct and culturally inferior minority, and confined them to a little niche in the labour force where they neither competed nor combined with white workers.

Since the mid-1960s, the marine industry has been in a depression from which it seems unlikely to recover. Meanwhile, a burgeoning mainland economy has drawn Islanders out of their isolation into the general labour force, while those left behind exist mainly on welfare payments and employment in government relief programs. Their plight is a familiar one throughout the world, and its social repercussions have been far reaching. However, this chapter focuses on the period when pearling was still the mainstay of the Torres Strait.

Internal colonialism seems an appropriate way to characterise the history of the Torres Strait, and indeed Rowley has already drawn comparisons between 'colonial Australia' and pre-independence New Guinea (Rowley 1971). But the notion has been applied to like situations elsewhere, in Central and South America, in South Africa and even in the British Isles, so that a general formulation is in order (e.g. see Gonzalez Casanova 1965; Stavenhagen 1965; Hechter 1974).

Colonialism, whether internal or external, places two territories on a footing of inequality in terms of power, economic exchange and status. These three 'dimensions' are always interrelated, but in a variable way. The metropolitan government usually has responsibility for 'colonial administration', while the exploitation of labour and resources is usually the province of private commercial enterprise. Colonial government usually protects and facilitates these interests, but it would be naive to imagine that it exists only for this purpose. If colonialism is primarily an economic phenomenon, it does not follow that every colony will be run for profit; some may be run at a loss as part of a wider strategy. How far the metropolitan society participates in the making of colonial policy and shares in the fruits of economic exploitation is another important set of variables. In terms of status, the metropolitan and colonial societies are ranked. The distinction is sharper when there is racial or ethnic difference, but is also apparent in attitudes towards the ne'er-do-wells and adventurers who become settlers, and their creole offspring. It may cut across emerging class divisions; however, colonial elites are not just the outcome of these two intersecting principles, but of the whole colonial matrix.

It was the pre-capitalistic societies of the world that proved most vulnerable to expansionist capitalism, hence the common association of colonialism with ethnic or racial difference. Colonialism tends to incorporate such differences, but varies in its response to the Indigenous mode of production, mainly according to whether it is oriented to the settlement of population, the extraction of natural resources or the exploitation of labour. Harold Wolpe (1975), in a discussion of internal colonialism in South Africa, shows how the 'normal' tendency of capitalism to destroy other modes of production may be checked by a counter tendency to preserve them when they can be harnessed to the industrial wagon. Thus it is the Bantu homelands that provide for the reproduction of labour, supporting the women and children, and the men when they are not in employment, while industry supports only its actual workers. The South African government's apartheid policy, then, may be said to maintain the articulation of the two modes of production.

Hartwig (1978) has proposed that this model should be applied to Australia. But, for Wolpe, internal colonialism occurs when capitalism develops predominantly by means of its relationship with non-capitalistic modes of production (Wolpe 1975, p. 244).[3] Certain Australian industries such as pearling and cattle raising have developed in this way, but the economy as a whole has not. Consequently, unless we regard Australian capitalism as monolithic, we cannot see government policy simply as a service for local industries without reference to other interest groups. In fact, we know little about the processes through which Australia's policies towards its Indigenous peoples have been formed. For much of the time, the big interest groups and the electorate at large have been uninformed and largely unconcerned. Legislators have variously evinced racism, humanitarianism and combinations of the two — sometimes preoccupied with the public purse, sometimes with Australia's standing in the international arena. The cattlemen and pearlers have had their lobbies, but they have often found it easier to modify policy by applying pressure at the local level. Career administrators, mediating between the parties and often the best informed, have been a major influence. Queensland in particular has been noted for its forceful administrators, one of whom, JW Bleakley, was called to advise other Australian governments during the 1930s.

In all the discussion of internal colonialism, little has been said about its implications for the development of a proletariat. Tribesmen and peasants do not immediately embrace the routines, rigours and scaled incentives of the industrial world: their tendency to withdraw when their immediate needs are met is notorious. Glossing Marx, Taussig (1977, p. 33) writes:

> the transition to the capitalist mode of production is only completed when direct force and external economic conditions, although still used, are only employed exceptionally. An entirely new set of conditions and habits have to be developed among the working class, to the point where common sense regards the new conditions as natural.[4]

This conversion process must to some degree be inhibited under internal colonialism, for the individual has repeatedly to choose between wage labour and subsistence production, between use and exchange value.

The account that follows is organised around the articulation of the subsistence and capitalistic modes of production in Torres Strait, and the role of government in regulating this arrangement. I shall be looking at the region as a whole, with its seventeen Indigenous communities centred on the commercial and administrative settlement at Thursday Island (see map); but focusing on one community, Badu, which more than any other committed itself to the pearling industry.

Sydney-based trepang boats were reported in the Torres Strait as early as 1846 (MacGillivray 1852, p. 308), but from 1868[5] until recently, pearl shell has been the staple of the industry, with golden-lip mother-of-pearl and trochus the most important varieties.[6] Both have been luxury products for alluring but fickle overseas markets. Trepang, otherwise known as bêche-de-mer, went as a culinary delicacy to the Chinese market, which closed at the outbreak of war in the Far East. Pearl shell, used mainly for ornaments and buttons, has had a worldwide market, which has been controlled by a few big dealers, first in London and later in New York. Though organised in an association, the Torres Strait master pearlers have had no control over prices, and so have been subject to market manipulations as well as the vagaries of fashion. They have also been limited in their capacity to expand by the availability of shell: one year's overfishing resulting in shortages for several years after. Bach (1961), the historian of the industry, wrote in its last phase that, 'The economy of the industry is precarious, with a record of recurrent financial crises over the last forty years.' (1961, p. 107) Pearling has had its prosperous times, but the rewards for capital and labour have always been uncertain.

Enterprises ranged from small, locally based operators to well-known metropolitan firms such as Burns Philp. Any tendency towards consolidation was offset by the excessive efficiency of large concerns — resulting in overfishing — and, on the other hand, the ease with which a small operator could start up. Just enough capital was needed to buy, fit out and provision a sailboat, usually a lugger or cutter, big enough to accommodate ten to twenty men. Diving equipment was needed for gold-lip, which was mostly below seven fathoms, beyond the reach of skindivers. Trepang and trochus were found at lesser depths, and all one needed was a few dinghies to carry the divers from the lugger to the reef. In short, pearling and trepanging were labour-intensive industries, with wages the major cost and the critical factor in determining profit margins. The recruitment and organisation of labour were thus of paramount importance.

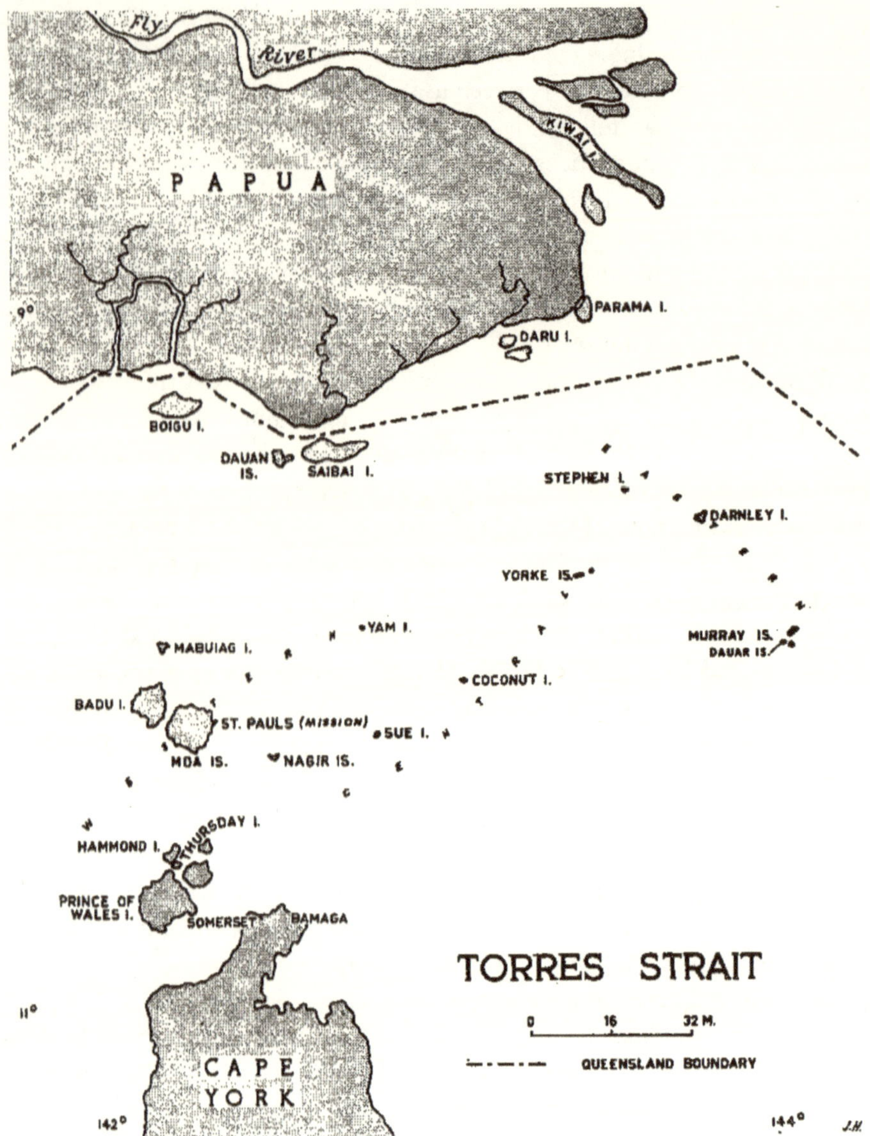

Map 5.1. The Torres Strait Islands

Veterans of the industry, white and black, all insist that the skipper's ability was critical: 'Better a good skipper with a bad crew than a bad skipper with a good crew.' He had to be familiar with tides, currents and winds, and to know where the fish was most abundant and most easily caught. He needed also to be able to keep up the pace of work for weeks at a stretch; to reduce tensions among polyglot crews living under cramped noisome conditions; and to keep in check the resentments of men who, particularly in the early days, had been subject to gross abuse.[7]

The owners of the boats rarely took charge themselves. They preferred to avoid the squalid conditions, the poor diet and the weeks of monotony, and still more the dangerous and debilitating deep-water diving. Fortunately, the masters could find able and reliable skippers at relatively low cost. In the 1870s, when the price of shell was still high, whites were attracted to the work in which a skipper-diver could make as much as £500 in a year (Somerset Magistrates' Letter Book, 3 April 1875). But as shell became scarcer and prices fell, employers looked to Asia and the Pacific Islands for workers ready to accept less money.

The skippers and divers of the 1880s were Rotumans and New Caledonians, Malays and Maniiamen until, in the 1890s, the Japanese arrived, ready to undercut and outwork them all. In 1907, in the wake of the White Australia legislation, a Royal Commission investigated the feasibility of replacing alien workers with Europeans, as had been done in the sugar industry (Queensland Parliamentary Papers 1908, p. lxi). But it was clear that no white man who could earn £8 a month as a coastal seaman would risk life and health for £8.17, which was the going rate for a diver (Queensland Parliamentary Papers 1908, p. lxiv).[8] The masters insisted they could not pay more and the Queensland government did not take up the Commission's proposal for a subsidy (Queensland Parliamentary Papers 1908, p. lxiv). As a result, the Torres Strait pearlers and trepangers, along with their colleagues in Western Australia and Darwin, remained exempt from the provisions of the White Australia policy right up to the outbreak of war with Japan. They were not allowed to resume when the war ended, but the labour — though local — was still cheap and coloured. It was Islanders who now filled the gap, not white men.

The 1907 Commission recognised that if white men could not be convinced to work as skipper-divers, there was no way that they would work as deckhands and skindivers at the going rate of £1 to £2 per month. These jobs could be given to Islanders, Aborigines and Papuans — who, it allowed, had 'natural rights to employment', as well as being 'tractable' (Queensland Parliamentary Papers 1908, p. lxiv). The first boats to work in the Torres Strait had come already manned by Pacific Islanders; other 'Kanakas' made their own way up from the Queensland cane fields, and even from Sydney.[9] But an industry liable to sudden booms needed to be able to expand its labour force at short notice. The Indigenous populations of the region could be made into a convenient labour reserve if they could be broken in. At first they proved unwilling to work for prolonged periods, and if kidnapped tended either to abscond or to succumb to exotic diseases. But with time they acquired immunity and became inured to remaining at sea for months on end. Moreover, they could be paid less than the more sophisticated Asians and Pacific Islanders. From the beginning of the century up to the outbreak of war in 1941, they made up more than half of the industry's labour force, with the Islanders constituting around 20 per cent.

Whether foreign or local, the workers were supported only while they were working, and there was little for their wives and children, and still less for the communities from which they were recruited. In other words, the reproduction of labour was left to the subsistence economies of Torres Strait and of the countries of Asia and the South Pacific, which thus became subordinated to the marine industry.

The Torres Strait marine industry did not become a basis for any kind of diversification. There being few other exploitable resources, profits were either ploughed back or invested in more promising fields elsewhere.[10] The industry may be said to have carried the Torres Strait to the threshold of the Australian economy and then left it there. After the initial developments of the 1870s and 1880s, it could neither expand nor diversify. Even this stunted development depended on continuing supplies of cheap labour. The labour supply itself depended on the back-up support of subsistence economies, and once foreign labour was excluded the Indigenous communities were largely responsible for the organisation of labour as well.

On the eve of colonisation, around the middle of the nineteenth century, there were between three thousand and four thousand Islanders distributed over twenty islands.[11] They lived by hunting turtle and dugong, fishing and either gathering or cultivating vegetable foods. The relative importance of these activities varied from one zone to another. In the Western Islands, men busied themselves with hunting the great sea mammals, while the women fished and gathered wild roots and berries; there was little or no gardening. By contrast, the small, fertile, densely populated Eastern Islands rarely saw dugong and got their turtle mostly during one season. Both men and women devoted themselves to gardening and some fishing. The tiny Central Islands provided little vegetable food, either wild or cultivated; their inhabitants spent their time catching turtle and fish, part of which they traded with the cultivating peoples to the east.

Social organisation was broadly the same throughout the islands and neighbouring New Guinea. Social relations were phrased in the idiom of kinship, with a patrilineal emphasis in the recruitment of residential and ritual groups. Economic activities dispersed and fragmented society. In the Eastern Islands, men gardened with their wives and unmarried daughters, or alone. Elsewhere, women gathered wild foods and caught fish alone or in small groups. Some cooperation was required to handle the big canoes that were used for hunting and trading, but the number never exceeded ten. This tendency to dispersal was offset by a rich ritual life that periodically brought together the people of one community — and sometimes several.

Pearlers and trepangers were the first foreigners to gain a foothold in the islands. They found the Islanders eager to trade for goods such as iron tools and cloth, and ready to work at least for short periods to get them. But if workers were unwilling, they were sometimes kidnapped, as were women to serve as prostitutes on the boats. Attempts at resistance only served to demonstrate the foreigners' superiority, so that when the London Missionary Society arrived in 1871 it met little opposition, and may have been welcomed as a protection against the rest.[12] Within a decade, the Society had won the adherence of the majority of Islanders, and begun the work of turning them into black replicas of the Victorian 'respectable working class'.[13] The Queensland government had completed its annexation of the islands by 1879, but lacking the means of administering them, it was content to leave the missionaries to guide the 'chiefs' it had appointed.

The missionaries regarded most of the pearlers and trepangers as a 'bad influence', and would probably have preferred not to let their flocks stray out of their sight, but they could scarcely stifle the demand for trade goods — and indeed, money was required to support the lifestyle they were introducing. Before long, they were encouraging communities to compete in the generosity of their donations to the mission, and in church building. Most of this money came from the wages of the young, unmarried men, who were most in demand with employers and most easily spared from their communities, being otherwise unproductive and a potent threat to sexual morality. The young men had their own incentive. Foreign workers in search of local wives had introduced marriage payments in the form of cash and manufactured goods: Islanders had to match them or miss out (Haddon 1908, p. 115).

Thus it was the young men who signed on for the boats, spending ten months of the year away from home while their fathers stayed back to guard the morals of their wives and advance themselves in the mission hierarchy. Combining their traditional authority as parents with their new authority as church leaders, they effectively nullified the young men's economic importance and succeeded in controlling most of the money that they brought back. Having right of veto over marriage, they delayed the event so that they could enjoy the work of their sons a little longer and hold out for a good price for their daughters.

The older, married men continued in subsistence production, gardening and fishing in the company of their wives and daughters, and hunting with their age mates. However, towards the end of the nineteenth century, they were buying small boats and working neighbouring reefs for shell or trepang. This seems to have reflected the growing demand for cash goods, including flour and rice, but did not amount to a complete abandonment of the subsistence production. Fish, dugong and turtle could still be caught on the way back from the working grounds. Not surprisingly, this arrangement proved more attractive to the hunting peoples of Western and Central Torres Strait than to the horticulturalists of the east.

The one difficulty with this arrangement was that it failed to provide for the 'hungry time' during the nor'west monsoon. The climatic conditions that caused a dearth of wild and cultivated vegetable foods, and made hunting and fishing difficult, also brought commercial fishing to a standstill. Flour, rice and canned goods could tide the people over, but money often ran out before the end of the season. Per capita cash income was still low and there were other calls on it: to support the church, and to finance ceremonial feasts and marriage payments. Clearly, then, more effort must be put into commercial production.

To deal with the problem, two missionaries formed a non-profit-making company, Papuan Industries, in 1904.[14] Its beginnings are described as follows:

> Revd. F. W. Walker, preaching at one of their church services, had reproached the Islanders for their apparent indolence. He pointed out the great wealth of marine produce at their very doors, the proceeds of which, if collected, would provide for the seasonal 'hungry times'. He was afterwards approached by a deputation of the people who explained that they had no money with which to buy fishing boats large enough to work profitably. (Bleakley 1961, p. 265)

For the next twenty-five years, Papuan Industries loaned Islanders the money to buy boats, selling their produce and marketing trade goods at fair prices. After a few years, the Queensland government went into partnership, taking over the company when its founders retired in 1930. Long before this date, it had taken effective control of what came to be called the 'company boats'.

The Queensland government's intervention was on too small a scale to threaten the masters, but still served to consolidate its hold over the Islanders. It seems to have been prompted by bureaucratic considerations, and as part of a statewide program for 'natives'. By 1890, the government had acquired the means for administering the islands, and began posting teacher–magistrates in the larger communities. This precipitated a struggle with the London Mission Society theocracy, which ended with the missionaries' withdrawal in 1914. The virtual takeover of Papuan Industries may have been one more move to reduce mission influence, but it was also in keeping with statewide policy. An *Aborigines Protection Act* had been passed in 1897, but the Hon. John Douglas, who had been Government Resident since 1886, believed that the Islanders were superior to Aborigines and not in need of it (Douglas 1899;

Queensland Parliamentary Papers, Chief Protector of Aborigines' Report for 1904). However, when he died in 1904, the incoming Chief Protector had them declared Aborigines for the purposes of the Act (Queensland Parliamentary Papers 1908, p. 408).

The White Australia agitation was at its height during these years, and the working-class fear of cheap labour was being expressed in terms of virulent racism. (The best account of this period is to be found in Evans et al. 1975.) The Aborigines were scarcely a labour threat, but they were included in the general opprobrium, as an offence to white sensibility and morality. They could not be deported like the Kanakas and Chinese, but they could be kept out of the way, 'for their own good' as well as that of the white majority. From this emerged a policy of protective segregation, whereby Aborigines would be confined on settlements and have as little outside contact as possible. The practice might better be described as *arrested segregation*, for there was never enough money to institutionalise everyone. Nor could the settlements be made self-sufficient, so that it was necessary to hire out the best workers to pastoralists — who, in any case, needed their labour. Since the government would have to provide if the worker was not paid or if he squandered his earnings, it had its own reasons for supervising employment and holding Aboriginal earnings. Under the tight controls that emerged, the government did not so much teach the Aborigines thrift as practise it on their behalf.

Islanders came under this regime after 1904. The commercial and administrative settlement on Thursday Island could not be rid of the Japanese, but Islanders and Aborigines were to be kept out as much as possible, and the surviving Pacific Islanders were to be settled elsewhere. The Torres Strait communities were to be made self-supporting, with the aid of the company boat system, but the masters were to be allowed to hire the best workers under government supervision.

It is hard to tell how far Indigenous entrepreneurship would have gone if the government had not taken over. Communities or community segments, called tribes, now worked off the price of the boats and became nominal owners; however, the protector, having legal rights of disposal over native property, could do with boats and produce as he saw fit. In reality, then, the means of production were in white hands, and if there was no master to skim away profits, there was the protector instead deducting large sums for various funds and contingencies.

The company boats became a continuing source of conflict between government and Islanders, who made the mistake of believing that, once paid off, the boats were theirs to use as they pleased, and when told otherwise gave up in disgust. Again, while it was understood that the boats could be used for hunting, they did not always get enough shell or trepang to cover running costs. The teacher–magistrates had to use stern sanctions before they could get the Islanders into line, and the Eastern Islanders, who had their fertile gardens to fall back on, remained refractory (Queensland Parliamentary Papers, Chief Protector of Aborigines, Report for 1910, p. 20; 1914, p. 12)

The government nevertheless persisted with the scheme, expanding its fleet to take advantage of the post-war boom, and persuading the men to divert their efforts from trepang and mother-of-pearl to trochus shell, which currently commanded a good price. In 1924, twenty-eight boats earned more than £20,000 and, with wages on the master's boat raised to between £3 and £4.10 a month, the communities were fully self supporting, if not well to do (Queensland Parliamentary Papers, Aboriginals' Department, Reports for 1925 et seq.). The number at work also increased, from 358 in 1921, when the population was about three thousand, to 587 in 1923, and it continued upwards through the 1930s. This was partly due to population increase, but mainly due to the expansion of the company boat fleet, giving employment to the older married men and the less fit.

The relative prosperity of the 1920s, during which Islanders increased their dependence on store commodities, came to an abrupt end with the Great Depression of 1930. The masters retrenched; the company boats worked on, but average per capita earnings for the year totalled only £8. The resentment that this aroused was not soothed by improving prices, and in 1936 the Islanders went on strike for four months (Queensland Parliamentary Papers, Aboriginals' Department, Reports for 1935–36). The private sector of the industry was unaffected. The grievances seem to have been various. The Chief Protector of the time supposed that the men wanted to handle their own money (Bleakley 1961, p. 170). Veterans of the strike cite the wretched pay, and the seeming lack of correspondence between effort and reward. Evidently officials did not bother to explain the complex system of deductions for debts incurred in earlier years, current running costs and various community and contingency funds. Some workers simply supposed that they were being robbed.[15] On the masters' boats they were assured of a minimum wage, and earnings were generally higher. This was partly because the masters took only the best workers, but the unfavourable comparison remained.

The government was able to bring the Islanders into line with a show of force, but knew it would face trouble again before long if earnings did not improve. The only solution was to increase productivity, and the only way of doing this was to build up a cadre of skippers who could step up the old, easy-going pace of work.

The Islanders had produced little in the way of leadership up to this point. Authority had not been much developed in the traditional society, and what there was had disappeared during the missionary reconstruction. The church leaders confined themselves to parish matters, and the local government councillors, who had replaced the old chiefs, were overshadowed by the government teacher–magistrates. As in other parts of Melanesia, ambitious individuals strove to aggrandise themselves only to be cut down by an egalitarianism that had been reinforced by the Islanders' lowly position in the colonial order.[16] The old-style company boat skippers were at most *primus inter pares*, elected by community or crew, and regularly replaced — perhaps 'to give someone else a chance', perhaps because they had antagonised the men. Many chose not to take the slightly larger share of the boat's earnings to which the system entitled them. Discussing such matters in later years, Islanders all agree that a boat could not do well when 'everyone boss'. In that case, it worked at the pace of the slowest worker, arriving late at the working grounds and coming back early, on one pretext or another. To work boat and crew at full capacity, and to get ahead of running costs, a 'tough skipper' was needed.

During the 1920s, a few 'tough skippers' had emerged, mainly from among the half-caste descendants of Pacific Island seamen, but their authority was personal. Only in Badu, in Western Torres Strait, did the skipper's authority become institutionalised, largely due to the achievement of Tanu Nona.

Tanu Nona was born in Saibai Island in 1900, the son of a Saibai woman and a Samoan seaman. His parents settled on Badu soon after and there he was raised along with his seven brothers and three sisters. He began with no particular advantages. His father was evidently a stern man and ambitious for his sons, but without wealth or influence. Tanu had to make his own way and, according to his own account, lost no time in doing so:[17]

> I got my first boat from Mr Luffman [a master pearler] in 1918. Then when I was nineteen I got the *Coral Sea*. I was going up to New Guinea to work out from Samarai, but my mother wanted me to stop and I took over as skipper of the island cutter. I've been a skipper ever since. Later the Poid people [a neighbouring community] made me captain of their lugger, the *Manu*. The government set me to race [i.e. compete] with Douglas Pitt from Darnley Island. In six weeks I got ten ton of trochus; Douglas Pitt only got five. That's how Badu got the *Wakaid*, the biggest lugger in Torres Strait. For six years we kept the cup [awarded by the government for the winning boat], until the competition was cancelled.

The *Wakaid's* success was not easily won:

> We stayed out sometimes for ten months on the coast, from Cape York to Gladstone [i.e. along the North Queensland coast]. You must have a strong captain to make those boys work. If they not get much shell I not let them into the dinghy to eat dinner, midday. They got to eat their piece of damper [bread] standing on the reef. Some skippers work only a half day, six in the

> morning till dinner time, then sail onto the next reef. That way they lose
> half a day. But I keep them there till six in the evening. We cook the shell
> and sail on to the next reef night-time. Making the crew work is the main
> thing. Also knowing the tides. But you must make those boys finish the
> reef. Bad skippers leave some shell behind.

The government was quick to recognise Tanu's ability and to advance him.
The competition, designed to take advantage of inter-island rivalries, probably
strengthened his hold over the crew and, when he won, enhanced his reputation.
The *Wakaid* would have been an added source of pride and, because of its size,
an asset in subsequent competitions. Nevertheless, the success was essentially
Tanu's and he is the one credited with 'teaching Badu to work'. No doubt
his forceful, not to say aggressive, personality was an important factor in
transforming the old easy-going routine, but he was also able to take advantage
of an unusual circumstance within the community. Towards the end of the
1920s, the community resolved to replace its decaying wooden church with
a cement building. Tanu, already elected a local government councillor, now
became a churchwarden and director of the project. He began by decreeing
that every able-bodied man should work full time on the boats, giving up a
portion of his earnings for the project. He next overrode the rule that a man
might only work on the boat belonging to his tribe, henceforth taking into his
crew the best workers, whatever their affiliation:

> I thought it silly that a good man couldn't work with others because he
> didn't belong to their tribe, and might have to work with other men who
> were no good. That was how *Wakaid* got all the best men.

With the benefit of hindsight, we can regard these minor innovations as the
opening moves in a process that was to transform Badu and have important
implications for other communities. However, it is unlikely that even Tanu
could see so far ahead. In the meantime, the innovations could be justified in
terms of established community values, principally the erection of a handsome
new church that rivalled the Thursday Island cathedral for size. If the young
men came home with more money than ever before, their mothers and
fathers and the church leaders were the main beneficiaries. Tanu remained
a community as well as an economic leader, with wide popular support. As
is often the case with innovators, Tanu's relationship to the community was
ambiguous (see Press 1969). Though Badu bred, he was not Badu born, and
while he had acquired fictive kin and affines there he had no true kin. Again,
as a 'South Sea half-caste', he could lay some claim to superiority over 'Torres
Strait natives' in terms of the prevailing ethnic stratification.[18] Finally, while
nominally an appointee of the community, he was developing an unusually
close relationship with the government, which was rumoured to pay him a
secret retainer over and above his skipper's share. This relationship was

strengthened by his refusal to join the 1936 strike, and his subsequent reward, the *Wakaid*, now to be worked as a family boat.

Normal life was interrupted in 1941 with the outbreak of war in the Pacific. Torres Strait became a field of military operations, though not of hostilities, and almost every able-bodied Islander served alongside white soldiers as members of a special volunteer contingent. Their contacts with the white troops were a radical departure from what they had known hitherto. At the outbreak of war they had been more cut off from the rest of Australia than they were at the turn of the century, their only contacts being with whites who were in authority over them. They now found themselves included in a new camaraderie and hearing ideas that challenged what they had learned in church and schoolroom. Having served 'King and country', they thought they would be entitled to the 'new deal' promised to Australian servicemen when the war ended. The Islanders supposed that this would mean 'freedom': the end of government supervision and segregation, and 'full pay'. As one veteran explained to me years later, 'We all came out of the army with swelled heads.'

In the new climate, the Queensland government found it difficult to restore the pre-war regime (Sub-Department of Native Affairs, Reports for 1946–47). However, boom conditions in the pearling industry, following four years of inactivity, eased its task and enabled it to offer certain concessions without making any structural changes. Taking advantage of the Australia-wide anti-Japanese feeling, the government insisted that the Islanders could and should provide the industry with all its manpower, including skippers and divers as well as crew (Queensland Parliamentary Papers, Sub-Department of Native Affairs, Reports for 1946–47). It also negotiated a new wage agreement that brought the basic rate to a little over 50 per cent of the national basic wage, with bonus incentives and higher rates for divers and skippers, who could now hope to earn as much as white workers.

The government had been negotiating wage agreements with the masters since 1904, as part of its statutory control over native employment. In 1907, Protector Costin had suggested that the Islanders were 'worth' £2 a month, though 'of course they have very inflated ideas of their own value' (Queensland Parliamentary Papers 1908, p. 60). In fact, he was going along with established practice that rated Islanders below Asians and Kanakas, but above Papuans and Aborigines. His successors arranged increases from time to time, sometimes in response to shifts in living costs, sometimes due to fluctuations in the industry. The employers, of course, insisted that increases were beyond their ability to pay, and more than the Islanders were 'worth'. But while these assertions can be taken with a grain of salt, it must also be recognised that the industry was predicated upon cheap labour, and had to compete with cheap labour producers such as the Philippines and the Cook Islands.

The gains made in the post-war boom years were soon swallowed up by inflation, and although the rates increased from time to time, there was a decline in real terms, and a widening gap between earnings in Torres Strait and those on the mainland. After two years of feverish activity, the markets were glutted and shell was once again hard to find. The number of boats and men at work declined, then picked up, reaching a post-war peak in 1950–51, slumping in the next year, partially recovering in 1956–57, then falling away, this time for good. In 1960 an economist observed that the industry seemed less viable every year (Bach 1961, p. 113), and within a few months competition from plastics had dealt it a mortal blow.

Trends within the government fleet were similar to those in the private sector. During the boom, it acquired forty boats, which the Islanders were quickly able to pay off from their wartime savings and post-war gratuities. But increasing stringencies forced one enterprise after another out of the race. The Island boats were left far behind when the master pearlers mechanised their fleet with engines and compressors. The government had to follow suit, but this meant a rise in running costs, so that more boats fell into debt. The government now adopted the policy of reducing its overall commitment and concentrating its boats in the hands of those who could run them most efficiently. By 1957, the fleet had dwindled to twenty-two, and by 1961 to fifteen, eight of them run by Badu's Nona company, which left some islands with no boat at all. By the mid-1960s, the six Nona boats were the only ones still working.

All these changes had important implications for the communities, both social and economic. The government boats had always worked out from their home islands; now the masters' boats often did so. This meant supplies of dugong and turtle at the end of each working spell, which might be every four weeks if the work was mother-of-pearl. With 600–700 kilograms of meat to supplement the fish and crops produced by those who stayed ashore, the income from the subsistence sector was considerable.[19] As Badu's fleet grew, so did its subsistence production, but at the expense of other islands, which became increasingly hard up.

There were other changes in the organisation of work. When Islander skippers took over the masters' boats, they brought with them the traditional norms that had already been adapted to work on the government boats. Most of the latter were owned by family companies like the Nonas. If additional labour were needed, the skipper mobilised his own kinship and affinal connections. Master boat skippers recruited in the same way. Initially, recruitment was mainly confined to the skipper's community, but as some communities lost their boats while Badu, and specifically the Nonas, acquired more, it became necessary to recruit outside and even outside the kinship circle.

As I noted earlier, the Nona company came into being after the 1936 strike, when the government made over to them the big lugger, *Wakaid*, which had previously belonged to one of the tribes. There were nine brothers, all but one of working age, and several already experienced in skippering boats. They initially joined forces to work the *Wakaid* under Tanu, but it was not long before the company expanded and they had boats of their own. The boats were lost during the war, but the company resumed work in 1946 with two new ones. Once again, the Nona family — which now included grown up sons of the older brothers — began by working together, hiving off as new boats became available. However, the expansion was too slow for some, who left to work for master pearlers. Most members of the family had the chance to prove themselves as skippers, either in the government or the private sectors, and while some failed, five of the brothers and four among the rising generation won solid reputations. However, Tanu continued to get the largest catch.

The company's quick expansion may have aided its survival. Other family companies, on Badu and elsewhere, foundered on internal rivalries — 'everyone wanted to be boss' — whereas the ambitious Nonas found an outlet before tensions reached danger point. Only the younger members worked under Tanu for any length of time, and even they sustained the hope of eventual advancement.

As well as skippering his own boat, Tanu acted as company head. He interfered little in the day-to-day routines of the other skippers, but advised the government on how the money was to be allocated. The younger skippers in particular had little idea of how their earnings were computed. Tanu also had a say in who should take charge of the boats. This was an area of considerable uncertainty, for the rights of company members remained undefined. In 1958, Tanu told me that he intended to divide the fleet among the branches of the family: one lugger to his most successful brother; one for two younger brothers; one to the family of a brother now dead. Three luggers belonged to him, but one of these should go to the family of his eldest brother, who had retired. This left out of account three brothers who were working for master pearlers, and who only benefited in the family's collective expenditures on weddings and memorials to the dead. They might, perhaps, have been accommodated in further expansion, but in the event there was no further expansion. Moreover, the family of the deceased brother failed to make a success of their venture and lost the boat to another branch. The son of Tanu's eldest brother resigned his command after some years, but was not replaced: the interest of this branch also lapsed. With the decline in pearling from the late 1960s, the number of Nona boats began to decline. After 1971 there were only two boats, skippered by two of Tanu's sons.

The company could run on in this uncertain manner because legally it was the government, not the Nonas, who owned the boats. In earlier reports, the government spoke of Islanders working off the price of their boats, becoming in some sense owners, though still under government supervision. Later reports make no such reference, and it would seem that the government was the real owner, although Tanu played an important part in management and was well paid for his services.

The Nonas trained skippers for both their own boats and the pearling companies. Masters and officials took Tanu's recommendations seriously, and were not often disappointed. Badu skippers had a clear sense of authority, in sharp contrast to the indecisive leaders characteristic of other communities. Tanu's harsh regime of the 1930s remained their legendary charter, but it was no longer a direct model since few now worked trochus. Mother-of-pearl fishing required tight discipline while the divers were down, but not long hours of gruelling work or prolonged absence from home. Diving could only be done for a few hours each day, and for about three weeks in the month. Nevertheless, the 'hard work' ethic persisted: skippers left for the working grounds before the water was clear and stayed out until it was too dirty for diving. They stayed neither for church service nor festival. Anyone who showed signs of lingering was said to be tied to his wife's apron strings. These standards were ultimately sanctioned by financial incentives and the risk of losing one's boat. But they were also maintained by the competitiveness among skippers, which ensured that any falling short would be noticed and commented upon. The Nonas were particularly jealous of their family reputation, and they all lived in fear of a rebuke from Tanu. The situation in Badu, with a dozen or more skippers at work, was quite different from that in other communities where there might only be one or two.

Throughout the Torres Strait, there was tension between skippers and their men, who always had some sense of being exploited. These feelings were not absent on the Badu boats, but were offset by other considerations. Divers certainly had something to gain by subscribing to the Nona regime. Skippers knew the value of a skilled man and showed appreciation in various ways. Although the Nonas generally preferred their own kinsmen, they did occasionally give other men recommendations that got them master boats. However, the divers' commitment was tempered by the realisation that it was the Nonas, and not the ordinary Baduans, who gained most from their labours.

Ordinary crew enjoyed the camaraderie of boat life, but got little in the way of prestige or money; they also bore the brunt of the senior workers' tensions. Skippers had no hesitation in punching a youth who was disobedient, and occasionally threw someone overboard. It is worth noting that they were all big men! There was no redress for these abuses. The island council was unsympathetic, being made up of Nonas, and the government referred complaints back to the council. Even parents might withhold support, for it was the custom for poorer families to ingratiate themselves with a skipper by sending a son to work under him. In return for this favour, they could ask for a free passage to Thursday Island and expect generous shares of turtle and dugong caught by the boats on their way home from the working grounds. The old company boats had shared the meat out equally among the tribe; latter-day skippers gave out meat or withheld it as they saw fit. A poor family, committed to a wedding or funerary feast, was wholly dependent on the generosity of a skipper for these festive foods.

The foregoing account is indicative of the changes taking place in Badu as a result of its commitment to pearling. The economic structure was also the power structure in a direct sense. An elected council would have found it hard to control the skippers, but in fact there had been no contest since 1947, when the government dismissed incumbents who were hostile to it and the Nonas. Thereafter, Tanu held office for life and secured the election of members of his family unopposed on his nomination.

The composition of the community, which now numbered about five hundred, had itself changed. There were relatively few people over forty, because many of the older generation had removed to Thursday Island, either to take up jobs ashore or get away from the Nonas, or because the Nonas had expelled them. But the skippers needed more young men than Badu could provide, and went recruiting around neighbouring islands that no longer had boats of their own. The Nonas' kin ties with Saibai proved useful here, as did their affinal connections with several other communities. Those who became their regular associates and protégés soon settled on Badu, swelling the ranks of their supporters. To accommodate them, the council abolished traditional land tenure, taking upon itself the right to allocate house and garden plots.[20]

The Nonas and their cronies became increasingly differentiated from the 'village people'. Their control of subsistence as well as cash production was reflected in their lifestyle. They occupied spacious modern houses on high land, back from the village, and maintained large households that included poor relations and hangers-on who helped around the place and ran errands. The largest share of dugong and turtle meat went to them, and they maintained large gardens, worked by their boat crews during 'dirty water time'. With all these resources, their wedding and funerary feasts were the most lavish in the Torres Strait.

Despite these changes, kinship remained the prevailing idiom of social relations. But people were also beginning to speak of 'skipper class' and 'crew class', and to regard the young Nonas as having better life chances. These young men were leaders among their peers, and seemed to be able to get away with misdemeanours that would have landed the others in prison. They married into the more important families in Torres Strait and showed a marked preference for wives with Pacific Island or Asian ancestry over 'Torres Strait natives'.

As the 'skipper class' rose in wealth and power, traditional forms of interdependence among ordinary Baduans dwindled in importance. Young people abandoned their parental homes for the more convivial and abundant households of their skippers, looking to them as marriage sponsors rather than their impoverished kinsfolk. The church, which had once provided the main source of prestige for older men, was now left to the women to run, with Tanu and a brother taking occasional major decisions. Religious festivals were still celebrated in the traditional way, but they were not always well attended, and the dancing was often perfunctory. The real conviviality went on up at the big houses above the village, where one went only by invitation.

While Badu was becoming fully committed to pearling, reducing subsistence production to a subsidiary activity, other communities were continuing in the old way. They sent their young men to work on the Nonas' boats, or those of the white pearlers, and themselves stayed at home to make gardens and fish. Although now getting an additional income from social service benefits, their incomes were well below what they had come to regard as their right as a result of the wartime experience. Even if they were to go to sea themselves, their earnings would not bring them appreciably closer to their goal. One heard such mutterings even in Badu, but the Nonas had a quick way with malcontents; elsewhere, however, protest was overt. To add to the problem, population was increasing while industry remained stagnant. The government expanded its building and welfare programs, providing work for some four hundred, but it could not expand indefinitely.[21]

The burgeoning economy and favourable labour market of northern Australia offered a safety valve for Torres Strait unemployment, but also posed a threat to the regional wage structure. Up to the outbreak of war, the government had confined Islanders to their reserves. After the war, it allowed them to settle and work on Thursday Island, but the few available jobs were soon taken up and the demand for employment was nowhere near satisfied. In 1947, a small party of Islanders went south to cut cane. The experiment was a success and was repeated in subsequent years. At the end of each season, some of the cane cutters found other jobs and stayed behind. Soon their numbers were augmented by young Islanders who had absconded from trochus boats at North Queensland ports.

Although by 1960 there were probably no more than five hundred Islanders living on the mainland, their presence there had a profound effect on the situation in Torres Strait. They were mainly concentrated in railway fettling, an occupation unattractive to whites but that did not have discriminatory rates for coloured workers. With overtime payments, a man could earn five and six times what he got at home, and the money was his to spend as he pleased, for the government did not extend its controls to the mainland. Islanders were soon in demand as first-class tropical workers (a marked change from the Torres Strait, where they were always told they were lazy). News of life on the mainland filtered back, increasing the restlessness of pearling workers, and of government employees whose wages were geared to those in the industry.

Further emigration was obviously a solution to unemployment, but if not controlled it could also deprive the pearling industry and the government of their labour supply. The government solution was to delegate the decision to island councils. Tanu was able to block emigration not only from Badu but from all the islands supplying him with labour, on the ground that Islanders were not yet ready to live without government protection.

In 1960, however, the industry suffered a permanent reverse. Plastics emerged as a cheaper competitor to shell in such fields as button manufacture. The trochus market collapsed and the demand for mother-of-pearl fell sharply. The industry was saved from extinction by the establishment of pearl culture stations, requiring supplies of live shell, but overall demand was still down and unlikely to expand. In 1960, eight government boats and five European-owned boats had worked out of Badu; in 1967, the numbers were six and two. With the population increasing, jobs declining and mainland employers ready to fly Islanders to construction camps in the Northern Territory and Western Australia, it was no longer possible for councils to say no. Some Baduans settled on the mainland; others alternated spells home and away. But those at home could be more selective about who they worked for. At the end of the year, skippers could be seen treating their men to drinks in the hope of recruiting them again for the next season. It was said that one particularly rough skipper had been forced out because he could no longer get crew.

Now, in 1977, the demand for shell has fallen still further. There are three luggers still working, all commanded by Nonas, but employing New Guineans. Those Islanders who have not emigrated can find work in various state and Commonwealth government programs. A number of Baduans work on their own crayfishing, using Commonwealth-funded boats and freezers.

Nonas still control the Island council and they have a foothold in several government programs, but they are not the power that they were since they are no longer large-scale employers and no longer have much dugong or turtle to dispense. The people now go hunting in their own small boats. Most of the younger Nonas are working on the mainland, and among the surviving brothers there is discord over the undistributed assets of the family business. Tanu is the only one to have invested his savings (in Brisbane real estate), and it is assumed that he will pass this, along with whatever else remains, to his own sons. Now that he is getting old, he is trying to secure his political office for a son, but the position is contested by a man of another family who has the backing of the village people and some of the Nonas as well.

In this chapter, I have analysed the Torres Strait's relationship with Australia in terms of a model of internal colonialism, focusing on the articulation of subsistence and capitalistic modes of production. I have taken the marine industry as the dominant mode, supported by the subsistence sector, and I have represented the Queensland government as regulating the articulation. This is not to suggest that they were under unified control: each had its own institutional autonomy, but in the local setting the two meshed into one another. Government policy may not have been designed with the needs of the masters directly in view, but it tended to their advantage in the long run. And when the government itself became an entrepreneur, with the aim of making the communities self-supporting, their immediate interests converged.

The industry's primary need was for cheap labour, which it either imported or recruited locally. It could keep wages low because the populations from which it drew its labour could support themselves by subsistence activities. Queensland's segregation policy not only kept Islanders away from whites, but anchored them to communities where they could support themselves without money.[22] There remained the problem of getting the Islanders to work regularly and at the required level of productivity — that is, to behave like ordinary workers without neglecting their subsistence base. This was relatively easy on Badu, where pearling and hunting could be combined, but difficult on agricultural Murray Island. Controlling both meat and money, Badu's skippers had a powerful base from which to consolidate their authority. Murray's split economy separated the men from the boys in a literal sense, leaving the skipper in the anomalous situation of being a man without a garden.

As Islanders took over the organisation of pearling, first on the company boats, then on the masters' boats, the conflict between use and exchange values became blurred. Men worked to put their island ahead of the others, or to build churches. The skipper–crew relationship became a service between kin, masking the trend towards inequality. These conditions existed throughout the Strait, but the Nonas were particularly well placed to take advantage of them because of their ambiguous place in the community.

Around the turn of the twentieth century, Islanders occupied an inferior position in the labour force, *vis-à-vis* Asians and Pacific Islanders as well as whites. With the elimination of foreign labour after 1945, they were able to become skippers and divers. However, almost all the top-notch skippers were part-Asian or Pacific Islanders, perhaps because the notion of foreigners being superior survived. This brought into existence a small elite who, like the Nonas, could earn at least as much as unskilled whites, and who enjoyed a much higher standard of living than other Islanders. Despite its class-like character, this elite was not an extension of mainland stratification but a colonial token, having no currency outside the Torres Strait. Its control of capital was tenuous at law and effective only under the peculiar conditions prevailing within the region. Similarly, the control of labour, on which it was primarily dependent, was achieved through the manipulation of kinship and communal ties. It is significant that a sizeable part of the Nonas' wealth went in lavish wedding and funerary celebrations that validated their status among their own people, but not among whites. In short, the elite was more firmly tied to Torres Strait than humbler Islanders, and it quickly moved into alliance with the government when the colonial structure came under threat.

We have seen that the colonial regime came under severe strain after 1945, due to the rupturing of isolation, a revolutionary rise in expectations under conditions of stagnation and a burgeoning population. The opening up of Thursday Island and of a new range of government jobs went only a short distance towards solving the problem, and boat companies, skippers and local government councils became increasingly subject to conflicting pressures. Cracks began to appear in the facade of kinship loyalty and communal solidarity.

The opening up of the mainland labour market provided a short-term solution to the problems of unemployment, economic frustration and political disaffection, but at the cost of undermining the colonial system. Those who remained became increasingly unwilling to work for small wages, or to accept the discrimination between black and white workers. Once Torres Strait workers had made their name elsewhere, the colonial economy's need for a labour monopoly came into direct contradiction with the mainstream economy's need for a free labour flow.

Commonwealth Social Service benefits, such as child endowment and old age pensions, introduced a further complicating factor after 1943. In the agricultural Eastern Islands, they relieved some men of the need to work on the boats. In the Western Islands, they probably reduced the pressure for subsistence production. In the quasi-urban conditions on Thursday Island, they complemented the inadequate wages of workers who could no longer grow crops, gather firewood or catch more than the occasional fish.

As in other parts of Australia, there was an increasing post-war inflow of special aid for Indigenous people, in the form of housing, health and education facilities, and development projects. With the decline of the marine industry, Torres Strait politics has increasingly focused on the distribution of government funds, and the old pearling elite have increasingly been displaced by new men with better education and wider horizons. Anchored to their communities, the

Nonas and others like them had little time for education or travel, and so are less well equipped to operate in the new conditions.

I do not think that the model of internal colonialism can be usefully applied to all Indigenous people in Australia, but it would seem to be appropriate to the northern cattle industry, which has long-depended on cheap, seasonal Aboriginal labour. 'Station blacks' have continued to maintain themselves by hunting and gathering at certain seasons, and have retained much of their traditional way of life. One could expect the mustering camps and droving teams to offer parallels with the pearling boat crews. But the prevailing tendency, particularly in the Northern Territory, has been for the government to concentrate population in large settlements so that only a small proportion could either obtain employment or live off 'bush tucker'. With rising rural unemployment, in the south as well as the north, the obvious comparisons are with under-developed regions of Western Europe and North America, rather than with the internal colonies of South Africa or the Andean republics.

Acknowledgment

The writer first worked in Torres Strait from 1958 to 1961 as a Research Scholar of the Australian National University, returning in 1967 and 1976 with assistance from Sydney University. Paul Alexander, Delmos Jones, Bruce Kapferer, Bob Reece and Kerry Levis have helped at various stages in the writing of this chapter. It was first published in 1977 in M Howard (ed.), *Aboriginal Powers in Australian Society*, Hawai University Press.

NOTES

1. The term 'under-development' can be taken here in the simple sense of the term, although it is used with Gunder Frank's writing in mind.
2. The agency has gone under many names: the Chief Protector's Department; Aboriginals' Department; Sub-Department of Native Affairs; Department of Aboriginal and Islander Affairs, and now Department of Aboriginal and Islander Advancement.
3. In a footnote, Wolpe (1975, p. 252) writes that, 'I leave open whether the notion of "internal colonialism" has any proper application in conditions of racial discrimination where, however, the internal relations within the society are overwhelmingly capitalist in nature, that is, where non-capitalist modes of production, if they exist at all, are marginal.' This is the issue taken up in Hartwig (1978).
4. Taussig's brilliant analysis of the proletarianisation of a group of Colombian peasants provides some basic insights into the Torres Strait situation, which I hope to take up in a later publication.
5. Captain Banner established a pearl shell station on Warrior Island in 1868, which seems to have been the first in the Torres Strait.
6. Black-lip mother-of-pearl and green snail shell have also been taken at times. Pearls provided a welcome bonus, but they occurred too irregularly and unpredictably to provide a basis for the industry.
7. In the early years, the Pacific Islanders had often been blackbirded, while Aborigines were shanghaied into the present century. For an account of labour abuse in the Torres Strait, see Evans (1972).

8. A report of the Northern Australia Development Committee, published in 1946, observed that: 'For many years, pearl shell fishing was a most hazardous occupation. One of the risks to which the whole crew was exposed was that of beri-beri, owing to the necessity for using preserved food with no fresh fruit or vegetables; another common hazard among the divers was that of divers' paralysis, a result of too rapid changes of pressure. Many men died of these diseases. The rough and ready life also took its toll. Living quarters were cramped and uncomfortable, the life was utterly monotonous, there was little provision for living while on shore. It was taken for granted that luggers' crews usually spent the last days of their lives as physical wrecks.' The report adds there was now more skill in the treatment of the bends, although fatalities still occurred from time to time.

9. The Somerset Magistrates' Letter Book for 1872–77 contains a number of references to crews recruited in various parts of the Pacific. From these sources and from the recollections of the descendants of Pacific Islanders born in the Torres Strait, it seems that the majority came from Rotuma, Samoa and Niue, and from various islands in the Solomon and New Hebrides groups.

10. During the early years of the century, several coconut plantations were established, but there seems to have been little or no copra production. For a few years after the Second World War, wolfram was mined on Moa Island. Otherwise the only resource has been fish, which to date has been exploited only on a small scale. For an analysis of the Torres Strait economy and its prospects, see Treadgold (1974).

11. This assessment, based on a number of sources, is discussed in Beckett (1972), which summarises the available data on the Indigenous Torres Strait. The primary source is the six-volume work edited by Haddon (1904–1935).

12. London Missionary Society Reports, September 1876.

13. For an account of the London Missionary Society in the Torres Strait, see Beckett (1971, 1978).

14. The 1897 Queensland Parliamentary Commission report indicates that Walker was helping Islanders to buy before the establishment of Papuan Industries. However, the London Missionary Society would not allow its missionaries to engage in trade. Walker was obliged to resign his position, but stayed on after the London Missionary Society withdrew in 1914. London Missionary Society Correspondence, 13 September 1896; see also Austin (1972).

15. This was alleged in the communist press, which took up the Islanders' cause (*Workers Weekly*, 21 January and 21 February 1936). The *Brisbane Telegraph* of 8 January 1936 reports a statement of the responsible minister to the effect that the Islanders 'were contributing something towards the support of Aboriginals on the Mainland'. Just what they were contributing and how was never made clear.

16. For a discussion of Torres Strait egalitarianism, see Beckett (1972).

17. I conducted two long interviews with Mr Tanu Nona in 1959.

18. Pacific Islanders married to local women were allowed to remain after their fellows had been deported. However, they were faced with the choice of becoming Aborigines under the terms of the Act, or removing to the St Pauls or Hammond Island missions where conditions were much the same as on the reserves. Their status nevertheless remained anomalous, and after 1945 their half-caste descendants were allowed to vote, take alcohol and travel as they pleased. These rights were still denied to half-castes living on the reserves.

19. Nietschmann (personal communication, 1977) found that a sample of forty-two dugong averaged 254.7 kilograms of butchered meat; a sample of fifty-four turtle averaged 191.1 kilograms. Badu luggers regularly brought back one or two dugong and several turtles each month, and would go out for more if there was a feast. With eight luggers working, Badu was well supplied with meat. For further data on hunting, see Nietschmann (1976).

20. It should be added that there was ample residential and gardening land. The change was made in order that those without hereditary rights should not be beholden to Baduan owners. See also Haddon (1904, pp. 284–91).
21. Reports of the Chief Protector and of the Aboriginals' Department indicate that the Islander population rose from 2368 in 1913 to 3765 in 1938. In 1948, the stated figure was 5000 and in 1960 it was 7250. Estimates by Caldwell et al. (1975), based on the Commonwealth Census, are considerably lower but record similar rates of growth.
22. The development of the island community in the colonial conditions suggests at least a loose parallel with the closed corporate communities of Meso-America and Java (see Wolf 1957).

REFERENCES

Austin, T 1972, 'FW Walker and Papuan Industries Ltd', *Journal of the Papua and New Guinea Society*, vol. 6, no. 1, pp. 38–62.

Bach, J 1961, 'The political economy of pearl shelling', *Economic History Review*, vol. 14, no. 1, pp. 105–14.

Beckett, J 1971, 'Rivalry, competition and conflict among Christian Melanesians', in LR Hiatt and C Jayawardena (eds), *Anthropology in Oceania*, Anthropological Society of New South Wales, Sydney, pp. 27–46.

—— 1972, 'The Torres Strait Islanders', in D Walker (ed.), *Bridge and Barrier: The Natural and Cultural History of Torres Strait*, ANU, Canberra, pp. 307–26.

—— 1978 'Mission, church and sect: Three types of religious commitment in the Torres Strait Islands', in JA Boutilier, DT Hughes and SW Tiffany (eds), *Mission, Church and Sect in Oceania*, University of Michigan Press, Ann Arbor, MI, pp. 209–29.

Bleakley, JW 1961, *The Aborigines of Australia*, Jacaranda, Brisbane.

Caldwell, JC, Duncan, H and Tait, M 1975, *The Demographic Report (The Torres Strait Islanders)*, vol. 4, CEAPR, Canberra.

Douglas, J 1899–1900, 'The islands and inhabitants of Torres Strait', *Queensland Geographical Journal*, vol. 15, p. 2540.

Evans, G 1972, 'Thursday Island 1878–1914: a plural society', BA (Hons) thesis, University of Queensland.

Evans, R, Saunders, K and Cronin, K 1975, *Exclusion, Exploitation and Extermination: Race Relations in Colonial Queensland*, ANZ Book Company, Sydney.

Gonzalez Casanova, P 1965, 'Internal colonialism and national development', *Studies in Comparative International Development*, vol. 1, pp. 27–37.

Haddon, AC 1904–1935, *Reports of the Cambridge Anthropological Expedition to Torres Straits*, Cambridge University Press, Cambridge, vols 1 (1935), 5 (1904) and 6 (1908).

Hartwig, MC 1978, 'The theory of internal colonialism — the Australian case', in EG Wheelwright and K Buckley (eds), *Essays in the Political Economy of Capitalism*, ANZ Book Company, Sydney.

Hechter, M 1974, *Internal Colonialism: The Celtic Fringe in British National Development 1536–1966*, University of California Press, Berkeley, CA.

London Missionary Society, Various dates, Reports and Correspondence, New Guinea boxes, microfilm, National Library of Australia, Canberra.

MacGillivray, J 1852, *Narrative of the Voyage of HMS Rattlesnake*, London.

Nietschmann, B 1976, 'Torres Strait Island hunters and environment', seminar paper presented to Department of Human Geography, Australian National University, Canberra.

Press, I 1969, 'Ambiguity and innovation: Implications for the genesis of the culture broker', *American Anthropologist*, vol. 71, no. 2, pp. 205–17.

Queensland Parliamentary Papers 1897, *Report of the Parliamentary Commission on the Pearling Industry*, Queensland Government, Brisbane.

—— 1908, *Report of the Royal Commission on the Pearling and Beche-de-mer Industries,* Queensland Government, Brisbane.

—— Various years, Reports: Chief Protector of Aborigines; the Chief Protector's Department; the Aboriginals' Department; the Sub-Department of Native Affairs; Department of Aboriginal and Islander Affairs.

Rowley, CD 1971, *Outcasts in White Australia*, Penguin, Ringwood.

Stavenhagen, R 1965, 'Classes, colonialism, and acculturation', *Studies in Comparative International Development*, vol. 1, no. 6, pp. 53–77.

Taussig, M 1977, 'The genesis of capitalism amongst a South American peasantry: Devil's labour and the baptism of money', *Comparative Studies in Society and History*, vol. 19, no. 2, pp. 130–55.

Treadgold, ML 1974, 'The economy of the Torres Strait area: a social accounting study', *The Torres Strait Islanders*, vol. 2, pp. ix–41.

Wolfe, E 1957, 'Closed corporate communities in Mesoamerica and Central Java', *Southwestern Journal of Anthropology*, vol. 13, pp. 1–18.

Wolpe, H 1975, 'The theory of internal colonialism: The South African case', in I Oxhaal et al. (eds), *Beyond the Sociology of Development*, Routledge & Kegan Paul, London.

Chapter 6

Rivalry, Competition and Conflict Among Christian Melanesians

Christian missions have been active in every comer of the South Pacific. Many anthropologists have made passing comments about the effects of their work, but few have described a missionised community as such. Ian Hogbin is among the first of these few, with his *Transformation Scene* (1951), an account of the Busama of New Guinea. Here and in his general book, *Social Change* (1957), he shows how Christianity has assumed a central importance in the life of such peoples, structuring their relations with the dominant Europeans and restructuring their relations with one another. This chapter explores similar developments on one of the Torres Strait islands.

Missions do not come alone but are part of a wealthy and powerful civilisation. In the new social order, the Indigenous people find themselves politically impotent, economically impoverished and morally degraded. Their political and economic plight cannot easily be remedied, but the mission seems to offer them the means of raising their moral standing. It thus becomes the main vehicle for their hopes and aspirations. Those churches that encourage active participation among their laity also become a vehicle for individual aspirations, and an arena for competition and conflict.

People of low status seem to resent the successes of their fellows in the wider society more than the successes of outsiders (cf. Foster 1965; Jayawardena 1968). Their resentment is most likely to be mollified if there is some promise of a collective benefit. This seems to be the case with many mission churches. But it often happens that the only outcome of all the zeal is an increase in internal differentiation without any corresponding gain in collective status. The rank and file find that, far from improving their position, they have fallen in the scale by allowing certain of their number to advance. When this happens, further cooperation is in jeopardy.

The community to be described in this chapter illustrates the trends I have outlined. Its status is low and there is a general resistance to individual advancement. The church provides virtually the only outlet for its aspirations in the wider society, and has become the focus of intense collective activity. However, cooperation does not run easily. People are at once pushing and over-quick to sense a slight. From time to time, resentments break out into open quarrelling and activities are disrupted.

The people are Melanesians, inhabitants of an island I shall call Kawa,[1] in the Torres Strait group. Like the other islands, it has been in regular though limited contact with the outside world since about 1860. During this period, much of the traditional culture has been lost and much has been adopted from Europeans. The institutions having the greatest importance in island life belong to the wider society and are dominated by white people. These institutions are governmental, religious and industrial. The Torres Strait islands are part of Australia and administered by an agency of the Queensland state government that has comprehensive powers in the fields of law and order, economic development, education, health and so on. The Anglican Church is established on every island, in all but one instance without rivals. The only industry of any consequence is pearling, which has provided Islanders with a meagre but nonetheless important source of cash.

Kawans stand low on the Australian social scale and they know it. They are poor, backward, black members of a prosperous, advanced, predominantly white society. Many whites consider them morally inferior and even question their potential for regeneration. They share these disadvantages with other Islanders, but even in this company they compare unfavourably. For Kawa is one of the most remote, least successful and least influential islands in the group. Its spokesmen are rarely heard when policy is discussed. Its pearling enterprises have failed and its prosperity has been declining for some years. Its population, less than 250, is no more than a rump of the old community, more than half of which has gone to live elsewhere. To the outsider, the village and the community have a depressed look, and the Kawans themselves are dismayed at their plight. As one of them said:

> We very worried people these days. We come a little bit good, but we look nothing change. Our houses are no good. We got no education. The boys can't find jobs. We like a bird shut up in a box. We want to come out and fly but we can't.

Other than emigration, they have no practical scheme for improving their material circumstances. But this does not prevent them from trying to impress their worth upon other Islanders and the few white people who come their way. If nothing else, they can show themselves to be good Christians.

Kawans first encountered Christianity in 1871 and had all become at least nominal converts by 1885.[2] The three generations that have grown up since that time have never known what it is to live without a church, its cycle of observances and festivals, and its code of morality. The church has also seemed to offer Islanders the readiest access to a worthy place in Australian society. They explicitly equate Christianity with 'civilisation'. It is what distinguishes them from their Papuan neighbours and identifies them with white people. In becoming priests, churchwardens, even communicants, they are becoming the formal equivalents of white Anglicans. Christian values are, they suppose, recognised throughout the civilised world, and provide a measure of human worth that cuts across differences of colour, culture, wealth and power.

Kawans not only want to be good Christians, they want to be recognised as such by their community and by outsiders, and they devote a considerable part of their time to this end. Being a good Christian entails right conduct and piety, which are individual matters, but also commitment to a church, which requires organisation. Kawans are not content to let each individual do as much as he pleases. Leaders have the task of exhorting others to further effort and pace setting. In the same way, conduct is not left to the individual conscience. Leaders must seek out wrongdoers and set a good example. These things are given an intrinsic value, but they also provide opportunities for demonstrating one's worth to others.

Opportunities for impressing outsiders are rare, and the formal courtesies that are observed when communities exchange hospitality tend to obscure responses. This creates uncertainty over how much is required to make the desired impression. There is no lack of opportunities for impressing other Kawans, but again it is hard to gauge their response. In such a small, isolated community, face-to-face encounters are hard to avoid, and interaction is usually conducted along what Goffman (1955) calls 'accommodative lines'. The response that one evokes is not, except incidentally, a recognition of true worth but of continued acceptance in a group, the product of tact, indulgence and politeness. Even boasting and bad manners may evoke the expected — or demanded — response, not because they are approved but because a rebuke would disturb smooth relations. When, as in Kawa, people are hungry for recognition but uncertain how much is due to them, they press their fellows' tolerance to the limits and sometimes beyond. This is what Goffman calls the aggressive use of face work.[3]

Although Kawans may be uncertain about their own rating, Christianity provides them with the measures by which to rate others. Similarly, the organised church provides a hierarchy of offices and of the qualities appropriate to them. Finally, long years of experience give each Kawan a notion of who is good and who is bad in terms of his own private interests. Any given action can be assessed in terms of Christian standards, the interests of the organised church and private interests. The conclusions are not necessarily in accord with one another. Some understanding of the confusion can be gained from Simmel's (1955) concepts of conflict, rivalry and competition.

Conflict, competition and rivalry

In his famous essay, *Conflict* (1955), Simmel distinguishes three kinds of situation in which people are pitted against one another. The distinctions are based on the aims of the participants, their relation to one another and the social value of what they are doing. In conflict, the relationship is central, with the aim of each being to inflict injury on the other. In competition, their relationship is incidental, with the aim of the participants being to gain some kind of prize. The contest may proceed 'as if there existed no adversary but only an aim' (1955, p. 58). But the prize in going to the winner is denied to the others. In rivalry, the participants are motivated by a 'jealous passion to surpass others' but the activity is valued in itself and there is lacking that characteristic of competition 'which is that the gain, *because* one obtains it, must be denied to the other' (1955, p. 70). Thus a group of pietists may strive to surpass one another in feats of devotion yet all attain salvation. Devotion carries its own reward and brings no additional reward because it happens to exceed that of another. By contrast, 'In every competition ... the significance of the success is determined by its proportion to the success of the competitor' (1955, pp. 70–1).

In rivalry, the actions of each contestant must be valuable to the others, since what they are doing is intrinsically good. In conflict, what is good for one is bad for another. In competition, either may be the case. Losers may gain from the outcome, as when divisions of an army compete in valour yet share in the victory. This can happen regardless of whether the motives of the competitors are altruistic or self-interested. Simmel writes (1955, p. 60) that, 'from the standpoint of society, it [competition] offers subjective motives as the means of producing objective social values; and from the standpoint of the competing parties, it uses the production of objective values as means for attaining subjective satisfaction'. Although Simmel does not consider the question, it is obvious that many contests may be seen in terms of all three of his types. The ethic of sport, for example, explicitly combines the principles of rivalry and competition. When Grantland Rice wrote in 'The Final Answer' (1955) that the 'One Great Scorer' records 'not that you won or lost — / But how you played the game', he was telling American college footballers that, in terms of good sportsmanship, the loser of the game might still be the equal of the winner. Similarly, Sir Henry Newbolt (1997) urged English schoolboys to 'play the game'. The hopeful belief of these writers was that the winners would be so filled with the love of their game that victory was scarcely more than incidental. Reality, of course, was otherwise, and the schoolboy literature of, for instance, Newbolt's period is filled with incidents in which the desire to win takes precedence over the game, or personal enmity intrudes.

It will be noted that Simmel's distinctions rest heavily upon motivation. The rival is moved by 'a jealous passion to surpass others'; the competitor is motivated by a desire to win the prize. Neither sets out to injure the others, though the competitor may do so incidentally. Now, in real life, motivation is a matter of inference and more than one inference may be drawn. I am not concerned here with the observer's inference, but those of the participants. The Kawans, for example, have a clear notion of competition and rivalry, and of the motives that underlie them. But they are distrustful of their fellows and sometimes suspect that what passes for the rivalry of religious devotion or civic piety is in fact a bid for the prize of public office or acclaim — or, worse still, a means of showing up and so injuring others.

Rivalry and competition are accepted norms in Kawan church life. The former serves to activate the congregation and the latter to select office-holders. But these benefits to the community have to be balanced against the differentiation that is created and the discomfiture of those who are surpassed. If it seems that the church is being used as a mask for self-seeking and malice, then cooperation — if not the institution itself — is in danger.

The community

All the people of Kawa live in a single settlement, strung out along more than a mile of foreshore. In this settlement are visible evidences of their connections with the outside world. The church is the only imposing edifice and the mission house, which accommodates the priest and other visiting clergy, is the largest and newest in the village. There is a small school, which also serves for meetings of the local council, and a store. Both are staffed by Kawans, but financed and directed by the Queensland state government. The money that goes into the store, towards the support of the church, and elsewhere comes from three sources. The first is the federal government, which distributes social services benefits in the form of child endowment and pensions. The second is the Queensland government, which pays small salaries to Kawan teachers, store assistants, councillors and police. The third is the pearling industry. In the late 1940s, one might have seen Kawan-owned pearling luggers anchored nearby. Now all these are gone, either wrecked or seized for unpaid debts. Those men — a declining number — who still work in the industry must work on boats belonging to others. But more than half of the able-bodied men stay ashore, living on social services benefits, the earnings of sons, gardening and fishing.

Torres Straits Islanders have few opportunities to rise in the world, particularly if they remain on the home island. The highest earnings are to be got as skipper of a pearling lugger, but positions are limited and not everyone has the required technical and managerial skills. Kawa has had three moderately successful skippers, the last of whom lost his command during my first visit.[4] Employment in government schools and stores carries some prestige and the work is relatively light, but the pay is little higher than can be earned by a pearling diver. Once again, positions are few — only four on Kawa — and only those who proved apt pupils in school are eligible.[5] The pay of a priest is even smaller, and many aspirants fail to complete the long period of training and probation. There are a number of Kawan priests, but it is diocesan policy that they should not serve on their own islands. Overall, economic differences within the community are small and not directly related to success. Two former skippers are among the wealthiest, though their savings are dwindling, but a married couple both drawing old-age pensions and with an unmarried son at sea are equally well off. The poorest would be those with no jobs, qualifying for no social services benefits and having no sons in employment, but I found no one in this unhappy situation.

Limited though it is, socio-economic differentiation has increased since 1946.[6] Kawans regard this development with ambivalence. They see it as a sign of progress, heralding their eventual entry into Australian society, but also as a force liable to disrupt relations within the community. For example, they see education as the key to success in the wider society and lament the limited facilities available to their children. Yet they say, 'Black people are different. They get a little more education and they get flash.'[7] When, at a drinking party, a government employee started to boast of his success, his brother replied, 'Don't try to come it over us black people. If you want to do that, go another place.' Kawan pearling enterprises also foundered on this contradiction. The usual verdict is that there were 'too many bosses'. Men recognised the need to have managers and skippers, but were never content with the current incumbents even when they had elected them. The post-1946 practice of paying skippers more than the rest caused bitter resentment: 'These skippers are too greedy. They leave nothing for the crew: that's why the boys won't work for them. The skipper doesn't do the real work, it's the crew.'

Disillusioned with their skippers, Kawans have given up work or signed with skippers from other islands whose success they seem to resent less. In subsistence production, the nuclear family is the regular work group. Wide cooperation occurs only occasionally and lacks clear patterns of command and obedience — even so, it is often disrupted by disputes.

The response to the island council and the parish organisation is much the same. But these bodies survive, supported by the government in the one case, and by the church in the other. Both are important for the way in which they represent Kawa to the outside world, while structuring relations within the community. They structure relations not merely through their establishment of formal offices, but also through the standards of conduct that they together maintain. These are the standards of generosity, hospitality, morality, piety and a vigorous church, which Kawans hope will make them appear to the outside world as good, Christian people.

Kawans maintain a high standard of religious observance, but in moral conduct they fall more or less short, while the vigour of their church fluctuates. In the last century, mission courts enforced moral conduct and sometimes religious observance with severe penal sanctions. But it is a long time since religious observance was enforced in this way, and a secular court composed of the two-man island council has assumed responsibility for enforcing good conduct. Fornication, adultery, swearing, gossip, quarrelling and other such offences are listed in the code of island by-laws and are punishable by fines and imprisonment in the village lock-up.[8] The church itself is no longer the place for the public exposure of sinners. Preachers discuss sin in general terms only. Confession and penance are a private matter between the sinner and priest.[9] A man who has been convicted of an offence that is also a sin loses any church office he may hold, but this judgment is foregone when he applies for another office after a decent interval, months or years later.

Those who have, or are believed to have, offended against the standards of Christian conduct are subjected to the additional sanction of gossip. Backbiting is endemic and severe, and there are few Kawans who do not engage in it. But, although the victim knows it is going on, nothing is said to his face. He may for a while avoid embarrassing contacts, but his fellows are likely to treat him as though nothing had happened, even those who formally condemned him. Given these conventions, the mention of his offence before others becomes a gross injury, which is itself a punishable offence. The victim is considered to have some excuse if he retaliates with violence, though he may simply recall some equivalent blot in his detractor's past.

Public comment on matters of individual conduct is the privilege of the court. The accused can defend himself, but he cannot challenge the court's authority without incurring further penalties. This arrangement has the combined effect of punishing offences and limiting punishment. Once the court has risen and the offender has paid his fine or served his sentence, the matter is closed and he is free to resume normal life in the community without fear of having the offence cast in his face.

The councillors are in an exposed position. They have the privilege or burden — and it is seen as both — of being the public censors. On behalf of the government, which has created the office, and the people, who elect them, they move outside the normal run of accommodative face work, exposing wrongdoers to the humiliating process of trial and punishment. However, they are not themselves immune from the same processes. The councillor who commits an offence automatically forfeits office. Furthermore, there are elections every three years, and for many years the Kawans regularly 'turned the rascals out'. By the end of a term of office, an incumbent had alienated a sizeable section of his former supporters. But there was, in any case, a common opinion that it was better for offices to circulate.

Shortly before my arrival in the community, a native official whom the government sent to conduct the elections persuaded the people to return the two retiring councillors.[10] The basis for this innovation was not their outstanding virtue but their somewhat superior education and familiarity with government affairs.[11] The people could see the force of this reasoning, yet they seemed uneasy about surrendering the offices to individuals on a more or less permanent basis. The incumbents themselves seemed uneasy in their new permanence. The junior councillor left public pronouncements and decision to the senior wherever possible. The latter seemed at pains to stress the bureaucratic aspects of his office, presenting himself as a mere instrument of the law, which he described several times as 'the schoolmaster that bringeth us to Christ'. He also instituted the practice of inviting the senior churchwarden to call the offenders to repentance to direct them back along the path of righteousness. This homily may have seemed irksome at the time, but it emphasised the regenerative aspects of the process, and so pointed the way back to normality.

Although the church is the doctrinal source and guardian of the Christian code, it is not otherwise active in the prosecution of particular offences. Its activities consist first in the organisation of regular religious services; second in the maintenance of church property and the raising of funds for parish and diocese; and third in the celebration of religious festivals. Although the ordained clergy occupy the higher ranks in the religious hierarchy, their activities within Kawa are largely confined to the first set of activities, particularly the administering of the sacraments, for which they are indispensable. Senior clergy visit rarely and stay briefly. The priest has another island parish in his care, and is often away. In any case, he is an outsider and, perhaps for this reason, the laity tends to exclude him from parish affairs. There are numerous lay offices, ranging from churchwarden, through lay reader and church councillor, to sidesmen and bell-ringer. Almost every mature male occupies an office of some kind. Most of the appointments are made, nominally, by the priest or the bishop on the priest's recommendation. In practice, the churchwardens have a considerable say in this, as in other parish matters. They hold religious services during the priest's absences, prepare rosters for various duties including preaching and reading the lesson, and organise working parties and celebrations in conjunction with the church councillors.

The church leaders seem to think it necessary to maintain a high level not only of religious observance but of other forms of church activity. However, the activities are voluntary and, since no sanctions can be brought against non-participants, the leaders must proceed by exhortation and example. After the Sunday services, people wait around in the churchyard in case there are any announcements to be made. Leaders often seize this opportunity to deliver a harangue. If the issue is important, they may call a special meeting. Although not all the leaders are given to public speeches, the practice is common and regarded as proper. Those in the older generation, in particular, have a certain relish for a strong speech, provided they are not the objects of castigation. But Kawans do not like bragging, hypocrisy or vindictiveness, although in the face-to-face situation such behaviour is given a good deal of licence. Leaders have the job of leading, not of self-aggrandisement or upsetting the people.

The maintenance of the code of Christian conduct and the promotion of the church as an organisation both provide the opportunity for rivalry. The homilies of local preachers and, even more, the pace-setting of church leaders are self-conscious attempts to stimulate rivalry in things that are intrinsically good. The contest is open to everybody — indeed, it is virtually impossible not to be a participant. Certain individuals may be still under the cloud of a recent court case, but while they may avoid the limelight, it is up to them to show that they are turning over a new leaf. Those few who have committed grave sins, such as sorcery or incest, leave the island. Less heinous offences, if not repeated, fade from public memory as fresher, more piquant, scandals take their place. Thus public sinners may, after a decent interval, become public censors, just as today's censors sometimes prove to be tomorrow's sinners.[12] In this rivalry of piety and zeal, virtue is its own reward, but it may in fact bring other rewards for which there is competition. In competition, the prizes are a higher place in the public regard, a right to take the limelight or perhaps high office in the community. Now the Kawans recognise that men of good character and forceful personality make the best leaders. But they also know that competition creates disappointment if not resentment among the losers, and that sometimes the leaders prove to be overweening hypocrites. In all events, those who find themselves discomfited by the success of others often find consolation in the thought that the leaders have unworthy motives. At worst, the winner is moved by the desire, not to do good or even to do well, but to injure others by placing them in an unfavourable light. The competition that takes place within the framework of the church and local government is not, then, based on what people really are, but on how they are made to appear by the manipulations of self-interested parties.

At one time or another, most of the present inhabitants of Kawa have come into conflict with one another. The issues might have been trivial and the parties now appear to be the best of friends. But there is a tendency for old rifts to reopen under the strain of cooperation. And, inasmuch as old quarrels are never completely forgotten, there remains the fear that they have never been completely forgiven. Thus some of my informants expressed fears that enemies whom they could not identify were making assaults on their reputations. Sorcery, which becomes an issue at rare intervals, is based on the belief that some people are gratuitously malicious. Kawans also seem to think of themselves as being caught up in a reputational rat-race. One explained that Islanders, 'because they had no education', were always 'trying to be over one another', at the least opportunity 'puffing themselves up like self-raising flour'. Given these beliefs, it is not surprising that they should be quick to impute unworthy motives, particularly to their leaders. Even if they do not believe what they say, it is a way of getting back at someone who is more successful.

Against the unjust councillor, there was — and in theory still is — the sanction of the election. One can also write anonymous letters to the authorities. But, in any case, court hearings are public and the accused has the chance to defend himself. I heard no complaints of wrongful conviction and doubt if it often occurred. In the parish the situation is different. Church leaders are much given to public peroration, the usual refrain being people's sloth and impiety. They name no names, but their reproaches are often interpreted as being directed against particular individuals. There is no opportunity for rebuttal. Similarly, there is no way of silencing the leader who uses the occasion to sing his own praises. Meetings are held on church ground and a wordy exchange would imply a lack of respect for the place.

A churchwarden may, of course, be unseated at the next election. But elections occur infrequently and, by the time they are held, the issue may well be cold. Moreover, an unseating is an impersonal act of anonymous voters, and so unsuited to the restoration of an individual's face. One can, however, absent oneself from voluntary activities, with the implication that one is avoiding further affronts to one's dignity. If one can find enough sympathisers, the action becomes a boycott.

It is the practice of the parish to celebrate occasions of religious rejoicing, such as Easter and Christmas, Rogation, Ascension and various saints' days, and visits by church dignitaries. Similarly, though less often, the council celebrates occasions of secular rejoicing, such as Labour Day, the Queen's Birthday and visits by government dignitaries. The mode of celebration is the same. The people assemble in the churchyard to enjoy a feast and a display of dancing. To provide meat, a party will go out in search of turtle and dugong, unless someone has already been lucky and is ready to donate his catch. If there is no wild meat to be had, the parish or council will have to go elsewhere and buy a pig. Otherwise, its cash outlay will be limited to a bag of rice or flour and a few packets of tea and sugar. Even these may be supplemented by private contributions. The food is prepared in the churchyard with the assistance of perhaps twenty men for two or three hours.

Kawan dancing is strenuous and, once it begins — typically at about nine in the evening — it will run on into the small hours, even until daylight, leaving the performers too weary to work the following day. It also requires preparation. If the occasion is important, Kawa's two choreographers devise new dances, which must be rehearsed over several nights. From time to time, the Kawans stage a whole cycle of dances, enacting some historical event, which requires more intensive rehearsal and the preparation of elaborate costumes and gear. Only men appear in these dances, which means that everyone is under pressure to participate, from his early teens to mid-fifties. At the time of my first visit, there were more than fifty males who could dance, but thirty-six of them were away working until Christmas, leaving at most twenty-six, the minimum number with which one could make a spectacular display.

Celebrations are of fairly frequent occurrence. In a period of ninety days, from the beginning of October to the end of December 1959, there were eight public feasts, thirteen dancing displays, two ceremonial welcomes and one formal presentation of gifts. There would have been three more feasts, and more dancing to mark the Christmas and New Year season, but for circumstances presently to be described. One should perhaps subtract from the ninety-day total twelve Sundays and Christmas Day, when neither work nor dancing was permissible. One might also mention that the public feasts were in addition to thirteen private feasts, to mark funerals, children's birthdays and family reunions, which engaged sections of the community. Those who live on Kawa do not have to work hard to maintain themselves — six men whose activities I checked were productively engaged on an average of only twenty-nine out of sixty-eight days. Even so, public celebrations make a substantial demand on people's time and energy.

In so small a community, which places so much stress on joint activity, the participation of each individual is important. In dancing, the absence of two or three can spoil the show. Even at feasts an absence is immediately apparent, and questions are asked. People feel under an obligation to attend. One man told me that he was tired of feasts and wanted to attend to his gardens, but would nevertheless come to the next feast lest people should talk. The kind of reproach he, and others like him, feared was that he showed lack of respect for those in office and the authorities they represented, or even civic or religious impiety. To absent oneself from church without good reason is a graver omission. Thus boycotting celebrations and, even more, church services is a measure which is not to be lightly undertaken. It is therefore something to be regarded seriously. It amounts to an assertion that the church is being so misused that its members are being prevented from doing their duty. In other words, it is a way of retaliating against those leaders who, from a position of privilege, have caused one to lose face. However, there is rarely any question of redress. Those who have given offence do not retract, leaving the dissidents with the problem of terminating their boycott. For, if it is too long continued, they incur the reproach of putting private pique before public interest and the church itself. The deadlock is broken by those who have remained apart; they duly note the protest and console the protesters with the thought that 'God knows who is right'.

I spent seven months on Kawa in two periods separated by an interval of fourteen months. During four of these seven months, the community was disrupted by public quarrels of the kind I have described, which several times culminated in boycotts. The Kawans were very ready to talk of their troubles, and in so small a community I was able to keep abreast of developments and hear the differing points of view. I shall now give an account of the two main sequences of quarrels, which were largely — though not wholly — unrelated.

The churchwarden who said too much

About a month after my first arrival on Kawa, a highly respected priest made a visit, providing the occasion for the first major celebration I saw. The Kawans were evidently intent upon making a good impression. There were five nights of feasting and spectacular displays of dancing which, on the last night, continued until the sun rose. After breakfast, each family presented the visitor with a gift, and a flotilla of canoes accompanied him on the first stage of his homeward journey. Within a few hours, I learned that there was dissatisfaction with the way the celebrations had been conducted. Apaga, the senior churchwarden, came to me complaining that he had paid for most of the store food consumed at the feast, while the rest had kept their money to give to the visitor so as to make a good impression. He singled out for criticism two of his fellow churchwardens, Sepal and Mataio, who he said were not pulling their weight in terms of either work or financial support. Neither had paid his church dues for several years. He made no allowance for the fact that, while he was relatively wealthy, the other two were nearly penniless. He made these and other derogatory statements to me only within the hearing of his two sons, but I think that other people were aware of the kind of things he was saying. They were certainly aware of the financial issue, because Apaga was in the habit of importuning people for church dues on store day. However, the affair did not come out into the open until later.

Most people seemed inclined to return to their own concerns for a while, but a minor church festival was due within three weeks, the Bishop was coming a fortnight after that, and then everyone was to go for a big religious celebration on a neighbouring island. When the church leaders called for preparatory work, the response was poor and I heard a lot of grumbling. No one produced a turtle for the feast and, when Apaga spent $20 of church funds on a pig, people complained that he had been extravagant. The feast took place and some of the young people danced for an hour, stimulated mainly by the arrival of visitors from a boat which had called. It was then that Apaga made a speech in which he complained that people gave presents to the visiting priest but would not bring food for church feasts. He also criticised the young people for performing the visitors' dances instead of their own. No one replied, but the dancers left immediately. Apaga also urged the people to make ready for the visit to the neighbouring island. But the following morning, many were declaring that they would not go, and parents forbade their children to attend dancing practices. Even Apaga was aware that his words had given widespread offence, but he insisted that it was his right and duty to speak out: 'I must give myself for the island, like Christ on the cross.' One of his supporters observed, 'Old people must talk like he does. Young people must take notice and not take offence.' Others had a different conception of the churchwarden's role: 'Sepal helps the church, too, but he does it on his own. He doesn't call everyone to help.'

Eventually, the churchwardens together called a meeting at which Mataio, another churchwarden, and Apaga reproached the people for their tardiness, with the Bishop's visit and Christmas so close. No one offered any objection, but Apaga noticed with annoyance that the brother of Sepal, the churchwarden, whistled quietly throughout his speech. The grumbling continued. Eventually, some older men who were not churchwardens and not closely linked with Apaga went about urging people to 'respect the church' and 'make the time happy', leaving God to decide who was right. Dancing practices resumed and all but a few went off to the neighbouring island. There, Kawa's dances provided the high point of the festivities, but people began to return before the end of the four days for which the celebrations were scheduled to run.

Shortly after the return, the church called a meeting to discuss plans for Christmas. Apaga promptly launched an attack on those who had left the celebrations early. The other churchwardens said little, trying instead to steer the discussion onto less controversial topics. At Christmas, almost no one came to celebrate at the churchyard. Instead, clusters of families celebrated Christmas in their own yards. Everyone admitted that this was not the proper way to celebrate Christmas, but put the blame on Apaga — or on those who would not heed him. Apaga and the senior councillor called the people to celebrate New Year on church ground, but it soon became clear that few would come and they abandoned the idea.

Not until Twelfth Night did people agree to dance in the churchyard. But, after the first round, Apaga arose and berated the people for not keeping Christmas in the proper way: 'Kawa has only one Bethlehem [i.e. the church yard]', he declared, and demanded to know whether they kept sorcery things in their private shelters — meaning that their behaviour had the odour of pre-Christian times. He ended by threatening to report everything to the Bishop. He then reminded the people that there would be a feast at which the priest would bless the new councillors' badges. When he had finished, the dancers removed their ornaments and went home.

The councillors' authority was now at stake. Hitherto, they had given Apaga tacit support, but remained in the background, since the celebrations had all been religious. Now they called a meeting at which they advised the people to forget their enmities and 'look for the silver lining'. There was no feast. Not until the arrival of an important official, who was known to favour the councillors and to be related to Apaga, did the Kawans come together and dance as a single team. For once, Apaga made no speech.

Obviously, it was churchwarden Apaga's sharp tongue and intransigence that sparked off the protests I have just described. But the conflict stemmed from a more basic and impersonal problem. Just how much time and effort should be devoted to festivals? Neither God nor the outside world, whom the Kawans would have liked to impress, gave any indication. The festivals themselves were indisputably good. Thus, given a situation of rivalry, the opportunity was open to men like Apaga to raise the ceiling above the level that others found tolerable. It is worth noting that Apaga was better off than his fellow churchwardens and so in a position to set the pace. But it was difficult for them to find religious or civic arguments for applying the brake, until Apaga's excess of zeal exposed him to the reproach of vainglory and malice, justifying a boycott. The arrival of outsiders provided the occasion for the boycott to be terminated, without loss of face and in the interests of expediency.

A church bazaar and the Christian way of marriage

When I revisited Kawa fourteen months later, I found the church preparing for a bazaar. The plan, copied from white churches, was to collect money and with it buy small luxuries from a nearby trading post that would then be resold at home. The profits would go to the diocese, the credit to Kawa. As a spur to the work, the church leaders divided the people into three competing teams, based on the normally unimportant divisions[13] between the eastern, middle and western sections of the village. For some reason, Wasaku, who was both senior councillor and store manager, chose to join with Middle Village instead of East Village, where he lived. He was a strategic member of any team because, being storekeeper, he controlled the limited supplies of cash available and could, if he wished, channel the greater part into his own team.[14] Later, when churchwarden Mataio boasted that Middle Village was outstripping the others, people muttered that the cash was indeed being monopolised.

In East Village, particularly, there were two extended family groups who felt themselves to be under attack. Churchwarden Sepal and his family had recently opposed the Bishop's proposal to reduce the number of churchwardens from four to two. They even opposed the election that was due. Sepal merely insisted that matters were very well as they were, but his critics said he was frightened of losing office. He and his family were also angry with the church councillors for setting the course of the Easter canoe race so as to discriminate against their build of canoe. The Tabu family, too, was angry with the authorities. The council had just convicted one of its number of adultery and dismissed him from the police force; the same man was alleged to have dabbled in sorcery. Thus, when members of the Tabu family were omitted from the list of those who were to keep vigil in church throughout the night of Maundy Thursday, they concluded that they had been slighted and made a noisy protest outside the church. It now chanced that the two families became allies in a new dispute.

Shortly before my arrival, the son of an important official from another island visited Kawa. Presently, he approached the priest and senior councillor with the request that they should help him to secure the hand of Sepal's daughter. They summoned the girl who expressed herself in agreement, but a few days later she retracted. It was generally understood that Sepal had dissuaded her. The priest and councillor declared themselves dissatisfied with this refusal, and spoke of calling in the official and the Bishop. The Bishop had repeatedly told parents not to obstruct their children's marriages. Apaga also identified himself with this view. His own son had married another of Sepal's daughters in the face of bitter opposition. Sepal was thus, once again, in the embarrassing position of appearing to flout the Bishop's authority. A few days later, he announced that his daughter would marry Peter, an adopted member of the Tabu family. This came as a surprise to everyone, since there had been no earlier signs of attachment between them. Those inclined to do so said that this was merely a device to block the other marriage, and that Sepal was now guilty of the un-Christian practice of forcing marriage. Sepal held an engagement feast for the two families and their close kin. He did not invite the priest, who took this breach of form as a snub, nor certain of Peter's kin who opposed the marriage.

Peter was in the unfortunate position of having to choose between his immediate family, who supported the plan, and other kin and friends — including his real father, the senior councillor and the priest — who opposed it.

Eventually, he told the priest that he wanted to break off the engagement. Sepal now turned the tables on his rivals by accusing them of obstructing marriages. The Tabu and Sepal families stayed away from church and skulked at their end of the village, visited only by those who had no declared position in the affair. Apaga now intervened to restore peace. On two nights he led singing parties, including the priest and the senior councillor but also many neutrals, up to East Village. Its houses were all dark, however, and everyone appeared to be asleep. The members of the offended party eventually agreed to hear Apaga's speech on my tape-recorder, but remained unmollified because they construed some of his parable to contain oblique criticisms of their behaviour. Finally, a man of Middle Village, who was related by marriage to Sepal, persuaded him to accept the gift of a turtle. The churchwarden reappeared in church and declared his anger at an end. But his party did not follow his example. A few days later, a member of this party quarrelled over a canoe with Peter's father, who also lived in Middle Village. We need not be concerned with the course of this quarrel, except to note that it helped to keep up ill feeling on either side.

The council now called upon the people to celebrate Labor Day. Middle and West Village exchanged feasts and dancing teams, but East Village people stayed at home. A week later came the celebration of Rogation Day. This being a religious festival, East Villagers attended — 'because otherwise people will talk behind our backs' — but sat by themselves until the food was cooked and ate only at their own tables or those prepared by West Village, none of whose members had been concerned in the quarrel. They went home without waiting for the dancing.

Kawa's saint's day was now approaching and, as usual, the days following it were to be given over to feasting and dancing. The people of a neighbouring island were expected to attend. With this in mind, the priest called together the Mothers' Union and addressed them on the theme of Christian forgiveness. Two dancing teams began to practise — one made up from Middle Village, the other initially formed by West Village and presently joined by men from East Village. The villages were also preparing displays of garden produce with which to decorate the church. Towards sundown of the evening of the big day, we heard the sound of drums and conches, and then the people of East Village appeared bearing an impressive display of produce, which they deposited in a big pile before the church. As they passed, one of them hissed a provocative challenge to Peter's father, who happened to be sitting nearby.

At the church service on the following evening, the priest devoted his sermon to the theme of Christian love and forgiveness but, as he later remarked, he might as well have saved his breath. No sooner had we emerged than Middle Villagers appeared, loaded with an even bigger display of garden produce. Churchwarden Mataio came at their head; reaching the churchyard, he flung his sugarcane into the air and dashed his taro on the ground, uttering boastful challenges. A few minutes later, East Village had formed a procession which marched, drums beating, up to West Village, where Apaga's family was hastily gathering its own display of produce. There ensued an angry conference at which the East Villagers unburdened themselves of their wrongs to the now sympathetic ears of Apaga. Mataio became the villain of the piece, not only for his recent conduct but for his provocative remarks concerning the bazaar. It was agreed that the trouble had started when the community had been divided into three competing teams, and had been aggravated by the senior councillor's defection. The priest was also criticised for his close friendship with several Middle Village men. Apaga then urged them to put away their anger, reminding them that God knew who was right.

This brought the affair to an end. The garden produce was put into a single pile and when, the next day, Apaga asked the assembled company whether they were now ready to forget their enmities, there was a murmur of assent. The visitors arrived for the celebrations and the Kawans directed their energies into the rivalry of the dancing ground.

This second series of disputes appears more diverse, but it can be understood as the attempt of the Sepal-Tabu faction (ten men and eleven women in all) to recover the face it had lost in several humiliating encounters, and to prevent further incidents of the same kind. The boycott and the statements uttered in private but repeated everywhere were also designed to counter the gossip which they knew, or supposed, to be directed against them. The whole operation was designed to vindicate these people in terms of the absolute values of Christianity, and to prevent Sepal's defeat in the churchwardens' elections.

Discussion

I have argued that church activities in Kawa are stimulated by the people's low status in the outside world. The church provides them with a ready means of contradicting this low status because it is already an established part of the community and can be maintained without too much strain on the members' economic and social resources. This adaptation has important consequences for relations within the community. Christian values create a field for rivalry. The need to appoint church officers and to have leaders creates an arena for legitimate competition. The intensity of competition and rivalry increases the probability that face work will be aggressive, while the frequency of public gatherings provides numerous opportunities for its practice.

Kawans are ready to recognise the value of rivalry and competition in the maintenance of their image of good, Christian people. But trouble arises when they suspect that what passes for competitive behaviour or behaviour inspired by rivalry is motivated by malice and intended to hurt. Kawans are prone to this suspicion because they are operating in a setting of multistranded relations, and I suggest that rivalry and competition will always be hard to maintain under these kinds of conditions. It is easy to suspect and believe in malice when a rival, still more a competitor, is, in another context, an enemy. Sepal and Apaga had quarrelled over a marriage. During the second series of squabbles, Sepal's family had been joined by a member whose educational achievements made him a possible competitor for Wasaku's position. The Tabu family was incensed against the council for convicting one of their number of adultery and dismissing him from the police. Wasaku himself had had a long history of squabbles with his East Village kin, squabbles he never mentioned during my first visit but frequently recalled during my second. The fact that he was storekeeper, councillor and team member introduced further complications. Even the priest could not preserve his neutrality because he was a remote kinsman of Peter's true father.

Although these tensions are never quite relaxed, the community recovers from its periodic crises and the church remains — overall — remarkably lively. When the stress upon competition and conflict becomes too great, there emerges a party of neutrals with the face-saving formula, 'God knows who is right'. Everyone can then turn his face away from his enemies towards higher things. In rivalry, at least, the contest cannot be rigged and the success of one is not at the expense of everyone else. Similarly, the occasion of an encounter with another community is a good time to remind the Kawans that their collective status is invested in the church.

All this is not to suggest that there is anything necessary about Kawan solidarity. As Leach (2000, p. 176) has remarked: 'It does not follow that those who have common interests are the most likely persons to act in co-operation; nor does the fact that two individuals are placed in the same category by third parties necessarily impose upon them any solidarity of interest or of action.' In terms of economic interests, in fact, the Kawans have little in common. Nor is there much sharing of political interest. Kawan solidarity stems from the existence of an isolated, compact, traditional community, in a social field where group identity and reputation is and has always been attributed on this basis. All the island communities manifest this notion of solidarity to some degree, and seem always to have done so. Church organisation followed closely the termination of warfare, channelling the sentiment into new outlets. However, political and economic developments since 1946 have made inroads upon this solidarity and reduced the church's importance. Communities have become more differentiated internally, with expanding economic opportunities and political outlets, and as islanders have gained admission to other kinds of association (Beckett 1965). For example, in one community, members of a war veterans' association formed the core of a faction opposed to another whose core consisted of government employees. The same community has undergone a religious schism. In another community, public affairs are dominated by a wealthy immigrant family with important outside connections. The rest of the people have either emigrated or remained as their employees and clients. The parish receives considerable financial support, but participation is largely confined to women and old men. In both communities, there is a declining regard for the old mission-inspired by-laws.

Kawa has largely escaped these developments, for reasons too involved to be set out here. Socially and culturally, as well as geographically, it is more isolated. External factors have not differentiated and divided its people to the same extent. The value of the church remains unquestioned. The conditions, then, are favourable to the persistence of a solidary ideology and its association with the parish. The people have no other means of proclaiming their worth to outsiders. They could, nevertheless, go on being good Christian people without devoting so much time to ancillary church activities. They could leave routine matters to the priest and a few old men, limiting their participation to the prescribed religious observances and financial contributions. There are also forms of piety that bypass the church as an organised body. Some people pray privately in the church or the cemetery, mostly late at night. There is a suggestion that one can gain healing and clairvoyant powers in this way. Members of the Tabu family, finding that they had been excluded from the prayer roster, marched off to the cemetery to conduct their own vigil. At present, those who engage in these practices are of lesser account in the community, and they continue to make the conventional religious observances. But widespread disillusionment with the church or the parish set-up might make these practices an attractive alternative. The collapse of the church would also mean an end to competition, with its attendant dissension. All that would survive would be a diffuse rivalry among individual pietists, with fewer occasions for aggressive face work and a lower threshold of tolerance in the face-to-face relations that do occur.

At the outset of this chapter, I noted without comment the tendency of low-status groups to resent successes of their own members more than those of outsiders. There have been various attempts to explain it. Foster has proposed a characteristic cognitive orientation, which he calls the 'image of the limited good' (1965). Jayawardena (1968) discusses groups whose deprivation is such that their common humanity is the only unaffected attribute left to them. This attribute and the suffering they all experience provide the basis for an egalitarian ideology that can be turned against those of their number who secure success in terms of the dominant values of the society. Such persons present a threat to the basic principles on which the group's solidarity is based. It is perhaps also true that the success of friends and neighbours is harder to bear than that of outsiders because these people have been so obviously like oneself but are so no longer, becoming instead a reproach on the very doorstep.

Jayawardena sees egalitarian ideology as providing a basis for a diffuse solidarity, even for short-lived collective actions such as riots. But its basic premise is antithetical to leadership and so to organisation. He leaves us with the problem of how such groups do, from time to time, achieve organisation. The Kawans provide an example of people who are of low status and whose tendencies are generally egalitarian, but who nevertheless maintain effective organisation. There is unconcealed resentment of those who are successful in economic activities, in education and careers. Such people become 'flash'. Christianity provides the only integrated ideology and its underlying premises are also egalitarian. These might be summed up in the twin doctrines: we are all sinners; we can all be saved. Even the punishment of offenders is in keeping with them. However, the Christianity of the Kawans requires the existence of an organised church, and so of offices and competition for them. It is here that we see the difference between Kawan Christianity and the simple egalitarianism of Jayawardena's examples. The irksome differences in status, authority and general achievement that organisation has produced are countered by the notion of rivalry. First, what is done is good in terms of transcendent values. Second, it is for the benefit of the whole community in its relations with the outside world:

> However, when they had been running half an hour or so, and were quite dry again, the Dodo suddenly called out 'The race is over!' and they all crowded round it, panting, and asking 'But who has won?'
>
> This question the Dodo could not answer without a great deal of thought, and it stood for a long time with one finger pressed upon its forehead ... while the rest waited in silence. At last the Dodo said '*Everybody* has won, and *all* must have prizes.'
>
> Lewis Carroll, *Alice's Adventures in Wonderland*

Acknowledgments

This chapter was first published in 1971 in LH Hiatt and C Jayawardena (eds), *Anthropology in Oceania*, Melbourne University Press, Melbourne.

NOTES

1. Out of consideration for the sensitiveness of my informants, I have altered the name of their community, as also of individuals.
2. The Torres Strait Islanders were evangelised by the Protestant London Missionary Society, which in 1914 handed over its flocks to the Anglican Diocese of Carpentaria. Its influence still survives at the parish level, particularly in the stress upon congregational participation in church government and activities. The history of the

Torres Strait mission can be recovered in some detail from the manuscript records and correspondence of the London Missionary Society.

3. Of aggressive face-work, Goffman (1967, p. 24) writes, 'When a person treats face-work not as something he need be prepared to perform, but rather as something that others can be counted on to perform or accept, then an encounter or an undertaking becomes less a scene of mutual considerateness than an arena in which a contest or match is held. The purpose of the game is to preserve everyone's line from an inexcusable contradiction, while scoring as many points as possible against one's adversaries and making as many gains as possible for oneself.'

4. It is doubtful whether any of these skippers earned more than $1500 in any year. Divers' earnings were probably about $500–$700.

5. At the time of the study, Islanders had access only to a rather inferior primary education. Since that time, many have proceeded to secondary education.

6. The war of 1941–45 in the Pacific provides a watershed in the development of the Torres Strait Islanders. As in many parts of the South Pacific, the war had a profoundly disturbing effect on the Islanders' view of the world and their place in it. Their aspirations and expectations rose while the Queensland government responded both to this and external pressures (cf. Beckett 1965).

7. 'Flash' is a nineteenth-century British and Australian cant word. In this context, it means 'putting on airs'.

8. The so-called island by-laws date from the early period of contact when the London Missionary Society had considerable influence in secular government. Some of the more repressive by-laws have been abolished, but many remain almost unchanged.

9. The London Missionary Society pastors made a practice of public denunciations. The Anglican Church did away with this practice. As the diocese has become increasingly 'high', it has emphasised confession more than is usual in Anglican circles.

10. I was not present at this election and am not entirely clear about what happened. The official in question carries considerable weight in the region and advice from him might well be taken as an instruction.

11. There is a general tendency throughout the islands to appoint the most sophisticated men to local government office.

12. Eaton (1963) describes a similar state of affairs among Hutterites, citing the case of a man who was elected to a top leadership position less than a year after excommunication for drunkenness and fornication. He continues (1963, p. 10): 'Persons who show peculiar or anti-social behaviour can count on receiving some recognition if they change. It is considered bad taste to speak publicly about the past transgression of any member.'

13. Normally unimportant because the basic divisions are clusters of close kin occupying adjacent lots. As it happened, however, the clusters of East Village were linked by a number of marriage ties, which held them together during the squabble.

14. The Queensland government controls the cash income of islanders (as of Aborigines). Purchases in the government store are commonly made by debiting the sum against the account of the purchaser. Only small quantities of cash are released, and cash is consequently at a premium.

REFERENCES

Beckett, J 1965, 'The land where the crow flies backwards', *Quadrant*, vol. 9, no. 4, pp. 38–43.

Eaton JW 1963, 'Folk psychiatry', *New Society*, vol. 48, pp. 9–11.

Foster, GM 1965, 'Peasant society and the image of limited good', *American Anthropologist*, vol. 67, pp. 293–315.

Goffman, E 1955, 'On face-work: An analysis of ritual elements of social interaction', *Psychiatry: Journal for the Study of Interpersonal Processes*, vol. 18, no. 3, pp. 213–31.

Hogbin, HI 1951, *Transformation Scene: The Changing Culture of a New Guinea Village*, Routledge and Kegan Paul, London.

—— 1957, *Social Change: Josiah Mason Lectures Delivered at the University of Birmingham*, Melbourne University Press, Melbourne.

Jayawardena, C 1968, 'Ideology and conflict in lower class communities', *Comparative Studies in Society and History*, vol. 10, pp. 413–46.

Leach, ER 2000 [1961], 'The hard core: Kinship and social structure', in S Hugh Jones and J Laidlaw (eds), *The Essential Edmund Leach*, Yale University Press, Harvard, MA.

Newbolt, H 1997 [1892], 'Vitaï Lampada', in S Chitty, *Playing the Game: Biography of Sir Henry Newbolt*, Quartet Books, New York.

Rice, G 1955, 'The final answer', in G Rice, *The Final Answer: And Other Poems*, Barnes, New York.

Simmel, G 1922 [1955], *Conflict and the Web of Group Affiliations*, trans. and ed. by Kurt Wolff, The Free Press, Glencoe, IL.

Chapter 7

Mission, Church and Sect: Three Types of Religious Commitment in the Torres Strait Islands

Christianity in the South Seas must, in the final analysis, be understood in terms of colonisation. Its fortunes have been inextricably bound up with those of the market and the metropolitan power, and it has been important in the structuring of the people's relations with these institutions. Dependence on the introduced religion has complemented dependence in the economic and political sectors. But Christianity must also be seen as mediatory, though in ways that change as relations between people and colonialism change, standing with white civilisation against heathen savagery, but with Christian natives against godless traders and government men. If it has been part of the colonial order, its representatives have always tried to determine what that part should be. For the people, then, conversion has always entailed a particular kind of commitment to the new order.

Christianity came to the South Seas in the form of a mission — that is, an agency of a church or sect. Church and sect, as I shall define them, occupy quite different places in the metropolitan society, and the strategy of their missions will vary accordingly. However, the mission, operating outside the metropolitan society, must be seen as distinct from either. In this chapter, I shall analyse Torres Strait religion in terms of these three kinds of religious organisation.

In its most general sense, mission means a sending forth of spiritual agencies to spread divine truth. In common parlance, it is the heathen who are to be the recipients of this message, but in ecclesiastical usage it may be Christians who have become separated from the main body — for example, the urban poor. The essential point is that there is a discontinuity between that main body of believers and those who are to be missionised. Here I define mission as a specialised agency of church or sect, having the task of attracting, instructing and directing people who are ineligible for immediate membership of the parent body. In most cases, membership is at least the long-term objective. But in the meantime, the people — however equal within the love of God — are deemed not equal within the *sight* of God.[1] This kind of charter allows the mission to organise itself along lines quite different from those of the parent body, creating roles and offices that have no currency in the outside world.

The inequality is due not simply to the people's ignorance of Christianity, but also to their ignorance of civilised living and their lack of the economic and technical means for sustaining it. In the frontier conditions, which are their typical milieu, missionaries find themselves undertaking uplift as well as religious work. They may themselves distinguish sacred from secular duties, but the people are not likely to do so. Thus the mission's influence becomes all-pervasive and, in the power vacuum that develops at the village level as a result of pacification, considerable. Petty theocracies are frequent in the history of the South Seas, and one may argue a tendency towards 'totalitarianism' in missions that is lacking, or much less pronounced, in the parent bodies. (I shall suggest in a moment that they share this tendency with sects.) Having used the emotive term 'totalitarian', let me add that mission regimes may be a welcome alternative to social and physical breakdown.

Much of the writing on sects is concerned with their internal structure and dynamics (as in Wilson 1967). Here I am concerned with the ways in which they structure their members' relations with the wider society. On this point, there is general agreement that a sect in some sense stands apart from the society that it either rejects or wishes to change. By contrast, a church or denomination 'accepts the standards and values of the prevailing culture and conventional morality' (Wilson 1967, p. 25). Viewed from the outside, a sect is deviant if not downright eccentric, whereas a church — even if it is not one's own — is normal and mainstream. As such, the sect is most likely to appeal to those who are deviant in terms of personality or social placement, since it explains and validates their alienation from the society in which they live. Thus sects tend to recruit their members from one social stratum, ethnic minority or subculture.

Although missionaries are often narrower in outlook than the clergy at home, a church mission transmits at least some of the values current in the society it represents. A sect mission stresses those that mark it off from the majority. A church mission might be considered a better preparation for entry into the wider society, but a thorough grounding in religion alone is not sufficient to secure acceptance. This is because churches have only an incomplete hold over their followers — in other words, religion is not everything. Sects, by contrast, have a totalitarian hold over their followers: religion *is* everything — or almost. Thus, while a sectarian mission will not prepare its members for entry into the wider society, it will prepare them for entry into the parent sect, where — whatever their other inadequacies — their religious accomplishments have overriding importance. For this reason, the gulf between a sect and its mission is relatively small.

The Torres Strait Islands, the focus of this chapter, were evangelised by the interdenominational Protestant London Missionary Society, beginning in 1871. Having worked in the Pacific since the beginning of the century, the London Missionary Society was by this time a thoroughgoing mission. Its members were all products of British non-conformity, but coming from the Congregational and cognate churches, they fell short of sectarianism.

The London Missionary Society withdrew in 1914, giving its flocks into the keeping of the Anglican Diocese of Carpentaria. The diocese was not organised for mission work and, unlike its predecessor, limited its activities to the religious sphere. In organisation and policy, it was a church. But because of the physical and cultural isolation, Torres Strait Anglicanism perpetuated certain elements of the mission at the community level. When, after the Second World War in the Pacific, islanders moved into white communities, they found standard Anglicanism unfamiliar, and also unrelated to the problems of adaptation then troubling them. Instead, they turned to a Pentecostalist sect, the Assemblies of God. Like a mission, the Assembly sought them out and provided practical help in coping with their new surroundings. Difficulty arose when converts carried the new religion back to their home communities. Here the sect came into conflict with the mission-like features of Torres Strait Anglicanism. Pentecostalism also became the religion of political dissent, whereas Anglicanism remained politically neutral.

The region and its inhabitants

The Torres Strait separates northern Queensland from the Trans-Fly district of Papua. In its waters are located many islands, small and not so small, some twenty of which were inhabited when Europeans made their first surveys in the 1840s. The islanders were Melanesian in appearance and culture, though with a variable admixture of Australian traits. At the beginning of intensive contact — around 1860 — they numbered some four thousand, falling to about half that figure by the turn of the century, but thereafter increasing to a present figure in excess of eight thousand.

European vessels strayed through the Torres Strait from early in the seventeenth century, but the traffic did not become regular until the foundation of the Australian colony, and remained transient until the mid-nineteenth century. By the 1840s, Europeans had begun to exploit the rich sources of trepang and pearl shell, and within twenty years there was a thriving industry, with fleets of schooners and luggers, shore stations and a labour force of around a thousand. Most of this labour came from the Pacific islands, but islanders and Aborigines soon played a part.[2] Thursday Island, which lies just off the tip of Cape York, became the centre of operations and then of government. The state of Queensland quickly established its jurisdiction over the offshore islands, but it did not annex the more distant ones until 1879, and had only nominal control until about 1885. Meanwhile, the islands were dominated by the pearlers and trepangers and, after 1871, by the representatives of the London Missionary Society.

The Coming of the Light

In 1871, the Reverend Samuel McFarlane and the Reverend AW Murray arrived with eight Loyalty Island teachers. The teachers were to do the pioneering work of evangelisation in the islands and along the Papuan coast, while their white directors set up the headquarters, which were to be the springboard for the Papuan campaign.

The teachers were themselves recent converts, but McFarlane argued that on this account they were better able to 'get at the heathen of their class' (McFarlane 1888, p. 138). Certainly there was a ready response. Just one year later, Murray declared that the Murray Islanders must be a people 'prepared of the Lord' (London Missionary Society [LMS] Reports 1872, p. 33):

> The entire population ... have attached themselves to the teacher. They treat himself and his family with great kindness, supplying their wants without charge so far as they are able and seeming ready to yield themselves implicitly to his guidance. No work is done on the Sabbath and the people come together from the three islands to attend the services, which except for the hymns and reading of the scriptures are conducted in the native tongue.

The work of the teachers was not everywhere so easy, and even the Murray Islanders had their moments of backsliding; seen in the long view, though, evangelisation progressed steadily.

Present-day islanders describe the 'coming of the Light' as though 'heathen darkness' was dispelled in an instant. Closer inquiry indicates that, although the missionaries claimed a religious monopoly, Christianity coexisted with Indigenous beliefs for a long time. But the teachers destroyed the old shrines, took away the sacred paraphernalia and put an end to the cults. By 1898, Haddon found difficulty in eliciting this kind of information, and concluded that much had already been lost.

McFarlane believed that the islanders initially welcomed the missionaries as a protection against the foreign boat crews who were plundering their gardens and abducting their women. Attempts at resistance had brought sharp reprisals. An observer reported that 'the once confident and fearless' people at Mabuiag had become 'cowed and sullen', taking flight as soon as a sail was sighted (Somerset Magistrates Book 1872). Even when their intentions were peaceable, the foreigners disrupted the tiny communities, luring away the young people with the promise of cloth, metal tools, flour and rice. Meanwhile, epidemics were decimating the population. As so often happened in the Pacific, the missionaries won their converts in the midst of catastrophe, bringing into spiritual dependence people who no longer had the means of independent existence.

Whatever the reasons for their conversion, there can be no doubt of the Islanders' commitment to the new religion. Not only did they come forward for baptism, but they went on to endure the rigours and abstinences required for church membership. Some even aspired to become deacons and teachers. Those who worked competed with one another over how much of their meagre earnings should go to the mission, and by the end of the century each community had built a substantial church for itself.

The significance of this commitment emerges when we look at the social context in which it was taking place. Like most Melanesians, the Torres Strait Islanders had no ranking system. Moreover, ceremonial exchange was not highly developed among them. Traditionally, men acquired prestige through success in headhunting, and gained respect through the control of physical and supernatural powers. The arrival of whites put an end to headhunting and degraded other traditional skills. In the new order, Islanders were always at the bottom of the scale, and there were few ways in which they could differentiate themselves from one another. The wages in the marine industry were small and went, at least initially, to the young men rather than to their elders. The mission opened up a hierarchy of religious worth and attainment, one that went some way towards redressing this economic imbalance, although it had no currency in the wider society.

The mission regime

The Queensland government exerted little control over the islands until around 1890. Up to that time, it did no more than back up the mission, which effectively ran the islands. Reverend Samuel McFarlane described the situation as follows:

> About 1878 Mr Chester [the government resident) advised the chiefs to appoint magistrates and police. In the presence of the Rev Mr Chalmers and myself the laws were formally inaugurated and the officers appointed by Mr Chester who publically [sic] requested Josiah [the pastor) to guide them in their administration (he being accustomed to a similar state of things in his own country) until they themselves were capable.
>
> These laws were, on the whole, equitably administered, Josiah being occasionally required to interfere in the interests of mercy, the native judges being inclined to severity. (LMS Correspondence, 17 July 1882)

In the same letter, McFarlane goes on to insist that it was the native judges and not the pastor who had had a coloured seaman and an island woman flogged for adultery. But whatever the facts of this case, it is certain that such severities were inflicted — particularly for sexual offences — into the twentieth century, and that the pastors were closely involved. They may not have been formally responsible, but the authority of the 'native judges' was not in practice distinguishable from that of the pastors. It is significant that when a government resident took over the running of one island, the pastor set up a rival court (Haddon 1908, p. 179). The white missionaries may not have approved these developments, but several served as justices of the peace. One was said to have shown marked partiality toward his church members (LMS Correspondence, 4 March 1889). It is worth remembering that the London Missionary Society had maintained some thirty years of stern theocracy in Rarotonga earlier in the century (Beaglehole 1957, p. 62).

Between them, the white missionaries, the coloured teachers and the native judges assumed wide-ranging control over people's behaviour. The by-laws that came into force during those years were by no means limited to the protection of person and property. Very early, the mission set about stopping infanticide and the 'revolting' mortuary practices; soon it was stamping out the old religion and whatever other traditional practices seemed offensive. The target was not simply paganism, but anything — such as dancing — that seemed licentious or immoral. As I have already noted, the traditional sexual freedom was countered by severe sanctions. These, together with a number of religious observances — such as the Sabbath — were enforced by the island courts. But beyond the limits of the law, the pastors denounced sinners by name from the pulpit, threatening divine punishment. The white missionaries themselves believed that God vented his wrath upon the living; the Pacific islands pastors were forever predicting it (see Haddon 1901, pp. 78–80).[3] On one occasion, the government resident on Thursday Island requested of the society that 'threats of excommunication involving damnatory consequences should be sparingly applied' (LMS Reports 1897).

Decline and fall of the mission

The Reverend Samuel McFarlane, who directed the mission for its first fifteen years, had hopes that the Torres Strait would become the springboard for the evangelisation of Papua. Convinced that recent converts were 'well adapted to fill the gap between the debased savage and the European missionary', he set about training teachers at a Papuan institute located on Murray Island (McFarlane 1888, p. 138). His plans came to nothing. Of the 100 students who enrolled in 1878, few were still in mission work a decade later, and McFarlane's colleagues thought little of them. More to the point, however, was the emergence of Port Moresby as an alternative springboard, and of the Reverend Mr Lawes as an alternative director. McFarlane withdrew in 1885, and those who followed him spent much of their time wrangling, so the Torres Strait became a backwater. From 1890 until his death in 1900, the Reverend James Chalmers (the famous 'Tamate') directed the mission from his headquarters on the Fly River. The pastors who were in effective control of the island congregation came mostly from Samoa and Niue, though a few Islanders also served.

By the time the Queensland government was in a position to assert its authority, it had only Pacific islands pastors with whom to contend. By 1890, it had installed a senior official — in fact, a one-time premier — on Thursday Island, providing him with the means of making regular tours. He, in turn, appointed white residents who would serve both as local magistrates and as teachers. The pastors held on tenaciously, but their superiors could not support them and alone they were no match for white officials (LMS Correspondence, 8 April 1914). In 1905, the Society again installed a superintendent in Torres Strait, but by this time it was too late. Queensland had brought in legislation giving it extensive control over the local government, property and movements of Islanders, and it bluntly refused the mission's request to take over education (LMS Correspondence, 8 October 1908). As if this were not enough, it went on to curb excessively generous donations to the mission and extravagant displays of hospitality at the annual LMS meetings, which extinguished thereafter (Bleakley 1961, pp. 265–7). Prevented by its rules from starting economic enterprises, the Society found little to absorb its energies.[4] Finally, in 1913, a government proposal to tax Islanders' earnings brought the London Missionary Society superintendent into open opposition (LMS Correspondence, 18 August 1913). He secured a reversal, but also the enduring enmity of government officials. Further cooperation was impossible. The prospect of giving way to the Anglicans had been considered as early as 1907 (LMS Correspondence, 6 December 1907). The Papuan Committee of the LMS recommended it early in 1914 and the transaction had been concluded before the end of the year (Goodall 1954, p. 420).

The church and the government

The Torres Strait Islands now came within the jurisdiction of the Anglican Diocese of Carpentaria, which had its headquarters on Thursday Island. The diocese was scarcely organised for mission work — in fact, it would probably not have taken responsibility for the islands had not the London Missionary Society completed the basic task of conversion and the Queensland government taken responsibility for all secular affairs. In the event, its resources were strained to provide for the people's spiritual needs.

The church, then, offered no challenge to the government's tightening control over the Islanders' lives. By 1920, Queensland had effectively confined the people to their island reserves, taken charge of their pearling enterprises and assumed control over any money they earned. They were allowed to elect local government councillors, but these were overshadowed by the white resident teachers.

The islanders did not welcome these restrictions on their freedom, and in the wake of the 1930s Depression, they refused to work on the boats the government managed on their behalf. In 1937, a strike leader approached the bishop with the proposal that he take over the running of the islands. The bishop gently declined, and in the years that followed the church continued to stay out of political affairs. Publicly, church and government appeared to be in harmony.[5]

The parishes were the Islanders' one haven of autonomy between the wars. Government officials did not encroach for fear of offending the church, but the diocese could not maintain the control to which it was entitled. Anglican organisation is not congregational like that of the London Missionary Society, but circumstances made it so in this case. The diocese could afford only two white priests to oversee thirteen island parishes, so it had to rely on the native churchwardens to hold the ordinary services, preach, collect dues and generally keep things going. This probably eased the transition from the London Missionary Society to the Church of England. By 1940, the bishop had ordained six island priests and a deacon, but these had been trained in a local seminary and were still imbued with the principles of congregationalism.

After 1936, the islanders restored another feature of the London Missionary Society regime. As a result of the strike, the government gave the island councils extensive autonomy. This they used to support the church and implement the old by-laws. Uniformed constables patrolled the village by night, armed with long flashlights for spotting courting couples or clandestine drinkers in the bushes. Those they apprehended came before the island court, though now the worst they could suffer would be fining or imprisonment. Once again, religion had a secular arm.

Torres Strait Christianity

When Bishop White made his first tour of the islands, he concluded that, under the LMS, 'the great mass of the people became not only Christians in name, but also to a large extent in practice' (White 1917, p. 23). The conversion may not have been quite so thoroughgoing as the bishop supposed. In 1913, a cargo cult had flared up briefly on the islands off Papua, though without creating any long-term disaffection from the church. People still believed in sorcery and magic — as many do today. But the public religion was Christianity in a relatively orthodox form. The old teachers had begun working in the vernacular very early, and the gospels were in translation before the century had ended. A number of islanders had undergone religious training in preparation for mission work. Consequently, the people had a vast repertoire of Bible stories and some grounding in doctrine, even though the more exotic or complex ideas would not have passed through the linguistic filter.

Nevertheless, the island parishes were still a far cry from those of white Anglicans on the mainland. The London Missionary Society had destroyed a great deal of the traditional culture, but there were too few whites to fill the gap with the culture of Victorian England. Instead, the vacuum had been filled by the Pacific islands pastors and seamen who had lived alongside the people over many years. Thus Polynesian styles prevailed in music, dancing, cuisine, house building and recreation. The hymns sung in church did not come from England, but were Samoan polyphony, introduced by some pastor in London Missionary Society times and continued. Under the less puritanical Anglicans, religious holidays were celebrated by Polynesian-style feasts and dancing on the church grounds.

The island parishes probably surpassed those on the mainland for the frequency, regularity and generality of religious observances. They probably also gave the church a larger proportion of their earnings. Finally, there was a far closer integration of church and local government.

Mission and church

The London Missionary Society in the Torres Strait was a mission not only in name, but also in the sense that I outlined earlier. Its congregations were not contiguous with those in the wider society. The Society claimed to be non-denominational, though in fact it received most of its support from British Congregationalists, a group scarcely represented in Australia and not at all on Thursday Island. The government officials and master pearlers usually belonged to the Anglican or Roman Catholic churches, a fact that McFarlane and his successors felt told against the Society. The pastors commanded small respect among the whites, and were in no sense deemed the equals of white ministers. McFarlane himself thought of them as 'bridging the gap between the debased savage and the white missionary'.

The Society was also a mission in the sense of its totalitarian tendencies. It was ready to take on secular administration, education and whatever else was needed. When the government pushed it out of these fields, it withdrew. As we have seen, the Church of England had no such pretensions and carefully avoided political involvement.

Anglicanism was also a church in the sense of being equally for white and black. There were Anglicans not only on the mainland, but among the officials and master pearlers of Thursday Island. It clearly had social importance, and it may have been for this reason that Islanders regarded the change as an advance.

In formal terms, black Anglicans were the equivalents of white Anglicans. The bishop had ordained the priests, appointed the churchwardens and Sunday school teachers, and confirmed the communicants in the normal manner. The forms of worship did not differ in essentials. Nevertheless, the church was part of a colonial order in which white dominated black. The priests were barely educated and had been trained at a local seminary: one white clergyman described them to me as 'good chantry priests'. They would not have been accepted in a white parish, still less their laity. They were inescapably placed on the wrong side of the colour line. The full force of this segregation was cushioned, however, by the isolation in which the Islanders lived.

The end of isolation

The Second World War in the Pacific released the Islanders from their isolation and overturned the established order. Although there was no actual fighting in the Torres Strait, it came under military administration and almost every able-bodied Islander was drawn into a local defence force, which was based on and around Thursday Island. Here they came into contact with white Australian troops, who were less imbued with prejudice than the local whites and, in many cases, were ready to meet Islanders on a footing of equality. The Islanders also heard talk of a 'better deal' that would be due to them when the war ended.

This experience had a profoundly disturbing effect on the Islanders who went through it. Fifteen years later, they looked back on those days with nostalgia, and their view of their rights in society was markedly different from that of other Islanders. With the war at an end, returning government officials discovered that the old order could not be restored in its entirety. There was a clamour for 'citizen rights', access to alcohol and control of earnings. The government was slow to grant these rights, and long before it did so the ex-servicemen had come to regard it as their enemy. But, perhaps to provide a safety valve, the government did allow Islanders to move onto Thursday Island and to settle on the mainland. For the first time, Islanders came to live alongside whites and to experience life in towns. Even those who remained on the reserves made frequent visits to Thursday Island for shopping and medical attention.

The situation on Thursday Island was unlike that on the mainland. The community was small, numbering about 2500, and almost all were employed in the marine industry or government service. Moreover, Thursday Island had a strongly hierarchical character. The small, all-white elite consisted of master pearlers, officials in charge of islanders' affairs, clergy and medical personnel. Ordinary workers and small businessmen were predominantly coloured, descendants of Pacific islanders, Malays, Filipinos and Chinese who had worked in the pearling industry in bygone years. The Islanders moved onto the bottom rung of the ladder and into the poorest paid jobs. Formally and informally, the groups stayed separate. Cultural differences were clearly recognised.

The Church of England went to considerable lengths to accommodate the Islanders in its services and organisation, catering for their distinctive likes and needs rather than expecting them to conform to those of whites. Senior clergy remained white, but island priests took their turn in celebrating communion and island lay readers alternated with whites. Island hymns alternated with English ones, and the organ was presently replaced with a drum accompaniment for both kinds. The church ground was opened for feasting and dancing on religious holidays. Some white Anglicans disliked these developments, and withdrew. By 1958, Islanders were in the majority at church services.

On the mainland, Islanders were a small, little-known minority, sometimes confused with the despised Aborigines. Widely dispersed, often working in remote places, and coming to town only on weekends, there was no possibility of the church accommodating them as Thursday Island had done. If they attended a service, they found the atmosphere alien and the congregations unwelcoming. Feeling out of place, they did not come back.

Despite the rebuff, it was unlikely that the Islanders could have stayed content with a purely secular existence. Uprooted from familiar surroundings and a highly organised way of life, they found themselves members of a migratory labour force that did not belong anywhere. A bewildering array of new opportunities and experiences surrounded them; they had more money than ever before. But there were no guidelines. With the government out of sight and the church ignoring them, life offered only the grossest kinds of restraints, such as might come from the police. Religion, which had structured their world, legitimised their values and engaged their emotions, was now absent.

It is uncertain whether, in the long run, the Islanders would themselves have organised to answer this lack. In the event, they were rescued by a Pentecostalist sect, the Assemblies of God, which had first emerged among uprooted and displaced rural folk in North America. Established in 1914 (Clark 1949, p. 106), the sect reached Queensland in 1929, where it became the largest Pentecostalist group, though still numbering only 6000 (Van Sommers 1966, pp. 167–9). In terms of Wilson's typology (1967, p. 27), it is a conversionist sect, putting a strong emphasis on the conversion experience and the acceptance of Jesus as a personal saviour. It is fundamentalist, but not adventist, and while condemning worldly pleasures, it is by no means opposed to the accumulation of property and material comforts. Meetings are enthusiastic and emotional – very much in the revival tradition. There is an absence of ritual and only the simplest of forms. Though a pastor conducts the meeting, he leaves ample room for the assembly to offer spontaneous testimonies, confessions, prayers and occasional outbursts of glossolalia (speaking in tongues). There is much singing of revival choruses and time out for anyone who is sick to come forward for healing.

The Assembly made warm approaches to Islanders on the mainland and found a widespread response. Converts evidently enjoyed the exuberant services, so different from Anglican decorum. They welcomed, moreover, the prohibitions on drinking, smoking and dancing, and responded eagerly to the offers of healing. They claimed for their newfound religion more 'power', greater 'holiness' and, through the prohibitions, a sure way to save one's money. They also appreciated the friendliness of the white 'brothers and sisters' who welcomed them into their halls and even their homes. This was 'proper love'.

The rally to Pentecostalism can be understood as a reaction to Anglican coolness, but also as a compensation for low status in white society.[6] Islanders might be earning more than they did at home, but they were for the most part filling jobs that others did not want, and the world around them was impersonal and unfriendly. Yet the whites who looked down upon them did not themselves live a Christian life — they broke the Sabbath, forgot their religious observances and practised adultery and fornication without check. The Islanders might perhaps have rejected all whites; instead, they identified themselves with the whites who did not look down upon them, but rather adhered to the values respected in the islands. In this way, Islanders modified the general identification with whites that had grown up during the war, instead becoming members of a sect.

Pentecostalism in the islands

Island Pentecostalists returning home struck trouble. They were free to follow the new religion on Thursday Island, but at home they encountered bitter opposition from the councils. Most succumbed to the pressure and reverted to Anglicanism, but on Murray Island the assembly gained a permanent foothold.

This move into religious dissidence may be seen as a development from Murray's long-standing political dissidence. Failing to satisfy their economic and political aspirations through the government, they were looking for alternative allies in the white society. Not surprisingly, they looked first to the church, only to find that it would not become politically involved. Murray Island had been the centre of the 1936 strike, and it was Murray's chairman who had unsuccessfully petitioned the bishop to take over the islands. By 1950, this same leader was the main antigovernment spokesman for all of the Torres Strait, and he had lately clashed with a senior official of the diocese over this matter. He had also quarrelled with the family of the parish priest over political and private issues. At this point, a Murray Islander returned from the mainland with the declared intention of establishing an Assembly in the community. The chairman did not join the sect, but gave his consent and a piece of land on which to build a meeting house. His actions caused a furore on Murray Island and throughout the Torres Strait, which resulted in his excommunication and removal from office. His main persecutors were pro-government island leaders.[7]

The Anglican synod resolved that religious dissent was unacceptable in the island reserves. The island councillors, many of whom were also members of the synod, echoed this resolve and gave it the force of sanctions, which they controlled through the island courts. No pastors would be allowed onto the reserves. No meetings would be permitted. And no Pentecostalist would be allowed to hold public office. This was enough to stifle dissent on every island except Murray, where it survived and, by 1960, amounted to some 29 per cent of the population. Without pastor or meeting house, and allowed only to sing together once a week, the Pentecostalists nevertheless held together and enjoyed, besides, a wide sympathy among rank-and-file Anglicans.

This development occurred in a context of economic impoverishment and political frustration. Murray's economic enterprises foundered; wages failed to keep pace with living costs; more and more young men were emigrating; and the long-promised 'new deal' was still remote. Everyone was affected, but perhaps the veterans felt it most keenly. It is remarkable that 60 per cent of the adult male Pentecostalists (fifteen out of twenty-five) were veterans, and that this age group had a much higher representation in the Assembly than in the general population. Of the forty-eight adult female Pentecostalists, twenty were the wives or widows of veterans. Pentecostalist veterans described the assembly as being opposed to the Queensland government as well as to the Church of England, prophesying that it would come into its own when they were delivered from the government's control. The majority of Murray Island veterans remained Anglicans, but they sympathised sufficiently with the Pentecostalists to prevent total suppression.

Murray Islander religion held up a mirror not only to Torres Strait political conflicts but to cultural conflicts as well. The Anglicans and the Pentecostalists represented different responses to the bicultural society in which they lived. The latter stressed modernity and Europeanism. They went to church wearing pants and shoes, whereas the Anglicans continued to wear waist cloths and go barefoot. They sang English-language chorus instead of vernacular hymns of Samoan origin. They eschewed — though with some difficulty — island dancing. Such things were 'not civilised'. In these terms, black Anglicans stood doubly condemned: not only did they belong to the wrong church, but they belonged to the uncivilised section of it! By contrast, black Pentecostalists were the same as white Pentecostalists. The Anglicans, for their part, were unimpressed by these pretensions to Europeanism, pointing out that in their tolerance of smoking, drinking and entertainment, they were more like ordinary white people than the puritanical Assembly of God.

The religious cleavage also reflected contradictions specific to the community, though reproduced in most other communities in the Torres Strait. As is often the way with groups situated at the bottom of the social scale, Islanders evinced a strong egalitarianism in their dealings with one another (Jayawardena 1968). At the same time, there was a strong streak of competitiveness, which revealed itself in eagerness for church and local government offices (see Chapter 6). The people tried to play down this competitiveness at the ideological level by stressing the values of selflessness and service to church and community; at the practical level, they ensured that offices circulated. But with the heightening of aspirations after the war, Islanders demanded more of their representatives than all but the ablest could provide. Consequently, circulation of the key offices was no longer possible and the communities came under increasing strain (Beckett 1967, Chapter 6). The Pentecostalists consisted of people who had little hope of holding public office: women, for whom no offices were open; men with low educational achievements and defective English; and some failed theological students and teachers. One might see their religious choice as an opting out of a race they had no hope of winning. One could also see it as an inversion of the inequality that was emerging in the secular sphere, allowing those who counted for least to claim moral superiority. Anglicans found this moral superiority particularly irksome.

The Anglican response to the contradiction between egalitarianism and growing differentiation was to multiply the number of minor offices to which anyone might aspire. The church set a limit to the number of churchwardens, who made most of the important decisions, but none to the number of lesser offices, such as lay preacher, church councillor, Sunday school teacher, chorister, sideman and so on. By 1960, there were so many that there were not enough duties to go around, even with careful rostering. Fortunately, many were content simply to have a title. Even so, on important festivals there were as many as twenty be-cassocked laymen at the high altar, to say nothing of the half-dozen altar boys.

Some 70 per cent of Anglican men over the age of thirty — which one might call the age of responsibility in the Torres Strait — held some kind of church office. It was less a matter of having a title than of not being without one. But people valued their titles, even when they were only empty honorifics. They were likely to join the Pentecostalists if deprived of a title, and several were drawn back into the fold with the promise of a position. It seems likely that the Anglicans inflated the number of positions as a means of stemming the drift.

With the exception of a few churchwardens, none of these officeholders thought of themselves as the exact equivalent of their opposite number in the white sector. Most were sensitive about defective English and some were barely literate. Theirs was local rank. But at least they were loyal workers for a church that was not only among the most important but also had Royal patronage. If all went well, the next generation would be better equipped to perform its duties. Murray's Anglicans, then, recognised that they were different from, and perhaps in some respects inferior to, white people. They might hope for a change to come in time, but meanwhile they were ready to put up with the situation.

Conclusion

The Torres Strait Islands are situated within the borders of a metropolitan power. This does not mean that they cannot be understood within the same colonial framework. However, the contradiction between the developed nation-state and its undeveloped enclave is perhaps more intense than that between a state and its external colonies.

The Torres Strait became a colony of Queensland when it proved to have valuable marine resources. The industry required a variable supply of cheap manpower, and so the islands became pools of captive labour under the control of the government. The London Missionary Society and later the Church of England worked within this framework, and more or less consciously legitimated the new order. Thus wage labour was not just an alternative means of satisfying material needs: it brought cash that could be given to the church. Similarly, the law was to be obeyed not just out of fear of punishment but because it was God's law.

The whole missionary effort was not devoted to this end, nor was this its only function. Its support came from people in Britain and in the cities of Australia who knew nothing of pearling, although they might approve of teaching the natives to be industrious and law-abiding. But while hymn singing and Sabbath observances might irk the hard-living pearler, they did not threaten his interests.

The missionaries' main effort went in reconstructing the island communities. The petty theocracies that resulted were certainly inspired by Anglo-Saxon Christianity, but they could only have existed on a colonial frontier. The pietistic Christian native they produced was scarcely less exotic to ordinary whites than his savage forebears.

The Second World War in the Pacific brought Islanders into direct contact with the outside world, and caused many of them to look critically at the existing order. Growing discontent, coupled with an expanding labour force and a demand for manpower in northern Australia, prompted the government to let them emigrate.

On the mainland, Islanders found a very different kind of life: free of the restrictions that irked them at home, full of novelty, but confusing and sometimes frightening. The government left them alone, but so did the church. The Anglicans did not try to transplant their Torres Strait regime; all they offered was a regular church adapted to the needs of comfortably settled whites. The uprooted and disoriented island worker found help he expected from the church in the Assemblies of God. Simply by accepting conversion, he could win white fellowship, a way of evaluating his surroundings and guidance in coping with them.

Back home, Pentecostalism assumed a different significance. Conditions were not anomic, and there were no white brothers and sisters to relate to. Instead, Pentecostalism became a religion of dissent, counterposing the restrictiveness of the government's regime in the Torres Strait to the self-restraints to be derived from Pentecostalism on the mainland. Moreover, it lumped the Church of England, which had combated religious dissent through the secular administration, with the government.

In fact, although the church was integrated with secular authority at the village level, this was not so further up the hierarchy. It had little influence, and for the most part left policy-making to the government. If one saw the church as politically neutral, as many Islanders did, there was no inconsistency in remaining an Anglican while opposing the regime. Pentecostalists, on the other hand, were always radical.

I have suggested that the Islanders' acceptance, in turn, of the London Missionary Society, the Church of England and the Assemblies of God needs to be understood in terms of concomitant socio-economic developments. The mission form 'fitted' the colonial situation in the Torres Strait; the sect 'fitted' conditions on the mainland. The Church of England started out as a church, as I have defined that term, but local conditions forced it into the mission mould. Events on the mainland indicated that, as an ordinary church, it had little to offer Islanders. Those who have stayed with the Anglicans in the Torres Strait may complete the transition from mission to church, but for those on the mainland the transition has been from mission to sect. Earlier I argued that the two forms were in many respects parallel, and in fact some older Islanders recognised the similarities between the London Missionary Society and the Assemblies of God.

Unlike Aborigines and most white workers, the Islanders have continued to look to religious organisations for solutions to their problems. The quest has not yet ended. After the completion of my study, large numbers of emigrant Islanders joined the World Church, a new sect formed explicitly to appeal to them and drawing extensively upon their folk Christianity. Its leader, however, is white. Evidently Islanders still like to take their religion ready-made, rather than making their own synthesis.

Acknowledgment

This chapter is based on twenty-four months' fieldwork in the Torres Strait, between 1958 and 1961, while the author was a research scholar of the Australian National University. It was first published in J Boutilier (ed.), *Mission, Church and Sect in Oceania*, Michigan UP, 1978.

NOTES

1. I have been unable to find a reference for this formulation, but recall that it was used by Archbishop Fisher on a visit to Rhodesia during the 1950s.
2. The pearling began by importing labour from the Pacific islands, ranging from sophisticated Rotumans to blackbirded New Hebrideans. Later in the century, Malays and Filipinos predominated and over the last decade Japanese became the diving elite. Islanders, Aborigines and Papuans became increasingly numerous in the years preceding the Second World War in the Pacific, and after 1945 Islanders and Aborigines made up the entire labour force.
3. Early in the mission, some Loyalty Island teachers were killed in Papua. On discovering that they had been involved in adultery, the Reverend Mr Murray commented that their fate would be a salutary warning to others.
4. Frustrated by this ordinance, Frederick and Charles Walker left the Society to form the Papuan Industries Company (PIC). Based on Badu, the company provided Islanders with boats, marketed their shell and sold them cheap goods. This enterprise inspired the government to form a similar company, which took over the PIC when the brothers retired in 1934.
5. It is interesting to note that most of the government officials in Torres Strait after 1930 were Roman Catholics.
6. Malcolm Calley (1955, 1964) reached similar conclusions in his study of Aboriginal Pentecostalists.
7. For a more detailed account of the politics of religion on Murray Island, see Beckett (1967).

REFERENCES

Beaglehole, E 1957, *Social Change in the South Pacific: Rarotonga and Aitutaki*, Allen & Unwin, London.

Beckett, JR 1967, 'Elections in a small Melanesian community', *Ethnology*, vol. 6, pp. 332–44.

Bleakley, JW 1961, *The Aborigines of Australia: Their History, Their Habits, Their Assimilation*, Jacaranda, Brisbane.

Calley, M 1955, *Aboriginal Pentecostalism*, Sydney.

—— 1964, 'Pentecostalism among the Bandjalang', in M Reay (ed.), *Aborigines Now: New Perspectives in the Study of Aboriginal Communities*, Angus & Robertson, Sydney, pp. 48–58.

Clark, ET 1949, *The Small Sects in America*, Abingdon-Cokesbury, Nashville.

Goodall, N 1954, *A History of the London Missionary Society 1895–1945*, Oxford University Press, London.

Haddon, AC 1901, *Head-hunters, Black, White and Brown*, Methuen, London.

—— (eds) 1908, *Reports of the Cambridge Anthropological Expedition to Torres Straits — Volume VI: Sociology, Magic and Religion of the Eastern Islanders*, Cambridge University Press, Cambridge.

Jayawardena, C 1968, 'Ideology and conflict in lower class communities', *Comparative Studies in Society and History*, vol. 10, pp. 413–46.

London Mission Society, 1872–1914, Reports and Correspondence.

McFarlane S, 1888, *Among the Cannibals of New Guinea: Being the Story of the New Guinea Mission of the London Missionary Society*, London Missionary Society, London.

Van Sommers, T 1966, *Religions in Australia*, Rigby, Adelaide.

White, G 1917, Round About the Torres Straits: A Record of Australian Church Missions, Central Board of Missions, London.

Wilson, B 1967, *Patterns of Sectarianism: Organisation and Ideology in Social and Religious Movements*, Heinemann, New York.

Chapter 8

'Knowing How to Talk to White People': Torres Strait Islanders and the Politics of Representation

Colonisation, which began in the 1860s, was not the catastrophe for the Islanders that it was for so many Aborigines on the mainland. It did not involve displacement from ancestral lands or the usurpation of the resources from which they had traditionally drawn their livelihood. Thus they were able to adjust to the new order at a leisurely pace, alternating between subsistence production and wage labour for white employers.

In this adaptation, the Islanders were guided by missionaries who reconstructed their communities along congregational lines. When the Queensland government took the Islanders under its care, it adapted this community structure to its own administrative needs, establishing elected councils as early as 1899 — well ahead of any other colonial authority in the South Pacific. Initially, councillors played only an advisory role in local affairs, but as government activity increased, they became important as channels of communication with the communities, and as agents for containing discontent. As government policy came under public scrutiny, councillors also became a device for legitimating its activities.

With the explosion of welfare capitalism in the 1970s, the conditions of Aborigines and Islanders became a national issue, giving rise to a new kind of Indigenous politics. In the process, both the strengths and the weaknesses of the Islanders' representatives became apparent: they knew better than Aborigines 'how to talk to white people' — specifically bureaucrats — but they were inexperienced when it came to mobilising public opinion.

The structure of representation and its significance in a Fourth-World setting

The essence of representation is that someone stands for some others in dealing with a third party. For this to occur, there must be a discontinuity between the two parties, which is not negated but rather reinforced by the act of representation. One major set of problems clusters around the relationship between the representative and his constituency. His existence amounts to the assertion that there is a group that is representable in terms of a collective will or set of interests. However, it is important to recognise that this is a form of alienation that is in no sense natural or automatic. No individual can be another, and the ways by which one comes to represent others are devious and obscure. Representation is mediated by the alienation of an individual by the society of which one is a part.[1] For an individual to be that society seems only to compound the condition. But there are both political and cultural processes for overcoming it: on the one hand, the group tries to control the actions of its representative; on the other, it tries to legitimate them, or the person who performs them, through symbolic processes ranging from election to the installation of an hereditary ruler. Legitimacy and political control are, to some degree, alternatives — and liable to conflict.

Legitimacy is important to both parties because the representative is rarely just an agent adhering to a precise mandate: processes of any complexity require a measure of discretion, in which he is trusted by his constituency and accredited by the others. In an extreme case, he is deemed to know better than his constituency what their 'true interests' are and how these are best served, either because he has access to information that they lack, or because he is in some sense forming those interests. One might call this quasi-representation. However, not everything that a representative does need be legitimate in this sense: in clientistic politics, for example, it is understood that he has a free hand to pursue his own or anyone else's interests, once he has acquitted himself of particular promises. Here the constituency is no more than an aggregate of private interests, brought together by an accident of geography. At the other end of the scale, where group consciousness is highly developed, he represents them totally even in his private life.

A second set of problems clusters around the functions of representation in the overall political process. Communicating the needs and aspirations of the constituency is always the ostensible purpose, but this may take second place to the function of legitimising the decisions of some superordinate body. In the Western democratic tradition, committees, councils, legislatures and assemblies must be representative, often in specified ways, in order to be legitimate. In consequence, representation is a political resource, to be controlled and manipulated, even through electoral fraud. We are all familiar, not least in the Fourth World, with pseudo-representatives answerable to, and appointed by, governments rather than to the constituency with which they are associated. However, to the extent that the representative body is important and the discontinuities between it and the constituents are great, there will be some tendency for cooptation. Aside from direct pressures, the forms of consultation and decision-making can subtly blunt intentions and divert them into harmless channels. Moreover, effective performance in such arenas may require the kind of expertise that can be acquired only outside the constituency, and that then distances the representative from his people. This leaves them alienated from yet still dependent on him. If one is to cope with these contradictions, it must be by exploiting the discontinuity with Janus-faced shifts in style and rhetoric.

Such problems are particularly characteristic of the Fourth World, where an Indigenous minority confronts not just other ethnic groups, but also the state, from a position of cultural inferiority and powerlessness. Representation, where it occurs, is part of the apparatus of government and sometimes little more than window-dressing.

The term 'Fourth World' comes to us out of practical politics rather than social science, but it is a useful way of characterising an historical phenomenon that cannot be defined precisely. One is not part of the Fourth World simply by belonging to what could be objectively defined as an Indigenous minority. There must be a consciousness of this status as an entitlement to particular rights, and a recognition in the wider society that such entitlement exists. Some of these conditions are met when expatriate colonies try to forge a nationalism that separates them from the mother country — as in, for example, the *indigenismo* of post-revolutionary Mexico. However, the Fourth World phenomenon seems rather to have come out of the welfare-capitalist phase of liberal democracy in the First World. Under welfare capitalism, the state redistributes wealth in the form of pensions, grants, the dole, scholarships and a variety of public services and programs. Whatever the ultimate motive of this expenditure, the rhetoric with which it is justified and which various groups use to bid for it is moralistic. Potential recipients are designated as 'disadvantaged,' 'deprived' or in some other way 'deserving'. This kind of political culture offers Indigenous minorities the possibility of transcending their small numbers and powerlessness, while giving governments the opportunity to demonstrate their humanity at what may be a relatively small cost.[2] Thus, in Australia, Aborigines as well as various immigrant groups have judged it more advantageous to follow this strategy rather than play class or party politics.

The politics of morality has not remained within the bounds of individual nation-states, but has spread into international arenas such as the United Nations and meetings of British Commonwealth heads of state. Perceiving the sensitivities of their governments to criticism from former colonial Third World states, Indigenous minorities have cultivated the politics of embarrassment. Thus the prime ministers of Zimbabwe and Vanuatu — both newly independent states — recently found themselves petitioned by Aborigines when they visited Australia. Similarly, Third World countries — which are commonly neither liberal-democratic nor welfare-capitalist — find themselves under attack for mistreating Indigenous minorities. The United States' recent attack on Nicaragua for alleged massacres of Indians is a case in point. However, the final act of the Fourth World drama must be played out between the Indigenous minority and its national government. It is my assumption that the prospects of the minority are most favourable when liberal democracy is combined with welfare capitalism. Governments that rule in terms of a national emergency, or are committed to a 'develop or die' strategy, are inevitably less responsive to external or internal appeals in terms of human rights.

It is not an easy task to achieve the cohesion necessary to be an effective Fourth World minority, even in favourable settings. The societies that make up the Fourth World were originally either acephalous or segmentary states whose boundaries broke up at conquest. In the years that followed, they suffered further fragmentation and the blurring of boundaries. And although, overall, the distinctions between native and settler, savage and civilised persisted, the individual was not always inexorably assigned to one or another. Policies of uplift and assimilation promised — if they did not always provide — escape from subordination and inferiority; legislative loopholes and administrative quirks permitted passing and gave rise to ethnological enigmas such as the Lumbee (Blu 1980). Confusions of culture and genetics gave rise to anomalous half-caste populations. Under such conditions, representation occurred only at the village level, if at all, while officials and missionaries interposed themselves between their native wards and the higher levels of government. Even locally, the levelling characteristic of the poor and the dispossessed inhibited the development of legitimating processes and cut down anyone who stood out from the crowd.[3] Often, as in the case of the Torres Strait, representative institutions were initially imposed from above, before the people were able to control or legitimate them.

The colonisation of Torres Strait

The traditional ethnography of Torres Strait need not detain us for long.[4] We can view it as a culture area that included coastal Papua and parts of Cape York, integrated through regular canoe traffic and trade. The economic adaptations that particular communities made to local conditions — be it by hunting, fishing, gathering and/or gardening activities — were influenced by the possibility of trading surpluses and making up deficiencies. The social organisation was broadly characteristic of coastal Melanesia in that it consisted of local groupings and cult activity. Leadership seems to have been manifested mainly in warfare and ritual, both of which ceased soon after contact. What survived was a tendency to utilise kinship connections in the formation of groups and action sets.

Although the first Europeans came to Torres Strait at the beginning of the seventeenth century, it did not become a regular waterway until the founding of the Australian colony in 1788, and there was no permanent European presence until the 1860s. This began with the arrival of small boats to work the rich deposits of pearl shell and trepang (bêche-de-mer). The marine industry, unlike the pastoral industry on the mainland, did not encroach on the Indigenous economy, since the resources it exploited did not form part of the native diet (see Chapter 5). Indeed, although it was slow to recognise the fact, the marine industry had an interest in keeping the island communities intact, since they could support a labour reserve without needing a cash economy. For the moment, however, the native population was suffering the impact of exotic disease, so the bulk of the industry's labour needs were being met by importation of workers from Asia and the Pacific.

The Queensland government established its jurisdiction in the wake of this economic development, initially to protect shipping and to secure its northern marches from the encroachments of foreign colonialism, but also to bring some order to an industry that was proving increasingly profitable. It had little interest in the Islanders themselves, leaving them to the care of the London Missionary Society, which made its appearance in 1871 (Beckett 1978).

The London Missionary Society quickly won the adherence of the Islanders and set about reconstructing their shattered societies and unifying the dispersed village populations around the church. The aim of the Society was to establish model Christian communities, and the congregational form of government it brought with them allowed it to enlist the help of native deacons. Offenders such as fornicators and adulterers were brought to trial before local courts, and then delivered over for punishment to a 'chief' who had been appointed by the government on the missionaries' recommendation. During the early years, white missionaries exerted considerable control over the communities, but by the 1890s they were leaving the work to Polynesian pastors. This proved unacceptable to the Queensland government, which was by this time better able, and more inclined, to intervene. Its first move was to post white teacher–magistrates to the main communities, and the conflict that followed resulted in the London Missionary Society handing its flocks over to the Church of England, which had no pretensions to secular authority.

Until the early years of the twentieth century, Islanders had been regarded as superior to Aborigines and not in need of special controls. In 1907, however, they were made subject to the authority of the newly appointed Protector of Aborigines and to the growing body of legislation regulating Aboriginal life (Bleakley 1961; Evans et al. 1975).[5] Like the other governments of Australia,

Queensland pursued a policy of first segregating its native population — ostensibly for their own good but usually in response to European pressure — and then controlling their labour power. Where the Queensland government differed from the others was in the comprehensiveness and effectiveness of its regime, particularly in the large, supervised settlements to which much of the population was soon relocated. In Torres Strait, however, there was no need for relocation: the island communities were already isolated and had already made their adaptation to the new order; moreover, there was a market for their labour which, combined with subsistence production, could make them self-supporting.

The inclusion of Islanders under the Protector's care seems to have been prompted by their growing importance as a reserve of labour for the marine industry. The White Australia agitation was then at its height, and bidding to cut off the industry's supply of cheap foreign labour. Meanwhile, the Islanders were acquiring a measure of immunity to new diseases and beginning to increase in number. Moreover, their intact subsistence economies could support the workers and their families during the periodic downturns in production. The problem was that whereas some communities were reluctant to get too deeply involved in the cash economy, others were too eager, developing needs for goods beyond what the industry was willing to support. The government undertook the difficult task of conserving the labour force: on the one hand, it ensured that subsistence production was not allowed to die; on the other, it kept a brake on the consumption of commodities by holding workers' earnings on their behalf and limiting their access to retail outlets. These controls were justified on the ground that Islanders were incapable of managing their own affairs and must be taught thrift.

The result was a regime that was no less restrictive than that of the London Missionary Society, though with different priorities. It included a European teacher–magistrate in residence, assisted by Islanders — just as the missionaries had been assisted by their deacons. At first these were the old appointed chiefs, but from 1899 there were two or three elected councillors. This was a surprising innovation, without precedent or parallel in the Australian administration of Papuans or Aborigines, but probably devised to counter the congregational forms of the London Missionary Society (Haddon 1935, p. 326). One of the functions of the councillors, in fact, was to enforce the old London Missionary Society code of conduct, which became a set of local by-laws. The cooptation of native councillors into the administrative structure, however, did not ensure the smooth implementation of government policy. There was periodic resistance, particularly during economic downturns, and in 1936 there was a Strait-wide strike against the regime.

The Queensland government took this demonstration seriously, and set about restructuring. It retained its controls over Islanders' employment, earnings and consumption, but exercised them from the commercial and administrative centre on Thursday Island, leaving the communities to run their own affairs. The councils proved more than equal to this task, satisfying the government in their maintenance of law, order and public health, and satisfying the people in their exercise of a degree of autonomy. Under this new regime, the Islanders, having only restricted contact with the outside world, were able to develop a rich creole culture around the church and council.

The councillor's role entailed a number of contradictions, however. He was simultaneously a representative of the government to the people and of the people to the government. This might mean having to implement programs such as compulsory medical treatment, which were unpopular. Fortunately, the distance to Thursday Island permitted a good deal of equivocation and procrastination. But if the authorities exerted pressure, he had to give way or lose his job and the tiny stipend that went with it. There were also internal contradictions relating to the impartiality required of the councillor and the partiality required of the incumbent as kinsman, so that a few years in office tended to alienate much of his support: non-kin through actual or supposed favours to kin; and kin through failure to meet their demands. The result was a fairly steady turnover in councillors. In other words, the Islanders dealt with the contradiction on a contingent basis rather than coming to a decision about principles. This was possible because the demands of office were not very great and the qualities required were widely distributed so that a regular turnover caused little dislocation. And if no particular individual represented the community to itself, there was nevertheless a close correspondence between any given councillor and the ordinary citizen.

Impressed by the momentary unity of the thirteen communities during the 1936 strike, the government set about institutionalising and controlling it. In 1938, it called the first conference of Torres Strait councillors, acceding to their request to be differentiated from Aborigines. In the following year, the Queensland parliament passed legislation that established the Torres Strait Islanders as a distinct Indigenous minority. Islanders, however, now had to learn the arts of external representation.

The development and control of representation

Although the councillors' work would lie mainly in the community for some years to come, the 1937 conference established the machinery for an increasingly active external representation in the post-war period.

It was the ex-servicemen who had served in the Second World War who began clamouring for rights. Their experience of military service articulated and legitimated a claim for citizenship and economic equality. The Queensland government, for its part, declined to relinquish its special powers over them, or to put wages in the marine industry on a par with those in the mainland economy. However, with Australia now entering a phase of welfare capitalism, it had a licence to upgrade facilities in the communities, effectively subsidising the low wages. Even so, the government faced the task of transforming the radical aspirations of the ex-servicemen into piecemeal reforms.[6] The representational structure provided the instrument.

The conference of councillors became a biennial event, presided over by a senior official and occasionally graced by the presence of the minister. Over-awed by these august presences, and hampered by a previously fixed agenda, radical representatives found it difficult to raise the broad issues that concerned their supporters, still less to demand the abolition of the administrative structure through which they had to work. They were likely to come home empty-handed, inviting unfavourable comparison with representatives — usually not ex-servicemen — who were prepared to settle for the limited but tangible benefits that the government was ready to concede. After the first few years, they became a small and largely ineffective minority.

The new representation, which had to operate in what might be called welfare politics, required a new set of skills. As one individual who had failed in the task remarked to me, 'You've got to be a smart man to be a councillor these days; not like before.' To compete with other communities for such amenities as piped water, housing, a new school, an emergency airstrip and so on required a grasp of English, an understanding of how government worked and an ability to negotiate the personalistic regime maintained by long-established officials. One had to 'know how to talk to white people'. Such skills were mainly to be found among the store managers, schoolteachers and boat skippers, who had dealt with white officials for some years. However, such individuals were, to some degree, dependent on the government for their livelihood and had accommodated themselves to it in the course of advancing in their occupations. As one man, himself a long-time government employee, observed, 'The councillors used to take off their coats to the government before. Not this time. They are all government men!'

The extent of the shift is well illustrated in the case of voting rights. In 1949, the Councillors' Conference had requested the franchise, without any result. In 1958, the councillors declared themselves to be unready for such a responsibility and so, by implication, content to be represented in parliament by the minister. Then, only three years later, when the federal government sent round a committee of inquiry into Aboriginal voting rights, every Torres Strait councillor was in favour. According to the report, the Queensland government had decided to drop its initial opposition and advised its trusted men accordingly.

As external representation increased and became more demanding, three elected delegates, representing the councillors of the three island groups (Eastern, Central and Western), took over the responsibility of dealing with the state government while the councillors retained their local government functions. Nominally the delegates were elected by the councillors immediately after the latter had been elected by the people. But since they acted as returning officers at the elections, they were in a position to influence the outcome, and it was well known that at least one of them did. In fact, two of the three who held office during the 1950s and 1960s had somehow been elected 'for life': as it happened, they were also well known to be friends of the government. However, the Eastern Islands delegate who took office in 1956 — and who still holds it today — submitted himself to re-election every three years and was regularly returned. Each of them, and those who succeeded in later years, developed a highly individual and personalistic style in dealing with officials, much of the time *in camera*. As far as their constituencies were concerned, their effectiveness was indicated by the benefits they wrought for them, combined with their own account of their role in getting it. If they sometimes claimed more credit than was strictly their due, it was probably in the government's interest that they should do so, since it strengthened their position. Certainly, over the years, both government and people became heavily dependent on the same delegates, so that the prospect of replacing them seemed increasingly difficult. Ordinary councillors could be turned over at regular intervals, as previously, but not the delegates. Murray Island, which has been noted for its turbulent politics, twice voted out a delegate only to vote him back in again, presumably as a rebuke and a way of reminding him of his dependence on their support.[7]

As expertise built up, as well as the need for it on the part of both the state government and the Islanders, representativeness became increasingly problematical. The cohort of ex-servicemen were inclined to reject those who worked with the government out of hand, and many more wondered to what extent representatives looked after their private interests rather than those of their constituencies, since the benefits they brought were few and far between. No one knew what went on when a delegate went into the office and closed the door, with the result that rumour ran riot. Delegates were becoming increasingly withdrawn from their communities as official business took up more of their time. By the end of the 1960s, two of the three delegates maintained a residence on Thursday Island. They still recognised ties to kin and were usually addressed by first names or kin terms, but the idiom was increasingly out of keeping with the power they wielded and their involvement with government.

Unofficial representation and political alternatives

By 1970, Islanders received most of the things for which the ex-servicemen had clamoured in 1946. Queensland had effected substantial material improvements in the communities, and with the collapse of the marine industry, it had relaxed its control over employment and movement. Some Islanders began working for regular wages on the mainland. But these changes had been a long time coming, and in the meantime many had lost faith in the government and its representative system. Radicals had long looked for white sympathisers outside the official framework: in 1946, the Communist Party looked to be a possible ally;[8] a little later, an Australian war veterans' organisation seemed to promise help;[9] some individuals took their problems to visiting members of parliament. In the 1960s, radicals looked to the Aborigines and Torres Strait Islanders Advancement League, a civil rights organisation based mainly in the southern states.

However, there had been a growing recognition that only the federal government could overrule the state. Hitherto it had remained aloof from Torres Strait affairs, but Islanders remembered that the army, which had given them their first sense of citizenship, was a federal body. Moreover, its 1960 intervention in the matter of voting rights suggested a more liberal attitude. When, in 1972, the newly elected federal Labor administration opened an office on Thursday Island, it looked as though a new era were dawning. This intervention was all the more timely because, with local industry at a standstill, government was the only source of funds.

The two governments quickly fell into an adversarial relationship, partly because they were of opposing camps, partly because of the issue of state versus federal powers and partly, perhaps, because of the possibility of oil in the Strait. With Australian welfare capitalism at its height, the two were virtually competing in the allocation of funds and for the support of Islander representatives.

Concerning the latter, the federal government came off second best in the first encounter. With the independence of Papua New Guinea imminent, it announced prematurely that three offshore islands, presently in the Torres Strait group, would be ceded as part of an adjustment to the old border, which ran to within two miles of the Papuan coast. Taking advantage of the alarm this caused throughout the islands, the Queensland Premier convened a Border Defence Committee, consisting mainly of councillors and the three delegates. Eager to make good its mistake, the federal government called the committee to Canberra for consultation. The committee went but publicly snubbed the

Minister for Aboriginal Affairs, and refused to recognise the delegation of Islanders that had arrived independently at his invitation. Obviously well drilled, the committee kept a predetermined position of no compromise, and refused to be drawn into a number of issues that were known to be a cause of contention between it and Queensland.[10]

In the event, no islands were ceded, although the committee and the Queensland government continued to protest the agreement on seabed rights.[11] By this time, the Labor government had been replaced by one of the same complexion as that of Queensland, but the rivalry did not abate, and the incoming Prime Minister personally visited the Strait to win over Islander leaders. The federal Department of Aboriginal Affairs maintained its office on Thursday Island, and the Strait's two members of the National Aboriginal Council continued to represent their people in Canberra. With the border virtually a dead issue, some leaders began to transfer their loyalties to the federal government, though the Queensland Director of Aboriginal and Islander Advancement continued to exert a powerful personal influence.

The old loyalties became strained when the question of land rights erupted in 1981. The federal government had for some time been facilitating Aboriginal land claims in the Northern Territory, which was under its direct administration. Queensland, however, resisted the idea of land rights, despite widespread criticism from politicians and Aborigines. The Islanders, for their part, took little interest in what they supposed to be an Aboriginal problem: having enjoyed uninterrupted occupation of their ancestral lands, they did not realise that their lands too belonged to the Crown, reserved for their use at the pleasure of the state. Islanders suffered a rude awakening when, in 1981, the Queensland Premier announced that all Aboriginal and Islander reserves would be turned into 50-year leases. Immediately the three delegates flew to Brisbane and, adroitly sidestepping the officials who usually mediated such contacts, secured an audience with the Premier. Given an undertaking that he would delay action until they had a chance to consult their people, they conducted a series of meetings at which all voted overwhelmingly for Perpetual Freehold Title. This information, together with a request for increased local autonomy, was submitted to the Premier by the Torres Strait Area Advisory Council, a group of councillors and representatives convened by the federal Department of Aboriginal Affairs.[12]

The local elections, which were due at the beginning of 1982, were hotly contested, with Queensland obviously anxious to secure the election of its friends. One critical result remained undeclared for some weeks, arousing widespread speculation; another was the subject of an appeal to the Supreme Court, lodged with the assistance of the federally funded Aboriginal Legal Service.

Soon after, the Premier proposed a Deed of Grant in Trust by way of compromise, but this too proved unacceptable. There followed a battle through the media over whether Islander and Aboriginal representatives were or were not in favour of the proposal.[13] In their campaign to oppose implementation of the proposal, Aborigines and Islanders collaborated for the first time, through the Queensland section of the National Aboriginal Council. The campaign reached a climax during the Commonwealth Games in Brisbane.[14] Nevertheless, the proposal received the approval of the state legislature.

Meanwhile, further debate had arisen over the revision of the *Torres Strait Islanders Act*. At the biennial meeting of Island representatives held in mid-1982, and at a subsequent meeting held in November, there was considerable support for a proposal to transfer administration of the islands to an island-controlled Torres Strait Affairs Commission. Queensland's Department of Aboriginal and Islander Advancement would be phased out, although the incumbent director would be asked to carry on in an advisory capacity.

Torres Strait representation and Fourth World politics

The Torres Strait Islanders were quick to emerge as a clearly defined, internally structured minority. Unlike most Aborigines, they came into the colonial world with their traditional communities intact, and these became the building blocks both of European administrative structures and of an emergent identity. Various historical circumstances combined to weld the communities, fourteen in all, into a single entity. The decision of the London Missionary Society to work with Islanders and Papuans, to the exclusion of Aborigines, established one boundary during the critical period of conversion. The drawing of the border between Queensland and the new colony of Papua divorced them from their northern cousins. Even when Queensland made Islanders subject to its Aboriginal legislation, between 1904 and 1939, there was always some notion that the Islanders were superior. By 1936, if not before, a shared experience of colonial conditions, combined with inter-community contacts through the marine industry, had imbued the Islanders with a sense of a distinct identity, and of the advantages of asserting it *vis-à-vis* Aborigines. Even today, Islanders relate much more readily to Pacific Islanders.

Representation had its beginnings in the needs of external church and government, rather than in the needs of Indigenous peoples. And though these needs have changed and become more complex with the years, representation must still be understood as part of the structure of European domination. Once representation was instituted, however, Islanders learned to use it for ends that were not always consonant with those of the regime, which then had to control what it had created. Islanders have often challenged the legitimacy of particular individuals, and some have felt alienated from the representative system itself, but its grounding in the exercise of local autonomy enabled it to take root during the early years. With the growth of welfare capitalism, representatives had to develop an expertise and a degree of collaboration with the authorities, who tended to distance them from their constituencies. This gave rise to intermittent conflict, but the underlying tension was, to some degree, offset by the increasing dependence on government and the consequent relaxation of community cohesion. If the delegates and councillors are today less representative of Islanders than their predecessors, they get more for them. Today's representatives no longer 'represent' their people in any total Durkheimian sense; at the same time, their upbringing and their situation within the web of kinship have saved them from becoming mere pork-barrel politicians.

Representation evolved in Torres Strait independently of political developments on the mainland. When the first conference of councillors was held in 1937, Aborigines were still politically inert, and white opinion uninterested. For this reason, however, Islander representation was normally contained within the Queensland administrative structure, if not actually coopted. With the collapse of the marine industry, the government became all-important in economic affairs. Consequently, the successful representative was one skilled in negotiating the personalistic labyrinths of the bureaucracy, and in making diplomatic approaches to senior officials and politicians. Such persons had little understanding of, or sympathy for, the kind of activism that overtook mainland Aborigines in the early 1970s. Long believing themselves to be different from, and superior to, Aborigines, they remained aloof from the struggle. Only with the intervention of the federal government and the eruption of the border issue did Islanders gain some sense of the national and international pressures to which the governments were responding. Even then, the representatives preferred the discrete official approach to the rhetoric of the open arena.

The problem with such a strategy is that the necessary skills and connections can be acquired only over a long period and, being exercised *in camera*, they are not communicable by example. They are thus confined to a small clique of long standing. The Eastern Islands delegate, who is also one of the National Aboriginal Council members, has held his office for 26 years. The Western Islands were likewise represented by the same man for thirty years, and are now represented by his son: his brother holds the other National Aboriginal Council seat.[15] There have been only three incumbents of the Central Islands delegacy, the present incumbent being the son of the second. Similarly, among the island councillors, almost half have been in office for more than twenty years, whereas emigrants returning from the mainland find it hard to get elected.

With more than half the population settled on the mainland today, there are also grave doubts about the representativeness of the old Queensland, community-based structure. According to one interpretation of state policy, the eight thousand Islanders who live in the cities and towns of northern Australia are ex-Islanders who have forfeited all rights to their ancestral communities. They cannot vote in council elections and may visit only with council permission. Islander representatives who have little or no experience of life on the mainland seem unwilling to include ex-Islanders in their constituency, even in voting on major issues such as the border or land rights. As a result, their base is dwindling, and they are creating a large body of dispossessed Islanders who may one day challenge their legitimacy.

For the moment, however, the expatriates are politically weak. Community loyalties are divisive in the urban situation, and the only over-arching organisations are the Islander churches, which compete for members. Although Islanders outnumber Aborigines in Townsville, the main centre, they have never succeeded in agreeing upon a candidate for the National Aboriginal Council. Nor have they succeeded in uniting with the Aborigines. In the organisations that the federal government has established for the two groups, such as medical and housing services, Islanders find themselves in conflict with Aborigines and at a disadvantage because of their defective English and inexperience of arena politics.

Political frustration resulted in the formation of a Torres Strait United Party in 1979, which sought independence for the Torres Strait by challenging the original Act of Annexation and by appealing to the United Nations.[16] According to some, this was really a strategy to get the Commonwealth government to re-annex the islands, while releasing them from the control of Queensland. Either way, it would mean an end to the old system of representation and open the door to the returning migrants. In the event, the High Court upheld the Act of Annexation,[17] but there can be little doubt that these urban Islanders will be making further forays into the realm of Fourth World politics.

So far, the official Torres Strait representatives have made sparing use of the tactic of appealing to higher authorities. Only during the border dispute did they make a broad appeal to the public, and this with the discreet support of the Queensland government. Yet it is obvious that the attentiveness of the state and federal governments to them, and their ability to attract substantial funds for their tiny communities, are consequences of worldwide concern for Indigenous minorities, and — indirectly — of the freewheeling agitation of Aboriginal activists farther south. In this sense, if in no other, the Torres Strait Islanders are part of the Fourth World.

Acknowledgments

This chapter was first published in 1985 in Noel Dyck (ed.), *Indigenous Peoples and the Nation-state: Fourth World Politics in Canada, Australia and Norway*, Institute of Social and Economic Research, Social and Economic Papers no. 14, Memorial University of Newfoundland.

NOTES

1. For an insightful exploration of these themes, see Murphy (1971, pp. 129–47).
2. Paine (1977, pp. 3–52) refers to welfare activities among minorities such as the Canadian Inuit as 'welfare colonialism'.
3. The authoritative work on this theme is Jayawardena (1968). For an exploration of the problem in a Torres Strait community, see Beckett (1971).
4. The principal sources for Torres Strait ethnography are the six volumes of *Reports* by Haddon et al. (1904–35).
5. Much can also be gleaned from various reports in the annual *Votes and Proceedings of the Queensland Legislative Assembly*.
6. See the report of the Sub-Department of Native Affairs for the year ending 1947, *Votes and Proceedings of the Queensland Legislative Assembly*.
7. For a detailed account of one community's politics, see Beckett (1967).
8. Communist journalists visited Thursday Island soon after the war and published a series of articles in the party newspaper the *Tribune*.
9. The *Australian Legion of Ex-Servicemen and Women*, under left-wing influence after the war, at one point took up the cause of Torres Strait veterans.
10. *The Australian*, 13 June 1973.
11. *Sydney Morning Herald* 15 June 1978.
12. Submission of the Torres Strait Advisory Council to the Premier of Queensland.
13. *National Times*, 11–17 April 1982.
14. *Sydney Morning Herald*, 25 May 1982, 13 July 1982.
15. The Torres Strait has two National Aboriginal Council members: one representing the old Islander communities and one representing Islanders living in the Thursday Island township and in government settlements on Cape York.
16. *Australian Financial Review*, 7 May 1981.
17. *Sydney Morning Herald*, 13 November 1981.

REFERENCES

Beckett, JR 1967, 'Elections in a small Melanesian community', *Ethnology*, vol. 6, pp. 332–44.

—— 1971, 'Rivalry, competition and conflict among Christian Melanesians', in LR Hiatt and C Jayawardena (eds), *Anthropology in Oceania*, Anthropological Society of New South Wales, Sydney, pp. 27–46.

—— 1978 'Mission, church and sect: Three types of religious commitment in the Torres Strait Islands', in JA Boutilier, DT Hughes and SW Tiffany (eds), *Mission, Church and Sect in Oceania*, University of Michigan Press, Ann Arbor, MI, pp. 209–29.

Bleakley, JW 1961, *The Aborigines of Australia*, Jacaranda, Brisbane.

Blu, Karen I 1980, *The Lumbee Problem: The Making of an American Indian People*, Nebraska University Press, Lincoln, NE.

Evans, R, Saunders, K and Cronin, K 1975, *Exclusion, Exploitation and Extermination: Race Relations in Colonial Queensland*, ANZ Book Company, Sydney.

Haddon, AC 1904–35, *Reports of the Cambridge Anthropological Expedition to Torres Straits*, Cambridge University Press, Cambridge.

Jayawardena, C 1968, *Migration and Social Change: A Survey of Indian Communities Overseas*, Geography Review, London.
Murphy, RF 1971, *The Dialectics of Social Life*, Basic Books, New York.
Paine, R (ed.) 1977, *The White Arctic: Anthropological Essays on Tutelage and Ethnicity*, Memorial University of Newfoundland, St John, Newfoundland.

Chapter 9

The Murray Island Land Case

Over the last year, the media and the politicians have put a new word into circulation: since the High Court handed down its decision on the case brought by Edward Koiki Mabo and three other Murray Islanders, 'Mabo' has come to stand for the whole issue of Aboriginal land rights, as in 'Mabo law', 'Mabo deal', 'Mabo show' and, of course, 'Mabo madness'; if it has not already become a verb, it soon will. There is a certain poignancy in all this, since Mabo, the principal litigant in the case that put Indigenous land rights on the front pages of the newspapers throughout 1993 and resulted in the passing of national land rights legislation at the end of that year, died before the High Court brought down its decision. There is also the irony that Mabo's creditability came under question to the point where his own claim was dropped in the final stages of the case. The High Court's decisions, not just in favour of the Murray Islanders, but of all Indigenous Australians, have overshadowed Mabo's fate, and indeed have overshadowed the long, drawn-out proceedings in the Supreme Court of Queensland, which the High Court directed to determine matters of fact in relation to Murray Island.

The hearings in the Queensland Supreme Court have not been quite forgotten, however. Some of the critics of the 'Mabo Bill' have argued that the High Court's decision was flawed, either because it was based on a misreading of 'the facts', or because the process by which the High Court directed that 'the facts' be determined was unsatisfactory. Thus a former Queensland governor, Sir Walter Campbell, has been reported as saying that a decision having major implications for mainland Australia should not have been based on a case concerning Murray Islanders, who were not Aborigines, but Melanesians, and not nomads but cultivators. Sir Walter quoted former Queensland judge Peter Connolly QC to the effect that the Murray Islanders were 'millennia ahead of the palaeolithics (Stone Age people) [i.e. Aborigines] in terms of social organisation' (*The Australian*, 27 October 1993). Along different lines, a Reader in Law at the University of Queensland, Dr John Forbes, has suggested that the evidence the plaintiffs brought in support of their claim was unsatisfactory in a number of respects (Forbes 1993). Some of these criticisms have been reproduced for readers in a scurrilous booklet by Tim Hewat (1993) entitled *Who Made the Mabo Mess?* Both works take off from certain misgivings expressed by Queensland Supreme Court Justice Martin Moynihan (1990) in his report on the facts to the High Court.

Koiki Mabo's cause (if not his own claim) was won when the *Native Title Act* was passed on 21 December 1993, but since the legitimacy of the High Court's decision and the new Act is still contested, it may be as well to respond to these criticisms, and in the process to review a case that stands apart from the rest of Australian land rights litigation. I shall do so not as a lawyer, but as an anthropologist who has spent many months on Murray Island — or, to use its Indigenous name, Mer — over more than thirty years, who advised the counsel for the plaintiffs in the later stages of the hearings, and who appeared in the Supreme Court as an expert witness. Briefly, I shall attempt to illuminate some aspects of the case that seem to be problematical, by viewing them in the context of Meriam culture and history. My response will also give me the opportunity to reappraise the standing of Koiki Mabo, whose credibility Justice Moynihan, and in turn Dr Forbes and Tim Hewat, have called into question. In thinking about these matters, I shall have occasion to review anthropological and other uses of such long-established but still unsatisfactory notions as tradition and cultural continuity.

The 'difference' between Islanders and Aborigines

There is some substance to the argument that there are cultural differences between Aborigines and Torres Strait Islanders, the group to which the Meriam belong. Indeed, before the High Court handed down its decision, it seemed to me possible that it would find in favour of the Meriam, but limit its decision to their island, or perhaps to Torres Strait. Islanders certainly regard themselves as different from Aborigines. At the same time, it does not seem that the differences are of such a nature as to render the two groups incomparable; what counts in the final analysis is that Aborigines and Islanders are both Australian Indigenous minorities with an interest in land that is different from that of other Australians.

The Meriam are related physically, linguistically and culturally to the people of southern Papua, and have maintained regular trading relations with them over centuries. Although they drew more on marine resources than these neighbours, they were also agriculturalists, growing much the same kinds of crops.

The adoption of agriculture has assumed a critical place in the theory of cultural evolution; viewed on the ground, as in the Torres Strait, it appears less as a historic watershed than as an option to which certain communities may have been led by — although we can only speculate — such factors as soil fertility, predictable rainfall and population pressure. The sedentary settlements and the substantial houses that the agricultural option facilitated provided European observers with the grounds for rating the Islanders as more advanced (that is, more like themselves) than the Aborigines, though scarcely for transposing the difference to the grand evolutionary scale and situating them 'millennia ahead'.

The difference in terms of social organisation is not all that striking. Both societies were organised in terms of kinship relations, and were further differentiated in terms of age and gender. Like both Papuans and Aborigines, the Islanders lacked hereditary chiefs; however, senior men gained power through leadership in certain religious cults, membership of which was hereditary. These cults were Papuan rather than Aboriginal in character, featuring the use of masks and drums, the cult of Malu-Bomai on Mer being among the most important in the Strait. Within Meriam society, the cult seems to have conferred status on certain groups (though it was by no means the only cult), and to have taken political form at least to the extent of sending out masked men to terrorise women by night, and killing women who discovered their secrets. The importance and character of this cult became contentious issues in the case, and I shall have to return to it.

Whatever the original differences between Aborigines and Islanders, they were increased through the form that colonisation took in the Strait. In particular, the Islanders (with the exception of those living round Thursday Island) were never displaced. Until the second half of the century, Europeans used the Strait only as a seaway. And when they established a permanent presence, it was to protect shipping and exploit the region's marine resources, principally pearl shell and trepang — activities for which they needed only enough land to repair their boats and process their catch. They used the Islanders as a labour reserve, but returned them to their gardens and boats when they did not require them. Thus it suited the authorities to reserve most of the islands for the use of the Islanders, taking only small lots for the building of churches, schools and stores.

The administration of the Strait also took an unusual form. Queensland did not annexe the outer islands until 1879, and did not establish effective control until the mid-1880s. In the interim, it left law and order to the London Missionary Society, which had arrived in 1871, directing it to work through the government chiefs (called *mamoose*). The London Missionary Society, coming out of the Congregationalist tradition, encouraged Islanders to participate in the running of the church, in the form of deacons and church councillors. When the Queensland government took charge, it was under the aegis of a former premier, the Hon John Douglas, who established an idiosyncratic benevolent despotism, very different from the regimes to which Aborigines were subjected. Regarding the Islanders as superior to the Aborigines, he instituted a system of government that was unique in the Pacific at that time, including elected island councils. These councils advised European resident magistrates (who were also teachers) and served as assessors in the island court. After 1939, they assumed a major part of the work of local government (Beckett 1987, pp. 45–60). The continuity in Indigenous control of community affairs was a major issue in the case.

Mer had as its teacher–magistrate one John Bruce, who had lived on the island for several years before his appointment in 1885, and who remained in the job until 1922. It seems that he acquired a command of the Meriam language and a considerable knowledge of Meriam custom, which he put at the disposal of the anthropologist AC Haddon, and the Cambridge University Anthropological Expedition of 1898.[1] He also brought this expertise to the hearing of the many land disputes that came before the island court, attempting it would seem to implement — though perhaps also to regularise — Indigenous rules about inheritance and local knowledge about boundaries. The court books, which record the decisions that he and later the island councils reached on these matters, were major exhibits in the Queensland hearings.

Enjoying unimpeded access to their islands, the Islanders were able to believe that they still owned them, and the Queensland Government encouraged them in this belief since until the 1960s it wanted to prevent them from moving to the mainland. Thus they saw little reason to join the Aboriginal clamour for land rights in the 1970s. Only in the early 1980s did they become aware that the land they lived on was reserved for their use, but belonged to the Crown (Beckett 1987, pp. 190–1). The island councils, by that time formed into an Island Coordinating Council, greeted this discovery with dismay: unanimously rejecting the Premier's offer of a thirty-year (later fifty-year) lease, they demanded inalienable freehold title. However, having had more than forty years' experience of dealing with the state government, they entered into negotiation, eventually settling for a modified version of a Deed of Grant in Trust, which gave them indefinite occupancy of their ancestral lands, reversible only by the Governor in Council. The Mer council was the only one to refuse, awaiting the outcome of the so-called *Mabo* case, which had been brought in 1982.

The origins of the case

The fact that it was Mer that held out was consistent with the island's strong attachment to land and its long history of resistance to government. Apart from the economic utility of land for the Meriam, it was a source of individual and family prestige, and thus of conflict. Its agricultural importance had been somewhat reduced by the 1980s, as the Meriam increased their dependence on the welfare economy, but it remained important for residential purposes, in a settlement that was becoming increasingly crowded. Mer's stand was also consistent with its long struggle to preserve its autonomy. However, it had no experience of legal proceedings, and would probably not have undertaken them had it not been for the initiative of Koiki Mabo, a Meriam long-term resident on the mainland.

Koiki Mabo, like many of his generation, had left the Strait at the beginning of the 1960s in search of work, adventure and freedom from government controls. Unlike them, however, he had moved outside Islander circles, meeting radical unionists on the North Queensland waterfront, Aboriginal activists and academics with an interest in Indigenous matters, such as Henry Reynolds and Noel Loos at James Cook University. These contacts came to the notice of the Queensland authorities, who advised the Mer council to bar him from the island. Reports that he had rejected Christianity would have strengthened them in this. He was not able to return until mid-1977.

Mabo had not joined with Carlemo Wacando and others in their legal challenge to the 1879 annexation of Darnley Island (Sharp 1993a, p. 279), but was well informed about it, since the Torres United Party that supported the action was based in Townsville. In 1980, Mabo attended a conference on land rights in Townsville, and it was there, in discussion with an anthropologist, Dr Nonie Sharp, as well as Dr HC Coombs and Professor Garth Nettheim, that the plan was laid. Also present was the Meriam Anglican priest, Father David Passi. Greg McIntyre and Barbara Hocking, who were also present at the conference, acted as barrister and solicitor respectively during the early stages of the case.

Mabo became the first plaintiff, but he did not proceed alone. To do so would have been to put his claim on a shaky footing, since the Mer council had resolved at one time that those who left the island forfeited their land. It did not adhere to this position in the case of anyone wishing to return, but the attitude lingered, with some even referring to emigrants as 'ex-Islanders'. To avoid this reproach, it was wise to include Mer residents among the plaintiffs. Mabo's father's sister, Celuia Salee, who was caretaking the family land, was an obvious choice. Father Passi persuaded his family head, Sam Passi, to become a plaintiff on their behalf. The two later withdrew, partly because of Queensland government pressure, partly through annoyance at a newspaper report suggesting that Koiki Mabo expected to become 'King of Murray' when he won the case. David Passi returned to the case in 1989. The fourth plaintiff, James Rice, was an island councillor.

The Passis were of particular importance as descendants of one of the hereditary leaders of the Malu-Bomai cult; Mabo claimed descent from another line. As we shall see, his claim was contested, but meanwhile, who the litigants were provided substance to claims in terms of continuity between the pre-colonial and colonial societies.

The statement of claim argued not merely that the plaintiffs and their forbears had been in continuous occupation of the island — a fact that was never contested — but that a system of ownership had existed 'from time immemorial', having been maintained within the framework of a mode of government. The supposed absence of such a system was a key assumption of the *terra nullius* doctrine.

The Queensland hearings

Although the case began in 1982, the determination of facts in the Supreme Court did not begin until 1989, the intervening time having been taken up by a variety of delays, including Queensland's attempt to abort the case by passing retrospective legislation, which the High Court by a narrow margin overturned on the grounds that it was in conflict with the *Racial Discrimination Act 1975*.

There had been no previous case of this kind before a Queensland court, so Justice Moynihan had to improvise when it came to hearing Islanders' evidence. Statements such as 'My father showed me the boundary' or 'My mother told me that this place belonged to her father' would normally have been regarded as hearsay and, as such, not acceptable evidence. This provided the Queensland counsels with endless opportunities to interrupt the plaintiffs' case, until the judge ruled that he would take their objections as heard, and decide the matter later.

Meriam evidence lasted many days, and in mid-1989 the court removed to Mer, hearing witnesses too old to leave the island, and visiting some of the places referred to in the hearings. The 1990 film *Land Bilong Islanders* records this visit.[2] Once the 'hearsay' question had been resolved, the witnesses seem to have been given respectful attention, although judge, lawyers and reporter must at times have had difficulty in following them. I am familiar with the Torres Strait English and the matters that were being discussed, but I have found sections of the transcripts incomprehensible.

Forbes (1993), by quoting selectively, manages to convey the impression that Justice Moynihan was concerned by the use of interpreters and perhaps suspected some kind of manipulation of evidence (1993, p. 52). Explaining that he granted an interpreter when this was requested, the Justice observed, 'On a number of occasions I soon gained the impression that the witness both understood and could speak English' (1993, p. 66). This rather loses sight of the possibility that the witnesses might have some acquaintance with English but, given the importance of the proceedings, might not want to risk misunderstanding or making fools of themselves (a matter on which Islanders are sensitive). While Mabo and Dave Passi spoke fluent, idiomatic English, most Meriam over fifty years of age were comfortable only in Meriam and Torres Strait pidgin (*kriol* or *broken*). However, Justice Moynihan did not attribute a sinister intent to the resort to interpreters, suggesting that the witness may have

> desired the opportunity to collaborate with the interpreter as a form of social support. The arrangement also gave an opportunity to, in effect, hear the question twice, and time for the witness to collect his or her thoughts and to 'collaborate' with an interpreter on an answer. I do not suggest that this process necessarily rendered the evidence unreliable — on occasion, it may have enhanced its reliability — but it has to be borne in mind. (1993, p. 66)

Forbes also puts a sinister interpretation on the Justice's observation that some witnesses (only one is named) may have been 'under some sort of constraint or pressure'. However, this is followed by a recognition that this was due either to culturally based considerations, or an unwillingness to be seen to take sides (1993, p. 67). When witnesses are members of a tightly knit community, it does not take a conspiracy for them to feel this way. However, it was not the case that all the evidence went in the plaintiffs' favour. The elderly gentleman in the pink lava-lava who speaks in the film (and who gave evidence for the defence) is complaining that Koiki Mabo has misstated the boundary between their properties.

The land claims

The claim that the Meriam people had been in some kind of continuous occupation of their islands 'from time immemorial' could not be contested (though it was argued that the church, the government and, in the 1930s, a sardine factory had occupied small parcels). This provided a solid foundation for the High Court's decision that 'the Meriam people are entitled as against the whole world to possession, occupation, use and enjoyment of the lands of the Murray Islands' (1992, p. 1). However, the plaintiffs brought action only for their own land, and while the general thrust of the counsels' argument was that they were standing for all Meriam landowners, in the Meriam context they were acting for themselves. Thus, while all Meriam subscribed to the principle of traditional ownership, some contested these particular claims. Mabo's own claims proved particularly contentious; indeed, some could see his case only in terms of self-aggrandisement.

Anyone who believed that custom was a matter of calm consensus would have been disappointed by this response, but it was entirely characteristic of the Meriam. The Murray Island court books bear witness to the contested nature of Meriam land tenure over almost a hundred years. There are various grounds for dispute. One of these is the location of boundaries which, because of the tiny areas involved and their use for growing crops, need to be exact. But while some are defined by fixed topographical features such as creek beds, others are marked by stones, stakes or mounds, which can be moved, or by trees, which can die or become confused with other trees, particularly when the land has not been cleared for a long time. Prolonged absences from the island may also leave owners uncertain as to where the boundaries lie. Since the area is divided into small, often tiny, parcels, with each owner having a number — sometimes on the nearby island of Dauar as well as on Mer — there is considerable scope for disagreement and perhaps cheating. Other disputes arise over inheritance.

Land almost invariably passes from parents to children, whether natural or adopted, or if there are none, to the next of kin. Beyond this, practice has been variable. Understanding Meriam practice is complicated by the rhetorical use of normative statements. For example, it is often asserted — as it was in the court hearings — that male kin are preferred over female kin (who may receive nothing more than a marriage portion), and that the eldest son should receive the largest share, if not all. But for the period covered by the court books, female children often inherited a share and brothers often inherited more or less equally. In the case of the Passi family, the eldest held land on behalf not only of his siblings, but of first cousins as well. However, this was a somewhat unusual case, since several of the other members were unmarried, while others (including David himself) lived away from the island for long periods. Moreover, there was no question that the other members were not entitled to the use of land. The High Court found this case difficult to construe, partly because David Passi explained the situation in terms of customary principle rather than contingency. The usual practice was either for parents to divide the land among their children, or for the children to do so after their parents' death; for cousins to hold land undivided was unusual.

The inconsistency between customary precept and practice was sometimes explained away as a consequence of change. Certainly, the move — mainly during the 1930s and 1940s — from the traditional villages around the circumference of Mer and on Dauar to one compact settlement near church, school and store, had been achieved by some improvisation outside the bounds of usual practice, including purchase. (The death of many of the original owners around the turn of the century had created the space for outsiders to come in.) Garden land was not subject to radical changes of this kind, but the pressure on land had certainly varied over the years, with fluctuations in population, and the degree of dependence on 'bush tucker' as against store foods; studies on Melanesian land tenure suggest that such factors affect the strictness with which rules are followed.

Contrary to the normative assertions of witnesses, however, the archival record suggests that practice was always fairly flexible. According to the *Cambridge Reports*, owners seemed to exercise a good deal of discretion, to the extent of disinheriting sons, and in the sharing out of the various plots among heirs (Haddon 1908, pp. 163–8). In later years, the council encouraged them to write wills, but often the determination of a deceased owner's intention depended on oral testimony.[3]

The widespread practice of adoption proved a particularly potent source of dispute. In principle, an adopted child — who ought to be of the same 'blood' as one of the adopting parents — acquired the same rights as natural children, simultaneously forfeiting any claim on its natural parents. In practice, its entitlements were liable to challenge in the absence of a written will. It might be alleged that the arrangement had been for fostering rather than adoption, or that the adoption arrangement had been aborted and the child returned to its parents. Some natural parents seem to have tried to entice their children back when they began earning. Some children ended up without an assured place in either family.

No one openly challenged the claims of Salee, Rice or Passi, though there were rival claimants for some of the places listed. But many challenged Mabo's claim. First, it was alleged that he had misstated the boundaries. Having left Mer at the age of fifteen and been absent for many years, it is easy to suppose that he had been guessing at them, or simply making them up, but his account was detailed and circumstantial, and he could give an accurate account of the places from memory. More seriously, it was alleged that he was not the adopted son, or had been disinherited. For the record, I had heard his adoptive parents refer to him as their son in 1958, and a senior man who had helped me put together genealogies had also described him as adopted. It seems possible that, as some alleged, his adoptive father had disinherited him when he was dying, since Koiki had not been home for many years, but this allegation came from a witness who had an interest in the matter. There was also a suggestion that he and his natural father had resumed a relationship when, as a boy, he stayed with the family over six months. When the government paid out supplementary wages to Islanders who had served in the army during the Second World War, or their heirs, Koiki Mabo had claimed from this man rather than his adoptive father, both of whom were by then dead. That he did so while the case was in progress led some to allege that he was knowingly misleading the court. I did not question him on the matter, but it is possible that he may have concluded that this was the appropriate course, since Australian courts did not recognise customary adoption.

The challenges to Mabo's own claim were serious, but they must be understood in the agonistic environment from which they came. In private conversation, I found Meriam expansive in their claims for land, and dismissive of the claims of others, but only occasionally did they test their claims in the island court. This may have been because the contestants were not sufficiently sure of their facts to come out with them, or because they suspected that the court, because of its composition, would be partial to the other side — court members seem sometimes to have been unwilling to decide against a large and influential family. An examination of the court books shows that, once the teacher ceased to participate in hearings, the court's decisions become less concerned with consistency in the application of rules and, seemingly, more responsive to the whole complex of considerations; they defer more cases indefinitely, and refer more to the Queensland administration.

As in mainland Australia — though more manifestly so — the Meriam legal system was politically embedded. In this respect, Mabo was in a weak position compared with the other plaintiffs, having been absent for many years and having few close kin on the island, none of them particularly important. As such, he was an easy target, particularly since the advancement of his claim through an Australian court looked to some like an attempt to by-pass the island court, thus threatening Meriam self-determination. His claims were no more expansive than those of some other Meriam, but he seemed to have made them without an appreciation of the resistance he would encounter and his lack of clout.

The question of continuity

The statement of claim makes repeated use of the phrase 'from time immemorial', representing the plaintiffs as descendants and heirs of the original inhabitants of Mer, the land tenure system as at least continuous with, if not the same as, what had been practised before the arrival of Europeans, and the contemporary culture and society as being in significant respects traditional. At a later stage, counsel for the plaintiffs spoke of these rights 'flowing along a continuum of a dynamic and flexible culture'.

In my book (Beckett 1987, p. 12), I had remarked on the profound cultural change that had overtaken Torres Strait as a result of 120 years of sustained contact, but I had also noted that among the Meriam there was 'a conscious effort to maintain continuity with the past, powerfully symbolized by the sacred drum Wasikor' (1987, p. 112). However, from the vantage point of the mid-1980s, Sharp (1993a, p. xv) 'began to observe an important continuity in which the sacred power or *zogo* of the Meriam culture heroes, Malo-Bomai, had been handed down into the present life of the Murray Islanders'.

Continuity, of course, is not an all or nothing affair, and it leaves hanging the question of whether what survives remains important, rather than mere folkloric curiosity. Moreover, old institutions may survive but assume a different character in a colonial context. Tradition, a term that also appears in the statements of claim and of the facts, is no less tricky. Such subtleties can scarcely be risked in adversarial statements, and are hazardous in the courtroom situation, yet they are bound to arise. I was called upon to comment on various statements I had made in my book when I was giving evidence, but I think they would have arisen anyway. Certainly Justice Moynihan gave extended consideration to them in his finding, choosing to emphasise the extent of change and the centrality of institutions such as the island court introduced as a result of colonisation.

The *Mabo* case raised a set of questions rather different from those arising in Aboriginal land cases. There was no question that the present-day occupants of Mer were the direct descendants of those who had lived there when the missionaries arrived in 1871, but their 'occupation' now included the supervision of inheritance and the settlement of disputes by an island court that, though manned by Islanders, had been established and was maintained by the Queensland government. The defence argued that this constituted a substitution of Indigenous practice rather than a continuation of it. The plaintiffs argued that the decisions of the court were informed by Meriam custom, but it was another matter to prove that the system of land ownership was 'the same' as the system that had existed a hundred and more years ago. An early visitor (Campbell 1827) had reported that there were boundaries between lots, but said nothing about the mode of inheritance. Strictly speaking, one could only argue that there must have been some kind of system, or life would have become intolerable, and refer the court to numerous accounts of similar systems of tenure in Papua New Guinea. Such systems were subject to change in response to such endogenous factors as shifting population pressures and warfare, but were nevertheless regarded by the colonial authorities and the Papua New Guinean government as customary. The defence nevertheless argued that the Meriam system had been radically changed as a result of external influences, at one stage proposing that since Melanesian inheritance was always patrilineal, the inclusion of female heirs was evidence of Polynesian influence.

This argument is anthropologically wrong, but if one wishes to be rigorous, as Justice Moynihan was inclined to be, it has to be admitted that hard evidence as to how land was owned and transmitted on Mer before the 1890s is thin. The first written account, by a missionary (Hunt 1899), contradicted in a number of respects the information included in the *Cambridge Reports* (Haddon 1908, pp. 163–8), which was closer to the plaintiffs' version. The account in the *Cambridge Reports* was based mainly on information obtained from the teacher, John Bruce — who, it will be recalled, knew the language and had a deep interest in and knowledge of the culture. However, even this source cannot be regarded as wholly reliable, since Bruce as administrator claimed to have regulated Meriam land tenure. Might he not, like many colonial administrators, have changed it in the process of making it more 'consistent' and 'fair'? Since the court's decisions were now backed by the power of the state, Bruce could also be said to have presided over the critical change from tribal anarchy to Western law.

Bruce did indeed claim to have eliminated the use of 'club law' in the settlement of disputes (*Report of the Chief Protector of Aborigines* 1912). Justice Moynihan gave some weight to this statement as perhaps indicating that, before the arrival of Europeans, disputes had been settled by force rather than anything that could be regarded as law. My own understanding is informed by the accounts of settlement disputes in stateless societies in Melanesia and elsewhere, but having worked in the Philippines, I have come to regard law as something that operates subject to (and is to a greater or lesser degree influenced by) politics and power, even when there is a government. The statement of claim, however, argued that there had been a system of arbitration, if not adjudication, by Indigenous authorities.

In the same document, several of the plaintiffs are described as 'descendants of the traditional leaders known as the "Aiets" of the Meriam people'. The statement of facts asserts that:

> Before annexation, disputes concerning land were resolved traditionally by referring them to the Aiets, being the religious and political leaders of the Miriam people, and to the heads of disputing families, for adjudication and decision according to traditional law. If no resolution was thereby achieved, the dispute could lead to feuding and open fighting. (1912, p. 43)

The reference to the 'Aiets' caused some discussion, since none of the nineteenth-century accounts refers to it, and I had not heard the name until Mabo mentioned it to me in the late 1970s. However, Ion Idriess's novel, *The Drums of Mer*, refers to Aet as one of the three leaders of the Malu-Bomai cult (1938, p. 7). Despite his lurid and romantic story, Idriess made a serious attempt at ethnographic accuracy; he is unlikely to have made the name up, but may have heard about it from Passi, whom his descendants refer to as Aet.[4] Whether or not it was a title rather than a name,[5] there is no doubt that the leaders of the various Meriam cults were referred to as *zogo le*, meaning those associated with supernatural power. What is less clear is the extent and nature of their authority, particularly in the case of the *zogo le* of Malu-Bomai, which was the most important cult.

As compared with nineteenth-century accounts, those of latter day Meriam place greater emphasis on the idea of hierarchy and formal authority, including terms such as 'chief', 'high priest' and even 'king'. Moreover, the Statement of Claim refers to only two *zogo le* or *aets*, of whom Mabo and Passi are said to be the descendants, whereas Haddon's account of the cult distributes the *zogo le* role among a larger number of descent lines, all of whose members had the right to wear the sacred masks (Haddon 1908, p. 286). Idriess's novel, by contrast, refers to a 'big zogo-zogo le', who is also a big sorcerer (1938, p. 6), and since the book has been circulating in the Strait for many years, it is possible that his 'heroic' view of Islander society may have influenced latter-day Meriam perspectives on what is now a remote past. *Drums of Mer* is also the only documentary source to mention a 'Council of *zogo le*' hearing land disputes (1938, p. 33).

The question of how many *zogo le* there were, and whether their powers were great or small, can be separated from the further question of whether the Malu-Bomai cult regulated social relations, rather than merely being a source of amoral supernatural power. Some confirmation for the first alternative comes from a series of injunctions couched in archaic language and known as *Malo-ra gelar*.[6] The word *gelar* is itself significant, since it has the connotation of a rule or law. Associated with the cult, it implies a supernatural sanction. The gist of *Malo-ra gelar* is that people should not trespass on one another's land or take one another's crops without permission, practices that were also prohibited by forms of *tapu*; although, if both parties to a dispute believed that they were the rightful owners, each would have argued that the prohibitions only applied to the adversary. What the injunctions indisputably affirm, however, is the principle of ownership over land and crops.

Justice Moynihan questioned whether Malu's law had survived the eclipse of the cult, suggesting that it had been rediscovered when Meriam got access to Volume VI of the *Cambridge Reports* through me in 1959. Although I heard it from several old men before the book arrived, I do not think it was widely known among younger folk before the court case. George Passi, in his evidence for the defence, suggested that this was the case, an opinion that was corroborated by a friend of mine who told me recently that he did not hear of Malu's law until he found it in a book of folk tales, published in 1970.

Nevertheless, the principle was generally understood and, I think, observed as long as gardening remained important. By this time, however, the council and the island police were the agents of law and order, and the question of whether, notwithstanding the ending of the cult, a belief in Malu was a factor in the observance of this principle is not easy to answer.

The statement of claim suggested that the 'Aiets' were still respected in the community, but it was not clear to me that membership of the two descent lines commanded respect in its own right. From 1971 to the present, some member of the Passi family had occupied a position of importance: Passi, the old *zogo le*, had been appointed *mamoose* soon after colonial rule was established; one of his sons was a highly regarded priest of the Church of England, though the other two held no office. Three of his grandsons had been councillors, one a long-serving chairman. However, the other line remained in obscurity until the court case. Koiki Mabo's claim to be a 'king', probably reported in an exaggerated form in *The Australian* newspaper, was not well received in a community that regularly cut down tall poppies and rejected know-it-alls from the mainland (Beckett 1987, p. 112).

The argument in the statement of claim that the Malu-Bomai cult remained important for Meriam in the 1980s also proved difficult to sustain, although in my judgment it was not altogether misconceived. The difficulty was that the Meriam had been at least nominal Christians from the 1870s, and from the time I knew them at least were regular church-goers and strict sabbatarians. Differences over competing brands of Christianity were matters of passionate and bitter dispute, whereas the Malu-Bomai cult entered the public domain only as folkloric entertainment. One of the plaintiffs, it will be recalled, was a priest of the Church of England. Early on, the missionaries had destroyed the Malu-Bomai shrine and burned one of the sacred objects; the sacred mask was said to have been buried by the officiants, and thus still on Mer, but the only surviving object was one of two sacred drums, which was used in church on feast days. Some of the songs and dances were also preserved in a modified form and performed occasionally as late as the 1970s. The performances were for fundraising; women and children and outsiders were not excluded, as they had once been, and no account was taken of the hereditary roles. And yet, looking back, it seems to me that these performances were more than just entertainment, if less than religious ceremonies: they were perhaps commemorations of the Meriam past and of an almost vanished autochthonous power.

During my first periods of fieldwork, between 1958 and 1961, the Meriam spoke of Malu and Bomai in the rhetoric of the mission as 'heathen or idol gods'. Sam Passi quoted his grandfather as saying, 'Malu was only a turtle shell. Now we have the true God.' But most spoke of Malu and Bomai as real spiritual beings. Although they had gone from the island, they had once existed and had supernatural powers, if not wholly for good. It was said that Jesus Christ and God were more powerful, though I noticed that some invoked Malu–Bomai when using magical spells for traditional kinds of activities such as dancing and gardening. Much later, Father David Passi, in the film *Land Bilong Islanders* and before the court, proposed that Malu was sent by God as a precursor of the Gospel (see also Sharp 1993b, pp. 68–9, 108–10). I did not hear anything of the kind during my first round of fieldwork, though it is possible that its seeds were there, waiting for the more liberal climate that the 1980s provided. The fact remains that, by this time, it was Christianity in one of a number of forms that organised people's daily lives. The Pentecostalist preacher in *Land Bilong Islanders* expressed no such regard for Malu. Perhaps people talk more about Malu Bomai and Malu's law these days, and they have recently erected a memorial in the church yard depicting the octopus — the form Bomai took in landing on Murray, and symbolising the eight Meriam tribes — but it is some years since the dances have been performed. The distinction between traditional and traditionalism is often hard to draw.

The creditability of Koiki Mabo

Justice Moynihan recognised the creditability of Rice and Passi, if he did not always accept what they said, but he was harsh in his assessment of Mabo:

> I was not impressed with the creditability of Eddie Mabo. I would not be inclined to act on his evidence in a matter bearing on his self interest (and most of his evidence was of this character in one way or another) unless it was supported by other creditable evidence. (1992, p. 71)

He also suggested that Mabo was 'quite capable of tailoring his story to whatever shape he perceived would advance his cause in a particular forum' (1992, p. 70). Reading between the lines, I get the impression that Justice Moynihan regarded him as not a real Meriam, but an urbanised political activist who, seeing the main chance, made up for his lack of roots by reading books. As compared with the oral tradition, such knowledge was inauthentic and liable to contaminate it.

I think that some of the claims that Mabo made but the Justice disbelieved could have been confirmed — for example, relating to his exclusion from Mer, and the belief that the Bomai mask had been buried at Las.[7] I have already indicated that I believe that he had indeed been adopted by Benny and Maiger Mabo, and that the doubts hanging over the continuation of this relationship were not unusual in such cases. I have suggested that his land claims were over-expansive and politically ill-advised, but the bases on which he made them were well within the Meriam canon. Nor was his use of particular arguments, such as that regarding the rights of the first-born son, more opportunistic than that of other Meriam in a similar situation; the difference was that he had to make all his claims at once, whereas normally people made their claims one at a time.

I first met Koiki Mabo in 1967, and met him from time to time from the mid-1970s. We talked a lot about Meriam culture, listened to my recordings of Meriam music and at one point worked together on an article about dancing. On his first visit home, in 1977, he took me to his village, Las, and showed me a place where he said the shrine of Malu-Bomai had stood. I have to admit that I was surprised that someone who had left Mer around the age of fifteen and had scarcely been back until his forties should know as much as he did. Some of it may indeed have come from the *Cambridge Reports* or from Idriess's novel, but much of it did not. He had, for example, an extensive knowledge of plants, including those used for various dance ornaments and implements, which was not to be found in print. Nor could he have got from books the vivid, detailed mind picture of the land that he presented to the court. A genealogy he recounted went back further than could be found in the *Cambridge Reports*.

Koiki may, as his own testimony suggests, have been a particularly attentive child, and he may have spent more time with his grandfather than small Meriam boys usually do. However, it would be a mistake to think that by leaving Mer he was forever cut off from the oral tradition. Although he said he was isolated during his early years on the mainland, by the mid-1970s there were many elderly Meriam living in or passing through Townsville. On several occasions, he and I interviewed such people in search of information. In the long run, I suspect, what he had heard as a child, what he heard in Townsville and what he read in books at the university became part of a single web of traditional knowledge. Inasmuch as many of the things included in the *Cambridge Reports* had been forgotten by the time he was growing up, he 'knew' more than other Meriam about their past. At the same time, he 'knew' it in a different way: not as something that had come to him just in the course of growing up on Mer, but as knowledge for which he had searched. At the same time, because much of this knowledge came from a vanished past, and because it was not constantly tested against everyday experience, it could feed his imagination. It led to him challenging the Queensland government in the High Court. His dream of being an Aet and a big landowner foundered, but he won the recognition of Meriam title. The Meriam will say that they knew this all the time, but now that he is dead they wear the t-shirt with his face against the map of the island.

Moynihan's conclusions

While Justice Moynihan, in his determination, declared himself dissatisfied with the confused and contested evidence supporting the plaintiffs' particular claims, his valedictory words to the Meriam community, recorded in *Land Bilong Islanders*, indicate that he was impressed by the strength of what one might call their culture of territoriality. In his determination, he is rather more cautious, stating that the Meriam

> succeed in conveying a strong sense of the observation of propriety in rela-
> tion to land ... The knowledge of boundaries is important in respect of
> those concepts of propriety and of the social behaviour respecting them ...
> Such attitudes are rooted in the precontact past ... (1990, p. 157)

However, the Justice is inclined to see these as something less than law:

> The attitudes I have mentioned are ingrained in the culture of the people
> are a part rather than objectively laid down and enforced by some distinct
> agency — rather like our (or more likely another age's) concept of good
> manners ... In this context, so far as the evidence reveals, I have little diffi-
> culty in accepting that the people of the Murray islands perceive themselves
> as having an enduring relationship with land on the islands and the seas
> and reefs surrounding them. (1990, p. 157).

Justice Moynihan concedes that 'the evidence establishes that Murray islanders recognise the continuance of claims to garden plots and recognise or dispute claims of entitlement by individuals in respect of those plots' (1990, p. 178). However, he seems to understand the process of inheritance and the decisions of the island court primarily as arrangements to distribute resources and avoid social conflict, characterised by some tendency to consistency, but — the implication seems to be — not amounting to law as it is understood in Australian society. He also prefers to suspend judgment on the question of the degree of continuity from a largely unknown pre-colonial culture and the present, and is sceptical of the suggestion that the Aets or any other authority decided land disputes in the old days, or that the island courts have been consciously applying Malu's law (1990, pp. 91–3).

Just how Justice Moynihan's determination influenced the High Court is not entirely clear. However, it should be noted that the Court did not recognise the particular claims of the litigants, even after Mabo's own claim had been dropped, and a reading of the transcripts suggests that the counsel for the plaintiffs were unable to persuade them on the point. At the same time, they found that that the Murray Islanders owned Mer 'against the whole world'. It is hard to believe that the judges were unaffected by the combined testimony of plaintiffs and witnesses, and perhaps Justice Moynihan's conclusion carried some weight — despite, or perhaps even because of, its caution. But perhaps in the last analysis the importance of the Murray Island case was that it provided the judges with the opportunity to right a two-hundred-year-old injustice.

The authenticity question

Although Justice Moynihan's findings enabled the High Court to overturn the *terra nullius* doctrine, they leave a cloud of inauthenticity hanging over the *Mabo* case, just as it hangs over so many Aboriginal claims on the mainland (e.g. Jacobs 1988) and, increasingly, over the scientific status of anthropology. Even if it is granted that a people once had an ordered relationship with the land, of what significance can this be after a century or more of colonisation? Are not these land claims anachronisms, the fabrications of Indigenous politicians and romantic anthropologists?

In part, this situation stems from anthropology's own difficulty in handling the question of cultural continuity, to which I have already referred. At different times, evolutionary and functionalist anthropologists, as well as the political economy tendency, have represented 'primitive culture' as irreparably transformed by contact with 'civilisation'. According to another view, such cultures survive against all the odds, encompassing alien influences, yet somehow remaining essentially themselves. But if the first view underestimates the resilience of Indigenous cultural reproduction, the second tends to a romantic essentialism that revives the fiction of the unchanging primitive. It also short-circuits understanding of cultural dynamics, obscuring such processes as cultural revival and the invention of tradition.

As people become aware of the presence and the possibility of cultural alternatives, their consciousness of their own culture becomes reflexive, and their customs and traditions become objectified, even fetishised. What were flexible principles become immutable laws which, ironically, become the screens behind which individuals and groups advance new interests.

These remarks apply in some degree to the Meriam. After more than a century of exposure to missionaries, schoolteachers and government officials, they cannot but have a relativistic view of their culture. Moreover, their sense of their past has been influenced in complex ways by the experience of being studied by a succession of anthropologists, and — particularly in recent years — by reading what the researchers have written.[8] It is ironic that, while anthropologists become creditable expert witnesses by writing, 'natives' render themselves inauthentic by reading: tainted with literacy, it seems they can't go home again!

But, to take one instance, even if it is true that the Meriam only rediscovered Malu's Law in the *Cambridge Reports*, this does not render their proclamation of it inauthentic. It was not seized upon opportunistically in the course of preparing the land claim. Its rediscovery (or, as I suspect, return to currency) occurred in the early 1960s, long before the *Mabo* case was thought of. The visits of three researchers in quick succession — myself, Wolfgang Laade and Margaret Lawrie — may have rekindled an interest in the Meriam past, but the interest would have been ephemeral had not it resonated with contemporary Meriam experience.

The experience to which I refer is summed up by the term 'occupation', in the sense of living on Mer among Meriam people. It refers less to the precepts and traditions by which Meriam sometimes represent themselves and their culture than to the sensuous everyday experience of being there. When I first lived on Mer, occupation included a steady round of gardening and harvesting, for prestige as well as subsistence, on land that had been inherited from ancestors, known and unknown, and that bore witness to one's relatedness to those who held adjacent lots. This occupation was in crisis, however, as the younger men, unable to earn money at home, looked to a new life among white people on the mainland. Those who still valued island custom (itself, by that time, a self-conscious mix of Meriam, South Sea and European practices) could no longer take it for granted, but must defend it. It was at this moment that, in Walter Benjamin's words, they 'seized hold of a memory as it flashed up at a moment of danger' (Benjamin 1969, p. 255). Twenty years later, gardening had lost much of its earlier importance, but when the Meriam discovered that it was the Crown that owned their islands, and all the government would offer them was a fifty-year lease, land became synonymous with the community's survival. Meanwhile, for those on the mainland, the dream of modernity had faded and many had begun to think of going home or, if that was not a possibility, to worry about their land, for to be an Islander — even on the mainland — one must have an island, and to have an island, one must own a piece of it. Once again they grasped their past as it flashed by and went to law.

Acknowledgment

This chapter was first published in 1995 in *Australian Journal of Anthropology*, vol. 6, nos 1–2. My thanks to Dr Nonie Sharp for her comments.

NOTES

1. Bruce's contribution is particularly evident in Volumes I (1935) and VI (1908) of the *Reports*.
2. *Land Bilong Islanders* was made by Sharon Connolly and Trevor Graham. It was released by Ronin Films, Canberra, in 1990.
3. I suspect that some parents delayed making a will in order to maintain control over their children.
4. Idriess also consulted Rev William MacFarlane, an Anglican priest who collected anthropological material in the Torres Strait between the wars, and wrote an introduction to the book.
5. Since hereditary titles are generally absent from the Torres Strait, it may be that *Aet* was a personal name, owned — like other names — by certain descent lines associated with the cult of Malu-Bomai. From such a practice, it is a short step to the idea of title.

6. The text is most readily found in Lawrie (1970, pp. 337–8).
7. I heard this story as early as 1958, and indeed it is probable that the custodians of the sacred mask would have attempted to conceal it from the missionaries, as they did the mask of Waiat (Haddon 1935, pp. 398–9).
8. Apart from the Cambridge Expedition in 1898, and the work of the missionary William MacFarlane in the 1920s, at least twelve researchers have visited Mer since my visit in 1958–61.

REFERENCES

Beckett, J 1987, *Torres Strait Islanders: Custom and Colonialism*, Cambridge University Press, Melbourne.

Benjamin, W 1969, *Illuminations*, Schocken Books, New York.

Campbell, J 1827, Letter to Captain Piper, 1 March, Piper Papers, vol. 3, p. 180, Manuscripts Catalogue, Mitchell Library, Sydney, No. A256.

Forbes, J 1993, '*Mabo* decision leaves some vital queries on evidence unanswered', *Financial Review*, 30 June.

Haddon, AC 1908, *Sociology, Magic and Religion of the Eastern Islanders: Reports of the Cambridge Anthropological Expedition to Torres Strait, Volume VI*, Cambridge University Press, Cambridge.

Hewat, T 1993, *Who Made the Mabo Mess?* Wright Books, Melbourne.

High Court of Australia 1992, *Order re Eddie Mabo & Ors (Plaintiffs) and the State of Queensland.*

Hunt, AE 1899, 'Ethnographical notes on the Murray islands, Torres Strait', *Journal of the Royal Anthropological Institute*, vol. 28, pp. 5–18.

Idriess, IL 1938, *Drums of Mer*, Angus & Robertson, Sydney.

Jacobs, JM 1988, 'The construction of identity', in J Beckett (ed.), *Past and Present: The Construction of Aboriginality*, Aboriginal Studies Press, Canberra.

Lawrie, M 1970, *Myths and Legends of Torres Strait*, University of Queensland Press, Brisbane.

Moynihan, M 1990, *Determination Pursuant to Reference of 27 February, 1986, by the High Court of Australia to the Supreme Court of Queensland to Hear and Determine all Issues of Fact Raised by the Pleadings, Particulars and Further Particulars in High Court Action B12 of 1982.*

Sanders, W 1994, *Mabo and Native Title: Origins and Institutional Implications*, Centre for Aboriginal Economic Policy Research, ANU, Canberra.

Sharp, N 1993a, *Stars of Tagai: The Torres Strait Islanders*, Aboriginal Studies Press, Canberra.

—— 1993b, 'No ordinary case: Reflections upon *Mabo [No. 2]*', *Sydney Law Review*, vol. 15, no. 2, pp. 143–58.

Chapter 10

Aboriginality, Citizenship and Nation-State

Gerald Sider (1987, p. 3) has recently observed that:

> If the expansion and consolidation of state power simply undermined, homogenized, and ultimately destroyed the distinctive societies and ethnic groups in its grasp, as various acculturation or melting-pot theories would have it, the world would long ago have run out of diverse ways of life ... To the contrary, state power must not only destroy but also generate cultural differentiation ... the historic career of ethnic peoples can thus best be understood in the context of forces that give a people birth and simultaneously seek to take their lives.

One should not, however, conclude that the state is in full control of the situation. Even the weakest people have their small ways of frustrating the plans of the powerful. However, the mode of their incorporation may be such that they are enabled actively to contest government practice — and may even be required to do so. If the state has in some sense brought such entities into existence, it is not therefore able to extinguish them at will, or fully control them.

Writing more generally of the United States, Frances Fox Piven and Richard Cloward argue that 'state policies have always helped create and nurture the political forces with which the state has then to contend' (1985, p. 184). Although they propose this as a general principle, exemplified by the manufacturing interests emerging as a result of protective tariffs or the railroad companies forming as a result of subsidies, they are principally concerned with the way the US welfare state has patterned popular political organisation, creating 'new organizations and collectivities — and therefore new political forces — through its welfare policies' (1985, pp. 184–5).

Piven and Cloward include among these groupings ethnic peoples of the kind that Sider (1987) writes about. All three writers implicitly call into question the status of a collectivity that is culturally defined in terms of essences and an existence extending back to time immemorial. But this is not a matter of challenging the authenticity of a people's cultural tradition, or of their historical experience as it is passed on to succeeding generations, so much as an insistence that these things cannot be understood apart from their relationship with the state. Moreover, if an ethnic — or Indigenous — person maintains his or her own sense of identity, and if families and communities continue to reproduce the social and cultural forms through which they redistribute the impact of their socio-political environment, they cannot control the definition of who and what they are in the wider society, any more than they control their lives. If what Sally Weaver (1984) has called 'private ethnicity' sustains a group's political actions in the wider arena, it also exists in tension with and in the shadow of the public ethnicity as it is practised in that wider arena, by ethnic as well as other actors.[1]

The state looms particularly large in the history of the Australian Aborigines over the last two hundred years. As the Australian nation-state has taken form, the situation of the Aborigines in relation to it has become a *problem*, in the sense of being something that requires the state to find a *solution*. In fact, Australia has been trying to *solve* this problem over a long period, and in the last thirty years has devoted considerable resources and concern to the task, only to find it looming yet larger and assuming new forms. And, as the country celebrates two centuries as a European colony of settlement, well-known publications such as *Le Monde Diplomatique*, *Time Magazine*, the London *Times* and the *New York Times* have qualified their congratulations with reports of the discrimination and deprivation that Aboriginal people experience in Australia. Aboriginal protestors have appeared on television screens throughout the world, while the Australian press has devoted daily space to Aboriginal issues. These facts are, at first glance, surprising. The poverty, ill health and oppression — both political and cultural — of Aboriginal people are real enough, but these do not in themselves explain the attention the Aboriginal *issue* commands. The wretched of the earth are, after all, legion. In any case, the Aborigines number less than 2 per cent of the Australian population, and are thinly dispersed through the remoter parts of the country, while their urban representation is virtually invisible. Non-Aboriginal Australians, like the rest of the world, 'see' Aborigines mainly through the media.

The media, however, construct Aborigines as a problem, whether of ill health, poor housing, unemployment, denial of civil rights and discrimination; or of parasitism, alcoholism, unacceptable conduct and vulnerability to agitators. Either way, the problem is laid at the door of the government, which is required to 'do something'. This attribution is understandable, since the government has numerous agencies and programs dedicated to dealing with such matters, which are paid for 'out of the taxpayer's pocket'. Moreover, such matters are periodically reported overseas, to the detriment of Australia's 'image', of which the government is supposed to be the guardian. That almost all aspects of the 'Aboriginal problem' are the concern of the national government helps to explain why the media devote so much space to it. For its part, the state is so inextricably bound up with the Aborigines, politically and administratively, that it cannot easily disengage; rather, each effort to solve the problem binds the two closer together. The implication of this is that the state is an integral part of the problem it is supposed to be solving.

To explicate this assertion I shall review the changing relationship between the Australian state and the Aborigines in terms of the concepts of colonialism and citizenship, and a blending of the two which, following Robert Paine (1977), I call welfare colonialism. I should make clear that I am giving a political definition to colonial, for while the expansion of Western capitalism may, in the last instance, be counted as economic, analysis solely in these terms may leave out of account military logistics, the pre-emptive seizure of territory, diplomacy and the maintenance of law and order, which may be the primary considerations in a particular time or place. Colonialism, then, refers to that aspect of Western expansion whereby new peoples are incorporated into a conquering state. Colonial relations derive from this event, as institutionalisations of the distinction between conquerors and conquered. Such relations, which have been characteristic of colonies of settlement as diverse as Mexico, the United States and Australia, become problematical when these territories become independent. The formation of a new state entails the definition of citizenship, which is to say participation (Turner 1986, p. 134), and poses the question of who is to enjoy it. Australia started out by reproducing existing colonial relations between the descendants of natives and settlers, making citizenship the privilege of the latter. Its recent attempts to extend citizenship to the Aborigines have run afoul of these pre-existing structures, giving rise to the curious hybrid of welfare colonialism. But in order to clarify these statements, we need to look briefly at the development of the Australian state itself.

Colony, state and nation

From the beginning, the state loomed large in the development of Australia as a European colony of settlement. The government of the United Kingdom originally established it as a penal colony, and though its grazing lands and mineral resources soon made it a valuable outpost of British capitalism, the authorities regulated access to these things. They also controlled the supply of labour, first in the persons of transported convicts, and subsequently and for much longer through sponsorship and exclusion of particular categories of immigrant. As government passed from Whitehall to the six colonies during the second half of the nineteenth century, these powers may have been exercised more closely in keeping with local interests, but they were for the most part retained.

Government in the colonies was already well established when Australia became a Dominion in 1901, and since the colonies retained most of their powers as states within the federation, the national government was left with a minor role in domestic affairs. However, one of its first acts was to stop the importation of cheap coloured labour, a measure with considerable implications for the domestic labour market, but justified in terms of defending a White Australia (De Lepervanche 1975). Canberra's responsibility for the national interest enabled it gradually to expand its internal authority, particularly during the Second World War. Conflicts between state and federal governments continue to characterise the Australian state, with Canberra able to offset internal against external political pressures, as the states cannot.

Despite strong trade unions and a broadly based Labor Party, Australia has stopped well short of state socialism, with only transportation and communications under direct ownership. However, the federal government has controlled immigration, and protected local industries through tariff control and subsidies. It has, at times, set a basic wage, and appointed arbitration courts to settle wage disputes. Although, compared with Scandinavia or Britain, Australia is scarcely a welfare state, it has supplemented incomes and subsidised the reproduction of labour through various kinds of welfare payments. It has also assisted special categories of people, such as newly arrived immigrants and people living in remote areas, as well as the disadvantaged — including Aborigines. State schools serve the majority of children, while parochial and private schools depend to a greater or lesser degree on subsidies. Tertiary education and research are almost wholly funded by the state, while sports and the arts receive substantial assistance.

The trade union-based Australian Labor Party (ALP) has ever been ideologically committed to state intervention, and its 1941–49 and 1972–75 periods of office have seen substantial growth in the welfare sector. But intervention — including welfare payments — has not been reduced significantly, and in some instances has been increased, during the long periods of conservative government; correspondingly, cutbacks have also been the response of ALP administrations to financial stringencies. Taking the long view, both right and left have oriented their policies towards broad constituencies such as the old, young families, widows and, in recent years, ethnic groups and Aborigines (see Macintyre 1985). One explanation for this may be that, despite rhetoric to the contrary, welfare has been rather a matter of compulsory saving on the part of the working class, against such contingencies as old age, sickness and unemployment, than a taking from the rich to give to the poor (Shaver 1987).

Whatever the case, government in Australia can be described as the application of liberal democratic institutions in the management of a small, relatively prosperous, semi-peripheral capitalist society. This management has been conducted in the name of a public interest, variously defined according to time and place in terms of economic development, social justice, national integration and external security.

Citizenship, as the term was used by the sociologist of post-war Britain, TH Marshall (1963, pp. 67–127), and as it has been used in Brian Turner's recent re-evaluation of Marshall's ideas (1986), brings certain key features of twentieth-century Australia into focus. Briefly, Marshall argues that while capitalism has given rise to naked economic inequality, it has also — at least in the liberal democracies — given rise to countervailing forms of civil, political and social equality, as embodied in the legal system, the franchise and the provision of services such as education, pensions for the aged and infirm, and basic medical care. In its developed form, the welfare state undertakes not only to prevent anyone from falling below some 'poverty line', but entertains a wide diversity of claims. While the rights of citizenship may, in the final analysis, have the function of maintaining capitalist hegemony, they are historically the outcome of political struggle, bringing material gains that are periodically threatened (cf. Turner 1986, p. 136). Again, while one may wish to derive this struggle from underlying class conflict, it must also be seen as an outcome of parliamentary government, based on universal suffrage, with diverse 'social movements' as the extra-parliamentary protagonists (Turner 1986, pp. 88–92; Piven and Cloward 1985).

By Federation, Australia had already instituted a variant of the British legal and governmental systems, including votes for all citizens – even women. There was already free elementary education, while the first social service enactments were only a few years off. But for whom were these privileges available? Turner (1986, p. 46) insists that national citizenship cannot be discussed 'without considering the constitution of the nation state', and he goes on to argue that the growth of citizenship in Britain entailed losses for the Celtic fringe. Similarly, the Australia that came into existence in 1901 was emphatically a white Australia, and it promptly established this identity by deporting indentured labourers from the Pacific islands. Taking the White Australia policy as its outer defence, the new nation set about forging its identity in terms of its primary relationship to the British Isles. In 1908, the Australian Labor Party stated as its platform 'The cultivation of an Australian sentiment based upon racial purity' (DeMaria 1987, p. 38).[2] Australia followed Britain into the First World War without hesitation, and while those of Irish descent opposed conscription, many volunteered to return to the old world to fight Britain's war. That Australia should create a ritual and mythology out of its soldiers' participation in Britain's disastrous Gallipoli campaign suggests that there was a cultural necessity for nationhood to be defined in relation to the 'mother country'.

Australia used the British national anthem until the 1970s, and still makes the Union Jack part of its flag; nevertheless, the British component in Australian national identity began to weaken after the Second World War. Among the factors in this change were no doubt Britain's military collapse in the Far East and its post-war decline, followed by its economic reorientation away from its former colonial territories and towards Europe. Australia, in turn, became a client of the United States and then of its old enemy, Japan. While it might hope for American protection against the Chinese communist 'menace', it came to recognise the necessity for good relations with the newly independent European colonies of South-East Asia.

Australia's need for immigrants to augment its tiny population and work in its developing economy soon forced it to look beyond the British Isles, first to northern and eastern Europe, then to the Mediterranean and the Levant, and Latin America. The dropping of the White Australia policy in the 1970s served the multiple purposes of improving relations with its South-East Asian neighbours and attracting Chinese capital, although in recent years the bulk of immigrants have been refugees from Vietnam.

Most immigrants had the option of becoming naturalised, and many of the benefits of citizenship were available to foreign nationals permanently resident in the country. Assimilation was the official doctrine of the program, with expectation that the children of immigrants, if not their parents, would embrace the 'Australian way of life'. By the 1960s, however, that way of life was changing, and with it the old forms of British identity. Although the idea might not be formally articulated — except satirically in Donald Horne's *Lucky Country* (1964) — what people in Australia (with the notable exception of the Aborigines) shared was a sense of participation in a process of ever expanding prosperity (cf. Lees and Senyard 1987). As White (1981, p. 195) has remarked, something called the 'Australian way of life' had replaced race and national type as the basis for Australian identity.

In Australia, as elsewhere, the later years of the long boom were characterised by a concern with style in consumption and leisure and an emphasis on cultural diversity in everything from religion to food. Among the many innovations proposed (if not always executed) by the Whitlam Labor government of 1972–75 was the doctrine of multiculturalism. Associated with the discovery of 'the ethnic vote', it celebrated the cultural diversity of the new Australia and encouraged the preservation of non-Anglo-Saxon cultural activities such as folk dancing and cooking. At the same time, elements of the old Australia were rediscovered and revived as folklore, in such media as the new Australian film industry and 'ocker' advertising. Effectively, the immigrant ethnicities cancelled one another out, while the Anglo-Celtic strain re-emerged as predominant when Australia was constructed historically — as it later was in the Bicentennial celebrations. In the process, however, Aborigines also acquired a historically privileged position as the First Australians, while emerging as the victims of colonisation to whom restitution must be made.[3] This development was made possible by the popular cultural pluralism of the period, but was also the expression of a radical critique of Australian society, which — as in the case of the women's movement — moved from a simplistic formulation of equality of opportunity towards a celebration of submerged and suppressed values.[4]

Outside the nation, inside the state

With rare individual exceptions, the six colonies had denied the Aborigines citizenship, and Federation did nothing to change their situation. Membership of the new nation was reserved for whites, preferably those of British descent. The Aborigines could not be deported as the Chinese and Pacific Islanders would be, but a 'Stone Age people' had no place in a modern Australia, and it was confidently expected that those still living would soon follow the many 'extinct tribes' into the past where they belonged. Meanwhile, they could be left in the care of the state governments, which had already made provision for their management, insofar as it seemed necessary. The national government concerned itself with Aborigines only to the extent of excluding them from its provisions, and when it took charge of the Northern Territory in 1910, it did rather less than the state governments (Larbalestier 1988).

The first Governor of New South Wales was under instruction to maintain friendly relations with the Aborigines, and in due course convert them into useful members of the colony. He did not, however, go so far as to recognise them as a sovereign people with whom treaties must be made, or as owners of the land on which they lived (Maddock 1983). Thus, once pastoralism began encroaching on Aboriginal land, violence was inevitable; and being unable to protect settlers on the frontier, the authorities had little option but to resort to punitive expeditions. Under pressure from humanitarian groups in Britain, they attempted to prevent the settlers from taking the law into their own hands, and in the case of the Myall Creek massacre, executed convicts who had killed blacks without specific provocation. However, the public outcry was so great that they looked the other way when killings were perpetrated in later years. The settlers who took control of the colonial governments in the second half of the nineteenth century had few compunctions about wholesale killings, though in the twentieth century they were more circumspect (Reynolds 1987; Evans 1975).

By the end of the century, Aborigines lived independently only in those parts of the north and centre of the continent that were inhospitable to European settlement. In many settled areas, there were no Aborigines, the original occupants of the land having been killed off or succumbed to the diseases the settlers had introduced. Tasmania pronounced its Aborigines extinct, despite the survival of a small population of part-Aborigines living on Cape Barren Island. Here and there, however, small groups survived in various forms of dependence on the settlers' enterprises. Many of the vast sheep and cattle stations of the interior included a 'blacks camp', which constituted a pool of casual labour and sexual partners for the white stockmen. Smaller groups — even single families — attached themselves to mines and farms, or travelled from place to place in search of work. But there were others who could find no place in the workforce, or who were too ravaged by disease, malnutrition and demoralisation to sustain the necessary physical exertion. The mixture of pity, fear and disgust that their squalid camps aroused among the gentrifying townsfolk, near whose homes they squatted, inevitably led to a clamour for something to be done (for a contemporary instance of the same response, see Sackett 1988).

The churches had early attempted to establish missions among the Aborigines, but they all foundered — usually because they lacked the funds to keep a flock together for any length of time. They were to establish a number of successful missions in the north during the early years of the twentieth century, among Aborigines who could partially support themselves by traditional pursuits, or find employment on European cattle stations or bêche-de-mer boats. But meanwhile, the destitute and the unwanted were left to government. The first gestures — the appointment of part-time officials, often local settlers, to distribute blankets and rations, and the allocation of small reserves — proved insufficient. What followed at various times and in various forms in the mainland states was the introduction of legislation, establishing government agencies that were to take charge of the Aborigines. These agencies were given powers over the persons and property of Aborigines, comparable only to those to which the orphan and the insane were subject.

Up to the 1930s, official policy might be termed protective segregation — though whether Aborigines were being protected from evil whites, as its advocates claimed, rather than respectable whites being protected from unwanted blacks, is open to question. The principal instrument of this policy was the supervised institution, to which Aborigines might be sent, and where they might be detained. These consisted of 'children's homes' and settlements where families might live throughout their lives. In some instances, the inmates also worked on these institutions, though in most cases the men and young women were sent out to work for white employers.

Although the bureaucratic impulse seemed to be for all Aborigines to be confined to such places, the resources were insufficient. Nevertheless, those who remained outside lived under the shadow of institutionalisation, since they were all subject to the special attention of police-protectors and welfare officers, and liable to confinement should some official so decree. During the twentieth century, church missions fulfilled a similar role, and received government subsidies for their services. Larger cattle stations were also permitted to maintain a number of Aboriginal families, and in later years were effectively paid for doing so (see Larbalestier 1988; Peterson 1985). Though varying in the extent and kinds of control they exercised, these institutions formed part of a total structure of domination orchestrated by the state.

The Aboriginal inmates of these 'total institutions' had something in common with the Anglo-Celtic inmates of orphanages or asylums for the destitute, inebriates and the insane, who might be confined involuntarily 'for their own good', but who should still be grateful for what was considered charity rather than a right. Orphans, however, were returned to society when they grew up, inebriates when they gave up and the insane when they recovered. Aborigines, like mental defectives, had no prospect of release.

As the name implies, the status 'Aboriginal' was derived from the initial encounter between 'native and settler', but between that moment and the time — a century and more after — when the states drafted their legislation, the distinction had taken on an arbitrary quality. In particular, the usual classification of the sizeable mixed-descent population — variously called 'half-castes' and 'mixed-bloods' — as Aborigines could only be achieved through a manipulation of folk-genetics.

The colonial status conferred on persons deemed to be descended from the original inhabitants of the country was opposed to the citizenship to which Australians of northern European, particularly British, descent were entitled. According to the prevailing social Darwinism of the period, Aborigines were an anachronism in a progressive nation, and in the natural course of events would soon disappear, leaving a white Australia. The half-caste posed a conundrum in this respect, although some eugenicists asserted that the results of racial mixture were inherently unstable and would either die out or revert to the lower type. Meanwhile, such persons were scarcely acceptable to a new nation that was eager to stand well with the Old Country, and which in moments of unease feared that life in the tropics would produce an Australian version of Latin America. It was doubtless such fears that led to the exclusion of Aborigines from the armed forces, and so from the 'nation-forming' experience of the First World War.

Aborigines were denied the franchise that was the automatic right of Anglo-Celtic Australians. They were also denied normal legal rights, being in practice subject to settlement supervisors, missionaries or station owners, who were simultaneously prosecutor, judge and jailer. Their participation in the economy was likewise different from that of other Australians, and subject to special restrictions. The concentration of Aborigines in unskilled casual and seasonal work may originally have been the preference of people still unbroken to labour discipline, but both workers and employers found it advantageous to keep them there. The cattle station system tied Aborigines to particular employers, who paid the camp rather than the individual, and in kind rather than in cash (cf. Larbalestier 1988). The supervisors of government settlements and missions also paid their workers in rations (cf. Rowse 1988), and often exercised control over their employment and wages. This control was most highly developed in Queensland, where protectors negotiated employment on the Aboriginals' behalf. There was a fixed wage — albeit a fraction of that earned by a non-Aboriginal doing similar work — but the protector held the money on behalf of the worker, releasing such amounts as he thought fit or simply debiting purchases against the money held.

Aborigines were likewise excluded from welfare entitlements. When the federal parliament passed the inaugural *Invalid and Old Age Pensions Act* in 1908, it rejected an amendment including 'Asiatics' and natives of various colonial territories, including Australia (DeMaria 1986, p. 26). It remained for the state protectors to provide for old and invalid Aborigines, at a more modest cost. During the Great Depression, Aborigines who had lived independently as rural workers were denied the unemployment relief given to whites and directed to the nearest government settlement, where they would receive rations and shelter. DeMaria explains such discrimination in terms of the White Australia policy. To leave it there, however, is to take the welfare system at its ideological face value. In part at least, the pensions and the dole were responses to pressure from the working-class movement, or perhaps to the threat of working class mobilisation. Aborigines were not part of this movement, being with rare exceptions excluded from union membership. Again, pensions must be seen as part of the apparatus for the reproduction of the labour force in a situation of population shortage: Aborigines were expected to die out.

Australians but not yet citizens

The idea that the Aborigines would die out seems to have relieved governments of the need to articulate a long-term policy for some time after the population decline had bottomed out. They were, however, aware of the burgeoning mixed-descent population, and were at times disposed to deny it the relief that had been designated for the disappearing 'full-blood'. But since most 'half-castes' had been raised with their black mothers, seeing nothing of their white fathers, and since they encountered much the same hostility in the majority population, they remained a charge on the state. However, their possession of 'white blood' allowed some officials to argue that, if removed from their Aboriginal relatives and subjected to intense 'training', they could become self-supporting in the wider community. Neville, the long-serving Director of Native Affairs in Western Australia, went so far as to propose a scheme of selective mating towards the end of 'breeding out the colour' and sparing Australia the racial problems suffered by the United States (Neville 1947). While his colleagues in other states stopped short of such eugenic engineering, they shared the same perspective, and regularly removed part-Aboriginal children to institutions, where they could be taught 'useful skills'. At a national conference in 1936 the officials in charge of 'natives' throughout Australia formally adopted what became known as the Assimilation Policy for the 'lighter caste' element.

The so-called full-blood Aborigines were not included in this policy, and in the view of both Western Australia and Queensland their future was perpetual isolation from the rest of the society. The federal government was itself trying to formulate a policy for the long-neglected Aborigines of the Northern Territory, particularly those of as yet undeveloped Arnhem Land, many of whom were only intermittently in contact with Europeans. Rejecting an anthropologist's recommendation that it leave the latter undisturbed, the government proposed to incorporate these Aborigines administratively. In 1939, it declared citizenship as the eventual status of all Aboriginal people (cf. Larbalestier 1988; Rowse 1988), a goal that was to be achieved through education and training in an institutional setting — in other words, through an intensification of colonial control.

Though assimilation, as this policy came to be known, may have appeared the logical choice, given the circumstances of the time, it was also a response to public pressure. Since the 1920s, small but persistent groups in the southern cities had subjected Australia's treatment of its Aborigines to critical scrutiny. Mostly church based, and headed by the clergyman-anthropologist, AP Elkin, they were able to speak with both moral and scientific authority, and having connections with Britain were in a position to embarrass the government. During the 1930s, there was also unrest in various Indigenous communities (see below) which, though easily contained, must have worried a nation living in fear of invasion from the north. A disaffected black population living along Australia's poorly defended and sparsely populated northern coastline could not but be regarded as a security risk, the more so since Japanese pearl divers had been in contact with that population for some fifty years (cf. Beckett 1987, pp. 62–5).

Although the war required that the new training programs be postponed, it provided Canberra with the opportunity for increasing Aboriginal participation. However, tentative moves in this direction soon became entangled in the web of colonial regulation. Though the law excluded the recruitment of Aborigines, the army formed a contingent of Torres Strait Islanders (Hall 1989) — partly, no doubt, because of their local knowledge of a strategically sensitive area, but also perhaps because their close association with Japanese divers before the war made it advisable to secure their loyalty. At the request of the Queensland government, however, the pay was pegged at a level consistent with earnings in the pearling industry, a fraction of what white soldiers received.[5] Aborigines — most of mixed descent — in the regular armed forces were paid at regular rates, but the numbers were relatively small and in some areas volunteers were rejected.[6]

The introduction of child endowment in the 1940s also provided an opportunity to include people who had previously been denied old age pensions. However, as William DeMaria (1986) has shown, Aborigines did not enjoy automatic entitlement until 1959. Before this, many were refused or had their money paid to some white authority. Queensland favoured the payment of benefits to people living on its settlements, no doubt welcoming the reduction in calls on its own resources. Since it held their money on their behalf, its powers were in no way reduced. Commonwealth officials, for their part, were often reluctant to release benefits to those who were already provided for by special agencies, preferring to include only those who were living independently. The states, however, protested that this provided an undesirable incentive for Aborigines to leave the settlements. Employers were no doubt alarmed at the prospect of their cheap labour force receiving alternative sources of income and 'learning the value of money'. Even after the legislation of 1959, Canberra diverted welfare money to the cattle stations and missions (Peterson 1985, p. 88).

It was not just bureaucratic prejudice that frustrated these reforms, but the contradictory nature of the Assimilation Policy, which used the goal of eventual entry into the community as a justification for segregating Aborigines on settlements, and the goal of eventual citizenship as a justification for curtailing their civil rights. Official propaganda celebrating the 'assimilated' Aboriginal, who lived like a white man, excelled at some approved activity and was 'accepted in the community', was also a way of stating the need to 'do something' about the Aboriginal living a dependent existence in some government institution.[7] As Barry Morris (1989, p. 1) has observed of New South Wales:

> The residues of the more metaphysical view of the Aborigine as the 'irredeem-
> able leper' trapped in his own inherent imperfections were progressively

removed. The disciplinary and surveillance policies of monitoring and correction of the 'redeemable plague victim' gained ascendancy during this new era of state control. The stress on environment as the source of the Aboriginal 'problem' underpinned the escalation of pedagogical/sociological intervention of state power.

The government settlement or church mission was the locus and instrument of this policy, and the number of Aboriginal people living under supervised circumstances increased during the period. Housing, schooling and medical care were provided for the inmates; these were of varying quality but generally better than what had been provided before. Personnel underwent training for service in the Northern Territory and on some missions.

A long-term objective of these programs was that Aborigines should come to adopt white Australian patterns of consumption, and acquire the working skills required to pay for them. But although occasionally successful, it came up against entrenched Aboriginal practices, such as sharing, as well as the long-standing use of cheap Aboriginal labour by powerful groups such as the cattle industry. Government had effectively to subsidise the low, and in some instances non-existent, wages — either by supporting the workers' families or giving funds to cattle stations on which Aborigines lived. Notwithstanding these payments, Aboriginal people remained on the average much poorer than other Australians, and their living conditions were often well below acceptable standards.

The need to solve the Aboriginal problem had in the meantime become more pressing. As Paul Hasluck, the architect of the federal policy, told his parliamentary colleagues, Australia could not raise its voice in world affairs if it had failed to solve this problem (Stone 1974, p. 194). More to the point, it could not win the respect of its new neighbours to the north if it appeared to perpetuate colonial practices and colour discrimination. At home, the continuing poverty and deprivation of Aborigines gave the lie to the ideology of ever-increasing prosperity for all (cf. Lees and Senyard 1987), while the American civil rights struggle, featured on television, brought new respectability to local protest movements. The most important of these, the Federal Council for the Advancement of Aborigines and Torres Strait Islanders (FCAATSI), formed in 1959, drew attention to the meagre achievements of the assimilation policy and the denial of civil rights that it entailed.

Increasingly pressed, the federal government began dismantling its colonial apparatus. It removed the restrictions on Aboriginal eligibility for various social service benefits in 1959. In 1962, it extended the federal franchise to Aborigines and set about removing the various legal disabilities to which they had been subject in the Northern Territory. Directly and indirectly, the states found themselves under pressure to follow suit, with New South Wales and Victoria actually dissolving their Aborigines Welfare Boards.

But while discriminatory laws could be removed from the statute book in a moment, the task of bringing Aborigines in from the cold — where the great majority remained — had scarcely begun, despite twenty years of assimilation programs. Not only were there no Aboriginal professionals and only a handful of university graduates, but few had completed high school or apprenticeships. While some Aboriginal people of European appearance lived in southern towns and cities, their foothold in the labour market was tenuous, and they remained socially isolated. The countryside was studded with Aboriginal enclaves — often government settlements — characterised by unemployment, poverty, ill health and hostile relations with non-Aboriginal neighbours. If this was the case after generations of coexistence, what was the prospect for assimilation in the north, where contact had been of shorter duration, and where the candidates were either peons on cattle stations or the recipients of rations on remote church missions and government settlements?[8]

Ironically, the legal reforms coincided with the first faltering of the long post-war boom, particularly in the industries for which Aborigines had provided cheap labour. The result was a decommodification of Aboriginal labour. An attempt to introduce equal wages in the Northern Territory and Western Australian cattle industry, coinciding with an economic downturn and other changes, resulted in the dismissal of long-serving Aboriginal workers and the dispersal of families long resident on the properties, who had nowhere to go but government settlements (cf. Peterson 1985). Contrary to earlier hopes, the new mines emerging in the north had little use for Aborigines. Moreover, according to Nicolas Peterson (1985, p. 92), once Northern Territory Aborigines received their social service benefits in cash, they found they could live from them at least as well as they had when they were employed, and often ceased to look for work. The depressed rural industries of the southern states also offered less of the seasonal and casual work by which Aborigines had lived in earlier years. In New South Wales, the government had tried relocating Aboriginal families to urban areas, but unemployment rates were already high among urban Aborigines, and employers were unlikely to hire unskilled Aborigines from the bush when they could obtain skilled and tractable labour from overseas.[9]

Relocation also posed problems of adaptation, not only for Aboriginal people but for their non-Aboriginal neighbours. In the recent past, the settling of a few rural families in country towns had evoked resistance from local residents; families coming in from remote settlements and cattle stations would be even less acceptable to northern townsfolk, particularly in the Northern Territory, where the Aboriginal component of the population was higher. In the previous period, the authorities had discouraged Aboriginal movement to the towns, and had the legal powers to remove them. But restrictions on movement were no longer acceptable and, while the general view was that town living was bad for Aborigines, unsightly and disorderly camps were growing up on the fringes of Darwin, Alice Springs and Tennant Creek (Rowse 1988; Sansom 1980). The white backlash that these developments presaged could itself be politically embarrassing for a federal government whose principal constituency lay in the southern cities, and that was concerned with opinion overseas.[10]

To add to the government's troubles, towards the end of the 1960s, the moderate white-led FCAATSI was giving way to a more aggressive urban Aboriginal leadership that had adopted the rhetoric of the United States Black Power movement. Though initially small, it developed quickly during the period of protest, and in 1972 it claimed to speak for all Aborigines when it established a Tent Embassy on the lawns of Parliament House in Canberra. The government attempted to ignore the embassy, but the opposition and other public figures accorded it recognition, and the media gave it full coverage. The government's attempts to evict it by force provided dramatic television footage, which was diffused throughout the country.

Although no one was yet ready to admit the fact, assimilation was at best a remote possibility. The immediate prospect was of Aboriginal enclaves eking out an existence by a combination of welfare payments and whatever could be got from hunting and foraging, which in some localities was very little. A government looking for a quick solution to an increasingly embarrassing problem must try something different.

Aboriginality restored

By the end of the 1960s, it must have been apparent that the only solution to Aboriginal poverty was a massive infusion of government funds into existing communities. It might be possible in some places to set up industries with some semblance of economic viability; in others, there could be nothing beyond government make-work programs. In either case, there was no alternative to providing housing, medical services and schools at the taxpayer's expense. An implication of this was that the institutions that had earlier been established as refuges for a dying race, or as transitional settlements pending assimilation, must now be reconstituted as permanent communities, which on some ground deserved special assistance. The justification for their existence would be that Aborigines were, after all, a culturally distinct people who, though free to move as they pleased, also had the right to live apart if they wished. Although they were not thereby to be divested of their newly won citizenship, their well-being would in practice depend on a special, collective relationship with the state, and particularly the federal government. Ironically, although no one may have intended it, the new dispensation provided a charter for Aborigines to live at a lower material level than other Australians: their poverty had been rendered exotic, and so no longer comparable to other forms of poverty. This cultural screen became important as the government discovered the difficulty of its task and the impossibility of completing it, given shrinking funds.

Initiatives emanated mainly from the federal government, but were intended to apply to the whole country, not just the Northern Territory. As such, they were part of the overall trend towards centralisation to which we referred earlier, and figured in the resulting struggle between Canberra and the states. In the case of Aboriginal affairs, the change can be traced back to the referendum that the conservative government submitted to the Australian electorate in 1967 (Bennett 1985).[11] In it, more than 90 per cent of voters approved changes to the Constitution which, though indirectly stated, in fact authorised the Commonwealth parliament to pass laws affecting Aborigines throughout the country. For the next five years, a three-man Council for Aboriginal Affairs, including the architect of post-war reconstruction, HC Coombs, the anthropologist WEH Stanner, and a former diplomat, Barry Dexter, conducted inquiries and made recommendations on national policy to the federal government. Until the election of the Whitlam Labor government in 1972, however, Canberra preferred to influence the states informally rather than intervene directly — see, for example, its attempt to persuade Queensland to liberalise (Nettheim 1981, pp. 6–7).

The election of the Labor government at the end of 1972, on a reform platform, provided an opportunity for a radical break with assimilation. Among its first measures was the establishment of a Department of Aboriginal Affairs and the setting up of branch offices throughout the country. In the months that followed, the government also established nationwide networks of government-financed legal, medical and educational services for Aborigines and Islanders, as well as agencies for fostering Aboriginal arts and crafts. This administration also convened a national assembly of elected Aboriginal and Torres Strait representatives to be based in Canberra. To complicate matters, the states maintained their own agencies which, although directly or indirectly financed by the Commonwealth, often acted in parallel to, and sometimes in competition with, the Department of Aboriginal Affairs (for the case of Queensland, see Beckett 1987, pp. 185–201).

Under the new dispensation, the state formally recognised the existence of the Aborigines, but left Aboriginal people to determine which individuals could and should qualify. Previous governments had formally defined Aborigines in genetic terms, while practically defining them through application of the special powers; now an Aboriginal was someone who identified as such and whose identification was recognised by other Aborigines. The implication was that Aboriginality was an honourable estate, entailing entitlements rather than disabilities, for which someone might freely opt. Many did opt for these entitlements, so that one might say that the government's working, if tacit, definition of Aboriginal was those who availed themselves of its services for Aborigines.

The fundamental entitlement of Aborigines under the new dispensation was to be recognised as a people — if not quite a nation — with their own values and culture, which they must be allowed to pursue as long as they wished. Indeed, as victims of colonial oppression, they must be assisted to do so. They must also be assisted to articulate and communicate their aspirations to those who handled their affairs. It was for this purpose that the National Aboriginal Consultative Council, composed of elected representatives from around the country, was convened. At an immediate level, there was to be consultation with the communities.

While the government might assist individuals to pursue a career or appoint them to positions in the emerging Aboriginal bureaucracy, its main strategy — as in other fields of social engineering at that time — was to develop the community. Conceived of as a primordial entity, though often as much the creation of colonialism, it was no longer a training institution for assimilation, but the locus of an Aboriginality that was to be a permanent presence in a multicultural Australia.

The reconstituting of the Aboriginal community coincided with the demand for land rights, which had become the focal issue for the Tent Embassy. The demand could be made in several modes: minimally as a plea for Aboriginal people to enjoy the same security of occupancy as other Australians — a serious issue in view of Queensland's relocation of the Mapoon mission a few years before; in terms of economic justice, as partial or token restitution for the original act of expropriation; and in religious terms, as a recognition of the Aborigines' spiritual relationship to the land, manifest in the performance of ceremonies by the 'traditionally oriented' in northern and central Australia, but also said to persist in the psychic makeup of Aboriginal people everywhere. Queensland was to recognise the first right in 1985; a few years earlier, New South Wales combined this with the principle of restitution (see Macdonald 1988); before any of the states, however, the federal government had instituted the religious right for the Aborigines of the Northern Territory.

Peterson (1985, p. 85) has asked how a capitalist nation-state could come to recognise or create non-capitalist forms of landholding. Indeed, one might ask how a conservative government that had voted down such legislation while in opposition could introduce similar legislation once in power, against the interests of several mining companies. Land rights, however, make sense in terms of the situation in which the federal government found itself in the Northern Territory. Not least importantly, the measure could be expected to look good overseas, and in particular strengthen the international authority of a prime minister who wished to play a part in solving the Rhodesian problem.[12] State governments, having no part in foreign affairs, could be expected to be less enthusiastic. There were also domestic considerations. Peterson (1985, p. 97) has described land rights as a welfare measure rather than compensatory justice, arguing that the new economic independence of Aborigines placed them beyond individual or family manipulation, necessitating a community strategy. Land rights served to anchor people — particularly those who had drifted away to follow a semi-subsistence existence. One might add that, since the authorities could no longer stop Aborigines from moving to the towns, the strengthened community and a guaranteed access to sacred and significant sites provided a counter attraction. It could also be argued that land rights for traditionally oriented Aborigines gave them a local interest that might be calculated to weaken the appeal of the urban-led national Aboriginal movement. Again, land rights being couched in spiritual rather than economic terms emphasised the cultural difference between Aboriginal and other Australians. On the one hand, it took the sting out of comparisons of their respective economic situation and, on the other, rendered the high expenditure on the support of non-productive communities more acceptable to the taxpayer. Indeed, this mode of managing the Aboriginal problem located it in a broader political context of causes such as multiculturalism and conservation, popular among both the electorate at large and a new generation of officials. The term 'managing' here should not be allowed to obscure the high ideals among many of those involved: the juxtaposition rather reflects the contradictory character of welfare colonialism.

Welfare colonialism

The term 'welfare colonialism' was first coined by Robert Paine (1977) to describe the situation of Indigenous people in Northern Canada. Juxtaposing terms that connote citizenship (welfare) and its denial (colonialism), he suggests a policy that is contradictory and unstable. Historically continuous with classic colonialism, it is 'solicitous rather than exploitive, and liberal rather than repressive' (1977, p. 3), yet it is still 'the colonizers who make the decisions that control the future of the colonized' and 'the decisions are made (ambiguously) on behalf of the colonized, and yet in the name of the colonizers' culture (and of their political, administrative and economic priorities)' (1977, p. 43).

In general terms, welfare colonialism is part of the political practice of the liberal democratic nation-state, which is aimed at maintaining a measure of social harmony and equity internally, and an image of moral rectitude in the world at large. Its specific application arises when, as in the case of Australia,

Canada or the United States,[13] the state finds itself embarrassed at home and abroad by the existence of a small Indigenous group, which it has constituted as a minority in the course of colonisation, but which it is unable to dissolve simply by declaring the members citizens. Cultural values and modes, whether originating before conquest or formed under conditions of colonial exclusion, cannot be cancelled by decree; moreover, the expropriation and marginalisation that are the common outcomes of colonisation have produced a level of poverty and deprivation that is beyond the capacity of the market or the welfare apparatus to remedy. The additional measures that are required make calls upon state resources that are subject to other claims. This poses the issue of equity, which is the ideological underpinning of the welfare system as a whole. Are the special measures to be justified in the same terms as other claims — for example, of social justice or material deprivation — or in terms of special needs that are not comparable with those of other claimants? Welfare colonialism follows the latter mode, rehabilitating the minority's distinctive identity as the possessors of a unique culture that must be preserved as part of the national heritage. In a sympathetic cultural environment, these arguments may justify substantial expenditure, but they also have the capacity to render poverty picturesque and social marginality an alternative lifestyle, reducing the necessity for remedial action.

While, as Paine (1977) notes, it is the colonisers who finally make the decisions, they can no longer impose them arbitrarily. Yet another contradictory feature of welfare colonialism is its need to secure the assent of its subjects as evidence of their political enfranchisement. This is required in terms of democratic values, once Indigenous peoples are included within the nation. It is also a practical measure, intended to avoid the frequent failures of government programs. Ironically, the subjects are often so politically weak and fragmented that the state is itself obliged to create the channels of political expression and articulate Indigenous aspirations. In other words, political incorporation of the Indigenous minority within the nation-state can be effected only through special structures, which institutionalise colonial distinctions while creating a political constituency that has simultaneously to be maintained and controlled.

The politics of Aboriginality

The Tent Embassy set up in 1972 amounted to a bid by a number of mostly urban Aboriginal people to speak for 'the Aboriginal nation'. Using the idiom of the United States Black Power movement, and employing the same methods as those protesting the war in Vietnam, they constituted a problem not merely for the conservative government, but for the reforming government that replaced it. A system of local self-management[14] would enable the government to deal with communities piecemeal, hopefully without risk of outsiders intervening, but at the national level the 'radicals' were rapidly assuming the role of national spokespersons, leaving the remote Aborigines all but voiceless. They were in the process of replacing the white directors of FCAATSI, and had succeeded in blocking a ministerially appointed advisory council (Cooper 1976, pp. 37–8, quoted in Weaver 1983, p. 2). But, given the impossibility of Aborigines acquiring electoral power,[15] the only alternative was a new national body. In 1973, the Minister for Aboriginal Affairs, Gordon Bryant, established the National Aboriginal Consultative Committee (NACC), consisting of 41 elected representatives.

According to Sally Weaver (1983, pp. 4–5), the National Aboriginal Consultative Committee was established as a means of stabilising Aboriginal pressure group activity and integrating it with the process of government. But, as she shows, it was scarcely a success on either count, failing to work with government to the bureaucracy's satisfaction or, given the diversity of Aboriginal people represented, to articulate an Aboriginal opinion. As in self-management organisations at the lower level (cf. Macdonald 1988), the requirement to make decisions — particularly regarding the distribution of insufficient benefits — brought pre-existing differences into the open and created the occasions for new ones. The attempt to reorganise the body as the National Aboriginal Conference (NAC), which Weaver (1983) documents, was scarcely more successful, and the government finally dissolved it in 1985.

The formation of the NACC may perhaps have prevented the development of an independent national Aboriginal body. Certainly its rise and that of other government bodies coincided with the decline of voluntary organisations such as FCAATSI and a weakening of ties with unions, student groups and churches, which had underwritten the Aboriginal movement of the 1960s. However, the result was not the destruction or co-optation of the Aboriginal movement. If no single organisation emerged, many Aboriginal people acquired political experience and contacts as members of such bodies and in public service positions. Nor did they have to surrender their freedom of action. Some used government-sponsored organisations, and even bureaucratic office, as a political base. Perceiving the government's need for Aboriginal officials and spokespersons, they demonstrated their independence by publicly criticising government policies, even attacking ministers, and by quitting their jobs, to be re-employed in some other capacity soon afterwards.[16] The licence that they enjoyed is well illustrated by the visit of a member of the Tasmanian Aboriginal Legal Service to Libya, prompting an outraged government to expel the Libyan People's Bureau from Australia while leaving the unrepentant official undisturbed. In other instances, government-funded bodies have taken legal action against the state.[17] Similarly, when in 1986 the federal government abandoned its plans to introduce national land rights legislation (see below), the protest was led by the two Northern Territory Land Councils, in alliance with similar bodies in the states.

Australia may be said to have to have created an Aboriginal constituency (cf. Piven and Cloward 1985) — if not quite as it, or perhaps the Aboriginal actors, intended. If there is still no national body with the authority to speak for Aboriginal people, there is no lack of spokespersons on whom the media can call for an opinion, and who can speak through the media when they have occasion to do so. The power of this constituency, however, is located mainly within the apparatus that the state has established for the management of Aborigines. Otherwise, as Beverley Gartrell (1986, pp. 11–12) notes, such minorities 'can only challenge the self-concepts of both bureaucratic and political office-holders, and the citizens of the nation', and this only if there is an audience receptive to such appeals. The politics of embarrassment has indeed become an important feature of Aboriginal politics, as in other parts of the Fourth World,[18] not a little fortified by the development of an international audience.[19] Indeed, Australia has had to send 'official' Aboriginal spokespersons to international conferences of Indigenous peoples. It would also seem that both the Aboriginal movement and the politicians went through to the early 1980s believing that the domestic audience of the earlier period still existed. Thus Aborigines, despite their heavy dependence on the welfare economy, were usually exempted from the attacks on 'dole bludgers' that became part of the political rhetoric during the financial stringencies of the later 1970s (Macintyre 1985, pp. 90–3).

Death and the Bicentennial

In 1983 the Australian Labor Party assumed government federally with a commitment to national land rights legislation, but in 1986 it abandoned the attempt. The decision was evidently influenced by a public opinion poll that, although the results were never published, was interpreted to show that the majority of Australians were indifferent to, if not actively hostile towards, Aborigines and the principle of land rights (Rowse 1988). This discovery followed on from a campaign against land rights by the mining industry, together with the governments of the Northern Territory, Queensland and Western Australia, which took the form of a critique of the special status of Aborigines. Whatever their cultural origins, and whatever they had suffered through colonisation, they should be given no more than other citizens. Implicitly, and sometimes explicitly, there was a turning back to the old assimilation doctrine (see, for example, the statement by mining executive Hugh Morgan in the *Sydney Morning Herald* of 19 April 1985).

This critique coincided with an attack on multiculturalism and Asian immigration, which were also said to be creating division in the community at a time when the federal government was endeavouring to achieve class consensus in the face of economic crisis. As the value of earnings declined, the welfare system itself came under closer scrutiny, and Aborigines joined young people as persons whose entitlement was suspect. While individuals might deserve public assistance, it was unacceptable for whole communities to make this a permanent way of life, particularly when they were also receiving other forms of assistance such as free housing and educational assistance.

The Aboriginal movement viewed these developments with dismay, particularly the abandonment of national land rights legislation. Since the dissolution of the NAC, the land councils had become the main centres of political mobilisation: they were now deprived of their political focus. Unexpectedly, however, they were overtaken by an issue of another kind.

Towards the end of 1986, the metropolitan press began featuring a series of incidents in which young Aboriginal men, who had been put in police custody for drunkenness, appeared to have killed themselves. The first cases occurred in Queensland, but soon similar reports were coming in from other parts of the country, until what came to be known as 'deaths in custody' took the form of a unitary phenomenon for which there must be a unitary explanation. One explanation offered was that the deaths were suicides, immediately due to the excessive intake of alcohol, but ultimately to the social and cultural breakdown prevailing in Aboriginal communities. Since the suicides appeared to be a new phenomenon, this carried the uncomfortable implication that, despite more than ten years of government expenditure, the situation of the Aborigines was worse than ever. The other explanation — that the deaths were the result of police negligence if not actual brutality — made better sense to Aborigines, who were in constant conflict with the police over drinking and drunkenness (cf. Sackett 1988). It also made good sense to the Aboriginal movement, since it indicated that, under Australian justice, the rights of Aboriginal citizens did not have the same value as those of whites. As new reports came in, and earlier instances were discovered, there was pressure for a federal inquiry at the highest level.

The federal government, with less than a year to go before the celebration of two hundred years as a British colony, seemed at first reluctant to take a decision that would give these embarrassing occurrences added importance, and keep them before the public for longer. But as the deaths continued to occur, it bowed to Aboriginal and media pressure, setting up an inquiry that focused on the role of the police.[20]

Even if the blame could be firmly laid at the door of the police, the deaths constituted a reproach to the self-congratulatory rhetoric of the Bicentennial. More practically, the authorities, having accepted that the Aborigines were not going to participate in the celebrations, were now fearful that they would disrupt them before the cameras of the world. A riot in a Queensland country town (which led to disclosure of deplorable sanitary and housing conditions, and racial harassment) seemed to provide a model of what might happen. Already there had been several unfavourable reports in the international press, and a critical report from the British Anti-Slavery Society, while Australia found its treatment of Aborigines used against it in a dispute with France over New Caledonia. Sections of the Australian press, notably the *Sydney Morning Herald*, also engaged in searching, if inconclusive, investigations of the Aboriginal problem. Even the Conservative weekly magazine, *The Bulletin*, included rueful cartoon comments on the issue.

In the event, Aborigines did not disrupt the celebrations, but world television diffused an Aboriginal protest march and a colourful mourning ceremony, performed by an Arnhem Lander. The dead were all those who had died as a result of colonisation, including those who had died in prison. In this way, the Aboriginal movement proclaimed the hypocrisy of those who said they should merely be citizens like other Australians, linked recent deaths to frontier killings and proclaimed that all Aboriginal people were the possessors of a distinct cultural heritage.

Conclusions

Occasions such as the Bicentennial occur rarely, and it will probably be some time before the Aboriginal movement finds itself in the world spotlight again. The long-term gains of its protest are also problematical, although they may include curbs on police abuse. But in less tangible terms, statements of commitment have been extracted from government that can be used in rhetorical appeals in time to come (cf. Gartrell 1986). The proposal to establish a new system of representation (Farrar 1988) suggests that the state once again perceives a need to 'stabilize and integrate' Aboriginal political activity.

Looking back over the last twenty years, Australia may be said to have transformed its Indigenous population from virtually passive colonial subjects, situated inside the state but outside the nation, to a political constituency consisting of citizens who are simultaneously a minority. This combination of statuses is the state's response to the presence of people who, as a result of colonisation, are poor, economically and socially marginalised, and politically disfranchised — notwithstanding the right to vote. Since this presence is embarrassing both overseas and, to a somewhat variable extent, at home, it constitutes a problem that, given the history of government in Australia and its long-standing responsibility for Aborigines, the state is called upon to solve. In the process of ameliorating physical and material deprivation, Australia institutionalised social and economic marginalisation through the rehabilitation of Aboriginality as both a way of life and an honourable status within the nation. The political disfranchisement correspondingly required the setting up of special consultative structures, while the rehabilitation of Aboriginality required at least a gesture towards self-determination.

The Australian state has formed its Aboriginal people into a constituency that, however, now exists in its own right. While its economic and political dependence is inescapable, its origin in the historic encounter between native and settler gives it a cultural legitimacy in terms that the state cannot wrest from it.

Acknowledgements

An earlier draft of this chapter was presented to the Anthropology Colloquium at the Graduate Center of the City University of New York in February 1980. I am indebted to the many colleagues and students who offered valuable comments and criticisms. This chapter was first published in *Social Analysis*, 1988, special issue no. 24. My particular thanks to Sheila Shaver for her help in preparing this chapter.

NOTES

1. For an extended discussion of this distinction, see Beckett (1988).
2. One reason for this extreme emphasis on race was that it provided a counter to the widespread belief that whites degenerated in the tropics. Significantly, racism was virulent in tropical Queensland.
3. For a preliminary analysis of the changing constructions of Aboriginality during this period, see Beckett (1988).
4. For a discussion of similar issues, see Macintyre (1985, pp. 118–19).
5. This did not prevent the Islanders from seeing military service as a form of citizenship, and they mounted a brief strike in support of a claim for higher pay (Beckett 1987, pp. 61–5).
6. The documentary film *Lousy Little Sixpence* includes newsreel footage of Aboriginal soldiers in training. The newsreel contrasts these soldiers with the Cummeragunga strikers.
7. The highly successful water colourist, Albert Namatjira, was made a national celebrity, and both officials and patrons went to great lengths to enable him to live 'like a white man'. His citizenship also foundered on the reefs of colonial regulation.
8. The importation of Central Australian Aborigines for fruit picking in New South Wales was unsuccessful, and not repeated (L Clack, personal comment).
9. The integration of Torres Strait Islanders into the Queensland railways and the northern construction industry was an exception to this generalisation (Beckett 1987, pp. 210–12).
10. Although systematic research is required, the author has the impression that the metropolitan press avoided reporting anti-Aboriginal manifestations among outback whites until the Moree shootings in 1983.
11. It is remarkable that what became the Aborigines' Bill of Rights should in fact be a mandate for state intervention in Aboriginal lives.
12. Macintyre (1985, p. 134) calls this a mock battle for land rights, noting that the program cost very little, and that Aboriginal assistance programs were severely cut.
13. New Zealand would appear to be a candidate for inclusion with these states. Unfortunately, paucity of information from New Zealand anthropologists makes a

judgement difficult. Since the Maori account for some 10 per cent of the population, and have a base in both the pastoral economy and the mainstream labour force, it may be that their situation is closer to that of the Indians in Mexico.

14. Representative local government existed at that time only in the Torres Strait, though Queensland maintained what were at best advisory councils on its Aboriginal stations. During the 1960s, the federal government had also experimented with councils on some of its Northern Territory settlements.

15. Although Torres Strait Islanders had a substantial representation in the federal seat of Kennedy (and a decisive voice in the state seat), Aborigines controlled no mainland constituency. Correspondingly, while one Aboriginal served one term as a Liberal senator for Queensland, no Aboriginal has sat in the House of Representatives, and only two in state legislatures.

16. As a result of this rapid movement, there are Aborigines with a comprehensive experience of politics and nationwide networks.

17. It should be understood that, in some instances, this provided the state with a means of getting points of law decided.

18. Vincent Crapanzano (personal comment) has insightfully remarked that such marginally situated individuals tend to assume a trickster role.

19. The abuse of Indigenous peoples has become part of international ideological conflict in recent years, thus the United States attacks Nicaragua for its mistreatment of the Mesquito Indians, Chile similarly assails Mexico, France attacks Australia and, lately, the Soviet Union comments on the situation of Indians in the United States.

20. It is worth noting that Canberra was able to distance itself from the deaths by this means, since the police were under the jurisdiction of the state governments.

REFERENCES

Beckett, J 1987, *Torres Strait Islanders: Custom and Colonialism*, Cambridge University Press, Cambridge.

—— 1988, *Past and Present: The Construction of Aboriginality*, Aboriginal Studies Press, Canberra.

Bennett, S 1985, 'The 1967 Referendum', *Australian Aboriginal Studies*, vol. 2, p. 31.

De Lepervanche, M 1975, 'Australian immigrants 1788–1940: Desired and unwanted', in EL Wheelwright and K Buckley (eds), *Essays in the Political Economy of Australian Capitalism, Vol. 1*, ANZ Book Company, Sydney, pp. 72–104.

DeMaria, W 1987, 'White welfare, black entitlement: The social security access controversy, 1939–59', *Aboriginal History*, vol. 10, pp. 25–39.

Evans, R 1975, *Exclusion, Exploitation and Extermination: Race Relations in Colonial Queensland*, ANZ Book Company, Sydney.

Farrar, C 1988, *The Origins of Democratic Thinking*, Cambridge University Press, Cambridge.

Gartrell, B 1986, '"Colonialism" and the Fourth World: Notes on variations in colonial situations', *Culture*, vol. 6, no. 1, pp. 3–16.

Hall, RA 1989, *The Black Diggers: Aborigines and Torres Strait Islanders in the Second World War*, Allen & Unwin, Sydney.

Horne, D 1964, *The Lucky Country*, Penguin, Ringwood.

Larbalestier, J 1988, '"For the betterment of these people": The Bleakley Report and Aboriginal workers', *Social Analysis*, vol. 24, pp. 19–33.

Lees, S and Senyard, J 1987, *The 1950s: How Australia Became a Modern Society, and Everyone Got a House and a Car*, Hyland House, Melbourne.

Macdonald, GM 1988, Self-determination or control: Aboriginal land rights legislation in New South Wales, *Social Analysis*, no. 24, pp. 34–49.

Macintyre, S 1985, *Winners and Losers*, Allen & Unwin, Sydney.

—— 2009, *A Concise History of Australia*, Cambridge University Press, Melbourne.

Maddock, K 1983, *Your Land is Our Land: Aboriginal Land Rights*, Penguin, Ringwood.

Marshall, TH 1963, *Sociology at the Crossroads and Other Essays*, Heinemann, London.

Morris, B 1989, *Domesticating Resistance: The Dhan-gadi Aborigines and the Australian State*, Berg, Oxford.

Nettheim, G 1981, *Victims of the Law: Black Queenslanders Today*, Allen & Unwin, Sydney.

Neville, AO 1947, *Australia's Coloured Minority: Its Place in the Community*, Currawong, Sydney.

Paine, R 1977, 'The path to welfare colonialism', in R Paine (ed.), *The White Arctic: Anthropological Essays on Tutelage and Ethnicity*, Memorial University of Newfoundland, St John, pp. 3–28.

Peterson, N 1985, 'Capitalism, culture and land rights: Aborigines and the state in the Northern Territory', *Social Analysis*, vol. 18, pp. 85–101.

Piven, FF and Cloward, RA 1985, *The New Class War*, Pantheon Books, New York.

Reynolds, H 1987, *Frontier, Aborigines, Settlers and Land*, Allen & Unwin, Sydney.

Rowse, T 1988, 'From houses to households: The Aboriginal Development Commission and economic adaptation by Alice Springs town campers', *Social Analysis*, vol. 24, pp. 50–65.

Sackett, L 1988, 'Resisting arrests: Drinking, development and discipline in a desert context', *Social Analysis*, vol. 24, pp. 66–77.

Sansom, B 1980, *The Camp at Wallaby Cross: Aboriginal Fringe Dwellers in Darwin*, Australian Institute of Aboriginal Studies, Canberra.

Shaver S 1987, 'Design for a welfare state: The Joint Parliamentary Committee on Social Security', *Historical Studies*, vol. 22, no. 88, pp. 411–31.

Sider, G 1987, 'When parrots learn to talk, and why they can't: Domination, deception, and self-deception in Indian–white relations', *Comparative Studies in Society and History*, vol. 29, pp. 3–23.

Stone, SN 1974, *Aborigines in White Australia: A Documentary History of the Attitudes Affecting Official Policy and the Australian Aborigine, 1697–1973*, Heinemann, Melbourne.

Turner, B 1986, *Citizenship and Capitalism: The Debate Over Reformism*, Allen & Unwin, London.

Weaver, SM 1983, 'Australian Aboriginal policy: Aboriginal pressure groups or government advisory bodies, part 1', *Oceania*, vol. 54, no. 1, pp. 1–22.

—— 1984, 'Struggle of the nation-state to define Aboriginal ethnicity in Canada and Australia', in GL Gold (ed.), *Minorities and Mother Country Imagery*, Institute of Social and Economic Research, Newfoundland.

White, R 1981, *Inventing Australia*, Allen & Unwin, Sydney.

Chapter 11

Contested Images: Perspectives on the Indigenous Terrain in the Late Twentieth Century

They were asked, 'And you, what are you committed to, politics or ecology?' 'We just want our companions to realize how they are suffering,' the actors replied. *All for All,* a Tzotzil-Tzetzal Tragicomedy. (Laughlin 1995)

The Zapatista uprising in Chiapas, Mexico, draws our attention to some of the distinctive features of Indigenous mobilisation in the late twentieth century. The eruption of the Zapatista Army of National Liberation (EZLN) was, of course, of immediate and vital interest to the Mayan peoples involved, and to their fellow Mexicans — particularly those metropolitan scholars who were concerned with the plight of such marginalised groups on the eve of Mexico's entry into the North American Free Trade Association, but who were nevertheless taken by surprise when it happened. However, this was not only an event for Mexico and its northern neighbours, where, apart from regular news reports, the *New Yorker* and *New York Review of Books* published long feature articles (Guillermoprieto 1994, 1995); Europe too paid attention, and a French hour-long television feature was in due course screened in Australia. The exotic setting, combined with the mystery surrounding the identity of the masked Sub-Commandante Marcos, no doubt made the story attractive to a spectacle-hungry media, but the rapidity with which the news of the uprising was diffused around the world (it reached Australia within twenty-four hours) indicates that there was already a transnational constituency, ready to receive and pass on the news through a network of concerned groups. This constituency was formed not in the first instance by a concern for the Zapatistas in Chiapas, but for Indigenous peoples generally.

This constituency is not, of course, unitary, nor is it always well informed; here and there it seems to be tainted with commercial ends. It is, however, grounded in the belief that Indigenous peoples not only have the right to be different from the rest of the world, but should be assisted to do so. They are the custodians of an alternative to modernity — particularly in their relation to the earth — which not just a particular nation, but humanity at large, needs to conserve. In the wake of the dissolution of the old imperial domains, and perhaps as a by-product of the Cold War between the communist and Western blocs, this belief has increasingly been accorded legitimacy — albeit selectively — by various international bodies such as the United Nations, the World Council of Churches and the World Bank.

Such notions are held at some distance from the Indigenous subjects, and reflect Western preoccupations — often to the point of self-indulgence. They cannot, however, be dismissed as irrelevant, since they make up part of a constituency that also includes concerned scholarship, liberation theology, human rights and social justice, to name but a few, and that constitutes what Arjun Appadurai (1990, pp. 6–7) has called 'a dimension of global cultural flow'. This 'flow' is not just a matter of disembodied ideas, but of information, including the exposure of repression and abuse that national governments may rather not have publicised. One does not have to buy into the image of Sub-Commandante Marcos composing his whimsical communiqués to the world on a laptop in the Lacandon jungle to appreciate how quickly news of the EZLN uprising reached the outside world. How much of a difference this exposure has made in moderating the reaction of the authorities is hard to say, but there can be no doubt that Indigenous mobilisations are increasingly aware of what Noel Dyck (1985, p. 18), writing particularly about Indigenous North Americans and Australians, has called 'the politics of embarrassment' (see also Urban and Sherzer 1991, p. 9).[1]

An implication of this complex field in which faraway friends provide an uncertain measure of empowerment to local struggle is that the Indigenous 'dimension of global cultural flow' — the indigeno-scape, to adapt Appadurai's (1990) suggestive metaphor (cf. Beckett 1995, pp. 422–3) — appears differently according to the position from which it is viewed. Position here, of course, implies not just physical distance from some critical point of reference, but different discursive environments and political agendas.

This field, then, is not homogeneous, but it is in some sense interactive. Some writers in the field of transnational identity have suggested that

> those about whom we write are both the subjects of our enquiry and subjects who, in relationship to what is being said and done around them, including the work of social scientists, and in relation to their own vary-ing motivations, act upon and change the world of our inquiry. We in turn observe these actions and are influenced by them. (Basch et al. 1994, p. 16)

I suggest that this insight can be broadened to include the whole field of advocacy and reportage — accurate or inaccurate.

I would also suggest that there is no one position that can be regarded as finally authoritative or determinative. Having said this, however, I would add that some voices are more easily heard above the others, and may on this account (though there is not a simple correlation) have greater bearing on outcomes. Daniel Mato (1996) in his introduction to the Chiapas dossier, points to the lack of space given to Mexican commentators in English-language outlets, and readers are indebted to him for assembling this panel of scholars, several of whom are actively involved in the political process. The Indigenous subjects are less easily heard (but see Campbell and Green 1993); for much of their history, they have been spoken for, often without their knowledge, while their own voices were inaudible beyond the bounds of their local communities — or, if heard, not fully understood. What is remarkable about Indigenous mobilisation in the late twentieth century is that these voices are able to reach not only their metropolitan constituency, but sympathisers around the world, and also other Indigenous peoples, giving substance to what one of them called the Fourth World.

For Parajuli (1996), recent developments around the world suggest a period of 'discursive contestation between ethnicities and democratic nation states'. In fact, ethnicities of one kind or another have been in evidence throughout this century — albeit sometimes overlaid or taken over by other kinds of ideology. It is nevertheless the case that, following a period of quiescence, ethnicity entered a period of salience, beginning in the 1960s and intensifying through to the present. This is not the place to look for the contributory factors, which no doubt vary from case to case, though the dissolution of the old imperial domains and the Cold War with its competition for the favours of the New Nations seem to have created a space in which minorities could embarrass their governments with accusations of racial discrimination and internal colonialism. The mass movement of labour to the developed economies is certainly another contributory factor, along with the disintegration of the communist bloc and with it the weakening of the communist parties. Whatever the critical factors, what Charles Taylor (1992) has called 'the politics of difference' confronts the nation-state, and indeed humanity at large, with the question of how much diversity of appearance and conduct they can contain and whether some degree of autonomy is the entitlement of those who claim to be different.

In the wake of this development, a number of the world's Indigenous peoples have been able to reassert their identity, their right to 'be themselves', and to make claims on the basis of their Indigenous difference. Indigenous identity takes on a distinctive form in relation to the nation-state. Immigrant ethnicities can claim kinship with (and sometimes support from) their states of origin (though this is only notionally the case with African Americans). Indigenous groups, by contrast, situate themselves inside the territory of the state in which they live, whether or not they consider themselves part of the nation. This Indigenous presence is characteristically defined in terms of an historical narrative that identifies a people as aboriginal or, to use a North American trope, 'first peoples' — a usage that gives a new meaning to older but cognate terms such as 'Native Americans'. This entails a claim to a territory, which can — or, if it has been taken from them, should — provide a base for the practice of cultural difference. A characteristic trope of indigenist discourse is survival — the physical survival of a people in the face of genocide, and their cultural survival in the face of development and modernisation; those who have survived, then, claim authenticity — a continuity, if not an exact similarity, with those who held it when the settlers came.

The idea of indigeneity took its present form from Europe's colonial project in the New World, and in particular from the European colony of settlement. For Les Field (1996), with Mexico particularly in mind, its source is to be found in 'the pivotal moment of European arrival ... [Indigenous] identity hinges on the position vis a vis that moment.' From that moment remains the assertion and the contestation not just of ethnic difference, but of inequality of achievement, moral capacity and destiny. Since then, Mexico, Ecuador and Europe's other settler colonies have become independent of the metropolitan power and attempted to a greater or less degree to imagine themselves as nations. In this project, the presence of the Indigenous constitutes a predicament: whether to be excluded as intractable obstacles to economic and political progress, 'civilised' into participation through some kind of pedagogical regime, integrated into some kind of cultural-cum-eugenicist *mestizaje* (in which the Creole remains the dominant partner), or allowed to retain their difference as some kind of folkloric (and touristic) anachronism.

As Parajuli (1996) shows, India — like other non-settler colonies, for example those of South-East Asia — faces an analogous predicament. Radical inequalities, which seem to have existed in some form at the moment of European colonisation, were ethnologised into 'tribes' under colonial rule and carried over into independence — where, so it seemed, their adherence to 'backward' practices made them obstacles to the same project of capitalist development and nation-building.

Without under-rating the courage with which Indigenous peoples have often resisted the assaults on their way of life, and defended the territory and resources on which it is based, I suggest that 'survival' has usually taken the form of negotiation with the dominant group. Although it is often understood in this way, Indigenous resistance to development has not always been in defence of the past, but often to changes that offered neither past nor future, beyond a marginal existence. By contrast, the two Ecuadorian initiatives discussed by Mark Rogers (1996) indicate a positive response (whether justified or not) to opportunities that seem to enable them to carry some of their past into the future.

Capitalism, while relentlessly expansionary and transformative in the long haul, cannot in any case be understood as a steady progression from simple to complex, or from isolation to incorporation, or from autonomy to subordination. It is often better understood as a series of tidal motions, invading Indigenous territory only to recede, leaving the 'natives' to pick up the pieces of their disrupted lives, before the next wave breaks (cf. Gudeman's 1978 study of rural Panama). Over more than a short period, the history of colonised peoples is likely to take the form of a series of accommodations and initiatives. In much of Chiapas, the land on which the Maya peasants currently conduct Indigenous lives may not be the land on which their ancestors lived, but other places to which they were assigned in some earlier negotiation, or which they settled in hope of a better life. Again, isolation rather than providing a 'region of refuge' may be a device to secure sources of unfree labour, which reproduce themselves outside the frame of the market (cf. Gonzalez 1965; Stavenhagen 1965, on internal colonialism in Meso-America). Even when simply a matter of inaccessibility, isolation and under-development have, ironically, become a lure for Westerners seeking alterity: the spiritual and eco-tourists, and the documentary filmmakers of recent years (cf. Rogers 1996), are the successors to the Christian missionaries, scientists and travel writers of earlier times (Thomas 1994), each producing their own kind of intrusion, but also perhaps a lifeline to the outside world in a time of danger.

The enhanced capacity in the later part of this century to reach outside audiences has in all likelihood intensified Indigenous consciousness, and emboldened Indigenous peoples to make their claims in the language of indigeneity. Rogers (1996), in his account of a community in Ecuadorean Amazonia, documents a shift from the ideology of development in the 1970s to an indigenist ideology in the 1980s. At the same time, one can ask whether people are likely to put the welfare of their families, and perhaps their lives, at risk simply for the sake of authenticity. Parajuli (1996) argues that the mobilisation against the 'eco-destruction' of marginal regions such as Jharkand takes ethnic form because there is a sense of a distinct ecological entity combined with an ethno-history (1996, p. 24). At the core of this 'ethno-history', perhaps, are the original 'tribal' inhabitants, such as the Santals, but Jharkandi ethnicity embraces people — now the majority — who came in at a later date.

While Parajuli's (1996) argument may not have direct application to the other instances of ethnic or Indigenous mobilisation included here, it encourages us to look more closely at accounts that treat these terms as transparent and natural. It also reminds us that, while regional autonomy might make political sense for the Jharkandis, whose quarrel is with outside interests, it may not make sense for other Indigenous mobilisations whose immediate problem is with a regional elite, whether of their own or the majority group. In such a circumstance, the best strategy may be to look for allies outside the region and perhaps the state. Of course, such support comes at a price, and local concerns must be weighed against the advantages to be gained either by identifying them with those of others like themselves, or merging them in broader political agendas.

Autonomous Indigenous mobilisations at the national level are difficult to sustain, if only for reasons of expense and logistics. Moreover, when they become an international embarrassment, or when for other reasons the Indigenous population is a charge on the state, the mobilisation is likely to become institutionalised as an arm of government. Such arrangements are — as in North America and Australia, and also Mexico — characterised by enlightened legislation and policies, and the fostering of Indigenous elites and cultural displays, but they do not necessarily reach down to the less 'visible' local level, whether because of insufficient resources or obstruction by antagonistic local interests. The same inadequacy of resources, and the historical and cultural differences among such a broad Indigenous constituency, fosters inequality and division, and a politics that is either bureaucratic or clientelistic.

The Jharkandi case also raises the problem of how to negotiate the division between Indigenous and non-Indigenous. In North America, it is in the interest of the beneficiaries of long-standing treaties to restrict the number of claimants, creating a situation where those who fall below the 'blood quanta' (cf. Field 1996, p. 141), or whose 'nation' has not been officially recognised, are excluded. This, of course, also reduces the claims on government resources. Australia, by contrast, recognises anyone who can establish some Indigenous ancestry as eligible for benefits, leaving it to community organisations to distribute the actual benefits, the supply of which is limited.

In Mexico, the Cardenista project of enabling Indigenous groups to enter the mainstream society — principally the agrarian sector (Barre 1983) — gave way in the early 1970s to a pluralistic — or what Diaz Polanco (1987) calls ethno-populist — project. The Instituto Nacional Indigenista (INI) became the official arm of this policy but, according to various studies, proved erratic in its identification of its Indigenous clients, while tending to avoid (or to be kept from) politically sensitive situations (Deverre and Meissner 1983; Friedlander 1975; Hill 1991).

It is remarkable that INI scarcely figures in the Mexican papers published here. The EZLN, and in a somewhat different way the Coalición Obrero, Campesino y Estudiantil del Istmo (COCEI), referred to in Campbell and

Green (1996; see also Martinez Lopez 1985), seem not to want to make too much of the Indigenous identification, although their claim to 'authenticity' is as strong as any group in Mexico. At all events, they do not include 'Indigenous' in their titles, but rather invoke the agrarian hero of the Mexican Revolution, Emiliano Zapata. The name of Zapata is of particular moment here because of his mediatory role between an Indigenous peasantry (particularly of Morelos) and the revolution of 1910–19 and, in post-revolutionary Mexican nationalism, between the mainly poor peasants and the Cardenista corporate state (Womack 1969). In view of the recent and impending upheavals consequent upon Mexico's entry into NAFTA, the invocation of Zapata identifies the particular suffering of the Tzetzal and Tzotzil with the plight of the rural poor, and the society as a whole.[2]

At the same time, their indigeneity is not without significance. Rather, the distinctive appearance and language of the EZLN becomes a reminder of 'Mexican history's collective and communitarian side', the unrecognised Mexico Profundo (de León 1996, p. 260), which is a perhaps unintended implication of cultural *mestizaje*. In his book, *Mexico Profundo*, the late Guilliermo Bonfil Batalla (1987) similarly found national salvation in the submerged qualities of Indianness, among which he includes care for the environment and spirituality.

While the business of the EZLN, and most other Indigenous mobilisations, is in the first instance with the state in which they are situated, several contributors have referred to the state's loss of legitimacy, while others have remarked on its weakening with the emergence of transnational hegemonies. The EZLN, through its networks, has certainly evoked sympathy in the metropolis, situating its local struggle in the broader disquiet about the direction in which Mexico is going, and its relations with NAFTA. At the same time, it has taken its case to a much wider constituency, including Mexico's NAFTA partners, but beyond them to an international constituency whose concern is with Indigenous peoples rather than the future of Mexico. In somewhat different mode, the COCEI, which during its two-year control of the city of Juchitán fostered a Zapotec cultural revival at home, maintained a 'foreign policy' stance of solidarity with the left regimes of Cuba and Nicaragua (Binford and Campbell 1993, pp. 16–17). The comparison is doubly interesting when one recalls that the United States was supporting the Mesquito Indian resistance to the Sandinista regime in Nicaragua at the same time.

The external constituency, towards which Indigenous mobilisations seem to be increasingly orienting their activities, exists not merely in the countries that have Indigenous minorities, but in the Western European states that have long since divested themselves of their colonies, and in supra-national, political and economic arenas such as the various United Nations bodies concerned with Indigenous rights, as well as a variety of non-government organisations (NGOs). Although, as I suggested earlier, it is hard to estimate their contribution to complex political processes, it seems that they have the potential to empower Indigenous mobilisation, and that Indigenous peoples are aware of this. However, this empowerment is ambiguous in the sense that the mobilisation must present itself in such a way as to appear 'Indigenous' to a constituency that, while sympathetic, may have inappropriate expectations of Indigenous alterity. Campbell and Green (1996) and Saynes-Vázquez (1996) show how Zapotec women have had endured centuries of misrepresentations, including feminist accounts that praise them for a 'liberation' of which they are unaware.

This paradox has been nowhere more dramatically acted out than in Brazil, with the appearance of the pop-star Sting with the Indian leader Raoni, resplendent in lip plug and feathers, in an Amnesty International concert diffused around the world. In this setting at least, the signs of indigeneity, which were once sources of shame, have undergone rehabilitation as the cultural capital of alterity. There is more to the story than this, however. Alcida Ramos (1994, p. 161) remarks that

> a tendency that has been around for a while in the indigenist circuit, namely the fabrication of the perfect Indian whose virtues, sufferings and untiring stoicism have won for him the right to be defended by the professionals of indigenous rights. That Indian is more than the real Indian. He is the hyperreal Indian.

Ramos makes it clear that this 'hyperreality' has *real* consequences for 'real' Indians, inasmuch as it may influence the decision of an NGO to support this or that project.

The predicament intensifies if claimants have to meet predetermined criteria in order to establish their 'tribal' status (Clifford 1988) or their right to 'tribal' land (Jacobs 1988). At this point, the judicial authorities are apt to call on anthropologists and ethno-historians to comment on the 'authenticity' of the claim — and perhaps the claimants as well (Beckett 1994). The appropriateness of this trope, along with cognates such as tradition, revival, construction, invention and essentialism, is raised in Rogers (1996), and taken up by Friedman (1996) and Mato (1996). The Native North American writer Vine Deloria (1969), with anthropologists particularly in mind, once complained: 'The more we try to be ourselves, the more you try to make us what we have never been.' The cryptic response of the Tzetzal-Tzotzil actors, which provides the epigraph to this chapter, can perhaps be understood as a more diplomatic attempt to deflect simplistic categorisation of their experience.

Acknowledgments

This chapter was first published in 1996 in *Identities: Global Studies in Culture and Power*, vol. 3, nos 1–2, pp. 1–13.

NOTES

1. More generally, it is remarkable how often television coverage of protests in non-Anglophone countries (e.g. Burma and Timor) includes placards and testimonies in English, no doubt with the intention of attracting overseas support.
2. The cover of the Mexican magazine *Proceso* of 11 November 1991, featuring the revocation of the *ejido* laws, displays his photograph, under the heading 'La Revolutión Mexicana va para atrás: tronó el campo'.

REFERENCES

Appadurai, A 1990, 'Disjuncture and difference in the global cultural economy', *Public Culture*, vol. 2, pp. 1–24.

Barre, MC 1983, *Ideologías indigenists y movimientos indios*, Siglo Ventiuno Editores, Mexico City.

Basch, L, Glick Schiller, N and Szanton Blanc, C 1994, *Nations Unbound: Transnational Projects, Postcolonial Predicaments and Deterritorialized Nation-States*, Gordon and Breach, New York.

Beckett, J 1994, 'The Murray Island Land Case', in G Cowlishaw and V Kondos (eds), *Mabo and Australia: On Recognizing Native Title After Two Hundred Years*, *Australian Journal of Anthropology*, vol. 6, nos 1–2, pp. pp. 15–31.

—— 1995, 'National and Transnational Perspectives on Multiculturalism: The View From Australia'. *Identities* 1, pp. 421–6.

Binford, L and Campbell, H 1993, 'Introduction', in H Campbell (ed.), *Zapotec Struggles: Histories, Politics, and Representation from Juchitán, Oaxaca*, Smithsonian Institute Press, Washington, DC, pp. 1–28.

Bonfil Batalla, G 1987, *México Profundo: Una Civilización Negada*, Secretaría de Educación Pública, Mexico City.

Campbell, H and Green, S 1996, 'A history of representations of Isthmus Zapotec women', *Identities: Global Studies in Culture and Power*, vol. 3, nos 1–2, pp. 155–82.

Clifford, J 1988, 'Identity in Mashpee', in *The predicament of culture*, California UP.

Deloria, V 1969, *Custer Died for Your Sins*, Collier-Macmillan, London.

Deverre, C and Meissner, R 1980, 'Les gigures de l'indien-probleme de l'indigenism Mexicaine', *Cahiers Internatiounaux de Sociologie*, vol. 48, pp. 149–66.

Diaz Polanco, H 1987, *Etnia, nación y politica*, J Pablos, Mexico City.

Dyck, N 1985, 'Aboriginal peoples and nation-states: An introduction', in N Dyck (ed.), *Indigenous People and the Nation-state*, Institute for Social and Economic Research, St Johns, Newfoundland, pp. 1–26.

Field, L 1996, 'Harvesting the bitter juice contradictions of Páez resistance in the changing Colombian nation-state', *Identities: Global Studies in Culture and Power*, vol. 3, nos 1–2, pp. 89–108.

Friedlander, J 1975, *Being Indian in Hueyapan: a Study of Forced Identity in Contemporary Mexico*, St Martins Press, New York.

Friedman, J 1996, 'The politics of de-authentification: Escaping from identity, a response to "beyond authenticity" by Mark Rogers', *Identities: Global Studies in Culture and Power*, vol. 3, nos 1–2, pp. 127–36.

Gonzalez Casanova, P 1965, 'Internal colonialism and national development', *Studies in Comparative International Development*, vol. 1, pp. 27–37.

Gudeman, S 1978, *The Demise of a Rural Economy: From Subsistence to Capitalism in a Latin American Village*, Routledge and Kegan Paul, London.

Guillermoprieto, A 1994, 'The shadow war', *New York Review of Books*, vol. 42, pp. 39–43.

—— 1995, 'Letter from Mexico: The unmasking', *New Yorker*, 13 March, pp. 40–7.

Hill, J 1991, 'Neca Gobierno de Puebla: Mexicano penetrations of the Mexican state', in G Urban and J Sherzer (eds), *Nation States and Indians in Latin America*, Texas University Press, Austin, pp. 72–94.

Jacobs, J 1988, 'The construction of identity', in J Beckett (ed.), *Past and Present: The Construction of Aboriginality*, Aboriginal Studies Press, Canberra, pp. 31–4.

Laughlin, RM 1995, 'From all for all: A Tzetzal-Tzotzil tragicomedy', *American Anthropologist*, vol. 97, no. 3, pp. 528–42.

Martinez Lopez, F 1985, *El Crepúsculo del Poder: Juchitán, Oax. 1980–1982*, Instituto de Investigaciones Sociológicas, Universidad Autónoma Benito Juarez de Oaxaca, Oaxaca.

Mato, D 1996, 'The Indigenous uprising in Chiapis: The politics of institutionalised knowledge and Mexican perspectives', *Identities: Global Studies in Culture and Power*, vol. 3, nos 1–2, pp. 205–17.

Parajuli, P 1996, 'Ecological ethnicity in the making: Developmentalist hegemonies and emergent identities in India', *Identities: Global Studies in Culture and Power*, vol. 3, nos 1–2, pp. 15–59.

Ramos, A 1994, 'The hyperreal Indian', *Critique of Anthropology*, vol. 14, no. 2, pp. 153–71.

Rogers, M 1996, 'Beyond authenticity: Conservation, tourism, and the politics of representation in the Ecuadorian Amazon', *Identities: Global Studies in Culture and Power*, vol. 3, nos 1–2, pp. 73–125.

Saynes-Vázquez, E 1996, 'Galán Pa dxandí'. "That would be great if it were true": Zapotec women's comment on their role in society', *Identities: Global Studies in Culture and Power* 1996, vol. 3, nos 1–2, pp. 183–204.

Stavenhagen, R 1965, 'Classes, colonialism and acculturation', *Studies in Comparative International Development*, vol. 1, pp. 53–77.

Taylor, C 1992, *The Politics of Recognition: Working Papers and Proceedings of the Center for Psychosocial Studies*, Center for Psychosocial Studies, Chicago.

Thomas, N 1994, *Colonialism's Culture: Anthropology, Travel and Government*, Polity Press, Oxford.

Urban, G and Sherzer, J 1991, 'Introduction: Indians, nation-states, and culture', G Urban and J Sherzer (eds), *Nation States and Indians in Latin America*, Texas University Press, Austin, pp. 1–18.

Womack, J 1969, *Zapata and the Mexican Revolution*, Thames and Hudson, London.

Index

___

Page numbers in italics refer to maps, 'n' after a page number refers to an endnote on that page.

www.ingramcontent.com/pod-product-compliance
Lightning Source LLC
Chambersburg PA
CBHW031054250726
48655CB00004B/1442